THE DOGMA OF
THE BATTLE
OF ANNIHILATION

THE DOGMA OF
THE BATTLE
OF ANNIHILATION

**The Theories of Clausewitz
and Schlieffen and Their
Impact on the German
Conduct of Two World Wars**

JEHUDA L. WALLACH

CONTRIBUTIONS IN MILITARY STUDIES, NUMBER 45

Greenwood Press
WESTPORT, CONNECTICUT
LONDON, ENGLAND

Library of Congress Cataloging in Publication Data

Wallach, Jehuda Lothar, 1921—
  The dogma of the battle of annihilation.

  (Contributions in military studies, ISSN 0083-6884;
no. 45)
  Bibliography: p.
  Includes index.
  1. Military art and science—Germany—History—19th
century. 2. Military art and science—Germany—History
—20th century. 3. Clausewitz, Carl von, 1780–1831.
4. Schlieffen, Alfred, Graf von, 1833–1913. 5. World
War, 1914–1918—Germany. 6. World War, 1939–1945—
Germany. I. Title. II. Series.
  U43.G3W35 1986   355'.00943   84-27942
  ISBN 0-313-24438-3 (lib. bdg.)

Library of Congress Catalog Card Number: 84-27942
ISBN: 0-313-24438-3
ISSN: 0083-6884

First published in 1986

Greenwood Press
A division of Congressional Information Service, Inc.
88 Post Road West
Westport, Connecticut 06881

Printed in the United States of America

10 9 8 7 6 5 4 3 2 1

Contents

Preface

During the years 1962 through 1965, when working at Oxford (England) on this study, many people expressed astonishment about the fact that I, an Israeli officer, delved into questions that obviously could be of interest only to Germans. It seems, therefore, to be appropriate to explain briefly why a soldier of the Israel Defense Forces (I.D.F.) has chosen such a subject.

As a soldier I was, above all, interested to investigate the relationship between theories of war and the practice of war, in order to establish whether theory exercises any influence on the conduct of war. It seemed to me that Germany was the most suitable country for such an investigation since it had in less than two centuries produced two such outstanding theorists of war as General Carl von Clausewitz and Field Marshal Alfred Count von Schlieffen. The world wars of 1914 to 1918 and of 1939 to 1945 could undoubtedly be considered suitable examples for the purpose of this study.

Moreover, the subject of this study was especially attractive for a soldier on active service in the Defense Forces of the State of Israel. The political and military problems that the German theorists of war—and in particular von Schlieffen—tried to solve may be compared with certain aspects of problems that have occupied the State of Israel since its foundation. Schlieffen and his successors considered Germany, in the center of Europe, as surrounded by hostile neighbors, bent on its destruction. They tried to solve the problem of how Germany, surrounded by superior enemies, could prevail. Because they also took into account the economic situation of their country, they strove for a victorious termination of a war that should be as short as possible. Israel was confronted with similar problems, of course, with certain differences, like the size of the country, the economic basis, the size of the population, the character and cultural background of the enemies, and the ratio of space and frontier. It was, therefore, interesting to establish why Germany lost two successive world wars, which in both instances—contrary to Schlieffen's teachings—were prolonged wars. I hope that I have succeeded, in the epilogue of this work, to draw from this some lessons for my country.

Without the assistance of certain institutions and personalities this study would never have been accomplished. Special thanks I owe to the Wiener Library (then in London and now at the campus of Tel-Aviv University). Without this library one can hardly deal with questions of contemporary German history. In Germany the Bibliothek für Zeitgeschichte, Stuttgart, rendered valuable help. The Director of this institute, Dr. Jürgen Rohwer, has provided valuable advice and contributed actively to the publication of the German edition in 1967. The Central Library of the Bundeswehr provided books that could not be procured otherwise. The librarians there made every possible effort to satisfy my sometimes unusual requests.

The Bundesarchiv/Militärarchiv (then in Koblenz and now in Freiburg im Breisgau) and in particular Dr. Count von Merveldt, the Berliner Hauptarchiv (former Preuss. Geh. Staatsarchiv), and the Militärgeschichtliche Forschungsamt, Freiburg im Breisgau, all allowed me to use their archivalia, take notes from them, and obtain photocopies and microfilms. Special thanks I owe to the late Colonel Dr. Meier-Welcker, then Director of the Forschungsamt in Freiburg, for clarifying various questions orally and in writing.

The Professors Dr. F. Fischer (Hamburg), Dr. W. Hahlweg (Münster/Westf.), Dr. G. Jäschke (Münster/Westf.), and Dr. E. Zechlin (Hamburg) have spent much of their valuable time in order to discuss with me certain questions of this study. I also owe thanks to Mrs. E. Schotte-von Moltke, a granddaughter of Colonel General H. von Moltke, who gave me access to her father's papers, and in particular to Mr. Jürgen von Grone, who made every effort to make available to me the scanty information concerning the younger Moltke.

I owe many thanks to the master of the theory of war and the history of war, the late Sir Basil H. Liddell Hart, who spent many hours of discussion with a novice in this field. He carefully read the finished manuscript, discussed it with me, and encouraged me to publish it. There can be no doubt that without the guidance of Professor N. H. Gibbs, then Chichele Professor of the History of War, Oxford (England), I would not have been able to master this matter. However, I would like to stress the fact that the responsibility for the ideas expressed in this book rests entirely with me.

This study would never have been accomplished without the assistance of the Ministry of Defense of the State of Israel, of I.D.F.'s General Staff, and of Tel-Aviv University, which provided the means for my studies at Oxford.

As for the other side of the Atlantic, I am extremely grateful to Professors Harold Deutsch and Jay Luvaas, and to Dr. James T. Sabin, Executive Vice President of Greenwood Press, for their interest in this study.

The following abbreviations for German Archives are used:

BA/MA   Bundesarchiv/Militärarchiv, formerly Koblenz, now Freiburg im Breisgau

MGFA   Militärgeschichtliches Forschungsamt, Freiburg im Breisgau

BHA   Berliner Hauptarchiv, formerly Preussisches Geheimes
          Staatsarchiv, Berlin-Dahlem

The English version of *On War* quoted in this study is taken from the following American edition: Carl von Clausewitz, *On War*, ed. and trans. Michael Howard and Peter Paret (Princeton, N.J.: Princeton University Press, 1976).

The English version of Hitler's directives quoted in this study is taken from H. R. Trevor-Roper, ed., *Hitler's War Directives 1939–1945* (London, 1964). The directives were published in German by W. Hubatsch, ed., *Hitlers Weisungen für die Kriegführung 1939–1945* (Frankfurt am Main, 1962).

J. L. W.

BOOK ONE
The Theories

Prologue: Some Reflections Upon a Theory of War

This study deals with certain German military theories and intends to trace their influence upon one combatant side in the two bloodiest wars of the twentieth century. One cannot, however, overlook the widespread suspicion regarding "theory, when applied to a business as practical and at the same time as uncertain as war."[1] It is obvious, as British military historian Cyril Falls stated, that the attitude toward a theory of war also depends, to a certain degree, on national character. He credited the Germans and the French with formulating and adhering to theories, but noticed that Britain did not produce theoretical writers.

As early as 1909 Major Steward L. Murray, trying to interest the British public in the theories of Clausewitz, held the opinion that "the wide and varied experience which the British officer gradually gains in so many different parts of the world, shows up the weak points of most theories, and produces a certain distrust of them."[2] This attitude has apparently not changed.

Cyril Falls revealed a remark of "a general who gained distinction in the Second World War, Sir Brian Horrocks, . . . that he had never been able to understand any military theory."[3] Falls regarded this as "a polite way of saying, that he thought it worthless and wondered why anybody took the trouble to compose or discuss it." Others put forward the argument that soldiers on the whole, as a professional body and independent of nationality, dislike theorists of war as well as theories of war. In a lecture delivered at the Wehrmachtakademie in 1935, a German staff officer stated that one often quotes theories but seldom reads them, and usually postpones the study of theories until the leisure time of retirement. Then one has the opportunity for meditating and for publishing essays on theory in professional periodicals. Until this time is reached, however, one prefers the role of a "man of action" and sneers at the "faded theory," believing that war is an art that cannot be taught and learned but must be an innate quality. And one, of course, is believed to be born with this capacity and therefore does not worry about theory.[4] This kind of reasoning, however, is refuted by Cyril Falls, who maintains that "if there is an art of war, it is impossible to study it without theorizing. Every art has its theories."[5]

If, on the one hand, people disbelieve in theory, and owing to certain national characteristics prefer an empirical attitude to war, and if, on the other hand, soldiers as a professional group tend to prefer an intuitive approach to war rather than an analytical one,[6] then the question must be raised whether theory is really contrary to practice.

THEORY AND PRACTICE

War can only be practiced in war. This seems to be a truism; notwithstanding, it bears grave consequences. It follows that in peace, neither armies nor commanders can be fully exercised. Sham battles fought in peacetime with blank ammunition and other such training makeshifts are but a poor and inadequate substitute for battle experience. As living memories of war fade with time, soldiers must look for guidance to written records of former campaigns. At their highest intellectual level these campaign records are distilled into theory. Thus theory becomes not bare of fact, but is derived from it. Hence a sound theory is essential both for the understanding of past wars and for a successful conduct of a future one. It approaches the substance of war analytically. Consequently, a certain kind of reciprocity emerges; the starting point of theory is the reality of war. Thus practice puts theory under a searching examination, and the latter guides the practice.

Clausewitz, the theorist, confessed in his introductory note to *On War* that his views of war "are the outcome of wide-ranging study: I have thoroughly checked them against real life and have constantly kept in mind the lessons derived from my experience and from association with distinguished soldiers." In the preface to his work he stated the relationship of theory to practice even more explicitly: "No logical conclusion has been avoided; but whenever the thread became too thin I have preferred to break it off and go back to the relevant phenomena of experience. Just as some plants bear fruit only if they don't shoot too high, so in the practical arts the leaves and flowers of theory must be pruned and the plant kept close to its proper soil—experience."

The process of constructing a military theory is by no means different from that developed in other arts and sciences. If one looks closer into military events, one will perceive that in war, as in other spheres of life, a certain constancy is ever present. Certain features constantly recur. Certain relations between mode of action and success often remain the same. Whereas certain events and moments have repeatedly proved decisive, one should nevertheless keep in mind that the mass of individual incidents bears the character of the changeable or accidental. The former, clearly separated from the incidental ballast of the latter, form a body of principles. It would, however, be misleading to consider these principles as rigid rules of action. It was again Clausewitz who most clearly outlined the fact that the creation of a positive system of rules is impossible. He said:

Give the nature of the subject, we must remind ourselves that it is simply not possible to construct a model for the art of war that can serve as a scaffolding on which the commander can rely for support at any time. Whenever he has to fall back on his innate talent, he will find himself outside the model and in conflict with it; no matter how versatile the code, the situation will always lead to the consequences we have already alluded to: *talent and genius operate outside the rules, and theory conflicts with practice.*[7]

He then reached the conclusion that theory must be of the nature of observation, not a sort of manual for action. It should be an analytical investigation leading to a close acquaintance with the subject, and when applied to experience—in this case to military history—it leads to thorough familiarity with it. Thus theory becomes a guide to anyone who wants to learn about war from books; it will light one's way, train one's judgment, and help one to avoid pitfalls. Moreover, an additional purpose of theory is the accumulation of knowledge and its proper arrangement "in order that each person need not have to clear the ground and toil through afresh."

If one attempts to lay down a simple definition of the relationship of theory and practice for a business so bloody as war, it seems that practice presents questions that theory tries to answer. But a sound theory renounces, *a priori*, the right to prescribe for practice a rigid line of action. At its best it draws attention to a certain lawfulness of events. In not accepting this posture and in regarding theory as a code of laws lies the danger of theory.

ON THE DANGERS OF THEORY

There was a time not so long ago when people believed that war might be conducted in accordance with a tabulated system. Methodical codes of rules and laws pressed military thinking into a Spanish boot. Military theorists tried to handle war as exercises in mathematics and geometry. The impact of irrational factors was completely ignored. Reality has always caused a shock awakening from these hallucinations. Yet in most cases the damage was already done. False doctrines have led armies to destruction and brought states to ruin. One of the most striking examples is doubtless the Prussian defeat in the battle of Jena and Auerstädt in 1806. In that instance it was an artificial conception of war, and not the inefficiency of the Prussian Army, that led to the disaster. Clausewitz, as an eyewitness of the debacle, drew the conclusion that "it was not just a case of a style that had outlived its usefulness but the most extreme poverty of imagination to which routine has ever led."

Although Antoine Henri Jomini, Clausewitz' contemporary, had shared the same experience, it did not prevent him from elaborating a systematic theory of war and constructing schemes from Napoleon's actual conduct of war, similar to the false method that had led to the Prussian defeat. Friedrich von Bernhardi, a German writing on military affairs prior to and after the First World War, scoffed at Jomini's teaching:

When we read him, there is apparently nothing problematical in war; rules and laws insuring success are laid down for every act, and we begin to think that the great Corsican gained his laurels merely by the fact that he conscientiously adhered to the rules constructed from his wars by his critics after the events. Jomini actually does the worst possible violence to the deeds of Napoleon. He—often quite arbitrarily—presses them into a system which he foists on Napoleon.[8]

This criticism presents perhaps an exaggerated view and does not do justice to Jomini's theoretical work, but by its distortion it draws attention to one of the possible evils of theory: the attempt to project backward, into past affairs, artificially constructed actions, which by no means guided the actors at the actual time of events.

One should also bear in mind that war, like any other sphere of social intercourse, is influenced by the progress of mankind in all fields of life. Theory has to pay homage to this fact, as well as to the impact of national characteristics on warfare. The wholesale transplantation of rigid and detailed theoretical rules from one epoch to another would be as much a folly as an uncritical transference of these rules from one nation to another.

An additional problem is whether theory can help in the actual conduct of battle. Theorists of the old school would probably answer in the affirmative, for otherwise it would be a pointless task to map out an elaborate system of "do and do not." Nobody has better defined the real purpose of theory in such an instance as Clausewitz, who held that theory "is meant to educate the mind of the future commander, or, more accurately, to guide him in his self-education, not to accompany him to the battlefield." He compared theory to a wise teacher who guides and stimulates but avoids leading his pupil by the hand for the rest of his life. Principles and rules crystallized from the theorist's studies should, however, "provide a thinking man with a frame of reference for the movements he has been trained to carry out, rather than to serve as a guide which at the moment of action lays down precisely the path he must take."[9] On the other hand, the only real proof of military theory is on the field of battle.

THE PROOF OF THEORY

Soon after the outbreak of the Second World War, at the climax of the Polish Campaign in 1939, a German military writer stated that many subjects which military authors wrote extensive treatises on from 1866 to 1914 turned out to be insignificant during the First World War. But he nevertheless maintained that there were still enough fundamentals from pre-war theory that were proved true by the war.[10]

In order to establish a theory that is able to weather the onslaught of real war, theory works again in two directions: It scrutinizes the past by means of military history and separates the essentials of permanent value from the accidental, and thus crystallizes principles. On the other hand it puts these principles time and again to the cruel test of war, and thus selects the permanent maxims from the ephemeral. In such a manner the experience of the past guides the speculation of commanders about the present and the future.

It follows that the history of war is the foundation of theory. One must, however, according to Clausewitz, distinguish the critical narration of history from the simple narration of historical events, which merely places events side by side and at best touches on their most immediate causal connections. There are three modes of critical narration. The first is the historical discovery and verification of questionable facts. This is historical research proper and has nothing in common with theory. The second is the relating of the effect to its causes, called by Clausewitz the "critical analysis proper. It is essential for theory." The third is the investigation and evaluation of means employed. This "is criticism proper, involving praise and censure. Here theory serves history, or rather the lessons to be drawn from history. In the last two activities which are the truly critical parts of historical inquiry, it is vital to analyze everything down to its basic elements, to incontrovertible truth. One must not stop half-way, as so often is done, at some arbitrary assumption or hypothesis."[11] By using this method Clausewitz concluded that there are a multitude of propositions that can be made clear without difficulty, and thus render possible the construction of a sound theory of war.

That military history should be understood in such a way was also stressed by British military thinker and historian Basil Henry Liddell Hart, who maintained that "most of the immortal victories of history" were psychological rather than physical,

with the actual fighting a secondary influence. For the profoundest truth of war is that the issue of battles is usually decided in the minds of the opposing commanders, not in the bodies of their men. The best history would be a register of their thoughts and emotions, with a mere background of events to throw them into relief. But the delusion to the contrary has been fostered by the typical military history, filled with details of the fighting and assessing the cause of victory by statistical computations of the number engaged.[12]

Another pitfall of theory is that, for the sake of clarity, it strives for perfect examples, whereas in battle the commander is often compelled to content himself more with fragments of evidence and, notwithstanding, must try to do his best to solve his problems.

In Book One the teaching of two German military theorists is investigated, and in Book Two an attempt is made to prove that these theories influenced the actual German conduct of both world wars. Military Germany, at least since the middle of the nineteenth century, maintained a highly developed interest in the science and art of war. The variety of military publications, dominated since the beginning of the present century by the quarterly of the Great General Staff, "Vierteljahreshefte für Truppenführung und Heereskunde,"[13] provides enough confirmation of this point. If the officers' corps of the troops were less concerned with the finer qualities of their art, most General Staff officers held it in high esteem. Most of the leading appointments, however, from divisional headquarters upward, were manned by members of the General Staff's Officers' Corps. Thus indoctrination of the higher ranks of the German Army (in both world wars) was almost assured. German military opinion considered the efficient type of modern commander and superior leader of troops to be a mixture of theorist and practical soldier. Friedrich von Bernhardi held the view that the pure practitioner of war is bound for failure as much as the pure theorist.[14] Both types lack a sense of reality. The first requirement for a military leader is, therefore, above all, common sense and a proper sense of proportion. But it is a mistake to conclude that a commonsense man of action, without proper previous training, practical as well as theoretical, could do the job. The combination of theoretical and practical knowledge is essential.

These preliminary reflections seem necessary in order not to lose sight of essentials when plunging into the detailed investigation of several military theories and two great wars that follows.

NOTES

1. Cyril Falls, *The Art of War*, London, 1961, p. 6.

2. Major Steward L. Murray, *The Reality of War*, London, 1909, p. 1.

3. C. Falls, *op. cit.*, p. 18.

4. "Kritische Untersuchung der Lehren von Douhet, Fuller, Hart und Seeckt," Vortrag gehalten am 29.11.1935 an der Wehrmachtakademie von Oberstleutnant des Generalstabes Matzky. BA/MA—W10–1/9.

5. C. Falls, *op. cit.*, p. 19.

6. One should, however, keep at the back of one's mind that in Germany a distinguished and specially selected group of officers, the Corps of General Staff Officers, was very much concerned with military theory. Cf. end of prologue.

7. In the second chapter "On the Theory of War" of the Second Book "On the Theory of War." Carl von Clausewitz, *On War*, II, 2, p. 140.

8. F. v. Bernhardi, *On War of To-Day*, London, 1912, vol. 1, pp. 55–56.

9. *On War*, II, 2, p. 141.

10. Generalleutnant W. Erfurth, *Der Vernichtungssieg*, Berlin, 1939, p. 77.

11. *On War*, II, 5, p. 156.

12. B. H. Liddell Hart, *A History of the World War 1914–1918*, London, 1934, p. 111.

13. Initiated, with General Schlieffen's approval, and edited by v. Freytag-Loringhoven, at that time Head of the Historical Department of the German General Staff.

14. F. v. Bernhardi, *op. cit.*, vol. 2, p. 221.

1

Carl von Clausewitz: Philosopher in Arms

"It was my ambition to write a book that would not be forgotten after two or three years." This passage was found among the papers of Prussian General Carl von Clausewitz (1780–1831) after his death. Even now, more than 150 years later, he is still regarded as "the high priest in the temple of Mars."[1] His influence in the science and art of war is still unrivaled, while the works of earlier, contemporary, and later writers have passed into obscurity.[2] In Germany his work gained general recognition soon after its first publication, and quickly became the "Bible" of the German officer and, to some degree, even of the German statesman. One of the purposes of this study is to discover to what extent Clausewitz was really understood by the Germans. The Anglo-Saxon peoples did not pay attention to his teaching until much later, and the British did not realize the importance of his theories for Germany's conduct of war until the eve of the world war of 1914–1918. The Americans first translated *On War* as late as the Second World War. On the other hand the French, who are more inclined toward theory in warfare, discovered him much earlier.[3]

Friedrich Engels (1820–1895) studied Clausewitz thoroughly and recommended him to Karl Marx (1818–1883). Engels was attracted not only by Clausewitz' comparison of war with trade,[4] but also by the theoretical aspects of warfare as stated in *On War*. Later on Lenin (1870–1924), the Russian Bolshevik leader, annotated an edition of this work with many marginal notes and comments, which was subsequently published.[5]

There is no intention here of narrating Clausewitz' biography; this may be found elsewhere.[6]

His complete works, containing ten volumes, were published by his wife after his death. It is clear that this was intentional when one considers his somewhat ambiguous position in the Prussian state and army. Being the outspoken ideologist of the so-called Prussian military and social reformers, and having preached dangerous ideas like "popular levy" and the "small war,"[7] he was highly suspect in the eyes of his royal master, who was one of the pillars of the "Holy Alliance."

The first three volumes of these works comprise the most famous treatise, *On*

War, generally regarded as dealing with the science of war, also labeled as the didactic part. The other seven volumes constitute war-historical studies. This classification does not indicate, however, the chronological sequence of Clausewitz' writing, or that the historical studies lack theoretical passages. But it is obvious that all the other parts of his work are focused on the centerpiece, *On War*, and were more or less preliminary or complementary studies intended to clarify its findings. In all, Clausewitz inquired into more than 130 campaigns in order to reach his conclusions.

As early as 1807 Clausewitz pointed out the importance of theory in warfare. At that time he was a prisoner of war in France, after the Prussian disaster of 1806. Yet, despite this collapse of the Prussian conduct of war, he still believed in theory. From Paris he wrote that "from all I have learned up to the present date about the art of war, I saw nothing at all being carried out on our side; nevertheless I recognized, in the reality of the war, the truth of all that theory had taught us, and convinced myself of the efficiency of its means."[8] This belief turned out to be the guiding principle for his future immense intellectual work.

Prior to an examination of Clausewitz' teaching in the various spheres of war, one should acquaint oneself with his definition of strategy and tactics.

STRATEGY AND TACTICS

"According to our classification, then, tactics teaches *the use of the armed forces* in the engagement; strategy the use of engagements *for the object of the war*."[9] That is Clausewitz' definition laid down in the first chapter of the book *On the Theory of War* (Book II). In the same book he stressed the theoretical importance of distinguishing the nature of means and ends in tactics and strategy. In tactics he regarded the "fighting forces trained for combat" as the means and victory as the end. The obvious sign of victory is the enemy's withdrawal from the battlefield.[10] On the other hand, for strategy, this victory, i.e., the tactical success, provides primarily only a means, whereas the events that may lead to peace present the ultimate object of strategy.[11] From this it is clear that strategy assigns the objectives to the particular engagements. Of course, the significance of each individual objective exercises a certain influence on the very nature of the victory. Consequently, if strategy is the use of the engagement to attain the objective of the war, "the strategist must therefore define an aim to the entire operational side of the war that will be in accordance with its purpose."[12] It follows that the strategy shapes the plan of war, arranges the sequence of actions that will lead to its fulfillment, maps the framework for the separate campaigns, and coordinates the different engagements. This immense task of strategy can be accomplished only if a theory is available that can provide, even if only on a small and limited scale, some principles and rules. It seems appropriate to outline the relationship of strategy and tactics in Clausewitz' own words: "Strategy decides the time when, the place where and the forces with which the engagement is to be fought and through this threefold activity exerts considerable influence on its outcome. Once the tactical encounter has taken place and the result—be it victory or defeat—is assured, strategy will use it to serve the object of the war."[13] But in his study of the campaigns in Italy and Switzerland in 1799,[14] he argued that the task of strategy does not stop with the first engagement, in order to leave its execution solely to tactics. He stressed that there are many engagements in which strategic combinations run their full course, and in such instances the general ought to understand which kind of actions and decisions the circumstances demand.

Clausewitz confined himself to the use of the armed forces when dealing with strategy and tactics. Although he was apparently aware that in war there are a number of important activities relating to the maintenance and supply of armed forces, he excluded these from his considerations. It appears that he did this for theoretical reasons: "discriminating between dissimilar elements." He exclaimed: "One would not want to consider the whole business[15] of maintenance and administration as part of the *actual conduct of war*."[16] This curious view of logistics is striking and runs throughout his writing.

The German usage of Clausewitz' theories was not confined to the division of the art of war into tactics and strategy. This two-level system had been superseded by a three-level system: "strategy," "operation," and "tactics." German General Hans Speidel argued that from the experience of the Second World War it was apparent that this threefold division is a necessity, *sine qua non*. By Speidel's definition, "strategy" embraces all military thoughts, decisions, and their execution that arise from the partnership of the intellectual, political, economic, and military managements in modern war. From this co-operation of the various leaders of a state or a coalition toward a common goal emerge strategic ideas in the military sphere, at the level of the high command of the armed forces and, according to circumstances, even at the level of autonomous theaters of war (or autonomous services: navy, army, or air force).

The "operation" is to be regarded as a subdivision of strategy. Its sphere is the conduct of battle at the higher levels, on the battlefield, and in accordance with the tasks presented by the strategic planning. Battle[17] is defined as a more enlarged engagement,[18] or a series of engagements dependent on one another in time, space, and effect. The engagement is the mere clash of arms.[19] Thus "tactics" is the conduct of troops toward and during the engagement.[20]

There is no intention here of discussing the pros and cons of such an arrangement, but as a matter of fact, many nations that did not accept these definitions found themselves using a similar triple division by adding "Grand Strategy" as a superior level above the normal (simple) strategy. From a superficial examination it seems that the results of this classification are not very different from the German one.

Let us now turn back to Clausewitz' teaching and start with an examination of its core: the relationship of war and politics.

WAR AND POLITICS

Many people who have never read a single word of Clausewitz' teaching know by heart and quote without hesitation the passage that "war is merely the continuation of policy by other means." But only a few know that with this statement they have embarked on a controversial subject that constitutes the principal part of Clausewitz' whole theory. If this component of his teaching were eliminated, the whole structure of his theoretical building would collapse. It seemed so vital to Clausewitz that he mentioned it again and again in different parts of his treatise and examined it many times from various angles. This incessant repetition led Cyril Falls to the unjustified accusation that "he does harp on the same string like a modern director of publicity."[21] But Clausewitz probably felt that this point would not be easily understood or accepted by his military compatriots. He learned it the hard way, from his sad experience, and would not agree to seeing the problems of war again handled by mere military experts and drill-masters lacking any political orientation and understanding. Moreover, he would, of course, not know how much would be written on this subject in the future.

Let us now trace Clausewitz' assumption in *On War*.[22] In the first book, *On the Nature of War*, he stressed that war is not only a political act, "but a true political instrument, a continuation of political activity by other means."[23] By applying the concept of end and means he reached the conclusion that political design is the end and war is the means. It follows that the means can never be considered separately from the end.

He returned to this subject in Book VIII. Unfortunately, this book exists only in fragmentary outlines but is nevertheless, even in this shape, an important contribution.[24] Chapter 6A is dedicated to the "Effect of the Political Aim on the Military Objective" and subchapter B reads: "War Is an Instrument of Policy." Here he derived from the assumption that war is only a branch of political activity, the concept "that it is in no sense autonomous."[25] He explained that although people know that war is caused by political institutions, i.e., governments and nations, it is generally supposed that political intercourse is broken off by war. He maintained, on the contrary, that "war is simply a continuation of political intercourse with the addition of other means."[26] And he again defined the dependence of means and ends by an analogy from the sphere of language and thought, by coining the famous phrase that "its grammar, indeed, may be its own, but not its logic."

Therefore, if war belongs to policy, it will naturally take on the latter's character. This decides the scale of the military actions, because wars vary in accordance with the nature of their motives and of the circumstances from which they arise. By starting with the nature of war and defining war "as an act of force to compel our enemy to do our will," the political object of war has nearly been "swallowed up" by this extreme statement. But the political object is easily recognized as the original motivation: "The smaller the penalty you demand from your opponent, the less you can expect him to try and deny it to you; the smaller the effort he makes, the less you need make yourself. Moreover, the more modest your own political aim, the less importance you attach to it and the less reluctantly you will abandon it if you must. *This is another reason why your effort will be modified.*"[27]

If we agree with this, then the political object, defined as the original motive of the war, will provide the standard for the aim and for the degree of military efforts alike. This equalization of the aim of the military action with the political objective explains why that action tends to diminish as the political object diminishes. In such a way a war may range from a war of extermination to a mere state of armed observation. Once the influence of the political objective on the war is tolerated, there will no longer be any limit to it, and we are compelled to include in its range even more threatening of the enemy or negotiation. In other words, war becomes but a specific case of the wider range of politics. On the other hand, war unrestrained by policy would always strive to the extreme: "The more powerful and inspiring the motives for war, the more they affect the belligerent nations and the fiercer the tensions that produce the outbreak, the closer will war approach its abstract concept,[28] the more important will be the destruction of the enemy, the more closely will the military aims and the political objects of war coincide, and the more military and less political will war appear to be."[29]

This principle of increasing power and violence may be applied in the opposite direction. A suspension in war is therefore no anomaly, and it is well known that there are many wars in which action fills only a small part of the time involved. In this respect political means also exercise an influence on the probable success without the need of defeating the enemy's armed forces but merely by disrupting the opposing alliance or paralyzing it or by winning new allies and favorably affecting the political scene and similar steps.[30] Often those actions may provide a much shorter way to peace, the ultimate goal of every military action.[31] Moreover, even if a final decision in a war has been reached, it should never be looked on as an ultimate one, for the defeated state often regards it as a transitory situation only, for which remedy might be found in new political action.

Clausewitz, however, did not only draw up the proper part of the military commander in the war-policy relationship, he also defined the role of the statesman. First of all, the politicians must share the responsibility for success or defeat in war and should not be allowed to put the blame on their military experts. This does not mean that the political element should penetrate deeply into the details of war. One does not, as Clausewitz put it, send out patrols during the war, or post sentries, on political considerations.[32] But the latter's influence is decisive in planning for war.

Policy, as Clausewitz wanted it to be understood, is the "representative of all interests of the community."[33] However, the question might be raised whether, for the sake of war planning, the political viewpoint should be subordinated to the purely military? Clausewitz rejected such an attitude completely and regarded it as an absurdity: "For it is policy that created war. Policy is the guiding intelligence, and war only the instrument, not vice versa."[34] The subordination of the military viewpoint to the political remains, therefore, the only acceptable solution. Thus if there arises any conflict between the political and the military interests, it should be regarded merely as imperfect knowledge, for if "policy could make demands on war which war could not fulfill; but that would challenge the natural unavoidable assumption that policy knows the instrument it means to use."[35] From this concept it follows logically that the art of war on its highest level becomes policy.

Defining the division of tasks between the statesmen and the generals, Clausewitz made one of his most controversial statements, arguing that "the assertion that a major military development, or the plan for one, should be a matter for *purely military* opinion is unacceptable and can be damaging. Nor indeed is it sensible to summon soldiers, as many governments do when they are planning a war, and ask them for *purely military advice*."[36]

On the other hand he also rejected violently as a complete absurdity the widespread demand of theorists that the available means should be laid before the military commanders, so that they may draw up a purely military plan for war. It was his opinion that war and its general outlines had always been determined by political institutions and not by military. One should therefore never speak, as has often been done, of the harmful influence of policy on the conduct of war. It is not this influence but the policy itself that should be found at fault. Conversely, if the policy is right, it can only affect war favorably. To avoid frictions between the politicians and the generals, and for smoother coordination of policy and military actions, Clausewitz suggested, in cases where the statesman and the soldier were not combined in one person, that the commander-in-chief be made a member of the cabinet, so that the latter could participate in the principal issues of the former's action. Nothing demonstrates the German soldiers' disapproval of this idea better than the fact that this statement of Clausewitz was altered deliberately, from the second edition, published in 1853, onward. It is the great achievement of Professor W. Hahlweg of having discovered this falsification.[37] Whereas Clausewitz' genuine definition illuminated the problem from the statesman's point of view, the forged statement enlarged the powers of the general, who was now made a member of the cabinet so that he could participate in decision making.[38] In fact, Clausewitz' opinion upside down! It is interesting that nowadays most countries have in fact adopted Clausewitz' concept for coordinating political and military policy at the highest level.

If, however, the conduct of war is really dominated by politics, then it is the government that decides on the size of the army and determines in this manner a vital part of strategy. The general in command must regard this absolute strength of the force as a given quantity.

At this point the question might be asked whether the relationship between German civilian and military leadership, especially in wartime, accorded with

Clausewitz' teaching? This important and delicate problem occupies a vital part of the second book of this study. It seems, however, to be of some interest to quote from the comment of the German Colonel W. von Scherff, who edited the 1880 German edition of *On War*: "The interference of policy in the conduct of war leads always to ruin. Policy sets the fashion *how* the house should be built, but it must not interfere with *the building process itself.*" Hence one will not wonder when a certain Rittmeister Bruno Pochhammer, editor of a popular German edition of *On War* in 1937, stated in an epilogue that "up to the First World War, war could be regarded according to Clausewitz as a mean of policy, nowadays every political measure becomes an expedient subordinated to the all-embracing war." This statement is, of course, no invention of Captain Pochhammer, who took it directly from General Ludendorff's (1865–1937) ideology of the "total war."[39] However, as the editor of Clausewitz' work, he did not dare to be as insolent as Ludendorff, who stated boldly that "all (!) theories of Clausewitz have to be thrown overboard. War and politics serve the survival of the people, but war is the highest expression of the racial will to life."[40] According to Ludendorff, total war is a product of demographic and technological developments, which means that the increased size of populations and the ever-improving efficiency of the tools for destruction have created the totality of war. Thus total war, without any political cause, absorbs policy.

Several other opinions existed among German soldiers. General L. Beck, Chief of the General Staff of the army in the period from 1933 to 1938, clearly stated, in accordance with Clausewitz, that among the preliminary conditions for the successful conduct of war, an efficient foreign policy ranks highest. (It should be noted that his opinion did not prevail at the time.) This creates the situation under which a state is involved in war and bears the responsibility for it. In case of failure, history will not record a continuation of policy by other means, but the bankruptcy of politics. In history one may find many a "war" that has been won or lost before it even began, and the reason for this has always been the conduct of policy. Beck stressed, again in strict accordance with Clausewitz' teaching, that the political objective should be apparent and this enables the military aim and the available means to be derived from it.[41]

Some modern writers tend to regard Clausewitz' postulate concerning the primacy of policy over war as obsolete in the age of thermonuclear weapons. Releasing the "bomb," they claim, would mean the ultimate bankruptcy of politics and its unconditional surrender to war. Even if one does agree with such a definition, this situation still appears to be covered by Clausewitz' theory of a wide spectrum of possible kinds of war, ranging from the hypothetical "absolute" war to merely armed observation. Nuclear warfare, reducing the share of policy to zero by its execution, would near the extreme "absolute" edge of the scale. One should, however, keep in mind that Clausewitz never demanded that war should at all times, in all cases, become the ultimate continuation of policy; he had only defined it as such, should it occur. On the other hand, nuclear weapons as a deterrent fit extremely well into Clausewitz' suppositions. Only more stress should be attached to the demand that the politicians must know perfectly well the nature of the instrument and the consequences of its release.

It seemed here necessary to deal at length with the problem of the relationship of war and policy, in order to stress the real importance and value of this particular part of Clausewitz' work.

THE OBJECTS OF WAR

In addition to the famous definition that "war is . . . an act of force to compel our enemy to do our will," Clausewitz also described war as "the impact of opposing forces. It follows that the stronger force not only destroys the weaker, but that its impetus carries the weaker force along with it."[42] According to Clausewitz' method of examining every phenomenon in terms of the concepts of end and means, he regarded the physical force[43] as the means, whereas the imposition of one's will on the enemy is the objective. For the achievement of this objective one must disarm the enemy, and it transpires that this disarming is by definition the proper aim of military action that takes the place of the objective. Moreover, from the theoretical point of view there is no limit to the application of that force. It follows, then, that if one's opponent is to yield to the former's will, the latter must be maneuvered into a situation more disadvantageous than the sacrifices demanded from him. Hence the disarming or overthrow of the enemy must be the aim of military action. This had led many students and interpreters of Clausewitz' teaching to the erroneous assumption that he preached what has been later called "the idea of annihilation."[44]

Clausewitz perceived a triple tendency in war:

1. The original violence of its elements, the hate and enmity, which are mainly the concern of the people;
2. the play of probabilities and chance, which make it a free activity of emotion and concerns primarily the commander and his army;
3. its subordinate character as a political tool, which makes it a concern of governments (and which has already been treated in the previous section).

In an instruction pamphlet prepared for the Prussian Crown Prince,[45] Clausewitz mentions the three main goals of every war:

1. To defeat the enemy armed force and destroy it. That means to direct the main effort first and always against the opponent's main army;
2. to take possession of the enemy's nonmilitary resources, i.e., occupation of the country or at least action against the capital and other important strong points;
3. to win over public opinion. This goal may be achieved by great victories or possession of the capital.

In his study of the campaign in Italy in 1796, he stressed the overwhelming importance of *one great* victory compared with the victorious outcome of a series of engagements, although the number of casualties on the defeated side might be equal in both instances.[46]

It is now time to put the question, was Clausewitz the prophet of annihilation? Many of his adherents would answer positively without any hesitation. Others would probably deny it. But what did he really mean? At the beginning of his treatise he claimed that "the aim of *disarming the enemy* . . . is in fact not always encountered in reality, and need not be fully achieved as a condition of peace. On no account should theory raise it to the level of a law. Many treaties have been concluded before one of the antagonists could be called powerless—even before the balance of power had been seriously altered."[47] Therefore, the enemy's outright defeat is not always necessary, but a variety of means are at the disposal of the belligerents to subdue the opponent's will: destruction of his forces, conquest of territory or temporary occupation of it, political schemes, or even the passive expectation of the enemy's attack.[48] Clausewitz recognized many gradations between a death struggle for political existence and a war that a strained and tottering alliance makes a matter of disagreeable duty. At a late stage of his work he defined "two kinds of war" and announced his intention to revise the first six books of *On War*.[49] The two kinds of war are either "to *overthrow the enemy*—to render him politically helpless or militarily impotent, thus forcing him to sign whatever peace we please; or *merely to occupy some of his frontier-districts* so that we can annex them or use them for bargaining at the peace negotiations."[50]

On the other hand, at a time when the *military* clash is unavoidable, it should be clear "that the primary object of great battles must be the destruction of the enemy's forces."[51] And that is true, of course, in regard to the goals of any individual engagement. But even then Clausewitz did not carry this point to its extreme, and asserted that not only engagements that had actually been fought, but also possible engagements should be regarded as real ones.[52] This explains how whole campaigns can be pursued with great activity, without the actual engagements playing any notable part in them. Furthermore, Clausewitz took into account "the negative side of the destruction of the enemy's forces—the preservation of our own." Both efforts of annihilation, the positive as well as the negative, are linked. While "the effort to destroy the enemy's forces has a positive purpose and leads to positive results, whose final aim is the enemy's collapse," it is obvious that "preserving our own forces has a negative purpose; it frustrates the enemy's intentions—that is, it amounts to pure resistance, whose ultimate aim can only be to prolong the war until the enemy is exhausted."[53] It follows that Clausewitz regarded the struggle for gaining time as a legitimate objective in war. Warning against half-measures he exclaimed: "Woe to the government, which, relying on half-hearted politics and a shackled policy, meets a foe who like the untamed elements, knows no law other than his own power! Any defect of action and effort will turn to the advantage of the enemy."[54] On the other hand it would obviously be a great mistake to deduce from this argument that a headlong rush must always triumph over skillful caution. Blind aggressiveness would destroy the attack itself, not the defense. Greater effectiveness relates not to the *means*, but to the *end*. This is the result of a simple comparison of the effect of different outcomes.[55]

Thus Clausewitz taught annihilation; it comprised but one component in a vast scale of other means that may lead toward the fulfillment of the aims of a particular war.

THE MORAL ELEMENT IN WAR

It will not come as a surprise that Clausewitz regarded war as a form of human intercourse, which settles a conflict of great interests by bloodshed. Thus the image of war would be freed from the fetters of previous artificial theories. Even his contemporary Jomini still dealt mainly with the possession of decisive geographical and topographical points and disregarded the moral elements, whereas the latter play a vital part in Clausewitz' analysis. Thus he managed to explain the tremendous phenomenon of Napoleon's successes more convincingly than any other theorist. His confrontation of moral forces with physical forces answered the question why an army inferior in numbers frequently prevailed over a numerically superior one. Moreover, he made it clear that in many instances exhaustion was more a matter of weariness of willpower than of physical exhaustion. If we aim, therefore, to destroy the enemy's power, this should not only be limited to the physical forces, but should also be directed principally against moral ones. This explains the tremendous impact of a great victory in paralyzing the still remaining, sometimes even intact, forces of the enemy. Sometimes, while the decision is still in the balance, victory comes to the side that has a small additional amount of moral power and is, as a matter of fact, not much affected by real losses or gains. Yet in his analysis of the campaigns in 1799 he stressed that every loss and fruitless effort had a more serious effect on the side that had already suffered more casualties.

As early as April 1807, being then a prisoner of war, he realized that "deliberate boldness,[56] a sense of innovation, rapidity promise justified claims for victory."[57]

His catalog of moral elements included, in addition to the virtues of generalship, the appreciation of popular forces (militia) as a supporting factor in the active army and the recognition that the "small war," i.e., guerrilla warfare, should be treated as equal to the "great war." In his "Memorandum of Creed" (Bekenntnisdenkschrift) of 1812, published at the climax of his rebellion against Prussian resignation to French overlordship, he had propagated the idea of the popular uprising.[58] In his final work, brought to maturity during the period of Restoration, he had more in mind a popular movement guided by authority, on the lines of the Prussian *Landsturm*.[59] But even this relatively tame idea gained no official favor for fear that it might escalate into a real revolution. Neither did the general approach to the "small war" in the sense of guerrilla warfare. It finally boiled down merely to the tactics and techniques of small, but normal, army units.[60]

The main credit, however, should be given to Clausewitz for his discovery of an additional factor closely connected with moral elements, namely, the friction factor.

ON FRICTION IN WAR

The term "friction" has now become an integral part of the modern military vocabulary. Even though Clausewitz compared the conception of friction in the military sphere with the same phenomenon in mechanics, he did not regard it as a mechanical process. He emphasized the human factor as mainly responsible for its occurrence. After all, the military machine, to use a technical term for the instrument of war, is composed of individuals, each of whom is the subject of human frailty. "Everything in war is very simple, but the simplest thing is difficult," said Clausewitz, and "action in war is like movement in a resistant element. Just as a movement which is performed with ease in open air becomes very difficult for men under water."[61] Thus friction distinguished real war from that planned on paper in the security of an office.[62] This explains why so many times plans fell short of the mark and why such tremendous powers are needed not to fall below the level of mediocrity. Friction in war is not reducible to a small number of points as may be done in mechanics, but covers a multitude of various circumstances—principally the moral elements, like danger, exertion, hardship, and many other physiological and psychological factors.

It is the great achievement of Clausewitz to have broken with the purely rationalistic approach to war of previous theorists, who tried to make us believe in mathematical and geometrical formulas, and having introduced—together with his concept of moral elements—the *irrational* in war.

Despite Clausewitz' penetrating investigation into most aspects of strategy, he did not pay much attention to the impact of logistics on strategy.

ON LOGISTICS

It is indeed striking to discover that Clausewitz has explicitly excluded the logistic factor from the necessary considerations for the conduct of war. He has even excluded such commonly accepted items as "supply," "medical services," and "maintenance of arms and equipment."[63] Would a modern commander, even on the lowest level, dare to disregard so vital a sphere? The explanation of Clausewitz' attitude in these matters might be found partly in the fact that the French in his time had freed the armies from the previous heavy burden of magazines and supply trains—Friedrich the Great's famous bread wagons—by shifting over to the system of requisition, the so-called "living on the country."

A further psychological reason may be found in his quarrel with his oversystematic and schematic predecessors and contemporaries in the field of military theory and their glorification of the importance of the base.[64] In order to uproot their geometrical maxims of the importance of bases and operation angles by turning the focus on the realities of war, Clausewitz had obviously over-reached the limit. He could not have foreseen the tremendous impact of logistics on the future mass-armies, eased and aggravated at the same time by means of mechanical transport, and, of course, the total mobilization of nations' whole resources. Nevertheless, the fact remains that in this matter Clausewitz failed to realize the full significance of the problem.

Leaving the sphere of strategy we shall now enter into the field of operations and tactics and first examine, with Clausewitz' guidance, the controversial subject of fighting on interior or exterior lines.

OPERATION ON INTERIOR AND EXTERIOR LINES

After a profound investigation of the matter in his campaign studies, as well as on a purely theoretical basis, Clausewitz did not provide the eager student of the conduct of war with a clear-cut solution. This is all the more remarkable because of the current popularity, thanks largely to Jomini's teaching, of interior lines as "the mysterious arcanum of victory."[65] In fact, Jomini allowed himself to believe that the inner line was the most essential secret of the art of war. On the other hand Clausewitz also stressed the advantages of a concentric attack, which he regarded in some circumstances as equal to attack on interior lines. Nevertheless, one may sense in his work some inclination toward the operation on inner lines, mainly on account of the inadequacy of communications in his time. In strategy, he argued, because "of the greater areas involved . . . the effectiveness of interior and therefore shorter lines is accentuated and forms an important counterbalance against concentric attacks."[66] Once the defender has decided to switch over to offensive action, i.e., to move (an act that he always starts later than the attacker but, it is supposed, always in time to break the fetters of paralyzing inaction), the advantage of greater concentration and shorter interior lines are shown to be decisive and are frequently more effective in obtaining victory than the convergent form of attack. The weaker party fighting on interior lines gains strength by concentrating strong forces toward decisive points in the assailant's dispersed deployment. However, in many situations the attacking forces are too numerous, and the defender, despite the assumed advantages of operating on interior lines, finds himself encircled and is eventually crushed under the attacker's overwhelming weight.

Clausewitz also offered an approach, novel in some respects, to the problem of concentration of force, especially if one keeps in mind that his attention was already focused on mass-armies created by popular levy, and not on the small mercenary armies of previous "Cabinet Wars."

ON CONCENTRATION OF FORCE

In the military pamphlets and manuals of today the postulate of concentration, both in space and in time, has become commonplace. But that was not the case in the eighteenth century. Time and again forces had been divided and dispersed without any apparently sensible reason "simply because he [the commander] vaguely felt that this was the way things ought to be done."[67] It is therefore no wonder that Clausewitz emphasized the concentration of force in its completeness as the norm, and every deviation from it as demanding explicit justification. This procedure seemed, in his opinion, the only safeguard against this widespread folly.

In regard to the concentration of forces in time (complementing the concentration in space), he formulated a law that "all forces intended and available for a strategic purpose should be applied *simultaneously*; their employment will be the more effective the more everything can be concentrated in a single action at a single moment."[68] Nevertheless, he also admitted that there exists the possibility of a successive use, but it depends on the level of execution: "In the tactical realm force can be used successively, while strategy knows only the simultaneous use of force."[69] Concentration of force also means the utilization of quantities.

ON SUPERIORITY OF NUMBERS

This issue would not have been considered in this study had not Liddell Hart described Clausewitz "historically as the Mahdi of mass."[70] Is this title justified? In order to answer this question one should refer to the following passage:

If we thus strip the engagement of all the variables arising from its purpose and circumstances, and disregard the fighting value of the troops involved (which is a given quantity), we are left with the bare concept of the engagement, a shapeless battle in which the only distinguished factor is the number of troops on either side.

These numbers, therefore, will determine victory. It is, of course, evident from the mass of abstractions I have made to reach this point that the superiority of numbers in a given engagement *is only one of the factors* that determines victory.[71]

And because this superiority has degrees, continued Clausewitz, it must be great enough "to counterbalance all the other contributing circumstances. It follows that as many troops as possible should be brought into the engagement at the decisive point."[72] He regarded this as the first principle in strategy. However, this statement was immediately followed by a list of battles that famous generals had won with inferior numbers. But it seemed to him "that in modern Europe even the most talented general will find it very difficult to defeat an opponent twice his strength."

But to fully understand Clausewitz one should note his conclusion that "to achieve strength at the decisive point depends on the strength of the army and on *the skill with which this strength* is employed'' (emphasis added). In other words: Generalship has a vital part in victory!

Clausewitz' observation that the size of an army is determined by the government[73] held a new challenge for the skill of the commander. Since by this the absolute size of the force is a given quantity, "consequently, *the forces available must be employed with such skill* that even in the absence of absolute superiority, relative superiority is attained at the decisive point.''[74]

Obviously the mainspring for the chapter on superiority in numbers was the elimination of the previously widespread notion, ''that there is a certain optimum size for an army, an ideal norm, and that any troops in excess of it are more trouble than they are worth.''[75] If by that Clausewitz heralded the emergence of future mass-armies, it only indicates that he had sensed the general trend.

If one pays attention to the fact that the chapters preceding and succeeding the chapter on ''Superiority of Numbers'' deal with such subjects as ''Moral Factors,'' ''The Principal Moral Elements,'' ''Military Virtues of the Army,'' ''Boldness,'' ''Perseverance,'' ''Surprise,'' and ''Cunning,'' and if one takes into account the importance that Clausewitz attached to moral elements, Liddell Hart's charge seems hardly to find ground. Superiority in numbers is but one factor among others in Clausewitz' theory!

While trying to lay down rules for the selection of the decisive point, Clausewitz again chose an analogical comparison with mechanics: *the* Schwerpunkt—*the center of gravity.*

THE CENTER OF GRAVITY

Deriving this from physics, Clausewitz said: ''A center of gravity is always found where the mass is concentrated most densely. It presents the most effective target for a blow; furthermore, the heaviest blow is that struck by the center of gravity. The same holds true in war.''[76] Therefore, ''a theatre of war, be it large or small, and the forces stationed there, no matter what their size, represent the sort of unity in which a *single* center of gravity can be identified. That is the place where the decision should be reached.''[77] This later led Field Marshal Paul von Hindenburg (1847–1934) to his famous saying that an ''attack without *Schwerpunkt* is like a man without character.''[78] It is therefore an essential component of good generalship to recognize this *centrum gravitatis*. Clausewitz offered various possibilities for the identification of such a center of gravity:

For Alexander, Gustavus Adolphus, Charles XII, and Frederik the Great, the center of gravity was their army. If the army had been destroyed, they would all have gone down in history as failures. In countries subject to domestic strife, the center of gravity is generally the capital. In small countries that rely on large ones, it is usually the army of their protector. Among alliances, it lies in the community of interest, and in popular uprisings it is the personalities of the leaders and public opinion. It is against these that our energies should be directed.[79]

By following up Clausewitz' arguments about the selection of the center of gravity, one learns that it is possible to direct a military action against a military objective in order to achieve a political aim and, vice versa, to undertake a political action in order to gain a military success. That applies, for instance, to a war waged against a coalition. In that case there are again two ways open for action: One may direct the decisive blow against the stronger (or sometimes the weaker) partner of the alliance in order to break up the coalition by means of defeat of one partner. The other possibility is by hitting along the seam of the Allied armies, dividing those armies physically one from another, and thus lending countenance to the political split of the hostile coalition.

However, even after identifying the center of gravity, there is still danger in overestimating the expected resistance and hence applying more force than required.

Another way of wasting force, according to Clausewitz, is dispersion for diversion. In his era, influenced by the predilection of the pre-Napoleonic period in favor of waging wars by "maneuvering" rather than by delivering real blows, it was still a common feature of generalship and a special hobby of statesmen, which Clausewitz condemned ruthlessly.

THE RELATIONSHIP OF DEFENSIVE AND OFFENSIVE

Book VI, *Defense*, comprises the largest part of the whole work *On War*. It covers thirty chapters, more than a quarter of the whole work. Moreover, the next book, dealing with the attack, is to be regarded as connected with this book; Clausewitz himself admitted in his note of 10 July 1827: "Book VII 'On Attack,' . . . should be regarded as the counterpart of Book Six."[80]

Clausewitz defined the conception of defense as the warding off of a blow and as its characteristic sign the awaiting of this blow. By this sign alone can defense, according to Clausewitz, be distinguished from attack. But pure defense seems to be an absurdity[81] and should therefore always be combined with offensive actions to ward off the blow actively. He defined the object of defense as preservation and protection, whereas the object of the offensive is conquest. This means that the defensive has a negative objective and the offensive a positive one. Although the latter increases one's resources, he reached the conclusion that *"the defensive form of warfare is intrinsically stronger than the offensive."*[82] His detailed explanation of this apparent contradiction was that "if defense is the stronger form of war, yet has a negative object, it follows that it should be used only so long as weakness compels, and be abandoned as soon as we are strong enough to pursue a positive object. When one has used defensive measures successfully, a more favorable balance of strength is usually created; thus, the natural course in war is to begin defensively and end by attacking."[83] Clausewitz did not argue that the defense is the most desirable form of war; but he did stress those conditions that compel one combatant party to remain on the strategic defensive, the most important being superiority of the opponent. This superiority may consist of numbers, morale, and equipment. But Clausewitz emphasized again and again the importance of offensive action in connection with the general defensive. He stated explicitly that "defense is . . . composed of two distinct parts, waiting and acting."[84] He made it clear that waiting and action, in the form of a counterstroke, are both essential parts of the defensive; without the former there would be no defensive, but without the latter there would be no war. However, every attempt to regard the counterstroke as belonging to the sphere of offensive and as entirely distinguished from and foreign to the defensive action, is contrary to Clausewitz' teaching.

It seems that a correct interpretation of Clausewitz' theory is to say that the strongest form of war is strategic defensive linked with tactical offensive. As a matter of fact, in chapter 9 of Book VI he explained "that the defender can fight a tactically offensive battle." The defender might choose either a completely offensive mode by attacking the adversary at the very moment of his crossing into the defender's theater of war, or a more delayed one by awaiting the adversary's appearance before his front; or the defender may actually await the enemy's attack on the defender's position and then engage him by a combination of local defense and limited counterstrokes.

The most extreme application of this approach of strategic defensive linked with tactical offensive is the retreat into the interior of the country, combined with a constant harassing of the pursuing enemy and attack on his outstretched supply lines until he is weakened to such an extent that he must stop his advance and is unable to overcome the resistance of the former defender. Finally the tide turns, the aggressor is exhausted, and his superior strength is diminished. This is the moment for the defender to fall on him from a well-chosen position and to attempt his complete destruction ("the flashing sword of vengeance" in Clausewitz' own colorful wording). That was the lesson learned from Napoleon's campaign in Russia in 1812 and since then reaffirmed many times.

To summarize, it is obvious that Clausewitz has by no means recommended any relations between the defensive and the offensive elements for winning a victory. However, he insisted on his assertion that an offensive essential part should never be lacking.

The case of the defensive retreat illustrates clearly that the time gained by such a withdrawal is to be regarded as an important advantage. As Clausewitz put it, "that time which is allowed to pass unused accumulates to the credit of the defender." This gain of time even increases if the exhaustion of the aggressor's forces is brought about by the difficulty of his own advance and the need to garrison decisive points along his line of advance, i.e., it is caused largely by self-weakening and self-attrition prior to the employment of the defender's main forces in a set-piece battle. But we should stress here the overall importance of fully utilizing this time in the sense of using the turn of the tide in the defender's favor; otherwise "wherever a victory achieved by the defensive form is not turned to military account, where, so to speak, it is allowed to wither away unused, a serious mistake is being made."[85] Connecting the time factor with the defense one may agree with Gerhard Ritter's interpretation of Clausewitz' concept of defense "that a delaying, defensive conduct of war makes sense, only if it may reckon on time as an ally and will one day become offensive."[86] But strange as it may seem, Clausewitz even believed that what he called "temporizing," i.e., the destruction of the enemy by means of "strategic holding back," had been a principal feature of many campaigns since the days of the famous Fabius Cunctator.[87] In his opinion this feature had been ignored by historians, although it comprised the true cause of many a decision.

No wonder that Clausewitz' presentation of the defensive as the stronger form was fiercely rejected by many German officers. One maintained sadly that he would have been much happier "had the great philosopher of war not written that passage." Colonel v. Scherff, the editor of the 1880 edition of *Vom Kriege*, confessed that this theory had violently divided German military opinion into two hostile camps. A German general exclaimed that "the decision to keep on the defensive is the first step on the ladder toward helplessness." German officers just could not reconcile Clausewitz' concept of "the application of force to the utmost" with his concept of the defense.

However, while dealing with this controversial matter, Clausewitz discovered another fact, called in the professional jargon "the diminishing force of the attack."

THE DIMINISHING FORCE OF THE ATTACK

This point has already been touched on in connection with the retreat into the interior of the country. Clausewitz really believed that an offensive in the depth of the enemy's country is supposed to become, sooner or later, a defensive. Or in his specific words: "Indeed, any attack that does not lead immediately to peace must end on the defensive."[88] It seems that even by the most vigorous advance, there might be reached a certain point beyond which every further penetration is liable to be checked. This point was called by Clausewitz the "Culminating Point," a term that subsequently became a classic. "The solution of this riddle," he said, "lies in the weakening which every strategic assault suffers *eo ipso* in its advance."[89] And in his section on "The Attack" he stressed even more explicitly that "there are strategic attacks that have led directly to peace, but these are the minority. Most of them only lead up to the point where their remaining strength is just enough to maintain a defense and wait for peace. Beyond that point the scale turns and the reaction follows with a force that is usually much stronger than that of the original attack."[90] That is the reason for the ancient truth that initial success of the assailant does not ultimately mean his final victory, because "there is only one result that counts: *final victory*. Until then, nothing is decided, nothing won, and nothing lost."[91] Needless to say, there exists a plain relationship between the numbers required for victory and the size of the hostile country.

ON ENCIRCLEMENT

The subject of encirclement would not have been touched on here had it not played so vital a part in subsequent German military thinking.

Meditating a "Plan of War Designed to Lead to the Total Defeat of the Enemy" (VIII, 9), Clausewitz reached the conclusion that "both in strategy and in tactics a convergent attack always holds out promise of *increased* results, for if it succeeds the enemy is not just beaten; he is virtually cut off. The convergent attack, then, is always the more promising; but since forces are divided and the theater is enlarged, it also carries a greater risk."[92] Comparing this situation with the relationship of attack and defense, he maintained: "The weaker form promises the greater success. All depends, therefore, on whether the attacker feels strong enough to go after such a prize."[93] In his letter of 22 December 1827 to Major Roeder he defined the encircling mode as the more decisive, promising greater results, but at the same time the more hazardous. However, success and risk form the dynamic law of war.[94] Elsewhere he drew attention to the paralyzing effect of the looming danger of being cut off, from which "arises an instinctive determination in the conduct of war and particularly in engagements, large and small, to protect one's own rear and to gain control of the enemy's."[95] It is important to keep in mind that this applies not only to the rear of the defender, as may seem from a superficial glance, but also in the same degree to the attacker's rear. Of course, it is much easier for the assailant to envelop the defender's position and cut him off, for the latter's position can be clearly identified; but on the other hand the defender, by means of having prepared himself for such eventualities, may have planned to utilize his reserves in order to catch the attacker's main force, or part of it, in flank and rear and to prevent his retreat while he is pinned down in front of the defended locality. It appears that encirclement is not solely the privilege of the offensive party. Attention has already been drawn to that fact in connection with the diminishing force of attack. It is an important point that should be kept in mind, for it is a widespread belief that encirclement is only an offensive device.

Clausewitz clearly distinguished between the execution of encirclement on the different levels of strategy and tactics. Whereas he had attributed to tactical envelopment all the advantages already mentioned, he was skeptical in regard to strategic encirclement:

1. The effect of cross fire is eliminated, since one cannot fire from one end of a theater of operations to the other.

2. There is less fear of being cut off, since whole areas cannot be sealed off in strategy as they can in tactics.

3. *Because of the greater areas involved in strategy, the effectiveness of interior and therefore shorter lines is accentuated and forms an important counterbalance against concentric attacks.*[96]

Obviously in strategy, encirclement can apply only to that side which has the initiative, i.e., the offensive. The defender seldom, if at all, can turn the tables on the enemy, as he may in tactics. On the other hand in many cases strategic encirclement may be out of the question, owing to the absolute lack of enemy flanks. Clausewitz, even in his time, envisaged a possibility that "the line of defense may run from sea to sea or from one neutral country to another. In this case, there can be no convergent attack; freedom of choice is limited."[97] With a visionary prediction of future events, Clausewitz warned against an exaggeration of the effects of cut-off lines of retreat and the danger of hampered or threatened lines. "Recent experience has made it plain that where the troops are good and their commanders bold they are more likely to break through than to be trapped."[98] Without doubt, in such circumstances the principle of creating a center of gravity opposite a weak spot in the enveloping line applies. Clausewitz further advised the utilization of the night for the purpose of breaking out.[99]

Clausewitz compared the mode of encirclement with the mode of by-passing an enemy position. Whereas encirclement strives for decision by battle on the strategic level as well as on the tactical, by-passing lies entirely in the strategic sphere. For "a position from which one can be manoeuvred out by means of sheer by-passing is not worthwhile to be captured."[100]

Clausewitz regarded encirclement as but one means among many for achieving the end. He regarded encirclement, however, as an effective expedient to force an enemy, anxious to avoid decision and trying to retreat, to accept battle by means of blocking his line of retreat.[101]

ON RESERVES

Reserves, according to Clausewitz, have two purposes clearly separated from each other: the prolongation of combat and its renewal. The first objective demands successive application of forces and falls therefore in the sphere of tactics and not of strategy. Developing his argument at this point, he reached the somewhat strange conclusion that strategic reserves are useless, "while the successive use of force in a tactical situation always postpones the main decision to the end of the action, in strategy the law of the simultaneous use of the forces nearly always advances the main decision, which need not necessarily be the ultimate one, to the beginning."[102] The idea of a strategic reserve became untenable for Clausewitz in connection with the main decision. The concept of a reserve of available active forces to be used or intended for use after the main decision has taken place, was considered by him to be absurd.

His concept of reserves in a defensive battle, however, was a modern one. For several reasons they should be located far behind the defended locality:

1. The reserves will not be under enemy fire during their waiting period;
2. it will be much easier to conceal them;

3. they are likely to counterbalance hostile encirclement movements by encircling in their turn the enemy forces carrying out the encirclement.

The time required for reaching the actual battle zone should not cause concern, Clausewitz held, because in modern battles the crisis occurs in an advanced stage of the fighting and the belated appearance of the reserve might serve its purpose much better.

Given the military situation today, it seems worthwhile to draw attention to a marginal subject in Clausewitz' writing that became important in the historical perspective: war against Russia on Russian soil.

ON WAR IN RUSSIA

One should remember in this context that Clausewitz witnessed Napoleon's invasion of Russia in 1812 while participating on the Russian side.[103]

During the winter of 1941–1942 German generals suddenly started studying Caulaincourt's (1773–1827) memoirs of Napoleon's retreat from Moscow.[104] It would, perhaps, have been much wiser if the "Führer" and his military advisors had recognized that in Clausewitz' writings they could find not only the impulse to annihilate the enemy, but also some clever remarks and references concerning an invasion of Russia. Some randomly chosen extracts may suffice to demonstrate this point: "The Russian campaign of 1812 demonstrated in the first place that a country of such size could not be conquered (which may well have been foreseen). . . . The Russians showed us that one often attains one's greatest strength in the heart of one's own country, when the enemy's offensive power is exhausted."[105] And in the description of the campaign in Russia in 1812 he stressed the vast dimensions of the Russian empire that allow it to "play at hide-and-seek with a hostile army." Under such circumstances the best defense against a superior enemy is therefore the retreat into the interior of the country and the allurement of the foe into pursuit. However, many territories remain in the invader's rear that he is unable to cover. Therefore, the defender can now change direction from retreat from the border into the heart of the country to an advance in the opposite direction, and thus both armies may reach the frontier simultaneously.[106]

The following reflections, that "a vast country with European culture can only be conquered with the aid of internal dissension,"[107] doomed Himmler's Gestapo treatment of the Ukraine in advance. Among the reasons for Napoleon's failure, Clausewitz mentioned that the destruction of his army was his own fault, not by having penetrated too far into the heart of the country—which was his objective and therefore unavoidable—but by starting the campaign too late in the year, by unnecessarily sacrificing the lives of his soldiers, and, above all, by his ignorance of logistics and of the security of his line of retreat and by deciding too late on his retreat from Moscow.[108] These reasons should have provided some warning to Herr Hitler before he embarked, on 22 June 1941, on his Russian adventure.[109]

Today some issues of Clausewitz' teaching seem quite commonplace, but at the time they represented revolutionary ideas. Some of his notions have lost their importance and even become obsolete, while others have retained their validity. A crude generalization suggests that many of his points on the tactical level have been superseded throughout the years, whereas those concerned with strategy and the nature of war have remained unimpeachable. That the modern student of his work regards many of his thoughts as of no special significance is perhaps Clausewitz' greatest success; it indicates that his theory has been absorbed.

Moreover, his work has outlived the other theories of war of his time. That is perhaps the ultimate test of its value. The main reason for that phenomenon is doubtless the fact that *On War* is not a technical guidebook for the conduct of war, but a treatise on the nature of war. That makes it difficult to digest sometimes. It should be recognized as an entirety, as a comprehensive piece of thought, and not as a compilation of quotations. The method used by Clausewitz was a structural analysis of that social phenomenon called war. Nevertheless, *On War* is not essentially theory. By linking appearance (the abstract war) with reality (the real war) it links theory with practice. Moreover, it shows the proper place of theory in relation to practice. Clausewitz' theory does not prescribe a particular course of action to be followed in practice, but draws attention to the fact that events happen by a lawful process.

Many soldiers would prefer to be presented with clear-cut instructions. Even a theorist like Jomini held the opinion that Clausewitz' approach had spread a theory of uncertainty, and that his way of handling problems might raise doubts. Many of Clausewitz' postulates were controversial and are still so today, for instance, the relationship of war and policy. The great clash between President Harry Truman and General Douglas MacArthur during the Korean War demonstrated clearly that even (or perhaps especially) in modern democracies this problem is still a live issue.

It is the great achievement of General Carl von Clausewitz to have been the creator of a comprehensive and modern theory of war. Nevertheless, it should not be forgotten that being a German of his time, his outlook was completely continental, and therefore his theory is restricted to one of war on land. Another omission in his otherwise thorough research is that he refused to inquire into the deeper undercurrents and causalities of war. He simply accepted war as a natural feature of social intercourse and left the problem of its justice (the problem of "just" or "unjust" wars as tackled by Lenin, for instance) to philosophers proper. That omission may also be explained by his German origin.

NOTES

1. Cyril Falls, *The Art of War*, London, 1961, p. 7.
2. For instance, Clausewitz' contemporary A. H. Jomini (1779–1869).

3. A description of translations into foreign languages is given by Dr. W. Hahlweg in the introduction to the 16th ed. of *Vom Kriege*, Bonn, 1952.

4. "The decision by arms is for all major and minor operations in war what cash payment is in commerce. Regardless how complex the relationship between the two parties, regardless how rarely settlements actually occur, they can never be entirely absent," *On War*, I, 2, p. 97. Or: "Rather than comparing it to art we could more accurately compare it to commerce, which is also a conflict of human interests and activities," *ibid.*, II, 3, p. 149.

5. For further details of Clausewitz' influence on Marxist doctrine, *vide* W. Hahlweg, "Lenin and Clausewitz," *Archiv für Kulturgeschichte*, Bd. 36 (1954), H.1, pp. 30–59; H.3, pp. 357–387; W. Hahlweg, "Clausewitz und die Gegenwart," in *Schicksalsfragen der Gegenwart*, Tübingen, 1957, vol. 2, and S. Neumann, "Engels and Marx: Military Concepts of the Social Revolutionaries," in E. M. Earle, ed., *Makers of Modern Strategy*, Princeton, 1952, and E. M. Earle, "Lenin, Trotsky, Stalin: Soviet Concepts of War," *ibid.*

6. For instance, Karl Schwartz, *Leben des Generals Carl von Clausewitz und der Frau Marie von Clausewitz*, Berlin, 1878, 2 vols.; Hans Rothfels, *Carl von Clausewitz. Politik und Krieg*, Berlin, 1920; R. v. Caemmerer, *Clausewitz*, Berlin, 1905, and many other more modern publications.

7. Synonym for guerrilla warfare.

8. Letter of 2 April 1807 from Paris, quoted in K. Schwartz, *op. cit.*, vol. 1, p. 261.

9. *On War*, II, 1, p. 128.

10. *Ibid.*, II, 2, p. 142.

11. General Fuller's fierce attack, that "of all Clausewitz' blind shots, the blindest was that he never grasped that the true aim of war is peace and not victory; therefore that peace should be the ruling idea of policy and victory only the means toward its achievement," seems to be totally unjustified. For the latter statement was exactly what Clausewitz was arguing. Equally unjustified is the assertion that "actually the word 'peace' barely occurs half a dozen times in 'On War.' " Cf. Major-General J.F.C. Fuller, *The Conduct of War, 1789–1961*, London, 1961, p. 76.

12. *On War*, III, 1, p. 177. Book III deals with "On Strategy in General."

13. *Ibid.*, III, 8, p. 194.

14. *Hinterlassene Werke des Generals Carl von Clausewitz über Krieg und Kriegführung*, vol. 5: *Die Feldzüge von 1799 in Italien und der Schweiz*, Berlin, 1858, p. 202.

15. In the German text Clausewitz used the word "Litanei" and the equivalent English translation should therefore be "litany."

16. *On War*, II, 1, p. 129.

17. The German term is "Schlacht."

18. The German term is "Gefecht."

19. General Speidel, in Ludwig Beck (ed. General Speidel), *Studien*, Stuttgart, 1955, p. 67.

20. General Günther Blumentritt, in his book *Strategie und Taktik*, Konstanz, 1960, pp. 7–8, suggested the following definition:

One may consequently denote strategy as the doctrine or art of moving and conducting strong forces, in large spaces, in order to achieve the strategic and i.e. the great object. A full-scale war is, from the military point of view, a strategic act, a campaign in that particular war is but an operative one; on the other hand, a battle or engagement is a tactical action.

That is the reason why divisions and army-corps were mainly regarded as tactical units, for use in the engagement, armies and army-groups as operative bodies and the armed forces as a whole as the strategic tool of the supreme policy.

Hence one should avoid any scheme. The conceptions often transit from one to another and do not like sharp demarcations. Everything is in a state of fluidity. If, for instance, an army-corps as part of an army or army-group is detached on a special mission, it may become an operative unit.
. . .

In modern times we would like to regard strategy as a substantial wider concept. Strategy by our perception is the summarization of all political, economic, intellectual, propagandistic and psychological factors into one multiformed unity.

21. C. Falls, *op. cit.*, p. 14.

22. The same subject is dealt with at length and on identical lines in Clausewitz' letter of 22 December 1827 to Major Roeder, printed in "Zwei Briefe des Generals von Clausewitz. Gedanken zur Abwehr," *Militärwissenschaftliche Rundschau*, März, 1937.

23. *On War*, I, 1, p. 87.

24. Clausewitz himself wrote in a note of 10 July 1827:

Book Eight, "War-Plans," will deal with the organization of a war as a whole. Several chapters of it have already been drafted, but they must not in any sense be taken as being in final form. They are really no more than a rough working over of the raw material, done with the idea that the labor itself would show what the real problems were. That in fact is what happened. . . . In Book Eight I also hope to iron out a good many kinks in the minds of strategists and statesmen and at all events to show what the whole thing is about and what the real problems are that have to be taken into account in actual warfare. *On War*, pp. 69–70

25. *Ibid.*, VIII, 6B, p. 605.

26. *Ibid.*

27. *Ibid.*, I, 1, p. 81.

28. This abstract conception was defined by Clausewitz as "absolute war" in contrast with "real war." It will be shown in Book Two, chapter 14 of this study that the conception of the "absolute war" has nothing in common with the concept of "total war" as preached by General Ludendorff.

29. *On War*, I, 1, pp. 87–88.

30. *Ibid.*, I, 2, p. 92.

31. The Cuban missile crisis of 1962 illustrated clearly what Clausewitz had in mind. It seems more that the "hot" or "shooting war" became but a special private case of war.

32. Nevertheless, in the era of the "cold war" and the deterrents, political considerations are involved even in posting sentries (for example, along the Iron Curtain) or sending patrols (air reconnaissance).

33. *On War*, VIII, 6B, p. 607.

34. *Ibid.*

35. *Ibid.*

36. *Ibid.*

37. Cf. W. Hahlweg's introduction to the 16th ed. of *Vom Kriege*, *op. cit.*, p. 24.

38. The English and the American translations before the present Princeton edition were based on the falsified text in use since the German 2d ed. The German respective versions (*On War*, VIII, 1B) are 1st ed.: "Soll ein Krieg ganz den Absichten der Politik entsprechen, und soll die Politik den Mitteln zum Kriege ganz angemessen sein, so bleibt, wo der Staatsmann und der Soldat nicht in einer Person vereinigt sind, nur ein Mittel übrig, nämlich den obersten Feldherrn zum Mitglied des Kabinetts zu machen, damit

dasselbe [i.e., the cabinet] teil an den Hauptmomenten seines Handelns nehme." The second part of this passage since the 2d ed. reads: "damit *er* [i.e., the general] in den wichtigsten Momenten an dessen *Beratung und Beschlüssen* teilnehme."

39. *Vide* Book Two, chapter 14, "Ludendorff's 'Total War.' "

40. E. Ludendorff, *Der totale Krieg*, München, 1935, p. 10.

41. Cf. L. Beck, *op. cit.*, pp. 60, 63.

42. *On War*, III, 12, p. 205.

43. He made it quite clear that "moral force has no existence save as expressed in the state and the law." *Ibid.*, I, 1, p. 75.

44. Schlieffen in particular interpreted Clausewitz in this respect, as may be learned from chapter 2.

45. The later King Friedrich Wilhelm IV of Prussia (1840–1861).

46. *Hinterlassene Werke*, *op. cit.*, vol. 4: *Der Feldzug von 1796 in Italien*, Berlin, 1899, p. 31.

47. *On War*, I, 2, p. 91.

48. *Ibid.*, p. 94.

49. *Ibid.*, p. 69, in the note of 10 July 1827. This particular statement of Clausewitz had set the stage for the future so-called "Strategy Controversy," which is dealt with in Book Two of this study at the end of chapter 9.

50. Clausewitz held the same posture in his letter to Major Roeder of 22 December 1827. *Vide* note 22.

51. *On War*, IV, 11, p. 258.

52. *Ibid.*, III, 1, p. 181.

53. *Ibid.*, I, 2, p. 98.

54. *Ibid.*, III, 16, p. 219.

55. *Ibid.*, I, 2, p. 97.

56. Today we would probably say "calculated risk."

57. Letter of 2 April 1807 from Paris, in K. Schwartz, *op. cit.*, vol. 1, p. 261.

58. Cf. Carl von Clausewitz (ed. Hans Rothfels), *Politische Schriften und Briefe*, München, 1922, pp. 105 ff.

59. Some kind of "Home Guard."

60. For further information about this part of Clausewitz' teaching *vide* W. Hahlweg, *Preussische Reformzeit und revolutionärer Krieg*, Beiheft 18 der *Wehrwissenschaftliche Rundschau*, September 1962, and W. Hahlweg, "Carl von Clausewitz," in W. v. Groote, *Grosse Soldaten der Europäischen Geschichte*, Frankfurt/Main, 1961, pp. 307 ff. The manuscript of Clausewitz' lectures, "Meine Vorlesungen über den kleinen Krieg gehalten auf der Kriegsschule 1810 u. 1811," is in the university library of Münster/Westf. Prof. W. Hahlweg has edited for the first time a publication of these lectures under the auspices of the Historical Commission of the Bavarian Academy for Science: W. Hahlweg, ed., *Carl von Clausewitz. Schriften—Aufsätze—Studien—Briefe*, Göttingen, 1966, vol. 1, pp. 678–750.

61. *Hinterlassene Werke*, *op. cit.*, vol. 7: *Der Feldzug von 1812 in Russland, der Feldzug von 1813 bis zum Waffenstillstand u. d. Feldzug von 1814 in Frankreich*, Berlin, 1862, pp. 152–153. Cf. also an almost identical version in *On War*, I, 7, pp. 119–120.

62. It is obvious that the discovery of friction provided an essential ingredient of the theoretical differentiation between "absolute" and "real" war.

63. *On War*, II, 1, p. 129.

64. Cf. Clausewitz' quarrel with v. Bülow, reprinted in Carl von Clausewitz (ed.

Eberhard Kessel), *Strategie aus dem Jahr 1804 mit Zusätzen von 1808 und 1809*, Hamburg, 1937. (The manuscript in Clausewitz' handwriting may be found in "Geheimes Staats-Archiv, Berlin-Dahlem" under Rep. 92, Nachlass Gneisenau M.52.) See also E. A. Nohn, "Clausewitz contra Bülow," *Wehrwissenschaftliche Rundschau*, Jg. 5, H.7 (1955).

65. Cf. F. v. Bernhardi, *On War of To-Day*, London, 1912, vol. 2, p. 85.

66. *On War*, VI, 3, p. 364.

67. *Ibid.*, III, 11, p. 204. The German text reads "bloss nach dem dunklen Gefühl herkömmlicher Manier," which seems to be an even more acid expression than the English translation quoted here.

68. *Ibid.*, III, 12, p. 209.

69. *Ibid.*, III, 12, p. 206.

70. Liddell Hart, *The Ghost of Napoleon*, London, 1933, p. 120.

71. *On War*, III, 8, p. 194, emphasis added.

72. *Ibid.*, pp. 194–195.

73. *Vide* p. 14.

74. *On War*, III, 8, p. 196, emphasis added.

75. *Ibid.*

76. *Ibid.*, VI, 27, p. 485.

77. *Ibid.*, p. 487.

78. Quoted in H. Rosinski, *The German Army*, Washington, D.C., 1944, p. 189.

79. *On War*, VIII, 4, p. 596.

80. *Ibid.*, p. 69.

81. On the other hand, Clausewitz said quite explicitly that "there is no greater absurdity than the desire to attack at all events." *Hinterlassene Werke, op. cit.*, vol. 5, p. 176.

82. *On War*, VI, 1, p. 358.

83. *Ibid.*

84. *Ibid.*, VI, 8, p. 379.

85. *Ibid.*, VI, 5, p. 370.

86. Gerhard Ritter, *Staatskunst und Kriegshandwerk*, München, 1954, vol. 1, p. 82.

87. Cf. *On War*, VI, 8.

88. *Ibid.*, VI, 3, p. 365.

89. *Hinterlassene Werke, op. cit.*, vol. 4, p. 280.

90. *On War*, VII, 5, p. 528.

91. *Ibid.*, VIII, 3A, p. 582.

92. *Ibid.*, VIII, 9, p. 619.

93. *Ibid.*

94. Cf. "Zwei Briefe," *op. cit.*, p. 39.

95. *On War*, IV, 4, p. 233.

96. *Ibid.*, VI, 3, p. 364, emphasis added.

97. *Ibid.*, VI, 4, p. 367.

98. *Ibid.*, V, 16, p. 347.

99. *Ibid.*, IV, 14.

100. Letter to Major Roeder of 24 Dec. 1827 in "Zwei Briefe," *op. cit.*, pp. 47–49.

101. *On War*, IV, 8, p. 246.

102. *Ibid.*, III, 13, p. 211.

103. Clausewitz' participation is mentioned in the second volume of Tolstoy's *War and Peace*.

104. Cf. W. Warlimont, *Im Hauptquartier der Wehrmacht, 1939–1945*, Frankfurt/Main, 1962, p. 237.

105. *On War*, III, 17, p. 220.

106. *Hinterlassene Werke, op. cit.*, vol. 7, p. 121. As early as 1804 Clausewitz wrote: "Should Bonaparte once come to Poland he will be defeated much easier than in Italy, and in Russia I would regard his fall to be decisive." C. v. Clausewitz (ed. E. Kessel), *Strategie, op. cit.*, p. 42.

107. *Hinterlassene Werke, op. cit.*, vol. 7, p. 152. Cf. also *On War*, VIII, 9, p. 627.

108. *On War*, VIII, 9, p. 628.

109. Napoleon, too, crossed the river Niemen in June.

2

Alfred Count von Schlieffen: Prophet of Annihilation

The "German Wars of Unification," consisting of the Prussian-Danish War of 1864, the Prussian-Austrian War of 1866, and the Franco-German War of 1870–1871, were the joint work of a Triumvirate acting under the King of Prussia[1]: Count Otto v. Bismarck (1815–1898), the Chancellor, representing the political leadership; General Albert v. Roon (1803–1879), the Minister of War, as the head of the military administration; and General Helmuth v. Moltke (1800–1891), the Chief of the General Staff, who was the actual strategist. These three successful wars completely changed the position and the status of the post of Chief of the General Staff. For example, even on the eve of the famous victory at Königgrätz (known outside Germany as the battle of Sadowa), many German generals did not know of General v. Moltke.[2] The next day, however, his fame spread not only through Germany, but throughout the whole civilized world. Until this date the Chief of General Staff had played only a subordinate role, as advisor to the King and the Minister of War, but from the Seven Weeks' War onward a royal cabinet decree empowered the Chief of General Staff to give operational orders directly to the commanding officers, thus eliminating the Minister of War entirely in matters of command and making the Chief of General Staff the supreme leader of the army in action.[3] This increase of power put the German General Staff in such a strong position that the Allies, at the end of the First World War, at Versailles, insisted on its dissolution and forbade the creation of a new one. The successor to Moltke, as German Chief of General Staff, was General Count Alfred v. Schlieffen (1833–1913), with whom this chapter is concerned.

Thus, right from the beginning, Schlieffen was in a much more influential position than Clausewitz, although he, too, suffered personal setbacks before he reached his high rank.[4] The lack of real power of command at the War Academy had led Clausewitz to concentrate on the theoretical-philosophical aspects of war. Schlieffen, on the other hand, was a typical product of the new industrial era, which introduced the new features of machines and masses into the ancient profession of the warrior. Thus the new type of expert in the military field emerged, personified by the anonymous staff officer.

Schlieffen, as Chief of General Staff, was concerned primarily with the solution of concrete problems and tried to derive from them general theories. His teaching lacked, therefore, the comprehension and depth of Clausewitz' work.

Since the German defeat in the First World War and, with much stronger emphasis, after the German failure in the Second World War, there seems to be no other controversial German military personality who has occupied the writers of "both sides of the hill" more than Schlieffen, despite the fact that he himself never had the opportunity of commanding a unit of any size in battle and never gained a striking victory or suffered a crushing defeat. But his name was and is connected with a plan that has dominated German military thought ever since its inception. As one military scholar has said, "his shadow hung over the first, as still over the second World War, and his influence on German military thought can hardly be over-estimated."[5]

One controversial issue is the question whether Schlieffen founded a new school of strategic thinking. Even his most ardent supporters frankly deny this, claiming that Schlieffen's teaching was firmly rooted in the soil of Clausewitz' theory and of Moltke's extensions and was concerned with their adaptation to new developments. Schlieffen was proud to state that he, like his teacher Moltke, had no system of his own, but always stressed that action should be in accordance with the circumstances of the particular theater of war and the available means.[6] One biographer even maintains that Schlieffen was afraid to construct a doctrine that could stand on its own.[7]

This practical, almost technical, approach to the problems of war earned for Schlieffen the accusation of one-sidedness by many of his contemporaries and by later writers. Walter Görlitz, the well-known author of the *History of the German General Staff*, argued that Schlieffen, like his Kaiser (Wilhelm II, 1888–1918), preferred obedient subordinates to brilliant original minds.[8] He has been admired by many of his partisans for his expertness and his exclusive concern with military matters alone,[9] but to many others these qualities seemed to be an expression of a craftsman-like approach. As early as 1912, during Schlieffen's lifetime, Friedrich v. Bernhardi, a famous military thinker of that time, warned in his book, *On War of To-Day*, that narrow-mindedness had taken possession of Germany military thought and pointed out the danger that the German Army was "on the high road of becoming slaves to such one-sidedness."[10] These remarks were clearly aimed at Schlieffen's military writings, which were having widespread publicity at that time. On the twenty-fifth anniversary of Schlieffen's death, Generalleutnant Eugen v. Zoellner[11] wrote that Schlieffen's thought was not one-sided, but that he taught "applied strategy" to the German Army, as opposed to the "philosophical strategy" of Clausewitz. It would seem, therefore, that this was a deliberate policy. Schlieffen himself stressed this point: Once Freytag-Loringhoven from the Historical Branch of the German General Staff mentioned to him that the continuous sharp accentuation of the annihilation idea might be looked on as being one-sided. Schlieffen's reply was: "Well, it might be boring; it always revolves around the stupid being Victory."[12] His followers regarded his historical studies only as a means of illustrating his "applied strategy." They therefore did not pay much attention to his misquotations and wrong explanations of historical facts. They claimed that he was not a teacher of military history, but a strategist and the propagandist of his applied strategy. For them it did not matter whether "the master" distorted historical events to conform with his opinion, or even "altered" geographical features. Even the editor of Schlieffen's letters[13] was compelled to admit that the description of Moltke's conduct of the battle of Königgrätz, in Schlieffen's "Cannae Studies," was more wishful thinking on Schlieffen's part than in accordance with reality. A famous contemporary military thinker, General Sigismund v. Schlichting, who also compiled many theoretical and practical manuals, accused Schlieffen of using a defective method. Wilhelm Groener (1867–1939) argued with regard to this accusation that Schlieffen never intended to write a history of war, nor to embark on scientific research work investigating the operational methods of various Great Captains.[14]

Schlieffen was admired primarily by the younger officers of the General Staff, who regarded him as a model, a demigod. In his conduct of staff rides, war games, and "end-of-year" problems,[15] he gave relatively low-ranking staff officers the opportunity to command at fairly high levels of divisions, corps, and armies. Many a German general of that time criticized this practice, but in one of his final discussions Schlieffen took the opportunity to present his point of view on this question:

It has been said that it is not the task of young officers to lead armies and great hosts. I cannot see any reason why in the future some of you, Gentlemen, should not be head of an army. Anyhow, I hope that you will be called on to lead a corps or a division, or at least to accompany a commander as his chief of staff or general staff officer. Then you ought to be able to judge the movements of an army. Only then will you be able to reach an independent decision for your own corps or division (which may occur frequently in a future war) which will favorably influence the course of events for the army as a whole.[16]

As one of his biographers put it: The main problems with which Schlieffen struggled were threefold: first, battle on several fronts or the battle on interior lines; second, battle against overwhelming odds; and third, the conduct of enormous hosts that, as a consequence of compulsory military service, grew to armies of millions and presented problems of leadership never faced before.[17]

But before embarking on these strategic, operational,[18] and moral problems, let us try to find out whether Schlieffen paid attention to the highest strategic level of war and policy.

WAR AND POLITICS

From what is already known about Schlieffen's personality and opinion, it should not be suprising to discover that the abstract problem of the relationship of policy and war never occupied his thoughts. Like many German soldiers after him, he proved himself to be completely "unpolitical" and totally disregarded Clausewitz' dictum that war has its own grammar, but not its own logic, which must be provided by policy. Schlieffen was probably a most efficient grammarian, but events proved that that was not enough. Nevertheless, Schlieffen should not be blamed exclusively, because this deviation from Clausewitz' postulate had already started under the elder Moltke's tenure of office. In an essay on strategy, circulated in 1871, the latter wrote:

Policy makes use of war to gain its objects, it acts with decisive influence at the beginning and the end of the war,[19] in such a way as either to increase its claims during the progress of war or to be satisfied with lesser gains. With this uncertainty strategy cannot but always direct its efforts toward the highest goal attainable with the means at its disposal. It thereby serves policy best, and only works for the object of policy, but is completely independent of policy in its actions.[20]

It is not surprising that Moltke, having a fine political sense, wrote such a passage, especially if one remembers that, at that time, he had still not recovered from his well-known conflict with Bismarck, when he was overruled by his king (now Kaiser) in the Chancellor's favor.[21]

Schlieffen, however, as Moltke's most devoted pupil, regarded his own strategic planning as a completely independent act. Therefore, strange as it may seem, the famous Schlieffen Plan is by no means a comprehensive plan for war, embracing all of its aspects—political, economical, and military—but is only the plan for the German ground forces in case of war. Liddell Hart, after reading Gerhard Ritter's interpretation of the famous Schlieffen Plan, charges Schlieffen with failing to warn the Emperor and his Chancellor that the chances of Schlieffen's plan succeeding were remote, and thus prevented the adjustment of German policy to that eventuality. He accuses Schlieffen of having taken "the technician's view that his duty was fulfilled if he did the utmost with the means available, and 'made the best of a bad job' in compliance with the customs and rules of his profession."[22]

Anyhow, every plan of war must be based on some definite political assumptions. The Schlieffen Plan was founded on the supposition that a state of war with France would exist prior to the outbreak of hostilities with Russia. Unfortunately, the events in 1914 evolved in reverse order, creating a complicated situation, because German diplomacy was compelled to conform to the needs of the military plan of deployment.[23] The policy was fixed into definite patterns, whether politicians and soldiers wanted it or not, and thus strategy did not adjust itself to the actual political situation; instead, policy was forced to act in accordance with a rigid and unalterable war plan. The General Staff prevailed over diplomacy. Of course, that was not solely the soldier's fault, but equally (or even more) the politicians'. In Gerhard Ritter's words, "the outbreak of the war in 1914 is the most tragic example of a government's helpless dependence on the planning of strategists, that history has ever seen. In allowing themselves to be drawn into this state of dependence, in regarding the planning of war as unreservedly the affair of military specialists, lies the historical guilt of Bismarck's successors."[24]

Let us consider Schlieffen's picture of the political situation in his famous essay, "Der Krieg in der Gegenwart" (On War at the Present Time): Germany was encircled by her enemies, headed by "jealous" England. There was no way to prevent this unavoidable clash. The "war-monger" Fritz von Holstein (1837–1909), a powerful and influential Assistant Undersecretary in the Foreign Office, who was dismissed by the Emperor for wanting a preventive war during the Agadir crisis of 1905, demonstrated in his papers the false nature of Schlieffen's essay.[25] Schlieffen asserted that "the powerful expansion of Germany's industry and trade earned her another implacable enemy [England]. This hatred of a formerly despised rival can neither be tempered by assurance of sincere friendship and cordiality, nor aggravated by provocative language. It is not the emotions but questions of debit and credit which determine the level of resentment."[26]

Holstein, on the other hand, showed clearly that the English hostility was not essentially a political necessity. Although it was natural that German commercial rivalry had aroused a certain amount of antagonism in English commercial circles, the English knew perfectly well that America could use a war between England and Germany to eliminate both protagonists from world markets. It was therefore in the English interest to avoid war, and English statesman Joseph Chamberlain (1836–1914) tried hard (in 1899) to construct an alliance between the greatest sea power and the greatest European land power. Schlieffen should have realized the significance of these facts. But they did not change his concepts, as it did not appear to have entered his mind that there was no ultimate necessity for the deterioration of Russo-German relations.

In this context it is interesting to learn, in a letter to Schlieffen from the younger Moltke (1848–1916), Schlieffen's successor to the office of Chief of General Staff, of the preliminaries for the publication of the essay "Der Krieg in der Gegenwart."[27] This letter shows that the author had sent a draft of his essay to Moltke before its publication. It had also been forwarded by Schlieffen to Karl v. Einem, at that time Minister of War, who suggested that its contents be discussed with the Ministry of Foreign Affairs, with regard to the fact that the author was the former Chief of the German General Staff.[28] Moreover, even the Kaiser had been presented with the draft and was so impressed by it that he ordered the essay to be read at the New Year gathering of the Commanding Generals (on 2 January 1909).[29] However, Schlieffen apparently did not find it necessary to comply with v. Einem's suggestion, and no discussion with the Foreign Ministry took place, although the political implications of the essay were obvious. However, after its publication a lively correspondence started on this issue between the Chancellor and the Kaiser.

The most striking example of Schlieffen's disregard of the primacy of policy over war was his attitude to the question of Belgium's neutrality. There is no doubt, from the legal point of view, that Prussia was one of the guarantor powers of Belgian neutrality, and there was also no doubt that the unified German Empire inherited the Prussian obligations. Schlieffen saw the problem of Belgium from the operational viewpoint alone. He reached the conclusion that the advance through Belgian territory was essential for the achievement of a German victory over France.[30] He therefore regarded the "salvation" of Germany as more weighty than any consideration for Belgium's neutrality. This train of thought was, to some extent, legitimate for the Chief of General Staff when presenting his plan to the responsible statesman. But the problem called "Belgium" was a real strategic issue, i.e., a political one. It was therefore the responsibility of the statesman to refuse acceptance for political reasons. Politically speaking, Schlieffen's plan meant a break with the established morality of Europe as the backers of Belgian neutrality. Public opinion in no country—including Germany—was prepared for such a violation.

The question arose whether the German political leaders knew anything about the Schlieffen Plan, for it is obvious that the political leadership was at no time a partner in shaping the plan, either in the original form or in its various alterations.[31] A German Chancellor of the Schlieffen period, Count Bernhard von Bülow (1849–1929), in a private letter written on 22 May 1928, denied any knowledge of the plan, whereas his successor to the office of chancellor, who was at that time Minister of the Interior, Theobald v. Bethmann-Hollweg (1856–1921), admitted it, as did the German Ambassador in London, Count Karl Lichnowsky.[32] On the other hand, among the documents at the German Foreign Ministry, a telegram from the Kaiser to v. Bülow as early as 1905 (a short time after the Björkö meeting of 24 July 1905) hinted of a German intention to advance through Belgium in case of war with France. There is no indication that v. Bülow objected to this idea.[33] It seems that the political administration at no time occupied itself with considerations of this vital issue. Perhaps it never entered the minds of German politicians that there might really be a war. Anyhow, contrary to the practice in other countries, the Germans never established an institution like the French "Conseil Supérieur de la Guerre" (Supreme War Council), in which statesmen and generals sat together and discussed war policy. The departmentalization was so deep-rooted that soldiers and diplomats never met to exchange information and to try to clear up common problems. Neither the Chief of General Staff nor the Chancellor made any attempt to establish a round table. The postulate of the primacy of policy over war seemed to be nonexistent. Or, as Otto v. Moser put it, it may be that the soldiers, inspired with the military victories of 1864, 1866, and 1870–1871, believed that the relationship of policy and war had changed in the latter's favor since Clausewitz wrote his treatise.[34] Therefore, when in July 1914 the crisis broke out, Germany had nothing but a plan for a military offensive whose rigid timetable robbed her diplomacy of any possibility of maneuver in the political field. Schlieffen's defenders, however, argue that he never intended to be the first to violate Belgian neutrality. He had a clever political maneuver in his mind: The German troops would array along the Belgian border without crossing it. This move would cause anxiety in the French High Command and result in an order to French troops to invade Belgium. Then the German troops would still have enough time to carry out the planned advance through Belgium, but the odor of aggression would rest with the French. Here is clear proof, claimed Schlieffen's partisans, of the master's political insight. He would have avoided Germany being labeled as the aggressor and would provide German diplomacy with a breathing space of some days for political activity.[35] Even Wolfgang Foerster, a keen admirer of Schlieffen, admitted that it was rather doubtful whether these political advantages would have resulted, for there was no obvious reason why the French and British should lose their nerve and violate Belgian neutrality before a German invasion.[36] It was apparent that the aggressor would meet Belgian opposition, whereas the other side would be invited in by the Belgian government and benefit from an undisturbed advance. Schlieffen's defenders also advanced the somewhat morally doubtful argument that, had the German troops been victorious, nobody would have objected afterward to the violation of Belgium's neutrality, and that all present-day critics would be full of praise for such a splendid plan.[37] The hypocrisy of this argument is so obvious that there would appear to be no need for any comment. But in this context Clausewitz' statement that even a final decision in war should never be regarded as an ultimate one, should be remembered, for the defeated state often regards it as a transitory situation only, for which a remedy might be found in new political action. We know from the historical evidence of the Second World War that the truth lies with Clausewitz and not with Foerster.

THE CANNAE CONCEPT AND THE IDEA OF ANNIHILATION

From a purely technical point of view, Schlieffen's Cannae concept might have been surveyed under the topic of "Encirclement," but nevertheless, the proper place for its investigation is here, considering it as Schlieffen's opinion on the objectives of war.

The problems that occupied Schlieffen's thought have already been mentioned. His solution to them is best illustrated by two of his own expressions. In a letter of 18 September 1909 he wrote that "the battle of annihilation alone is the desirable battle."[38] This statement is complemented by his stating that the attack against the flank is "the essential substance of the whole history of war."[39] In his works he tried to support these conclusions by historical examples, but a comparison of the dates of publication of his various essays with the dates of his exercises and the staff rides conducted by him, reveal that he did not first derive the idea of encirclement from history, but rather approached history to discover in its pages justification for his concept. Moreover, in 1903 he ordered the Historical Section of the General Staff to undertake a study to discern by what means success in battle had been achieved in European wars since the time of Friedrich the Great.[40] He summed up the results of this investigation in words that confirmed the ancient truth, that the launching of a thrust into the enemy's flank and the endangering of his rear leads to success. This was a supplement to Moltke's conduct of war at Sadowa. Moltke himself defined his method, in the regulations for the conduct of troops, as follows: "The situation is much more favorable if it is possible to concentrate the forces from different points towards the battlefield on the day of the battle, and to conduct the operations in such a way, that from all quarters a last, short march leads into front and flank of the adversary. Then is strategy at its best and great results are to be expected."[41] This rule is a further development of Friedrich the Great's flank march on the battlefield and Napoleon's pre-prepared flank marches. We should remember that Moltke had the advantage of superiority of numbers in all his battles, as a consequence of Bismarck's superb statesmanship. The problem that confronted Schlieffen was how to prevail against grave odds. Moreover, he did not wish merely to injure his adversaries; he wanted to destroy them. As early as 1899, summing up a staff ride in the East, he said:

While we had numerical superiority in the battles of 1870 and partly in 1871, we had always the ability to occupy fully the French front and simultaneously to encircle one or both wings, to press on their lines of retreat and in such a way to achieve a real decisive success, a procedure, which found its most brilliant expression in the battle of Sedan. Such a possibility will never be offered to us in future wars with respect to the strength of our opponents. We must, therefore, conduct one small host in such a way, as not only to attack with the utmost possible strength one hostile wing, but also to endanger seriously and simultaneously the adversary's line of retreat which sensibility is ever increasing with the growth of armies. That is the only way to achieve decisive results and the quick end of a campaign and such results are indispensable in our case of war on two fronts.[42]

He regarded the total annihilation of the hostile fighting forces as a success that, from a military point of view, could not be surpassed and must therefore be looked on as the utmost attainable. Total destruction of the opponent is always the most advantageous because it sets the whole of the victor's forces free for other duties, and that really counted in a war on two fronts. Obviously, he believed that the best way to achieve the enemy's annihilation is encirclement and attack in the rear. Whereas the enveloping of both wings demands large numbers, a small force may be satisfied with action against one flank only. Thus very early Friedrich the Great's battle of Leuthen became the desirable prototype that "revealed the secret of victory." Only from 1909 onward, after studying Hans Delbrück's description of the battle of Cannae,[43] did Schlieffen evolve the concept of complete encirclement, i.e., the attack from four directions: front, flanks, and rear. Hannibal showed, in Schlieffen's opinion, how to destroy completely a numerically superior enemy, not only to beat him as had been done at Leuthen. Suddenly, Cannae became the model. Schlieffen maintained that, although 2,000 years had elapsed since this battle on the shores of the Aufidus, the "main conditions of battle remained unaltered. The battle of annihilation may be conducted today in accordance with the same plan Hannibal had contrived in those forgotten times.''[44] The recognition of the possibility of achieving a striking victory with unequal forces was Schlieffen's contribution to the modern theory of war. (It should not be overlooked, however, that the stress on cutting off the enemy's line of communication constituted a certain reintroduction of a geometrical principle into the art of war, from which this art had been freed by Clausewitz' theory.)

From this moment on he compared every military action of the past and judged every future plan by the battle of Cannae. In his famous ''Cannae Studies'' he maintained that all the great commanders of history had aimed at the Cannae plan, even if they did not know this battle.[45]

According to the basic feature of Cannae, a broad line of battle advances towards a narrower one, which is arrayed in depth. The overlapping wings wheel against the flanks, the preceding cavalry against the rear. If the wings by some reason or another were divided from the center, there is no necessity to draw them nearer in order to carry out a joint march. They may proceed direct by the shortest routes into the flanks or rear.[46]

It is risky, of course, but effective and worthwhile. Most generals refrain from acting in such a manner out of fear that the divided parts might be beaten separately. However, by doing so they renounce their chances of gaining an important victory. Moreover, ''a perfect battle of Cannae rarely occurs in history. There is on one side the need for a Hannibal, on the other for a Terentius Varro, who both co-operate in their manner for the achievement of the great purpose.''[47] Sometimes in place of Hasdrubal, the cavalry commander acting in the enemy's rear, a natural obstacle or the border of a neutral state may be substituted.[48] In order to gain the fullest effect from the flank assault, a frontal attack is necessary to tie down large numbers of the enemy. While the decision is effected by the enveloping wings, the main weight of force must be shifted from the front to the wings. Hannibal had acted in such a way, when reducing his center to a third of the opposing center and exposing it to the danger of being pushed back by overwhelming strength. But this retrograde movement of the center, in fact, supported the enveloping move of the wings. Schlieffen admitted that it is not too easy to copy such a maneuver with modern mass-armies. But ''even today it is possible, as it was at Cannae, to reduce the center to a line without too much support—but with a lot of ammunition—and nevertheless to attack.''[49] The modern battle will therefore be a struggle for the flanks even more than it was before, and so reserves must be shifted beforehand directly to the wings, by a pre-arranged plan of deployment, from the railheads.

There were, and still are, many objections to this concept. First of all, Schlieffen, excited by his discovery, had overlooked the political consequences of Hannibal's victory as Delbrück had presented them: ''He who wants to wage war according to the principle of throwing down the enemy, must be able to follow up the victory unceasingly, until the siege and capture of the hostile capital, or at least, if the latter will not lead to peace, until *debellatis*, after the enemy's main force was found and beaten in the open field. For such an attempt Hannibal was too weak.''[50] It did not occur to Schlieffen that the battle of Cannae, in the wider aspects, besides its tactical moves, presented a classic example of the dependence of war on policy. There was no political exploitation of Hannibal's striking victories. Schlieffen did not even realize that in the long run Hannibal and the Carthaginians lost the war despite these victories. Neither did he grasp that it was Roman sea power that brought Carthage's final downfall.

It has been doubted whether such an early event in the history of mankind and wars might provide any guidance for the actual conduct of modern battles. It has been argued that the Punic flank echelons are by no means analogous to the deployment in depth of modern armies of millions. Further discussion on this issue is deferred until chapter 3, in which Clausewitz' verdict on the value of historical examples is examined.

It is obvious from all the essays compiled in Schlieffen's "Cannae Studies" that he tended to simplify history and projected modern ideas—his own practical solutions of actual problems—into the historical facts. He did not even refrain from acting in such a manner when dealing with recent events. He assigned, for instance, to Moltke thoughts, plans, and aims that could by no means have been Moltke's at that time.

The strongest objections have been made to the Cannae concept as the "secret of victory" and the "philosophers' stone." F. v. Bernhardi argued against paragraph 392 of the "Infantry Training" pamphlet, in which Schlieffen's theory had been set out, and which reads: "The combination of frontal with enveloping attack best insures success."[51] "That sentence is wrong," he declared.

It only proves correct with perfectly arbitrary notions about the strength and attitude of the enemy. But that sentence is also dangerous; for not only does it render it difficult for the Commander to strive after victory by other methods which, from immediate circumstances, seem perhaps more expedient, but it also makes it easier for the opponent to adopt suitable counter measures, if he can with some certainty count upon the opposite party always acting on the same principles.[52]

Bernhardi also objected strongly to the concept of thinning out the center and, in spite of it, ordering his forces not only to "occupy" the enemy, but also to attack. He pointed out that such a procedure can be attempted, with regard to modern armaments, only at the cost of disproportionate losses and does not promise success. For

if we advance with weak forces against the hostile front we come already at the distant ranges under superior fire of the enemy and a real action begins. If we give up any further advance, the enemy sees through the game, and adopts his measures accordingly. But if we continue to advance, we suffer destructive losses and shall soon be unable to advance further. It will then not be long before the enemy again discerns the character of the feint attack and he will weaken his own front accordingly, or defeat the weak attacking forces by a counterstroke, long before the enveloping attack can have attained its object.[53]

He maintained that a halfhearted attack or a feint attack always carried the germ of defeat, and the solution therefore should be to confine ourselves to defense or to elude enemy blows where we do not attack decisively. There remains, of course, the possibility of deceiving the enemy by various means, strategically and tactically as well.

By adopting the Cannae concept Schlieffen eliminated any other form of attack and preached encirclement as the only possible solution. He strongly opposed all thought of a frontal attack and break-through. The break-through is the desired objective of a frontal (also called "head-on") attack. It aims to split the hostile front and thus to pave the way into the rear and flanks of the enemy from the center. To carry out a break-through normally entails assaulting a defended front, but if the assailant succeeds in detecting a weak point in the enemy's positions, he may be able to pierce a wide gap and pour prepared reserves through it.

Schlieffen rejected frontal attacks; time and again he criticized them in his final discussions of exercises, war games, and staff rides by emphasizing that, at best, an "ordinary victory" might be achieved. (An "ordinary victory" in Schlieffen's vocabulary meant a victory without annihilation of the enemy.) In 1901 he summed up:

The trend of the present time is, strangely enough, aimed at frontal attacks. The previous century started with a campaign against the hostile lines of communication and a battle with reversed fronts. An Emperor's crown[54] was the prize of victory. At the beginning of this century entirely contrary opinions prevailed. A long series of exercises, reports of corps' staff rides and publications coincide with this, and leave no doubt about the train of thought. The essential principles, for the conduct of armies, were sought in the gathering and thorough basing of all forces, followed by their seeking out the hostile front. A satisfactory situation was only reached when the heads of columns had wheeled until the right wing was addressed exactly to the enemy's left, the left wing to the enemy's right. A problem of how to conduct an attack in face of the devastating effect of modern weapons greatly troubled leading intellects.[55] The driving thought behind this procedure was based on the understandable desire not to be beaten. This wish will only be fulfilled if the opponent acts by a similar system. But it will result in undecided battles and long drawn out wars. Armies of millions make this intolerable. . . . Another motive must supersede this one; it is not the wish not to be beaten, but the burning desire to beat the enemy which must determine the decision.[56]

In his final discussion of the war game in 1905 he explained:

Everyone strives to envelop and therefore extends his front. Everyone strives to avoid encirclement and therefore extends his front likewise. Both these endeavours might lead to overstretched lines and to a possible break-through. We are told that Napoleon always carried out this break-through, but, as a matter of fact, he seldom executed it.[57] If today a new Napoleon wanted to break through, he might not find the windmill from which to watch the battle and to discover the weak spot.[58]

The experience of both world wars refuted Schlieffen's postulate. However, as early as 1911 v. Bernhardi strongly opposed Schlieffen's exclusion of penetration from military thinking and military planning. He made it clear that break-through, followed by "rolling up" the enemy's lines on one or both sides of the penetration point, has its advantages.[59] "If strategic outer lines lead to tactical envelopment, a successful tactical penetration brings us strategically on the inner line . . . successful penetration . . . obliges the enemy to change front so as to be able to oppose some forces to the penetrating assailant. But changes of front of this kind are difficult to execute, and always liable to the danger of local defeats."[60] He argued with some foresight that "under the conditions obtaining in a war of masses and owing to the breadth of the strategic front, neither envelopment nor flank attack will be possible under any circumstances."[61]

It seems essential to pick out one special by-product of Schlieffen's envelopment theory for the fateful consequences it exercised on both world wars: the danger of gaps. In the war game of November/December 1905, when evolving the annihilation idea, he insisted on the means "to summon all forces in order to close every gap through which the misery and desperation of the enemy could find an escape-route."[62]

While discussing the prospects of break-through, he argued that it can succeed only in the special case, when the adversary's front presents gaps. Thus he pointed out the perils of gaps during the staff ride (East) of 1897, in the final discussions of the staff ride of 1902, in the Imperial war game of 1901–1902, and at many other occasions. He hammered this fear into the heads of the German commanders and officers along with his other theories.

Concluding this section one should point to a certain determinism in Schlieffen, which found its expression in what he called "the unalterable laws," according to which things "must" occur.[63] Or in another phrase, during the speech at the unveiling of the Moltke monument, he mentioned the general "who learned from the book of the past what might come and must come."[64] The same feature reappeared, in a speech on the one-hundredth anniversary of the Prussian War Academy, that the study of the history of war reveals "the knowledge how everything has come, how it had to come and will come again."[65] The same attitude appears in the phrase about the "secret of victory," which is in the General Staff's custody.[66],[67] It is therefore not to be wondered at that his disciples thought on identical and even more mystic lines.

From Schlieffen's preoccupation with his Cannae concept it is obvious that he was compelled to deal with the problem of fighting on interior or exterior lines.

OPERATION ON INTERIOR OR EXTERIOR LINES

The problem of operation on interior lines forced itself on Schlieffen because of Germany's geographical and political situation in the heart of Europe. There was a time, during the wars of Friedrich the Great and Napoleon, when operating on the interior line against two or more adversaries was thought to be the acme of generalship. But considered from the viewpoint of a quick decision and a short war, the situation appears very different. Friedrich's wars, despite many successes on the inner line, lasted many years and were eventually victorious only because of changes in the composition of the hostile coalition, not to mention that Napoleon's final defeat on the battlefield was twice caused, when he himself acted on interior lines. Schlieffen therefore argued that an "ordinary victory" over one of the opponents is not enough; complete destruction is necessary in order to prevent, once and for all, its recovery and the possibility of a rush to its ally's aid.[68]

From the first year of his accession to office he frequently presented exercises exposing the problem of action on inner lines to the young officers who were posted to the General Staff.[69] He explained in detail the difficulties arising from operations on interior lines. He quite rightly rejected the opinion of some historians that Napoleon lost the battle of Leipzig, the battles in the spring of 1814, and the battle of Waterloo—which were all conducted on inner lines—as a consequence of physical and mental illness. He analyzed Napoleon's failures mainly in terms of the too-early transference of force against a second opponent, before the destruction of the first. It should be remembered that Moltke's great victories had been achieved by fighting on exterior lines, and the general trend of the generation was the foundation of a Moltkean school of thought opposed to Jomini's school of interior lines, and as narrow-minded as this. Moltke's followers believed that by concentric action on exterior lines against an enemy operating on inner lines, ultimate envelopment and destruction could be achieved. However, in Moltke's time, owing to Bismarck's policy, there was no imminent danger of a war on two fronts. In the reign of Wilhelm II the situation had changed completely. Schlieffen had to reckon with war against a Franco-Russian coalition at least, and he had to find a solution. He solved the problem with the famous Schlieffen Plan, by acting strategically on interior lines (first move against France and then a shift to the east), and operationally and tactically on exterior lines (encirclement in the Cannae style).

Even after having already sensed what might have been called Schlieffen's somewhat mechanical approach to war, one is nevertheless struck by how little attention he paid to the moral element. In this sphere he dealt mainly with the problems of generalship.

ON GENERALSHIP

Besides some mystical utterances about "the drop from the consecrated oil of Samuel," which ought to be the lot of a general, he defined the general's task as "to destroy or to throw down completely an opponent, even a superior one, upon whom he does not know where he is located, where he goes, what his intention is."[70] Owing to the concept of attack in front, flanks, and, if possible, in the rear, it is the duty of the higher commanders to make the necessary arrangements for shortening the unavoidable interval between the clash in the front and the arrival of the enveloping forces in flanks and rear. Schlieffen heaped the whole burden of coordinating the different parts of this risky concentric assault onto the shoulders of the supreme leader. The task of the subordinate leaders is to march in the ordered direction, to engage the enemy, and to attack without any further support. According to Schlieffen, subordinate leaders have to be well trained in their profession, strive for an understanding of their superior's intentions, and obey. The coordination of the different parts and their harmonious interaction rests with the general. Schlieffen demanded from the general the ability to recognize his adversary's failures and utilize them fully.[71] On the other hand the general must know to what extent he himself may disregard the laws of science.[72]

While examining the various factors by which an inferior army may prevail over a superior one, he included among them the need for "an aim-conscious leader, an iron character, with an obstinate will for victory and troops which clearly understand the issues at stake." But in his opinion these are not enough; "there is still the need for the enemy, surprised by the suddenness of the attack, to become more or less confused, thus following up his rash decisions with a hasty execution."[73]

In order to make the attack really surprising and maximize the shock effect, all available force must be concentrated.

ON CONCENTRATION OF FORCE

As early as 1866 Moltke was committed to his principle of not squandering any force on secondary missions: no corps of observation and no armies where there was no actual enemy. In 1866 he left no covering forces in the West, and during the Franco-Prussian War no such forces were retained in the East, or elsewhere. Schlieffen, because of the changed political circumstances, could not be as daring as his teacher. He planned, however, to reduce the forces posted in the secondary theater of war to a minimum, to the embarrassment and indignation of his contemporaries and epigones. "To achieve a victory you need the concentration of superior forces at one point." "It is a rule to gather all available forces for one thrust." These are some of Schlieffen's maxims. In his "Cannae Studies" he praised Napoleon for regarding as the most vital feature the need "to be the stronger party. All the forces must be drawn into the battle. One single Battalion may be decisive. As long as this last battalion has not yet arrived, the attack on the adversary will be delayed."[74] That was the lesson to be learned from the great Corsican. But Schlieffen made it clear that "when I recommend concentration on the battlefield, I nevertheless oppose those people who demand concentration prior to the battle. The latter concentration leads, as a rule, to a frontal battle and, moreover, is almost impossible on a large scale. I would recommend, therefore, adherence to the great models of Königgrätz and Sedan.''[75] It follows logically that in a battle of encirclement, overwhelming forces should be concentrated on the wheeling flanks. A Napoleonic *bataillon carré* of 100,000 men and more must be formed on one wing, at least, he claimed, and this would also create the desired pressure on and threat to the enemy's rear. This idea provided an important part of his final plan for war against France: the superstrong right wing.

Faced with the strategic problem of fighting against odds on two fronts, Schlieffen had to decide not only where to deliver the first blow, but also how to accumulate superior forces at the decisive spot in order to deliver it. This consideration leads to the strategic ''Schwerpunktbildung'' (the formation of a center of gravity or thrustpoint).

THE CENTER OF GRAVITY

The importance of this notion follows logically: If there is a desperate need for a quick decision, and if forces must be shifted from West to East (or vice versa) in consequence of a war on two fronts, and if the first enemy to be engaged must be completely destroyed before turning to the next, then it is necessary to insist on a radical solution at one single blow. This is, of course, sometimes difficult to achieve, but there remains the need to settle all campaigns in as few major actions as possible. That was Schlieffen's conclusion from the Schwerpunkt theory.

ON OFFENSIVE AND DEFENSIVE

''No battle can be won purely by occupying positions but only by movement''—that was one of the rules Schlieffen propagated. In his various war games and exercises he rejected every thought, even in case of tremendous inferiority, of exchanging offense for defense.[76] He agreed that it was tempting for the weaker force to seek refuge in a strong position, in face of enemy superiority, and wait for the latter's assault. He supported his rejection of this attitude by many examples taken from history, demonstrating the danger to the defender of being surrounded by overwhelming forces or at least forced into a difficult and disastrous retreat. Instead of this solution, Schlieffen stressed his ''patent prescription'' for the inferior force: flank movement and encirclement of the enemy. He even maintained that the purpose of modern fortresses is not to facilitate defense, but to enable the inferior force to take offensive action. He agreed that even in the future a general would have to take fortifications into account, their role being to attract an irresolute enemy and by these means to bring him to a standstill, thus facilitating encirclement.

While putting great emphasis on fire power, Schlieffen completely overlooked the great advantages of modern long-range and quick-firing weapons for the defender. He pointed out that the modern battle formation depended on increased performance by the individual marksman. But unfortunately, this performance improved for the defender as well as for the assailant. It is quite certain that the improvement in firearms chiefly benefits the defender.

With respect to Schlieffen's Cannae concept, the question arises whether the flank attack really surprises the opponent, or whether the enveloping columns of the assailant will be opposed by a new defensive front. The latter would mean a new frontal attack. One may grant the assailant the advantage of the ground being perhaps here less favorable to the defender than on the actual front the latter had selected; but this advantage, too, is doubtful, for since the defender can count on the envelopment as an event that will probably occur, he will have selected and prepared his ground for this also. It seems also erroneous to think that the nature of envelopment with a synchronized frontal attack affords the assailant a superiority by itself; rather, the opposite is true, since the defender, using modern arms, can spare more forces in front and may, consequently, meet the enveloping movement by superior force.

The retreat, an essential feature of Clausewitz' concept of strategic defense, played but a minor and insignificant part in Schlieffen's teaching. Colonel Dr. Meier-Welcker ventured the opinion that Schlieffen might have regarded it as too complicated a form of battle.[77] Moreover, Schlieffen had doubts whether the enemy would respond to a retrograde movement and "enter the trap." He simply objected to any thought of surrendering the initiative to the enemy and playing a "last hand." In his critique of the exercise of 1897 he argued about delaying actions and maintained that

this method of occupying positions and breaking off combat may suit a detachment, a division, in some cases even an army-corps, but cannot be applied to an army, consisting of four to five army-corps, which cannot be observed adequately from one point. The commander-in-chief will hardly succeed in recognizing the crucial moment for retreat, even less so, in dispatching the opportune marching-orders to the troops and in ordering the latter to march off in due time.[78]

Nevertheless, in the final discussion of the staff ride of 1905 he admitted that, from the experience of the Russo-Japanese War, it seemed advisable for a force threatened by encirclement to withdraw quickly in order to renew battle at a more suitable locality. He rejected vigorously the notion that the "honor of arms" demands to be slaughtered in one's position, rather than to retreat.[79]

ON RESERVES

There remains the question whether the general should retain reserves to cope with unforeseen emergencies, or whether, by so doing, he goes against the principle of concentration of force. Schlieffen's point of view in 1894 was:

since a direct conduct of battle rarely occurs, it is therefore usually impossible to ensure a decisive result by using reserves. The lines are too extended for a timely arrival of the reserves at the decisive spot, and the field too large for recognition of this decisive point, if it is not predicted in the general plan of operation. In a modern battle of encirclement, the reserves consist of the wheeling wings. Thus we should regard the Second Army at Königgrätz, the XIIth Corps at Gravelotte . . . as the decisive reserves. To lead such reserves is not in the Supreme Commander's power, except when moving in person to their location. As a rule, the role taken by Napoleon, when advancing his Guards, has now passed to the General commanding at the decisive spot. On the latter's understanding, by moving his troops to the right spot, may depend on the decision of the day.[80]

He rejected the holding back of any general reserves because they would never reach the decisive place in time. He maintained that Moltke at Königgrätz did not hold back reserves in the vicinity of Sadowa, but had moved them in the opponent's flank right from the outset; neither had he horded forces at Gravelotte on 18 August 1870, nor spared the Prussian guards at St. Privat. On the other hand Napoleon had withheld his guards at Leipzig. In such a manner, concluded Schlieffen, one wins a Königgrätz or loses a Leipzig. Nevertheless, he supported the use of local reserves on the tactical level.[81] In 1909, however, in his essay "On War in the Present Time," he reached a more advanced stage in his conception of reserves:

Instead of accumulating behind the front reserves which must remain inactive and will be missed at the decisive spot, it is better to attend to a plentiful supply of ammunition; cartridges brought up by lorries form the best and most reliable reserves. All the troops formerly retained to bring about the decision can now from the outset be led forward to attack in flank. The stronger the forces which can be brought up with that objective, the more decisive the attack will be.[82]

It seems, as v. Bernhardi so rightly stated,[83] that Schlieffen reached a false conclusion. First of all, in Schlieffen's time, because of mechanical difficulties, lorries could not follow the attacking infantry into action and supply new rounds; they therefore could not substitute for reserves. Second, fighting troops do not spend ammunition alone; they also spend physical and moral strength and suffer losses. This consumption of force can by no means be made up by ammunition alone. If there is, therefore, a need for any reserves, a fact that Schlieffen did not deny, then it could only mean real reserves of fighting units (and, of course, maintenance of all supplies), which can take the place of the men whose strength is spent. However, Schlieffen's new posture in regard to reserves was adopted by him when shaping his last version of the Schlieffen Plan in December 1912. No reserves were kept at the disposal of the Supreme Command.

Schlieffen's main literary work began after his retirement from the office of Chief of General Staff on 1 January 1906. One of the central pieces of his work is, without doubt, the famous essay "Der Krieg in der Gegenwart," published for the first time in the *German Review* (Deutsche Revue) in January 1909.[84]

THE MODERN WAR

Even earlier than the publication of this programmatic article, Schlieffen meditated on the problems of modern war. He recognized the armies of masses and
the difficulty of handling them efficiently as one of the most outstanding problems
of modern times. In a letter to his sister Marie[85] he embarked on the question
of whether modern armies could be properly led and marshaled. He mentioned
that, at the end of the previous century, it had been maintained that an army
should not exceed 40,000 men. Napoleon immediately refuted this opinion,
however, in face of a horrified Europe. ''Now,'' he complained, ''Bismarck
says that 200–300,000 is the highest number. In 1870, the German Army numbered twice this number and Bismarck did not complain, while beleaguering
Paris, that we had too much.''[86]

In the final discussion of a staff ride in 1894 he stressed the difficulty of
conducting a vast army.[87] There was no longer any possibility of coordinating
battle with aides and ordnance-officers alone. It even seemed doubtful whether
a special order for battle could always be issued. An assault-order might be
substituted for a march-order, which leads eventually to a clash with the enemy.
Schlieffen's extreme belief in planning led him to the assertion that if everything
progresses well, there will be nothing left for the corps to do but to charge. The
pattern of the battle would follow from the direction of the approach-march
intended by the general. To ensure maximum exploitation of the existing forces,
deployment should be in breadth and not in depth. Marching abreast of one
another was raised to the status of a principle. Some of Schlieffen's critics
regarded this as a return to linear tactics and even the creation of a new linear
strategy. But Schlieffen maintained that this deployment in breadth would meet
all the demands of modern times: It allowed full use of the railway net and
maximum utilization of modern, quick-firing arms.

As far as infantry combat was concerned, infantry should advance while
exchanging fire in a loose single line, without a strong reserve, making the most
of natural cover (that was the lesson drawn from the war in the Far East). Open
ground, swept by the enemy's fire, could be crossed only with the aid of the
spade. The crowding of troops would cause unnecessary losses. The improved
rifle would substitute for the density of former lines. All these circumstances
would, by sheer necessity, lead to a vast extension of the battlefield and the
theaters of war. As fronts broaden in action, columns should march toward the
battlefield in the same breadth that they are to occupy afterward in battle. Corps
should be deployed alongside one another. The deployment area should be pushed
as far forward as possible, leaving only a little space of operation between the
hostile lines. The advance to battle would begin, therefore, the moment the
troops detrained. Corps and divisions would have to reach the places apportioned
to them in the battle line from the railheads, and seek battle immediately. Concentration for the battle loses importance; where the troops encounter the enemy,
they must enter the battle.

The tasks assigned to other arms would also change considerably: Artillery should still support the infantry combat, but owing to the devastating effect of improved artillery fire on attacking infantry, artillery must first destroy the hostile artillery; not until then are its forces free for their main task.[88]

With regard to the development of air reconnaissance, cavalry might become freed from reconnoitering. Its task would now be to carry its firearms into the rear of the enemy (Hasdrubal's feat at Cannae!). In order to get there it would first have to beat the enemy cavalry, which in turn would probably be on the move into their rear, in a separate duel.

The air force, including dirigible airships, captive balloons, and aircraft, would have to carry out its own duels with the hostile air force prior to a successful and, as far as possible, unmolested air reconnaissance.

One should assume that all European armies were on an approximately equal level of military value. This might result in a great frontal collision over an extensive area. Deployment in breadth might lead to an almost equal distribution of force on the whole front. There would then appear to be no factor of superiority, either tactically or strategically, but Schlieffen aimed to achieve this by encircling, and reinforcing one (or both) wings, by weakening his strength on the hostile front. Lateral shifting of troops would meet grave difficulties, and this massing of encircling forces at the wings must be planned beforehand.

The commander-in-chief, after assigning the routes to the different columns and setting them in motion, is almost redundant. Once the mechanism is set in motion it works almost automatically. Even his freedom of planning is very much restricted by the rigid railway network. For the "modern Alexander," as Schlieffen put it, connected with the troops from his office by wire, wireless, and motorized messengers, it remains only "on each fresh day to urge the armies and corps already engaged in action to new exertions, to keep in their direction of march those not yet engaged, or to direct them into new ones if the situation has changed."[89] Bernhardi called this a mechanical concept of war.[90] One must acknowledge Bernhardi when considering Schlieffen's thoughts about the requirements for leading mass-armies in battle and their conduct: He strove to lead armies of millions just as Friedrich the Great had led his small host at Leuthen, "in long lines, i.e., dress and alignment." "There is definitely more need for action according to the drill-regulations, for some 'eyes left!' and dress to the right." Summing up an exercise in 1905, he argued: "We have to become used to unified conduct of armies. The temptation often rises of saying to the Army-Commanders: Would you, please, align your men and put out 'right markers'! There was such a mess! Those chaps who invented dressing were, no doubt, great pedants, but they had the concentration of their forces and unified action in mind. One ought rather to strive for a drill-like advance."[91]

One military writer perceived the essence of military theory, before the First World War, in two closely connected ideas: an exaggerated cult of offensive and a belief in a short war.[92] Both ideas were strongly fostered by Schlieffen. He maintained that "a strategy of exhaustion is impossible when the maintenance

of millions [of soldiers] necessitates the expenditure of milliards [of Marks]."[93]
He therefore mistakenly regarded prolonged wars as an impossibility in modern
times, owing to the need of nations to maintain undisturbed their commerce and
industry. His teacher, the aged Moltke, foresaw much more clearly the prospects
of a future war of seven or even thirty years.[94] Schlieffen, a Prussian aristocrat,
never understood that economic forces may complement the mobilization of the
masses.[95] He, watching as Chief of the German General Staff the wars of his
time in South Africa and the Far East, should have recognized the tendency of
modern wars to drag on. His search for a short war was among the deciding
factors in his plan, whether to attack first in the West or in the East.

THE SCHLIEFFEN PLAN[96]

It is perhaps surprising to discover that Schlieffen's detailed plan was a deviation from an established usage of the German (Prussian) General Staff. Karl
Wilhelm von Grolmann, the Prussian Chief of General Staff in the years after
the Wars of Liberation, stressed the following opinion: "In the dispositions and
plans for a future war, only the first general order, with regard to the exact
knowledge of the theater of war, should be fixed. The preparations of offensive
as well as for defensive must be made. We must limit ourselves to these; to
design a plan of operation for years from the office-table is nonsense and belongs
to the sphere of military novel."[97] Moltke understood a plan of operation as
"the military utilization of the available means." The main difficulty in drawing
a plan lies in the fact that our will is soon opposed by the enemy's independent
one. The latter can only be broken by tactics, i.e., the battle. It follows that
"no plan of operation can extend with any prospect of certainty, beyond the
first clash with the hostile main force. Only a layman can pretend to trace
throughout the course of a campaign the prosecution of a rigid plan, arranged
beforehand in all its details and adhered to to the last. All successive acts of
war are therefore not pre-meditated executions but spontaneous acts guided by
military tact."[98]

Besides this basic diversity of opinion with regard to military planning in
general, Schlieffen's definite plan differed from Moltke's plan of war on two
fronts. Moltke did not believe in the possibility of a short war in France; he
learned this the hard way in 1870–1871. He had decided, in case of war against
a Franco-Russian coalition, to deliver the main offensive in the East; in the West
he would maintain a strategic defensive, and he was even prepared to withdraw
east of the Rhine, temporarily ceding the annexed territories of Alsace and
Lorraine. Although he believed in the prospect of a successful defense in the
West, he thought the eastern frontier, stretching 750 kilometers, as undefendable
by any but offensive measures. He also had in mind for that front a joint action
with the Austro-Hungarian Army. He doubted the probability of a total victory
on both fronts; he would be satisfied with favorable alterations of the border
line.[99]

Schlieffen based his plan on the Cannae concept. "The great Punic contrived it in ten-thousands, Moltke in hundred of thousands: Schlieffen devised it in millions!" acclaimed one excited biographer.[100] It was the basic idea that big armies are more vulnerable in their flanks, and against these the main blow should therefore be delivered.[101] An encirclement, to be executed successfully, must be combined with a frontal offensive action: "In strategy as well as in tactics the same rule obtains: he who strives for encirclement must firmly attack in front, prevent there every enemy movement and thus render possible the effect of the encircling wing."[102]

This operational and tactical solution based on concentric action was, of course, linked to the strategic necessity of fighting on interior lines; in this case it meant war against a Franco-Russian coalition. On the occasion of the staff ride in the East, in 1901,[103] Schlieffen explained:

Germany has the advantage of lying between France and Russia and of separating these allies. It would lose this advantage if it were to divide its army and thus be inferior in numbers to each single opponent. Germany must strive, therefore, first, to strike down one of the allies while the other is kept occupied; but then, when the one antagonist is conquered, it must, by exploiting its railways, bring a superiority of numbers to the other theater of war, which will also destroy the other enemy. The first blow must be delivered with the utmost power and a really decisive battle (Entscheidungsschlacht) must take place; a Solferino will bring us nothing; a Sedan, or at least a Königgrätz, must be fought.[104]

Nevertheless, the first decision should be sought in the West.[105] Schlieffen shrank from the prospect of becoming bogged down in an endless war of attrition in the immense Russian territory.[106] He also realized the implications of the improved Russian railway network and the tremendous fortifications erected by the Czar. On the other hand, with regard to the French fortifications, he considered that "an attack by the Germans upon the French fortresses did not seem advisable in a war on two fronts."[107] In the end the solution he reached was at the expense of a neutral country. There were two possibilities: Switzerland on the French right flank or Belgium on the left. Topographical considerations led to the violation of Belgian neutrality.

In addition to these arguments, which demonstrate the purely military-technical considerations for Schlieffen's plan, his partisans attempt to maintain that economic factors likewise had a decisive effect on the plan. Adherence to the elder Moltke's plan would have robbed Germany of its "most important sources of power . . . like the industrial areas of Lorraine and the Saar-basin . . . and it would partly immobilise them, as in case of the industries of the Rhineland and Westphalia."[108] G. Ritter disproves this: "I have not found such considerations in Schlieffen's own memoranda, and their soundness is questionable, for there was still the Ruhr, the whole of Upper Silesia and, if necessary, the Swedish ore mines. The truth is, that the considerations which decided Schlieffen were probably exclusively strategic, and this in the narrowest sense of the word."[109]

The main feature of the plan, besides the encirclement idea, was Schlieffen's endeavor to fuse mobilization, operational, and tactical decisions, i.e., the battle, into one single act, in which the hitherto clearly separated elements lost their separate identity. Kessel called it "a tremendous increase in methodology."[110] According to this scheme, battles became subordinate incidents in a total campaign, in which only the whole counted. The difference between operational movement and tactical action became blurred. The mainspring for such an approach was, of course, the striving after a quick decision.[111]

The Schlieffen Plan of 1905, presented here in rough outlines, deployed four army groups against France. The first group on the extreme right wing was the strongest component of the array: the famous *battaillon carré*.[112] It was echelonned in depth and consisted of five cavalry divisions; seventeen corps (including reserve corps); six so-called Ersatzkorps, which were to be levied and formed immediately on the mobilization of the German Army; and many brigades of Landwehr and even Landsturm. This force was to deploy in the sector opposite Brussels–Namur, cross the Somme between Abbeville and Chaulnes, pass westward of Paris, and then wheel in an eastern direction into the flank and rear of the French forces. This group should be permanently supported by additional reserve divisions and reserve corps made available from other places. The Ersatzkorps had to beleaguer Paris from the west and south. In Schlieffen's opinion, this right-wing group could never be strong enough.[113]

The second (central) group in the section Namur–Mézières was preceded by one cavalry division and consisted of six corps followed by some Landwehr brigades. It was meant to advance in close contact with the first group, between Chaulnes and La Fére, and engage a French position that Schlieffen expected on the Oise between La Fére and Paris. If this position was not occupied, then Schlieffen would use the forces of this group for the encirclement of Paris from the north and east, and for the reinforcement of the first and third groups.

The third group (the most southern of the right wing) had two cavalry divisions, eight active corps, five reserve corps (including the garrison and "main reserve" of Metz), and some Landwehr brigades, and was located opposite the section of Mézières–Verdun. It was intended to encounter the enemy expected on the Aisne and Aire in the line La Fére–Verdun and move southward, enveloping Verdun west of the Meuse.

The German left wing, the fourth group, consisted of three cavalry divisions, three active corps, and one reserve corps. There were also to be two Ersatzkorps formed on the left wing, but if it was possible to transport them by railway to the extreme right wing, they would not remain with the fourth group. This group was to deploy east of the Moselle opposite Verdun–Nancy and by attacking this line, tie down as many French forces as possible. In case of a strong French counterattack they were to avoid the blow. South of Strasbourg there remained only three and a half Landwehr brigades covering the line of the upper Rhine to the Swiss border and one Landwehr brigade in Lower Alsace.

The proportion of the right wing to the left was 7:1. This gigantic phalanx was to wheel around the pivot of Metz–Diedenhofen, crush and sweep before it all French resistance, and close like a revolving door on the French armies trapped between it and the German left wing, or compel them to escape into neutral Switzerland, and thus eliminate them in this way.

The designer of this plan hoped that this immense task could be accomplished in six weeks. He believed that the situation in the East, where only a small force would remain to stem the Russian tide, would not worsen militarily. A swift transfer of forces from the west to the east would begin a march of conquest there.[114]

The Schlieffen Plan also included a detailed timetable. For instance, on the thirty-first day after mobilization, the German right wing should reach the line Abbeville–Verdun. All the traffic and logistic problems had been studied in exercises time and again.[115]

The plan took into account the possibility of a French attack across the Rhine into southern Germany. Schlieffen maintained that "if the Germans persevere in their operations, they can be sure that the French will hastily turn back, and not to the north, but to the south of Metz, in the direction whence the greatest danger threatens. The Germans must therefore be as strong as possible on their right wing, because here the decisive battle is to be expected."[116] Again the expression of a fervent belief in this super-Cannae!

Schlieffen also had English intervention in mind.[117] The intention was to include the small British Expeditionary Force in the destruction of the French Army right from the beginning. The strong and deep German right wing, the *bataillon carré*, could cope with an English landing without losing too much of its momentum.

After his retirement from office, and after spending his leisure time on historical studies, he returned, just before his death, to the problem of the actual war plan. The 1912 version of the Schlieffen Plan differed from the older plan in three main points:

1. In a more outstretched movement of the right wing, which was to swing out far beyond Paris up to the coast. "If you march into France," he is reported to have said, "see to it that the grenadier on the utmost right brushes the Channel Coast with his sleeve." To deploy the necessary forces, the operation would involve in addition to Belgium the whole of (neutral!) Dutch territory.

2. In an offensive on the whole line in order to engage the enemy everywhere and to uncover weak points.

3. To compensate for the inferiority in numbers by reorganizing the German Army. Schlieffen regarded the corps as a too-cumbersome formation. The active corps lacked infantry, whereas the reserve corps and reserve divisions were insufficiently equipped with artillery. He proposed to combine both types and thus to attain a more balanced force. That would mean divisions well equipped with artillery and with full-strength infantry battalions. By abandoning the corps organization he intended to assign a former corps mission to every division of the new type. It was also believed that this arrangement would shorten the march columns.[118]

Many deficiencies of the plan were obvious prior to the crucial test of actual war. Some have already been mentioned. Among the others perhaps the most striking is that, from a purely technical viewpoint, the plan left no space for what Clausewitz had called "friction." In its elaborately calculated timetable, as well as in its basic design, it did not reckon with the tremendous difficulty of regulating such an enormous sweep by such vast numbers, even when composed of the best-trained troops led by the most efficient commanders. It was, in G. Ritter's well-founded opinion, "never a sound formula for victory," but "a daring, indeed, over-daring gamble, whose success depended on many lucky accidents."[119] It is surprising that Schlieffen, in fact, knew of this weakness in the plan and expressed it in the final discussion of his last war game in 1905:

Since the danger of a war with France and Russia is imminent, the theory of a decisive battle (Entscheidungsschlacht) in the West plays a vital role. The theory runs approximately thus: we shall enter France with all forces, there engage in a decisive battle, which of course turns out in our favor, and on the evening of the battle, or at least the next morning, the trains are ready to carry the victors eastwards to give a new battle of decision on the Vistula, the Niemen or the Narew. Wars are not waged in such a manner today. After battle, as may be read in the text-books, there follows the pursuit which sometimes lasts a very long time.[120]

Nevertheless, he did not himself draw the necessary conclusions from his own insight.

Another essential part of any criticism is the accusation that Schlieffen took into account forces not yet existing. All the verbal acrobatics of his followers to make one believe that these forces could be available, if the Socialists in the Reichstag and the fainthearted government had not prevented their establishment, only underline the fact that these formations were pipe dreams at the time the plan was drawn.[121] Schlieffen, however, recognized what Clausewitz had called the "diminishing force of attack." In his memorandum of 1905—the Schlieffen Plan—one reads: "We shall find the experience of all earlier conquerors confirmed, that a war of aggression calls for much strength and also consumes much, and that this strength dwindles constantly as the defender's increases, and all this, particularly so, in a country which bristles with fortresses."[122] Holding a vast occupied country, guarding long-stretched lines of communication, and enveloping many fortresses and defended towns would exercise a heavy drain on the German forces. If we add to this Schlieffen's estimation that the siege of Paris would absorb about seven corps, the question arises whether the plan was too extravagant for the available means. This does not even include the fact that the way Schlieffen intended to deal with the British Army was completely inadequate.[123]

Friedrich v. Bernhardi strongly opposed Schlieffen's proposal in 1912 for the creation of sufficient formations. The more "new Reserve and Landwehr formations, by training Ersatz-Reservists and such-like makeshifts" that we establish, "the more inferior they will become, and the more they will weaken the regular army, which must be drained of its blood to infuse any life at all into the new formations. We must rather resolve to limit these inferior formations as much as possible, and only establish the number absolutely necessary for containing the general levies of the enemy on the secondary strategic fronts."[124] By praising the value of regular troops, v. Bernhardi took, of course, the professional soldier's view, opposed to the idea of a "Volk in Waffen" (a nation in arms).

Another point that needs consideration is the question whether the French would really be subjugated by one single move, as planned by Schlieffen. First of all, they could avoid battle and even retreat south of the Seine. Such a move would render doubtful the possibility of an early transfer of troops to the east; and what, in the meantime, would be the situation in East Prussia and Silesia? In the war game of 1905 Schlieffen had such a situation in mind: "If we intend to wage war in France for months, we cannot, on the other hand, disregard the Russians completely. We cannot just watch them crossing the Vistula, Oder, Elbe and, in spite of that, continue to wage war in France. This is completely out of question."[125] The conclusion? Nothing but a fanatic belief in the Cannae miracle. The greater issue, now obvious in retrospect, whether a defeat of France would have meant a final victory, remained unanswered. Schlieffen's purely military mind was not bothered with such an "academic" problem. But he believed that a French defeat would lead England to enter peace negotiations and even deter Russia from continuing the war single-handed.[126]

The question of Belgian neutrality and the Schlieffen Plan has already been dealt with. But it seems worthwhile to note some further points. Schlieffen's defenders rejected every reference to the plans of the elder Moltke, who never considered a violation of Belgian neutrality. The circumstances had changed, they argued. However, "quod licet Jovis non licet bovis": Two of Schlieffen's biographers mentioned that he had compared his plan with Friedrich the Great's "Reflections upon Campaign-plans," written in 1775, and was excited that Friedrich thought, in case of a war with France, of using the route from the north, enveloping Dunkirk and leaning his right wing on Abbeville. From this he gained confirmation of his plan to advance in an outstretched arch on the northern shore of the Meuse.[127] This analogy is sheer nonsense, and a purely mechanical approach with respect to absolutely different political circumstances. The same is true with regard to Schlieffen's comparison of his plan with that contained in Clausewitz' main work (Book VIII, chapter 9), which includes a movement of combined British, Prussian, Dutch, and North German forces through Belgium toward Paris. This comparison, too, does not hold water, for then, in 1828, Belgium was still part of the United Netherlands, and therefore a combatant partner on the Allied side.

From both sides the question has been raised whether Schlieffen himself, if he had still been alive in 1914 and had led the German Army, would have been victorious. This is, of course, a hypothetical question. Schlieffen's partisans never doubted that he knew the "secret of victory" and would conquer.[128] Wilhelm Groener exclaimed:

When Fieldmarshal Count Schlieffen closed his eyes on 4 Jan., 1913, he bequeathed, as a legacy, the secret of victory in a war on three fronts. . . . Seven years earlier, he had left his sphere of activity at the Königsplatz—the General Staff—in firm possession of the secret of victory. . . . Simple and clear was the operative idea which contained the secret of victory: the quickest and greatest decision of war against our strongest and most dangerous enemy in the West. Gigantic, strategic Cannae! The left wing kept back and firmly anchored at the Moselle position Metz–Diedenhofen with withheld flank. The right wing formed in a powerful bataillon carré; direction of march through Brussels toward Abbeville–Amiens, from the sea to the Moselle "left-wheel march!"—in Friedrich's fashion—to the tunes of the "Paris Entrance March." Then further across the lower Seine, in sufficient force, in order not only to envelop Paris from the West, but also to carry on the operation against the flank and rear of the French army even in the direction of Orléans or Le Mans. Should the bataillon carré of the right wing, on its way, encounter the English, landed at the Flemish coast, or the French, then the wheeling will come to a temporary stop, the English will be beaten and rendered harmless and then "quick march!" again.[129]

Very simple, isn't it? Especially with the accompaniment of military brass bands playing the "Paris Entrance March"!

On the other hand Eberhard Kessel rightly maintains that, with the present knowledge and experience of the Second World War, it is quite certain that even a proper handling of the Schlieffen Plan would not have finished the war. Kessel avoids further discussion by saying that this knowledge enables one to pass from the Schlieffen Plan debate to the order of the day.[130]

There still remains the question whether Schlieffen was too mesmerized by his own 1905 plan to be able to adapt it to the changed circumstances of 1914. Liddell Hart maintains that "it is hard to find reason for the way he has so long been regarded as a master mind, and one who would have been victorious if he had lived to conduct his own Plan."[131]

It seems important to draw attention again to Schlieffen's tremendous influence on his environment. His operational expertise—revealed only in such exercises as war games, staff rides, and never tested on the battlefield—has been acclaimed by most of his subordinates. They accepted all his clever, biting, and sarcastic utterances as eternally "right." There was, of course, a minority that was deeply annoyed by his mechanical schematism.

The most striking feature, however, is the fact that although he had retired from office in 1905, his plan for war maintained a firm grip on German military thinking. This plan is therefore in history correctly associated with the name of its designer as the Schlieffen Plan. For it was the single-handed work of this one man, bearing alike the imprints of his qualities and his deficiencies.

NOTES

1. Wilhelm I (1861–1888).

2. Field Marshal v. Schlieffen mentioned in his speech when unveiling the Moltke monument in Berlin, that a German corps commander had received an order signed by Moltke and had asked the officer delivering the message from the High Command: "Who is this General Moltke?"

3. Decree of 2 June 1866. Cf. F. v. Cochenhausen, *Soldatische Führer und Erzieher*, 2d ed., Hamburg, 1942, p. 111. From Colmar von der Goltz it may be learned that such orders, although bearing the signature of the Chief of General Staff, were regarded as royal decrees. Cf. Colmar von der Goltz, *The Nation in Arms*, London, 1906, p. 91.

4. As in chapter 1, it is not intended to deal here with Schlieffen's biography. This may be found elsewhere, especially in the following books: Hugo Rochs, *Schlieffen*, Berlin, 1926; F. v. Boetticher, *Graf Schlieffen: sein Werden und Wirken*, Berlin, 1926; F. v. Boetticher, *Schlieffen*, Göttingen, 1957; H. v. Freytag-Loringhoven, *Generalfeldmarschall Graf v. Schlieffen*, Leipzig, 1920; E. Bircher and A. W. Bode, *Schlieffen: Mann und Idee*, Zürich, 1937; Gerhard Ritter, *The Schlieffen Plan*, London, 1948; and many others. It is notable, however, that the biographies of Schlieffen (studied so far) are divided into those that praise Schlieffen without any reservation and those that underline strongly his personal shortcomings. Human nature seldom, if ever, expresses itself exclusively in black and white but includes all possible intermediate shades. This effect on Schlieffen's biographers is a clear indication of his controversial character.

5. Hajo Holborn, "Moltke and Schlieffen: The Prussian-German School," in Edward Mead Earle, ed., *Makers of Modern Strategy*, Princeton, 1952.

6. Cf. Wilhelm Groener, *Das Testament des Grafen Schlieffen*, Berlin, 1927, p. 241. A modern writer, however, E. v. Kiliani, "Die Operationslehre des Grafen Schlieffen und ihre deutschen Gegner," *Wehrkunde*, H.2 (1961), p. 71, maintained that Schlieffen's *Dienstschriften* (service papers) and his publications after his retirement from office had formed a body of theory.

7. F. v. Boetticher, "Der Lehrmeister des neuzeitlichen Krieges," in F. v. Cochenhausen, ed., *Von Scharnhorst zu Schlieffen 1806–1906*, Berlin, 1933, p. 290.

8. Walter Görlitz, *Der Deutsche Generalstab*, Frankfurt/Main, 1955, pp. 172–173.

9. Most of his biographies are interspersed with "funny" stories, for instance, how he presented his subordinates with military problems as Christmas presents, which had to be solved and sent back by Boxing Day; or the brisk answer to a young adjutant who, during a staff ride, expressed admiration for the beauty of the Pregel valley, that "it is an insignificant obstacle" etc. Cf., for instance, Hermann v. Kuhl, *Der deutsche Generalstab in Vorbereitung und Durchführung des Weltkrieges*, Berlin, 1920, pp. 132–133.

10. Friedrich v. Bernhardi, *On War of To-day*, London, 1912, vol. 2, pp. 92–93.

11. Generalleutnant a.D. v. Zoellner, *Schlieffens Vermächtnis*, Berlin, 1938.

12. "Ja, es mag ja langweilig sein; es kommt eben immer auf das dumme Gesiege heraus!"

13. Generalfeldmarschall Graf Schlieffen (ed. Eberhard Kessel), *Briefe*, Göttingen, 1958, p. 312, footnote 4.

14. W. Groener, *op. cit.*, pp. 237–238.

15. It was the usage of the German Army to present to junior officers commissioned

to the Great General Staff an operational problem at the end of the year that ought to be solved by them.

16. A. v. Schlieffen, *Dienstschriften*, Berlin, 1937–1938, vol. 1, p. 118.

17. F. v. Boetticher, *Graf Schlieffen, op. cit.*, p. 23.

18. It is widely assumed that Schlieffen was the creator of the level of the operative art between strategy and tactics. Cf. Ferdinand M. v. Senger und Etterlin, "Cannae, Schlieffen und die Abwehr," *Wehrwissenschaftliche Rundschau*, Jg. 13 (1963), H.1–2, p. 27.

19. It is interesting to trace the younger Moltke's credo, that the beginning and the end of wars are the business of politicians, whereas the strategy of war itself is the domain of the General Staff and evolves independently from politics, to this essay of his great uncle. Otto von Moser quoted in his book *Die obersten Gewalten im Weltkrieg*, Stuttgart, 1931, p. 10, a marginal note of Wilhelm II on a copy of the "Frankfurter Zeitung": "Politik hält im Krieg den Mund bis Strategie ihr das Reden wieder gestattet" (Policy keeps its mouth shut during war until strategy allows it to speak again).

20. Quoted in Lt. Gen. R. v. Caemmerer, *The Development of Strategical Science During the 19th Century*, London, 1905, p. 85.

21. The controversy was over the early bombardment of Paris, demanded by Bismarck for political reasons and rejected by Moltke for military ones.

22. B. H. Liddell Hart's foreword in G. Ritter, *The Schlieffen Plan, op. cit.*

23. "Plan of Deployment" is used as the translation of the German technical term "Aufmarschplan."

24. G. Ritter, *The Schlieffen Plan, op. cit.*, p. 90.

25. Cf. *The Holstein Papers* (ed. Norman Rich and M. H. Fisher), Cambridge, 1955, pp. 159–167.

26. "Der Krieg in der Gegenwart," in Generalfeldmarschall Graf Alfred v. Schlieffen, *Cannae*, Berlin, 1936, p. 283.

27. The letter is dated 3 Dec. 1908—Berliner Hauptarchiv (BHA), the former "Preussisches Geheimes Staatsarchiv," under Rep. 92, Generalfeldmarschall A. v. Schlieffen, Nr. 12. The letter is also printed in Generalfeldmarschall Graf Schlieffen (ed. E. Kessel), *op. cit.*, but owing to a reorganization in the BHA the reference numbers given by E. Kessel are now superseded.

28. BHA—Rep. 92, Generalfeldmarschall A. v. Schlieffen, Nr. 12—Letter of the Minister of War, 16 Dec. 1908.

29. Holstein, who is supposed to know, claimed that the essay was inspired by encouragement from the Kaiser's entourage.

30. The operational and tactical considerations will be examined in due course.

31. Cf. Th. v. Bethmann-Hollweg, *Betrachtungen zum Weltkriege*, Berlin, 1919–1921, vol. 2, p. 7. There is no supporting evidence to Dr. Friedrich-Christian Stahl's claim, in his article "Der Grosse Generalstab, seine Beziehungen zum Admiralstab und seine Gedanken zu den Operationsplänen der Marine," *Wehrkunde*, Jg. XII, H.I (1963), p. 7, that since 1904 the Chancellor was currently informed about military planning and asked to give his and the Foreign Ministry's opinion.

32. Joh. Victor Bredt, *Die belgische Neutralität und der Schlieffensche Feldzugsplan*, Berlin, 1929, p. 56. Bülow's letter was a reply to an investigation of the author. V. Bethmann-Hollweg knew it officially, at least, from the younger Moltke's famous memorandum of Dec. 1912 (this memorandum is printed in Ludendorff, *Urkunden der Obersten Heeresleitung*, Berlin, 1922, pp. 51–60), and obviously, Ludendorff was referring

to that fact when he write that "the Chancellor was entirely informed about the military plans." Ludendorff, *Kriegführung und Politik*, Berlin, 1922, p. 66, footnote.

33. Cf. Walter Kloster, *Der deutsche Generalstab und der Präventivkriegsgedanke*, Stuttgart, 1932, p. 77.

34. V. Moser, *op. cit.*, p. 10.

35. The German "Reichsarchiv" (States Archives), however, replied to an inquiry of Groener (letter of 28 Jan. 1924) that "there is no evidence at all in the files of the former General Staff and in Count Schlieffen's papers kept at the Reichsarchiv, that the latter had pursued in his operational plan the intention to lay the odor of violating Belgian neutrality on the French or the British. Count Schlieffen maintained the opinion that the French and English would never be at a loss for a pretext to invade Belgium." BA/MA—H08—46/41:5.

36. Wolfgang Foerster, *Aus der Gedankenwerkstatt des Deutschen Generalstabes*, Berlin, 1938, pp. 15–16.

37. *Vide* W. Foerster, *Graf Schlieffen und der Weltkrieg*, 2d rev. ed., Berlin, 1925, pp. 80–81.

38. Letter to Freytag-Loringhoven. BHA—Rep. 92, GFM A. v. Schlieffen Nr. 6, printed in A. v. Schlieffen (ed. E. Kessel), *op. cit.*, p. 310.

39. Letter to Freytag-Loringhoven of 14 Aug. 1912. BHA—Rep. 92, GFM A. v. Schlieffen, printed *ibid.*, p. 317.

40. The work was subsequently published in the series *Studien zur Kriegsgeschichte und Taktik*, Herausgegeben vom Grossen Generalstab, Kriegsgeschichtliche Abteilung I as vol. 3: *Der Schlachterfolg, mit welchen Mitteln wurde er erstrebt*, Berlin, 1903.

41. Quoted in W. Erfurth, *Der Vernichtungssieg*, Berlin, 1939, pp. 43–44.

42. A. v. Schlieffen, *Dienstschriften*, *op. cit.*, vol. 2, p. 171 (Generalstabsreise Ost—1899).

43. *Vide* Hans Delbrück, *Geschichte der Kriegskunst im Rahmen der politischen Geschichte*, 2d rev. ed., Berlin, 1908, vol. 1, pp. 317 ff.

44. A. v. Schlieffen, *Cannae*, *op. cit.*, p. 3.

45. *Ibid.*, p. 254.

46. *Ibid.*, p. 257.

47. *Ibid.*, p. 262.

48. *Ibid.* We may recognize in this the beginning of the modern "hammer and anvil" conception.

49. *Ibid.*, p. 217.

50. H. Delbrück, *op. cit.*, p. 346.

51. D.V.E. Nr. 130—Exerzier-Reglement für die Infantrie (Ex. R. f.d.I.) vom 29. Mai 1906. §392: "Die Verbindung von frontalem und umfassendem Angriff verbürgt am sichersten den Erfolg."

52. F. v. Bernhardi, *op. cit.*, vol. 2, pp. 92–93.

53. *Ibid.*, p. 61.

54. Viz., Napoleon I.

55. In a lecture about the Prussian defeat of 1806, delivered in Oct. 1905, Schlieffen said: "The question, still not solved, at present, was then raised for the first time: How to attack a quick-firing enemy, located in a covered position?" BA/MA—H08–43/63.

56. A. v. Schlieffen, *Dienstschriften*, *op. cit.*, vol. 1, pp. 86–87.

57. Among Schlieffen's papers is a document of thirty-one typewritten pages entitled "Über die Aussichten des taktischen und operativen Durchbruchs auf Grund kriegsges-

chichtlicher Erfahrungen'' (On the prospects of the tactical and operational break-through, based on war-historical experiences). The purpose of that paper was to demonstrate the superiority of encirclement over break-through. BA/MA—H08–43/88.

58. Quoted in W. Groener, *op. cit.*, pp. 241–242.

59. ''Rolling-up'' is used as the translation of the German military term ''aufrollen.'' It seems that in the British and American military language an equivalent term does not exist.

60. F. v. Bernhardi, *op. cit.*, vol. 2, pp. 76–77.

61. *Ibid.*, p. 320.

62. Quoted in F. v. Boetticher, *Graf Schlieffen*, *op. cit.*, p. 19. The original text sounds as curious as the English translation: ''alle Kräfte aufzubieten um jede Lücke zu schliessen, durch welche das Elend und die Verzweiflung des Feindes einen Ausweg finden können.''

63. A. v. Schlieffen, *Cannae*, *op. cit.*, p. 373. Schlieffen's speech on the one-hundredth anniversary of Moltke's birthday (25 Nov. 1900).

64. *Ibid.*, p. 377.

65. *Ibid.*, p. 380.

66. *Ibid.*, p. 389. Farewell speech to the officers of the General Staff (30 Dec. 1905).

67. The same kind of arrogant determinism is demonstrated by his statement regarding the development of weapons in his time, that ''the conceivable has been achieved'' (Das Denkbare ist erreicht), contained in his essay on the future war.

68. A summary of the Staff Officers' exercise in 1896 reads: ''In operations of this kind against two separated enemy corps, it is not enough to push back one of them but it must be thoroughly beaten before we may turn to the other.'' A. v. Schlieffen, *Dienstschriften*, *op. cit.*, vol. 1, p. 39.

69. Almost every final exercise for staff officers during the years of office (1891–1905) revealed this problem. *Ibid.*, vol. 1: *Die taktisch-strategischen Aufgaben, aus den Jahren 1891–1905*.

70. A. v. Schlieffen, *Cannae*, *op. cit.*, p. 264. K. Justrow maintained rightly that this is to be regarded as a highly problematic advice for a General in modern times. He stressed that it is the task of the General, by utilizing all the means at his disposal, to establish the whereabouts of his enemy and his intentions and not to rely solely on the fallibility of his ingenious insight. K. Justrow, *Feldherr und Kriegstechnik*, Oldenburg, 1933, p. 42.

71. With typical arrogance he stated that ''the whole history of war consists in a series of mistakes and naturally every war-situation is the product of failures.'' A. v. Schlieffen, *Dienstschriften*, *op. cit.*, vol. 1, p. 123, exercise of 1904.

72. *Ibid.*, p. 123.

73. *Ibid.*, p. 243.

74. A. v. Schlieffen, *Cannae*, *op. cit.*, p. 315.

75. A. v. Schlieffen, *Dienstschriften*, *op. cit.*, vol. 1, p. 21. The tactical-strategical exercise of 1893.

76. Schlieffen's disciple, v. Freytag-Loringhoven, who served under his turn of office as Head of the Historical Branch of the Great General Staff, wrote in 1905 in a Clausewitz study that ''only by offensive battles and not by choosing unassailable positions, which the Austrian Cunctator [viz., Fieldmarshal Daun, 1705–1766] used to select so skillfully, and by the little tricks of manoeuvre, could the final objectives of war be reached.'' Frhr.

v. Freytag-Loringhoven, *Die Macht der Persönlichkeit im Kriege. Studien nach Clause-witz*, Berlin, 1905, p. 3.

77. H. Meier-Welcker, "Graf Alfred Schlieffen," in W. Hahlweg, ed., *Klassiker der Kriegskunst*, Darmstadt, 1960, p. 349.

78. A. v. Schlieffen, *Dienstschriften, op. cit.*, vol. 1, p. 45.

79. BA/MA—H08–46/111:3.

80. A. v. Schlieffen, *Dienstschriften, op. cit.*, vol. 2, p. 50, staff ride East—1894.

81. The same view was propagated by Colmar von der Goltz, as early as 1883, in his famous book *The Nation in Arms*: "Every reserve presents a dead force. . . . A situation is even conceivable in which it would be quite correct to entirely dispense with a reserve; for instance, when the enemy's strength is exactly known, and his forces have been deployed in their entirety. However, such eventualities never occur in reality, and, there-fore, we must never fight a battle completely without reserves. But the fact remains, that *strong* reserves are invariably not the most practical, but rather reserves which correspond to the existing situation. Excessively strong reserves are not the result of a good, but of a decidedly bad, system of economy, being a simply wasteful dispersal of forces, which frequently remain unemployed, whilst they might have ensured a favorable issue of the battle." (pp. 326–327)

82. A. v. Schlieffen, *Cannae, op. cit.*, p. 280.

83. F. v. Bernhardi, *op. cit.*, vol. 2, p. 45.

84. A. v. Schlieffen, *Cannae, op. cit.*, pp. 273 ff. Schlieffen was asked by the editor of this Review to contribute an article on the preservation of peace, and curiously enough, he wrote the essay "On War at the Present Time."

85. Letter of 13 Nov. 1892, quoted in GFM Schlieffen (ed. E. Kessel), *op. cit.*, pp. 296–297.

86. Alfred Vagts, *A History of Militarism*, London, 1959, p. 201, provides the following data: Montecuccoli (1609?-1680) had considered an army of 30,000 men the maximum size; Turenne (1611–1675) regarded an army of 50,000 as "inconvenient for him who commands it and those who compose it"; Marshall Saxe (1696–1750) and General Moreau (1763–1813) believed that an army should not outgrow the number of 40,000; Gouvion Saint-Cyr (1764–1830) thought that an army of 100,000 exceeded the moral and physical strength of one single leader; the Franco-Prussian War was opened on the German side with 480,000 men against 300,000 French.

87. Cf. A. v. Schlieffen, *Dienstschriften, op. cit.*, vol. 2, pp. 49–50.

88. Whereas many of Schlieffen's critics did not realize the importance of the "ar-tillery duel," as stressed by Schlieffen, both world wars confirmed his opinion.

89. A. v. Schlieffen, *Cannae, op. cit.*, p. 279.

90. Cf. F. v. Bernhardi, *op. cit.*, vol. 2, p. 163. Schlichting, another German con-temporary military theorist, maintained that "the defect of Schlieffen's doctrine is always that he generalizes, for application's sake, lessons and experiences which suit a single particular case," and that "he—Schlieffen—labors throughout only with mechanical apparatuses in breadth and depth. With their aid, the exercised battle of Friedrich may be constructed, if need be, sometimes the organized battle of Napoleon; for the battle of today they are useless at all command levels." Quoted in Siegfrid Mette, *Vom Geist deutscher Feldherren. Genie und Technik 1800–1918*, Zürich, 1938, p. 200.

91. F. v. Cochenhausen, ed., *Von Scharnhorst, op. cit.*, pp. 292–293.

92. Cf. Hoffman Nickerson, *The Armed Horde*, New York, 1940, p. 202.

93. A. v. Schlieffen, *Cannae, op. cit.*, p. 280.

94. The ninety-year-old Moltke's speech in the Reichstag on 14 May 1890: "If war should break out, this war which has now been pending like a sword of Damocles over our heads, for more than ten years, nobody may estimate its duration nor predict its end. The greatest powers of Europe, armed as never before, will fight each other. None can be thrown down so completely, in one or two campaigns, that it would declare itself vanquished and be compelled to accept hard conditions for peace without any chance, even after a year's time to renew the fight. Gentlemen, it might be a seven or even a thirty years' war—but woe to him who sets fire to Europe and first throws the match into the powder-barrel!" Quoted in Hermann v. Kuhl, *Der Weltkrieg 1914–1918*, Berlin, 1929, vol. 1, pp. 106–107. (First printed in Graf Moltke [ed. F. v. Schmerfeld], *Ausgewählte Werke*, Berlin, 1925, vol. 3, p. 345.) Even earlier (1883) Colmar von der Goltz wrote in his *Nation in Arms*, *op. cit.*, pp. 150–151: "Our conception of a future campaign presents the picture of rapidly progressing operations, the idea of decision upon the battlefield in uninterrupted succession, of a swift penetration deep into the heart of the enemy's country, and a propitious peace thus speedily obtained. It was so in 1866 and also in 1870, let us hope that it may be the same in future. Such are the principles according to which good leaders should always strive to conduct any fresh war." But then he probably had second thoughts, and added on p. 159: "It is absolutely certain that in future wars, events will not march with anything like the rapidity peculiar to our last campaigns."

95. That was, however, not only confined to Germany, as will be learned in Book Two, chapter 4 of this study.

96. For the student of the Schlieffen Plan and its estimation, the works of G. Ritter, *Staatskunst und Kriegshandwerk*, *op. cit.*, and *The Schlieffen Plan*, *op. cit.*, are invaluable. The latter work especially eliminates a deficiency to which General Speidel had drawn attention, in his comment on General Beck's essay "West- oder Ost-Offensive 1914?" in L. Beck, *Studien*, *op. cit.*, p. 141: "Moltke's ideas of strategic defensive in the West and joint operations with the Monarchy of the Danube against Russia had been forgotten too often, just the same as the fact that at the time of the last formation of the so-called "Schlieffen Plan," Russia was tied up by Japan in the Far East. It seems curious that this idea was neither mentioned in German nor in French or other foreign literature upon Schlieffen's studies." Excellent maps and diagrams demonstrating the development of the Schlieffen Plan may be found on pp. 263–267 of F. v. Cochenhausen, ed., *Von Scharnhorst zu Schlieffen*, *op. cit.* The original manuscripts of the Schlieffen Plan are now stored in the Dokumentenzentrale des Militärgeschichtlichen Forschungsamts (MGFA) at Freiburg in Breisgau, contained in three files of "Nachlass GFM Graf v. Schlieffen." References in this study, however, will be mainly made to the English edition of G. Ritter's publication, except in cases where Ritter is in error.

97. Quoted in F. v. Cochenhausen, ed., *op. cit.*, p. 118.

98. GFM Graf Moltke (ed. F. v. Schmerfeld), *op. cit.*, pp. 77–78. Colmar v. d. Goltz held the opinion that "no plan of operation can with any safety include more than the first collision with the enemy's main forces." C. v. d. Goltz, *op. cit.*, p. 187.

99. Up to 1877 Moltke planned offensive action in the West and defense in the East. From 1880 (the ratification of the Austro-German Alliance) he reversed this plan and thereafter held to this change. Cf. W. Groener, *op. cit.*, p. 85.

100. H. Rochs, *op. cit.*, p. 37.

101. Cf. A. v. Schlieffen, *Dienstschriften*, *op. cit.*, vol. 1, p. 46, exercise of 1897.

102. *Ibid.*, vol. 1, pp. 108–109, exercise of 1903. Cf. also p. 94, exercise of 1902.

103. *Ibid.*, vol. 2, p. 222.

104. Schlieffen regarded Königgrätz as an imperfect, and Sedan as a perfect, battle of encirclement.

105. There the well-developed railway network, German as well as French, would render possible a quick deployment of huge masses of troops.

106. The debacle of Napoleon in 1812 still had an iron grip on human minds!

107. A. v. Schlieffen, *Dienstschriften*, *op. cit.*, vol. 2, p. 222.

108. W. Foerster, *Aus der Gedankenwerkstatt*, *op. cit.*, pp. 58–59.

109. G. Ritter, *The Schlieffen Plan*, *op. cit.*, p. 39.

110. "Eine ungeheure Steigerung der Planmässigkeit." GFM v. Schlieffen (ed. E. Kessel), *op. cit.*, p. 16.

111. As a matter of fact, this merging and overlapping of different stages was not Schlieffen's invention, for many of Napoleon's campaigns show identical features.

112. In his lecture "Die Operationen in der ersten Hälfte des Oktobers 1806," delivered in Oct. 1905, at a conference of General Staff officers (*vide* BA/MA—H08–43/63), he explained in detail Napoleon's concept of the *bataillon carré* but added that now such a formation must be even stronger and more compact. V. Freytag-Loringhoven, who attended the staff ride of summer 1905, in which Schlieffen had tested various aspects of his final plan, immediately recognized the connection of the ideas expressed in the lecture, with the Schlieffen Plan. (Entry of 11 Dec. 1905, in v. Freytag-Loringhoven's minutes-book of his conferences with Schlieffen. BHA—Rep. 92, GFM A. v. Schlieffen, Nr. 6.)

113. It was told that in his last moment of life he murmured, "Macht mir den rechten Flügel stark" (Strengthen the right wing). Cf. General W. v. Hahnke's letter to v. Freytag-Loringhoven (5 May 1924). BHA—Rep. 92, W. v. Hahnke, Nr. 6/12, p. 10.

114. As a matter of fact, owing to the political situation in the East in 1905, Schlieffen devised the plan with regard to the West only, and the topic of his memorandum was "War Against France." In the 1912 version of his plan he intended to strip the eastern front of all German forces, saying "that Austria's fate is to be decided on the Seine and not on the San."

115. Groener, for instance, conducted in 1912 a transport exercise in order to explore the problems of transferring four army corps on the thirtieth day after mobilization (M + 30) from France to the eastern front. W. Groener, *Lebenserinnerungen*, Göttingen, 1957, p. 133. For further details of logistic problems, *vide* Book Two, chapter 4 of this volume.

116. G. Ritter, *The Schlieffen Plan*, *op. cit.*, pp. 147–148. This is the final passage of the 1905 memorandum.

117. This issue will be investigated in detail in Book Two, chapter 6 of this study.

118. The same idea is also expressed in a letter to v. Freytag-Loringhoven of 14 Aug. 1912 (BHA—Rep. 92, GFM A. v. Schlieffen), quoted in GFM Schlieffen (ed. E. Kessel), *op. cit.*, pp. 317–318.

119. G. Ritter, *The Schlieffen Plan*, *op. cit.*, p. 66.

120. Quoted in W. Foerster, *Aus der Gedankenwerkstatt*, *op. cit.*, p. 51.

121. Moreover, many of Schlieffen's supporters, who accused the younger Moltke of "watering-down" Schlieffen's grandiose plan and of not demanding further enlargements of the German Army, forget, when dealing with the Marne disaster, their claim that the forces mentioned in the plan were a reality, and explained that exactly the eight corps,

whose formation was demanded by Schlieffen, would have turned the tide (had they existed, of course!).

122. G. Ritter, *The Schlieffen Plan, op. cit.*, p. 141.

123. *Vide* in more detail in Book Two, chapter 6.

124. F. v. Bernhardi, *op. cit.*, vol. 2, pp. 448–449.

125. Quoted in W. Foerster, *Aus der Gedankenwerkstatt, op. cit.*, p. 52. F. v. Bernhardi stressed, as an additional disadvantage of the plan, that "to transfer a large German army after having beaten the French, from the western border of Germany to its eastern boundary, takes weeks to depart and to arrive; during that time a superior and victorious Russian army may have penetrated deep into the heart of Germany. But during this time, the French, against whom only weak forces would have been left behind, might have returned to the attack. The space separating the two armies operating on the exterior lines would be likely to decrease very materially during the weeks the German army is being transported by rail.'' F. v. Bernhardi, *op. cit.*, vol. 2, pp. 85–92 passim.

126. W. Groener even held the opinion that "Italy and Rumania at least would have pursued a very peaceful policy impressed by the victory in the West. And America could have been harnessed to the peace-wagon quite easily by a skillful German Chancellor.'' W. Groener, *Das Testament, op. cit.*, p. 217.

127. Cf. H. Rochs, *op. cit.*, p. 85, and v. Freytag-Loringhoven, *GFM Graf v. Schlieffen, op. cit.*, p. 77. This is also confirmed in a letter of W. v. Hahnke, Schlieffen's aide-de-camp and son-in-law, to Groener (16 April 1926). BA/MA—H08–46/38:1.

128. Cf. F. v. Boetticher, in F. v. Cochenhausen, ed., *Von Scharnhorst zu Schlieffen, op. cit.*, pp. 299–300, and F. v. Cochenhausen himself in the same book, p. 317; W. Groener, *Das Testament, op. cit.*, pp. 235–236; General Werner v. Fritsch (at that time the Supreme Commander of the German Army) in his introduction to the 3d edition of *Cannae*; and others.

129. Wilhelm Groener, *Der Weltkrieg und seine Probleme, Rückschau und Ausblick*, Preussische Jahrbücher, Schriftenreihe, Nr. 1, Berlin, 1920, pp. 16–18 passim.

130. GFM Schlieffen (ed. E. Kessel), *op. cit.*, p. 14.

131. Liddell Hart's foreword in G. Ritter, *The Schlieffen Plan, op. cit.*, p. 9.

3

Schlieffen versus Clausewitz: A Confrontation

The teachings of these two military thinkers are not on the same intellectual level. Whereas Clausewitz' thoughts circled on the highest level of a philosophy of war and strove for the understanding of the eternal nature of war, Schlieffen tried to solve concrete problems of the conduct of war in his time. However, despite this disparity, the comparison seems necessary for two main reasons: first, because Schlieffen regarded himself as a disciple of Clausewitz.[1] It probably never entered his mind that he deviated in the slightest degree from Clausewitz' theory. And, second, although the impact of both men on future wars will be judged in Book Two, a proper evaluation of them should be made here.

Liddell Hart, whose criticism of Clausewitz is not always just, was right, however, when he pointed out that the latter's main work should be regarded "as a treatise on the nature of war, instead of as a practical guide to the conduct of war."[2] This seems to be a proper interpretation of Clausewitz' own aim. Schlieffen, on the other hand, understood Clausewitz' *On War* in the latter sense, stressing, in his introduction to the fifth edition, that "the permanent merit of the work 'On War' lies, in addition to its high ethical and psychological value, in its emphatic accentuation of the annihilation-idea. Clausewitz regarded war as being under 'the sole and highest law of decision by arms.' It seemed to him that 'the destruction of the hostile forces is the most commanding purpose among those which may be pursued by war.' This is the doctrine which led us to Königgrätz and Sedan." Although Schlieffen looked at Clausewitz' work as a practical guide for the conduct of war, there remains no doubt that in his own teaching he aimed at nothing but practical instructions for combat.

In other words, Clausewitz presented his readers with the tools with whose aid the phenomenon of war can be examined and its relationship to other social phenomena evaluated. The intelligent student can derive a sound estimate of any concrete (or hypothetical) situation from them. Schlieffen presented rules of "do and do not." As Wilhelm Groener, one of Schlieffen's most eager disciples, put it: "In Count Schlieffen's writings you will never find spacious, theoretical discussions on strategy and tactics, nor scientific evolution of theories and maxims, but only life and reality."[3] This is the same attitude of "applied strategy" as opposed to "philosophical strategy."[4] This comparison also comes from a great admirer of Schlieffen,[5] and one cannot resist a certain feeling that its author wished to express his esteem for Schlieffen's practical outlook as compared with Clausewitz' "philosophical."[6] However, apparently owing to Schlieffen's own appreciation of Clausewitz, the same author thought that both complemented each other and should therefore be studied together, thus providing the German officer with a comprehensive guide.

WAR AND POLITICS

When dealing with Clausewitz, great stress was put on his concept of the relationship of war and policy. This was not accidental, for this concept comprises one of the most essential components of Clausewitz' whole theoretical edifice. He denied explicitly the independent existence of war. The main features of all great strategical plans are principally of a political nature. A plan of war emerges from the very existence of both belligerent states and their relations with others. The plan of war decides the plan of campaigns and therefore policy is interwoven into every war-like act. It follows that there is no purely military judgment of a strategic issue, and no purely military plan for its solution. It is absurd to strive for the separation of the military from the political implications of a strategical plan. In a letter to Major C. F. Roeder, Clausewitz revealed his belief, later to be found in his main work *On War*, that "war is nothing but a continuation of political endeavor by other means. On this opinion I base the whole of strategy, and believe that he who refuses to recognize this necessity does not understand what really matters. This principle explains the whole history of war and without it, all is full of absurdity."[7] It is striking that Schlieffen also expressed a credo of his own about "the essential substance of the whole history of war." But being, to use Clausewitz' phrase, a grammarian of war and not a logician, Schlieffen stressed that this essence is the attack against the flank.[8] Being thus obsessed by his encirclement mania, Schlieffen could never raise a question like Clausewitz and ask "how is it possible to draw a plan of campaign for one theater of war or more, without regard to the political situation of the states and their constellation to each other?"[9] According to Clausewitz, the foremost question that the strategist must ask is the ultimate object of a war, or a campaign, for all the main lines of his plan lead toward this object, or at least are decided by it. There is no single standard solution (for instance, annihilation), but the volume of one's efforts is decided by the aim.[10] It follows that one should not regard war as a mere act of violence and destruction, which might lead by a logical consequence to a series of conclusions far from the appearance of the real world, but that one should regard war as a political act, a real political instrument, directed by one hand. This hand is embodied by policy. The intensity of the issues at stake decides the degree of violence. A war of survival is therefore reduced to the essential concept of violence and destruction, as an *ultimo ratio*, and seems to be nonpolitical. Nevertheless, it does not lack the political principle; but the latter coincides only with the violence and destruction, and is therefore hidden from recognition.

Clausewitz' concept of the primacy of politics over war is still unaltered today, despite the social changes during the past 150 years that have elapsed since Clausewitz' time. To the same extent, history has proved true his theory of a variety of means for gaining the political end; at least the modern "cold war" is nothing but one nuance in the scale of probable means.[11] Clausewitz should be ranked top among military thinkers for this one maxim alone.

Schlieffen, as we already know, was never troubled by such "theoretical" considerations. On the contrary, he may serve as a fine illustration of Clausewitz' opinion "that the assertion that a major military development or the plan for one, should be a matter for *purely military* opinion is unacceptable and can be damaging. Nor indeed is it sensible to summon soldiers, as many governments do when they are planning a war, and ask them for *purely military advice.*"[12] Indeed, "the available means" had been allotted to the military commander, i.e., to Schlieffen as the German Chief of General Staff, and he had drawn a purely military plan. No coordination of the war aims and war needs, on the one hand, and the available means, on the other hand, ever took place. The army was kept as a "state within the state," sanctioned by the crown, and planning was conducted from purely military-technical points of view, without consulting any of the political agencies.[13] The ideology behind this attitude is clearly indicated by the forgery of Clausewitz' passage with regard to the relationship of the general and the statesman.[14] The question about the political consequences of the military plans had never arisen. That was so with respect to the invasion of Belgium, and to the same degree Schlieffen had never considered the question of what would be the attitude toward Great Britain after a French defeat. Although he regarded England as the "ringleader" of the anti-German coalition, he never considered an invasion of the British Isles. His whole plan disregarded completely the importance of the British Empire and its main military instrument, the Royal Navy, and their obvious political influence on the continuation of the war. Therefore, his famous plan was never a comprehensive and balanced one, for he took into account only the part to be played by the German land forces. Moreover, as Walter Görlitz has so rightly observed, "the Schlieffen plan, in its original form as well as in its alteration, would not secure the winning of the war but at its best give a victory in an initial operation, viz. the battle of France. The belief that this victory would coincide with the final winning of the war was a typical military error of judgement."[15] There is no doubt that Schlieffen can serve as the prototype of a new kind of un-political soldier, who was completely absorbed in his profession and impervious to anything outside its narrow technical scope.

It seems, therefore, to be logical that the respective views of both men differed, too, concerning the objects of war.

THE OBJECTS OF WAR

Whereas Clausewitz recognized various degrees in the selection of war aims, Schlieffen confined his theory to one sole object: annihilation of the adversary. This complete destruction, he taught, can be achieved by encirclement alone,[16] the shibboleth of victory. He rejected any idea of break-through, even on the tactical level, as was indicated and supported by his special study,[17] because he thought it was not enough to be decisive, i.e., annihilative. Moreover, it is difficult to follow Schlieffen's Cannae concept, owing to the uttermost confusion of the different levels of execution.[18] In all his essays one seldom knows whether he related his ideas to strategy, operation, or tactics—it is all one hotchpotch. Clausewitz, in his study of the campaigns of 1799, had already observed the mode "of pulling over from tactics into strategy, the principle of attacking the enemy, as far as it was possible, from many points and sides simultaneously."[19] It seems as if he had predicted this future nuisance. Clausewitz had not ignored the possibilities of encirclement, but he stressed that strategy and tactics should fit the nature and conditions of the particular war in which one is engaged. In order to gain one's objective, he rejected all forms of systemization.[20] He admitted that encirclement is always a more decisive move, promising the greatest success, but that it is, at the same time, a riskier one, with the least prospect of success. Success and danger are linked and form the dynamic principle in war, thus he wrote in a letter to Major Roeder. If one wants to increase the first, one has always to accept an increase of the latter and must therefore decide whether the circumstances suit such an increase. One may try it if one has the advantage of a great physical and moral superiority.

Because encirclement is an action on exterior lines, Schlieffen had completely overlooked the fact that the antagonist has all the advantages of a fight on interior lines on his side.[21] Or in Clausewitz' definition:

The other form of envelopment and cutting the line of retreat entails a division of forces. The danger here lies in that division itself, for the enemy has the benefit of the concentration of his internal lines and can thus bring superior numbers against any individual part of his opponent's force. This hazard cannot be eliminated and only three main causes justify one's exposure to it:

1. A previous division of forces which makes this type of operation obligatory if one wishes to avoid a major loss of time.[22]
2. Great physical and moral superiority, which will justify taking drastic measures.
3. A loss of impetus on the enemy's part once the assault has run its course.[23]

One cannot resist the acceptance of the criticism of Schlieffen's contemporaries, that in stressing of the attack and encirclement alone he "lost sight of the infinite variety of the military challenge in favor of a one-sided tendency" (Field

Marshal Gottlieb Count Haeseler).[24] This one-sidedness was also criticized by F. v. Bernhardi: "He who makes war following a fixed system for victory will hardly twist the laurels around his temples."[24] In contrast with this, Clausewitz provided the student of warfare with the widest range of possibilities in accordance with circumstances.

ON HISTORICAL EXAMPLES

Schlieffen tried to back his teaching by historical examples. The battle of Cannae became the catchword of his theory.[25] He tried to make us believe that, although 2,000 years had elapsed since the battle on the shores of the Aufidus, the main conditions of battle remained unaltered.

In Clausewitz' theory, historical demonstrations played an important part too. He had examined 130 campaigns, which had consequently been published in his collected works. But his approach was more critical and selective. He maintained that

historical examples clarify everything and also provide the best kind of proof in the empirical sciences. This is particularly true of the art of war. . . . Historical examples are, however, seldom used to such good effect. On the contrary, the use made of them by theorists normally not only leaves the reader dissatisfied but even irritates his intelligence. We therefore consider it important to focus attention on the proper and improper uses of examples.[26]

Clausewitz distinguished four points of view for the use of a historical example:

1. It may be used as an *explanation* of an idea.
2. It may serve as an *application* of an idea.
3. One can make special reference to historical fact in order to support what has been advanced, i.e., one wishes to prove the *mere possibility* of a phenomenon or effect.
4. Deduction of some theory from circumstantial presentation of a historical event and from the comparison of several of them. In this case the testimony presents the true *proof*.

In the latter case

care must be taken that every aspect bearing on the truth at issue is fully and circumstantially developed—carefully assembled, so to speak, before the reader's eyes. To the extent that this cannot be done, the proof is weakened, and the more necessary it will be to use a number of cases to supply the evidence missing in that one. It is fair to assume that where we cannot cite more precise details, the average effect will be decided by a greater number of examples.[27]

This latter procedure, however, has its disadvantages and is frequently misused. Instead of presenting a detailed case, often a number of instances are touched on, which give the semblance of strong proof, but in fact they may prove nothing, since there are cases in which one may present a dozen examples to support a certain occurrence as well as the same number of examples that had the opposite result. Clausewitz compared a superficially mentioned event with an object seen at great distance, in which the details cannot be distinguished and therefore may serve to support the most conflicting opinions. Moreover, he also maintained that in order to establish a new—or doubtful—opinion, one single event, thoroughly analyzed, may be much more instructive than ten that are superficially treated. The danger in a superficial treatment lies in the fact that in most cases he who acts in such a manner "has never mastered the events he cites" and therefore "such superficial, irresponsible handling of history leads to hundreds of wrong ideas and bogus theorizing."

Clausewitz then passed sentence on the use of examples from ancient history by excluding it almost entirely from consideration, and by reaching the conclusion "that examples should be drawn from modern military history, insofar as it is properly known and evaluated." In more distant times conditions and ways of waging war were different and therefore bear fewer practical lessons for our time. With the passage of time these historical examples also are bound to lose a mass of essential minor elements and details, and the picture becomes blurred. He argued that with respect to the conduct of war at his time the wars since that of the Austrian Succession (1740–1748) are the ones to be considered. "The further back one goes, the less useful military history becomes. . . . The history of antiquity is without doubt the most useless and the barest of all."[28] It is striking to discover that Schlieffen, Clausewitz' ostensible disciple, disregarded this advice; but one wonders whether he had in any way acknowledged Clausewitz' brilliant analysis of the Second Punic War (218–201 B.C.). For Clausewitz has drawn much more valuable conclusions from this occurrence than has Schlieffen's encirclement theory. He stressed that "the peculiar way in which Rome fought Carthage in the Second Punic War—by attacking Spain and Africa while Hannibal was still victorious in Italy—can provide a most instructive lesson: we still know enough about the general situation of the states and armies that enabled such a roundabout method of resistance to succeed."[29] Instead of a doubtful tactical maneuver, which attracted Schlieffen to Cannae, Clausewitz' eye was caught by the broader strategical and political issues and their lessons. The latter were completely disregarded, or ignored, by Schlieffen. The final verdict of Clausewitz leaves no doubt what his judgment would have been had he known of Schlieffen's use of Hannibal's battle at Cannae: "Unfortunately, writers have always had a pronounced tendency to refer to events in ancient history. How much of this is due to vanity and quackery can remain unanswered; but one rarely finds any honesty of purpose, any earnest attempt to instruct or convince. Such allusions must therefore be looked upon as sheer decoration, designed to cover gaps and blemishes."[30]

THE MORAL ELEMENT IN WAR AND FRICTION

In Schlieffen's writings the so-called moral factors played a small part. Schlieffen's attitude is the more surprising when one remembers the vital part accorded to this element by Clausewitz. After all, Schlieffen was the head of this new kind of conscripted service army, about which Clausewitz had said that "war is today a war of all against all. No more a king wages war against another king, nor an army against another one, but one nation fights another and the nation includes also king and army. . . . War was given back to the people, who had partly been removed from it by the professional armies."[31] Clausewitz had realized that a national army, fighting on its own ground and soil for its highest interest of national survival, is very different from the mercenary-type armies. He was therefore not afraid to make use of a common uprising, an idea that horrified many of his noble compatriots. From this recognition of the moral elements he gained the understanding of the vital factor of "friction" for warfare. Armies and units consist of many individuals with their different qualities and shortcomings, and all are likely, in one way or another, to exercise influence, in addition to other factors, on the working of the complicated machine of war. Schlieffen's "planfaithfulness," however, overlooked the tremendous impact of friction on warfare. In the design of the Schlieffen Plan no tribute was paid to this vital factor. Clausewitz had cleared the sphere of military thought of the rigid rules of rationalism and given due notice to the irrational realism of war— boldness, daring, genius of leadership, friction, danger, fear, and an additional variety of irrational factors; Schlieffen had restored a certain amount of rationalism by his "unalterable laws," his disregard of friction in his plan for war and the task assigned to the commander as "director of battle."

THE RELATIONSHIP OF DEFENSIVE AND OFFENSIVE

Whereas Schlieffen presented his Cannae concept as the solution for the success of inferior force, Clausewitz turned to the investigation of the relationship of the defensive and offensive to find an answer to the question how unequal adversaries can wage war. His conclusion that the defensive is the strongest form of war was not a consequence of an ethical preference for defense, or lack of offensive spirit, but a cool calculation of facts. Schlieffen completely rejected every thought of the defensive. Although he worshiped Friedrich the Great, he never grasped the fact that Clausewitz recognized, that during the Seven Years' War (1756–1763) the Prussian King was strategically on the defensive. Schlieffen maintained that even the inferior, or only the inferior, has to attack—always and everywhere.[32] This belief was utilized in the 1912 version of the Schlieffen Plan: From the Swiss border to the North Sea the German Army was to attack and thus to "dictate the law" to the adversary. The selection of the thrust toward Paris, the "pit of the stomach of France," was to force the opponent to accept battle. This notion was exemplified by Schlieffen's lecture on the campaign of

October 1806, when he enlarged on the criticism raised against Napoleon's march, directed from the coast toward Berlin: "The most decisive feature of the war was therefore, Napoleon's advance from the right wing toward Berlin, with the explicit intention to push away the enemy from its communications, reinforcements, allies and consequently, to cut off his possibility to carry on the war."[33] Schlieffen also denied the advantages, stressed by Clausewitz, of gaining strength by retreating into the interior of the country, a procedure that his predecessor, Moltke, intended to carry out in southern Germany in case of a war against a Franco-Russian coalition. Schlieffen had not believed that the enemy would become "trapped."[34] His disregard of defense led, during his turn of office, to a complete neglect of any defensive training of the German Army, a fact that bore grave consequences for the future.

Up to this point many issues of disagreement between Clausewitz and Schlieffen have been mentioned. It now seems appropriate to touch on some points of harmony.

THE DIMINISHING FORCE OF ATTACK

Schlieffen's expression on the diminishing force of attack in the final version of his famous plan for war against France—which runs: "We shall find the experience of all earlier conquerors confirmed, that a war of aggression calls for much strength and also consumes much, that this strength dwindles constantly while the defender's increases . . . "—may be considered exactly identical to Clausewitz' point of view concerning this subject. Nevertheless, in the Schlieffen Plan no indication whatsoever can be found that concrete conclusions had been drawn from that insight.

ON CONCENTRATION OF FORCE

Even though Clausewitz emphasized the concentration of force in its completeness as the norm, and every deviation from it as demanding explicit justification, although Schlieffen adopted Moltke's procedure of concentration from different quarters on the battlefield, there seems to be no basic discordance of opinion. What might look different is, as a matter of fact, Schlieffen's application of modern means of communication to the old concept of concentration.

ON RESERVES

There is complete harmony of opinion with regard to reserves. Both deny any need for strategic reserves; both agree as to the usefulness and necessity for tactical ones. But Schlieffen, in a more advanced stage of his thinking, would have liked to have substituted reserves of lorry-borne ammunition for human reserves. This perhaps demonstrated a more advanced understanding of logistics so far as Schlieffen was concerned; but on the other hand, as already mentioned, it showed a complete ignorance of moral factors.

In chapter 2 the argument was propagated that Schlieffen was a product of the era of the Industrial Revolution. This statement was not intended to indicate, however, that Clausewitz' ideas were obsolete. On the contrary, we are convinced that Clausewitz' theory is still applicable, whereas Schlieffen turned war into a trade and the commander into a mechanic by his overemphasis of the outward conditions of modern war, such as the effect of arms, masses, means of inter-communication and railways as the main lines of communications. War, yielding to these conditions, without any attempt to find a modern form for a concept basic to the very nature of war, ceased to be an art. The commander-in-chief only puts the army, or armies, in motion in accordance with the network of railways and roads, "greases" the mechanism, and adds mechanical power by means of logistics. This mechanical conception, already mentioned, limits the commander's will and subjects him almost entirely to the force of outward conditions. Rarely anything remains of Clausewitz' ingenious conception of the "genius for war," its free scope of command, and his claims to master the material conditions of warfare spiritually. To the same degree, the overemphasis on detailed over-all planning hampers any flexible freedom of thought at every level of command. Even Ludendorff, the High Priest of "Total War," objected strongly to Schlieffen's approach to this matter.[35]

Summing up, it appears that the three generations that passed from the days of Clausewitz until Schlieffen's death, in 1913, had not made any essential contribution to the science of war, and that Clausewitz' thoughts remained unmatched and unmastered. But have German soldiers held this opinion? It is obvious that they were not so attracted by Clausewitz' approach of looking at war at the high level of contemplative theory. They longed for a more concrete approach, for clear-cut guidelines. As F. v. Rabenau, Hans v. Seeckt's biographer and Head of the Historical Branch of the post-World War I German Army, put it: "Clausewitz is the outspoken representative of the absolute war, that is, the pure war, as we could call it in analogy to Kant's pure reason. . . . Schlieffen, I am drawing a parallel to Kant's practical reason, has developed a practical theory of war, namely, of that particular war which in his imperturbable opinion was imminent as a struggle of destiny since 1905."[36] Schlieffen's striving for military-technical perfectionism, his "prescription for victory," his creation of simple dogmas appealed much more to the German soldiers than did Clausewitz' reflections on the nature of war. This is the reason Clausewitz, the deeper and brighter intellect, was nevertheless almost outshone by Schlieffen.

It is the purpose of the following book to trace the influence of both theories on the events of the two major wars of the twentieth century.

APPENDIX A

The following extracts, from German pre-World War I instructions, aim to demonstrate the effect of Schlieffen's ideas on the practical day-to-day preparations of the German Army for war:

I. *D.V.E. Nr. 53—Grundzüge der höheren Truppenführung vom 1, Januar 1910 (Principles of Higher Troop Conduct)*

6. The assembly of vast masses of troops cannot be tolerated for long. The army assembled in a narrow space can hardly be fed and billeted; it can neither march, nor operate and cannot exist at all in the long run, it is only able to strike. To assemble forces, for other purposes than for a decision, is therefore a mistake. For such a decision, of course, one can never be strong enough; to call on the last battalion at the battlefield is imperative. However, he who wants to be the first to approach the enemy should not confine his advance to one or a few roads. The art of conducting great masses consists in keeping them separated for as long as possible, while operating, but to concentrate them for the decision at the right time. . . .

8. The character of the present-day conduct of war is typified by the tendency towards a big and quick decision. The levy of all able-bodied people, the size of armies, the difficulty of feeding them, the expense of maintaining an armed establishment, the interruption of commerce and communications, trade and agriculture, the ready-for-battle organization of the armies and the ease with which they can assemble—all these press for a quick termination of the war. . . .

12. . . . It is of decisive importance, to maintain uniformity in the operations of armies right from the beginning. The Commanders-in-Chief of the armies should carry out their measures, in such a manner that they will lead to the execution of the joint objective of all parts of the Army, in accordance with the aims of the Supreme Command. The difficulties of conducting modern mass armies may only be overcome, if all Commanders-in-Chief of the armies are always aware of this aspect of belonging to a whole. In a future war we can reckon neither on superiority of numbers, nor on being better equipped than the opponent. Only superior leadership and quality of troops will win the day. . . .

16. The dimensions of front-lines in battle become considerably extended in accordance with the increased fire-effect of modern weapons. This applies above all to the defense; but the attack, too, demands a greater deployment of space than previously. The ground and the effect of hostile fire, as well as the martial quality of the enemy here play a part. Too broad a front entails the danger of a break-through, a too narrow one of becoming encircled and out-flanked. . . . Wherever the battle is conducted in a delaying manner, and the ground is favorable, small forces may cover great spaces. Moreover, a strong artillery may compensate for the weakness of infantry. . . .

19. The utmost goal of every martial act is the annihilation of the enemy. That must always be striven at. Surrounding,[37] or, under certain circumstances, encircling,[38] present

annihilation as the price of victory. The ultimate goal may not, however, always be attainable. . . .

If, after a victory, in whose wake the adversary was thrown back frontally, a pursuit is carried out to the full, then this may also lead to great results. Nevertheless, only in the rarest cases can a final decision be reached by it; almost always one will find the opponent, beaten in a frontal battle, after a shorter or longer period, again in front of ourselves. Lasting results may be achieved only where one succeeds in barring the enemy's withdrawal or pushing him completely away from his communications, to the rear.

20. The strength of the hostile front, and the attempt to divert the assault into a decisive direction, necessitates leading it against one wing or, if possible, against a flank of the hostile position. Should this be attempted with undivided force, it will suffice for that purpose, that small units will slightly change their direction of march. On the other hand, turning an army's flank will demand a day's march or more. This will postpone the decision and provide the opponent with the necessary time for his withdrawal or a change of front. Instead of the intended attack in the flank, the assault will be met by a new front and lead to a frontal attack. It is therefore necessary to tie down the adversary, if one attempts to assail his flank. That is only possible by occupying his front with part of the force, while advancing the other parts for the purpose of enveloping his flank. Engaging the front may be achieved in the most decisive manner by attacking; at the same time it will certainly prevent a hostile superiority against our flank attack. At all events, one must remain sufficiently strong opposite the enemy's front, in order not to be overpowered here before the flank attack becomes effective. . . .

32. Should it be possible to occupy a position which the enemy is likely to attack for military, political or other reasons, it may be advisable, for the time being, to exploit the advantages of the defensive and only then to resort to the offensive. One should, however, keep in mind, that even a short postponement of the decision might entail disadvantages which will completely counter-balance the advantages of the tactical defensive.

II. *D.V.E. Nr. 130—Exerzier-Reglement für die Infantrie (Ex. R.f.d.I.) vom 29 Mai 1905 (Infantry Training Regulations)*

392. The combination of frontal with enveloping attack best insures success. A preliminary condition for the envelopment is the tying down of the enemy's front. Hence rough handling is the most effective.

One should nevertheless consider that a frontal assault might lead to a setback, if the encirclement cannot succeed in good time. Thus, if there are not sufficient forces for a rough handling in the front, or if there are other reasons for desisting from a frontal attack, a skillful action may give the impression of envelopment, by means of delaying combat, or even by merely threatening an attack.

393. The simplest way of conducting an envelopment, is to direct the march of the units allotted to it, from far away, directly into the hostile flank. It is much more difficult to undertake this at time of deployment or with withheld reserves.

Shifting troops in the front echelons may render envelopment possible only in the case of particularly favorable ground and will, even then, generally lead merely to outflanking by fire. . . .

396. Simultaneous encirclement of both wings presupposes a considerable superiority. Otherwise it will lead to a detrimental dispersal.

III. General Konrad Krafft von Dellmensingen[39] drew attention to the fact that during the Schlieffen era, the term "break-through" completely disappeared from all official pamphlets and publications.

NOTES

1. That was also the opinion held by some subsequent writers: "One thing is certain, namely that Schlieffen's ideas about war correspond to the image of an annihilation-war, drawn by Clausewitz." R. J. Leinveber, *Mit Clausewitz durch die Rätsel und Fragen, Irrungen und Wirrungen des Weltkrieges*, Berlin, 1926, p. 169. "At last the long controversy of scientists of war came to an end and thus since Schlieffen the way back to Clausewitz was found." Generalleutnant W. Erfurth, *Der Vernichtungssieg*, Berlin, 1939, p. 58.

2. Liddell Hart, *The Ghost of Napoleon*, London, 1933, p. 124.

3. Wilhelm Groener, *Das Testament des Grafen Schlieffen*, Berlin, 1927, p. 11.

4. *Vide* the discussion of "applied strategy" that appears early in chapter 2.

5. Generalleutnant a.D. v. Zoellner, *Schlieffens Vermächtnis*, Berlin, 1938, pp. 11–12.

6. When German soldiers used the term "philosophical," they rather wanted to say that it was of no use.

7. Clausewitz' letter of 22 Dec. 1827 to Major Roeder, published in "Zwei Briefe des Generals von Clausewitz. Gedanken zur Abwehr," *Militärwissenschaftliche Rundschau*, März, 1937.

8. *Vide* Schlieffen's letter of 14 Aug. 1912, to Freytag-Loringhoven, quoted in the preceding chapter, note 39.

9. In Clausewitz' letter mentioned in note 7.

10. Clausewitz' theory of end and means is examined in detail in chapter 1.

11. It seems worthwhile to read again Clausewitz' *On War*, Book VIII, Chapter 6, and become impressed by the solidity of his thoughts. In this respect, a part of his letter of 22 Dec. 1827 to Major Roeder is also of interest: "It is not necessary to prove that there is a possibility of wars, the aim of which is even more unimportant, a mere threat, an armed negotiation or, in case of an alliance, a mere sham-fight. It would be entirely unphilosophical to claim that such wars were outside the scope of the art of war. As soon as the art of war is compelled to accept, that logically, there are wars, which have other objects than the most extreme, the throwing down and destruction of the opponent, then it must settle down on many possible gradations which might be demanded by politics. The task and right of the art of war toward policy is mainly to prevent politics from demanding things which are against the nature of war and thus avoid mistakes arising from ignorance of the effects of the instrument."

12. *On War*, VIII, 6B, p. 607.

13. W. Hahlweg discovered that commencing the scholastic year of 1858–1859, the subject "Logic" was cancelled from the curriculum of the Prussian War Academy in Berlin, which indicates the technical trend. W. Hahlweg, "Clausewitz und die Gegenwart," in *Schicksalsfragen der Gegenwart*, Tübingen, 1957, vol. 2, pp. 197–199.

14. *Vide*, chapter 1.

15. Walter Görlitz, *Der Deutsche Generalstab*, Frankfurt/Main, 1955, pp. 199–200.

16. His critics had coined the slogan that he was infected with "Umfassungssucht"

(mania of encirclement) as General v. Fritsch mentioned in the introduction to the 3d ed. of *Cannae* in 1936.

17. *Vide* note 58 of chapter 1.

18. General M. v. Gallwitz, Schlieffen's contemporary, maintained that there are quantitative restrictions to the Cannae idea, namely, that the latter may apply to tactics only. Quoted in W. Erfurth, *op. cit.*, p. 82.

19. *Hinterlassene Werke des Generals Carl von Clausewitz über Krieg und Kriegführung*, Berlin, 1858, vols. 5/6, p. 357.

20. As early as 1814 (in an obituary of his teacher Scharnhorst) he accused a famous military writer of his time, v. Bülow, of charletanism; his reason being that v. Bülow had considered encirclement to be the only true principle of combat, and that he (v. Bülow), in accordance with the then-prevailing fashion, had evolved a geometrical system from it. Quoted in Carl v. Clausewitz (ed. Hans Rothfels), *Politische Schriften und Briefe*, München, 1922, p. 130.

21. Clausewitz' concept of locating reserves in defense provides a perfect answer to Schlieffen's threat of encirclement.

22. That was the case in the Prusso-Austrian War of 1866.

23. *On War*, VI, 24, p. 466.

24. Quoted in W. Erfurth, *op. cit.*, pp. 56–59.

25. Alfred Vagts writes in his *History of Militarism*, London, 1959, p. 27, that "to call a battle of today, 'Cannae,' is about as much justified as naming a brand of synthetic parfume 'Psyche.' "

26. *On War*, II, 6, p. 170.

27. *Ibid.*, pp. 171–172.

28. *Ibid.*, pp. 172–173.

29. *Ibid.*, p. 174.

30. *Ibid.*

31. C. v. Clausewitz (ed. H. Rothfels), *op. cit.*, pp. 118, 130.

32. Clausewitz, in his campaign studies, criticized the method of the French Revolutionary Army of attacking everywhere, along the whole front. Cf. *Hinterlassene Werke*, *op. cit.*, vol. 5, p. 367; vol. 6, p. 24.

33. "Die Operationen in der ersten Hälfte des Oktobers 1806. Besprechung durch den Chef des Generalstabes der Armee. Berlin, Oktober 1905." BA/MA—H08–43/63. That Schlieffen really had in mind a comparison of Napoleon's move on Berlin, with his own plan for Paris, is confirmed by v. Freytag-Loringhoven when recording a conversation with Schlieffen in his minutes-book (entry of 22 Sept. 1905): "Hohenlohe erred when he reproached Napoleon with the intention of marching to Berlin in 1806, i.e. toward a geographical point. He [viz., Hohenlohe] did not consider that it actually meant the direction into the flank and rear of the enemy. One should choose points, as Paris, for example, by us." BHA—Rep. 92, GFM A. v. Schlieffen, Nr. 6.

34. However, he would consent to a retreat of his weak left wing in case of enemy pressure there because of his fervent belief that the fate of the whole war would be decided by the *bataillon carré* of the right wing, even after a temporary setback in Alsace–Lorraine.

35. Cf. General E. Ludendorff, *Der totale Krieg*, München, 1935, p. 93.

36. F. v. Rabenau, *Operative Entschlüsse gegen einen an Zahl überlegenen Gegner*, Berlin, 1935, pp. 6–7.

37. In the original text: Einschliessung, here indicating a complete surrounding from all quarters.

38. In the original text: Umfassung, here used for enveloping the flanks only.

39. Konrad Krafft von Dellmensingen, *Der Durchbruch*, Hamburg, 1937, pp. 11–12.

BOOK TWO
The Practice

Theorists generally define their opinions in clearly understandable formulations (otherwise they would have difficulties in finding followers). Although later readers may quarrel over the proper interpretation of one postulate or another, it is nevertheless not too difficult a task to sum up theories. However, it is much more complicated to track down the influence of theory on actual events. Generals, as men of action, seldom proclaim that a certain course was chosen by them under the guidance of a particular theoretical consideration. In order to prove that, notwithstanding this, theory *was* involved in war, it has been necessary to put together various pieces of evidence. The method used here is of looking at the events as they had been observed by the acting personalities themselves, whether it was the younger Moltke, von Falkenhayn, Hindenburg and Ludendorff, and, finally, Hitler and his advisors, or as perceived at the time of the occurrence by people who had an incisive knowledge of what was going on in the High Command. Not so much consideration is given to the events themselves, interesting as they are, but the focus is more on the presence of theoretical considerations that they convey. If, therefore, for instance, the strained relationship between Schlieffen and the younger Moltke is touched on, or the controversy between Falkenhayn and the Supreme Command East, it is not these quarrels themselves that are of interest in that context, but the theoretical implications that lie at the bottom of these events. One should keep that aspect in mind before embarking on the following pages.

Part I

The War of 1914–1918: Implementation of Theories or Hotbed for New Ones?

4

Case 1: The Younger Moltke and the Execution of the Schlieffen Plan

SCHLIEFFEN'S SUCCESSOR

On 1 January 1906 General Helmuth von Moltke, a nephew of the "great" Moltke—the victor of Königgrätz and Sedan—succeeded Colonel-General Alfred von Schlieffen as Chief of the German General Staff. The "younger" Moltke, as he is generally known, was, and still is, blamed for the German retreat that resulted from the battle of the Marne in September 1914. For many Germans he became the scapegoat for the German defeat in the First World War. Most of Schlieffen's partisans were convinced that, had Schlieffen conducted the opening phase of the war in 1914, Germany's quick victory over the French-Belgian-British Armies would have been assured. It is therefore a general tendency not only to trace Moltke's failures during the war, but also to deny completely his ability as general. Schlieffen's adherents (and probably Schlieffen himself) had circulated the fact that not only Schlieffen but the whole German Army was surprised by Moltke's appointment. It was rumored that Kaiser Wilhelm II had chosen v. Moltke because of his name and for having been a courtier for many years. Considerations of such a kind no doubt played a part. Nevertheless, the expressed astonishment is completely unjustified and hypocritical, for as early as the end of 1903 the question of succession to Schlieffen had been discussed by the Military Cabinet, in charge of senior-rank appointments in the German Army, and the Kaiser had decided on Moltke. Consequently, Wilhelm II posted the latter, at the beginning of 1904, to the Great General Staff, for him to get acquainted with the problems of his future job. In a letter to Schlieffen suggesting such an arrangement the Kaiser referred to Moltke's "honorable name,"[1] but he also stressed that Moltke commanded the "necessary qualities of leadership, the necessary daring, energy and the readiness to take responsibility."[2] It has been asserted that Moltke had refused the office but was persuaded by the Kaiser to yield to the appointment. Wilhelm Groener gave publicity to this assertion by entitling one of his books dealing with the events of the initial phase of the First World War *The Reluctant General*.[3] This was, no doubt, a crude lie. Moltke was quite ready to accept this high-ranking office and, feeling himself obstructed by Schlieffen's intrigues, decided even to fight for the appointment.[4] Moltke's papers, partly published by his wife,[5] reveal that he had a serious conversation with the Kaiser[6] in connection with his pending appointment, and demanded that in the future the Emperor should refrain from any further interference in maneuvers and war games and from taking an active part in them. This was a frank and forthright demand, which Schlieffen had never dared to make, although Wilhelm's predilection for picturesque cavalry charges had spoiled many maneuvers, and his love of commanding personally one of the opposing parties compelled Schlieffen always to let him win whatever moves were made.

On account of this attitude, Schlieffen has been accused (with a certain degree of justification) of "Byzantinism" by many German officers. Moltke wanted the maneuvers and war games to present unbiased situations, as close as possible to the reality of war. He hoped that this measure would eliminate the Emperor's arbitrary actions in case of war and force him to consult the Chief of the General Staff. In order to enable the Kaiser to test his abilities, Moltke had suggested that he be entrusted with the conduct of the Imperial Maneuvers in 1905, prior to his appointment as Chief of General Staff at the beginning of 1906. Wilhelm II agreed to that proposal, but Moltke came to loggerheads with Schlieffen over this issue. In a letter of 23 July 1904 Moltke wrote to his wife: "On the way the Kaiser harangued me about the manoeuvres etc. I had to stand up for Schlieffen. I realize more and more how difficult the inheritance will be for his successor. But that is without doubt Schlieffen's fault."[7] Notwithstanding, he remained loyal to Schlieffen, and 21 July 1905 he wrote: "The Kaiser wanted me to deliver the speech, on occasion of the unveiling of uncle Helmuth's[8] monument, but I argued that this should not be inflicted upon Old Schlieffen, and he consented to leave him in office until then. I am far too busy to prevent his hasty dismissal, which would be very unjust to this meritorious general."[9]

Many writers, soldiers, and historians have, since the autumn of 1914, minimized Moltke's qualities and virtues. He has been described as inexperienced in General Staff duties, unqualified in operational matters, without any knowledge of military history or even of Clausewitz' work (not to mention his preoccupation with spiritism and anthroposophy and his suffering from a split personality and ill health!). Schlieffen's biographer, Rochs, who was Schlieffen's former regimental medical officer, recalled that, when on 1 January 1904 Moltke had reported to the General Staff, Schlieffen had uttered in desperation: "What shall I do with this man who has not the slightest notion of operational thinking?" However, Moltke's adjutant, Friedrich von Mantey, disclosed in 1948[10] that on 1 January 1905 Schlieffen had submitted the annual qualification report concerning Moltke, in accordance with German General Staff's routine, and stressed explicitly Moltke's "practical thinking." Unfortunately for Moltke, as v. Mantey regretted, this document was never published. This "practical thinking" found its subsequent expression not only in conducting more realistic maneuvers, but also in a more balanced doctrinal approach to war. To the horror of Schlieffen's disciples he ordered frontal attack, in addition to encirclement, to be included in the training schedules of the units. To a great extent the Imperial Maneuvers of 1910 dealt with the difficult issues of assault on and defense of fortified field defenses.

Nevertheless, Moltke was held responsible for many errors in the German preparations for war and in its conduct. First of all, Moltke was presented by his predecessor with the famous memorandum of December 1905—known since as the Schlieffen Plan—"the definitive formula for victory." With this inheritance he should have entered the war in August 1914 and won it. Despite Schlieffen's plan, Germany faced defeat. Why? Because Moltke had deliberately "watered-down"[11] this ingenious plan, it has been argued. What was the nature, however, of these "dilutions"?

MOLTKE II AND THE SCHLIEFFEN PLAN

According to v. Mantey, as early as March 1904, that is, before the final formulation of the Schlieffen Plan, Schlieffen and Moltke had discussed the progress of a future war on two fronts and reached a mutual understanding that France must be the enemy to be destroyed first, by means of a quick, at least partly decisive, blow, in order to free forces as early as possible for a contest with the expected "Russian steam-roller."[12] After thorough examination they reached the conclusion that the only way to carry out this intention with some prospect of success was by advancing through Belgian territory. In this early exchange of ideas Moltke had already mentioned the necessity of possessing an intact railway network in the direction of Paris. A letter of 18 June 1904 from Moltke to his wife reveals the clash of opinion between the two men: "From time to time Schlieffen asks for my opinion, and this is almost never in accordance with his own. One could not imagine a greater contrast than in our two ways of looking at things. However, I air my view quite frankly and he receives it with grace and dignity."[13] In the published memoirs there is no hint of what kind of controversy caused this letter to be written. Schlieffen's adherents, headed by the triumvirate of Wilhelm Groener, Hermann von Kuhl, and Wolfgang Foerster and supported by Schlieffen's son-in-law, W. von Hahnke, tried to make one believe that the clash was actually over trifles. However, it can be learned from v. Mantey that there were heated arguments between them during a staff ride in the West and again in connection with the railway situation to be expected in this future theater of war. Moltke had pointed out the distance to Paris and the probability that the enemy might destroy its railway network, as happened in 1870, and that Liège blocks the main line. Schlieffen referred to this difference of opinion in his usual rude manner at the final discussion of the staff ride in Koblenz: "It has been said that in case of war we might find a destroyed railway network in Belgium. My opinion in this matter is different. The Belgian railway is the best link between our railway net and the French" (for reference, see note 10). Here clashed two completely opposed viewpoints: on one hand the belief that France, on account of her alliance with Russia, was compelled to strive for the offensive against Germany and therefore would prevent the destruction of the Belgian railway system; whereas Moltke, on the other hand, was convinced that the French would recognize before long the deployment of the main German forces in the West. Therefore, they would try to evade the initial encounter by retreating into their own country. Such a move would doubtlessly be accompanied by obstructions. The actual run of events in 1914 vindicated Moltke.

At this point one should raise the question whether, in the final analysis, Moltke adhered to Schlieffen's plan, or tried to construct his own plan of war. It should be quite clear (although some writers will not concede the fact) that in his capacity as Chief of the German General Staff, he was completely justified in undertaking modifications of the existing war plan. Moreover, it was his express obligation to adapt the plan, from time to time, to changing circumstances. Any denial of this right would mean a stupid elevation of Schlieffen's plan to the sphere of an infallible dogma. Moltke's son, Adam von Moltke, in an open letter to Walter Görlitz,[14] confirmed that his father, on entering on the duties of his new office, took on himself the execution of Schlieffen's plan. "But while judging the different circumstances brought on by the course of time, he changed his mind upon the steps to be taken, and was therefore compelled to create a "Moltke Plan" corresponding to his strategic considerations." Hermann Gackenholz,[15] one of the few German writers to undertake an unbiased investigation into Moltke's conduct of the war, stressed similarly that Moltke had never regarded himself as the executor of Schlieffen's will but always as a general in his own right and with his own responsibility. Moltke's plan, Gackenholz held, was the result of a train of thought not only independent from, but even opposed to, Schlieffen's.

On the other hand many of Moltke's subordinates were firmly of the belief that he stuck to the Schlieffen Plan, and that his alterations were merely an adaptation to changed circumstances and not of a basically different nature.[16]

A third view is offered by many who believe that Moltke disagreed with Schlieffen's plan but lacked the necessary space of time to carry his point. K. Mayr, for example, maintained that "what still remained to be liquidated of the Schlieffen era was so huge, that, until as late as 1914, it prevented an appropriate reappraisal, fully corresponding to Moltke's views."[17] Ludendorff argued that Moltke, although opposed to Schlieffen's planning and altering it here and there, lacked the necessary decisiveness to set himself completely free from Schlieffen's influence.[18]

It seems that the truth rests with those who maintain that Moltke adhered to the Schlieffen Plan. His memorandum of December 1912 should be considered a clear indication of this.[19] That he was really an admirer of Schlieffen is confirmed in the unpublished memoirs of his son, Adam von Moltke. The latter remembered that "my father gave me, in order to prepare myself for the entrance to the War Academy, the great standard-edition of Schlieffen's "Cannae" and urged me to study it diligently."[20]

Consequently, the younger Moltke's alterations were only intended to improve the master plan and, above all, to secure its proper execution.

The first time that Moltke altered a basic feature of the Schlieffen Plan was in 1909. At this juncture he changed the ratio between the right and the left wings. He added forces to the left wing, thereby creating the Sixth and Seventh Armies in Alsace and Lorraine. There was later to be a tremendous outcry over this step by the Schlieffen school, headed by General Groener. But in 1909 nobody objected to this alteration, or regarded it as a "capital piece of folly" (that was the attribution awarded by Groener), not even Groener, who, in 1912, accepted the appointment of Chief of the Railway Department in the Great General Staff, and whose responsibility it was to ensure the deployment of the forces in accordance with the plan. Had he really objected to it, he would have refused the appointment to the General Staff and asked for a field appointment. Moltke's alteration was based on insight and the knowledge gained from intelligence sources, that the French would no longer restrict themselves to defense, as was rightly anticipated in 1905, but would now take to the offensive and probably in the direction of Alsace–Lorraine and the Upper Rhine.[21] This is also illustrated by the fact that in all staff rides and war games conducted by Moltke— except the staff ride of 1911 and the war game in the winter of 1913–14—the French took to the offensive, even despite a German advance through Belgium. For Moltke, therefore, the defense of southern Germany and the industrial areas on the Rhine became an explicit objective. That was also the reason Ludendorff, at that time Head of Operations Department, agreed to the alterations and stood by them.[22] One remembers that Schlieffen had not been troubled by a French advance toward the Upper Rhine, and had believed that the impact of the German right wing, wheeling through Belgium and northern France, would be felt at an early stage. The final paragraph of his memorandum reads: "If the French cross the Upper Rhine, resistance will be offered in the Black Forest. . . . If the Germans persevere in their operations, they can be sure that the French will hastily turn back." However, Ludendorff doubted whether this assumption was correct. He wrote: "Had the German left wing, as shaped by Count v. Schlieffen, been pushed back, on account of its weakness, by strong superior French forces, as were in fact deployed in 1914, the late success on the German right wing would no longer have made itself felt."[23]

Moltke was accused of having deliberately weakened the German right wing in the West, Schlieffen's famous *bataillon carré*, in favor of the left wing. Groener, v. Kuhl, Foerster, and others argued that the initial ratio of 7:1 had been "watered-down" to 3:1. This is, of course, a misleading and insincere presentation of the facts. It will be remembered that Schlieffen had dealt with still nonexisting forces in 1905.[24] Furthermore, Ludendorff, who was strongly in favor of a policy for strengthening the German Army, charged Schlieffen, in 1926, with not having pressed the importance of this issue vigorously enough.

In an article on the German deployment in 1914[25] he wrote that "it is hardly understandable why Count Schlieffen did not deal energetically with the enlargement of the Army, and, throwing into the scale the whole prestige of his office, did not demand this from the Minister of War, the Chancellor of the Reich and the Kaiser. Had he not, too readily and frequently, reckoned, during his staff rides, with forces we did not really possess!"[26] As a matter of fact, in the Moltke era, more forces were at hand. And these additional units were used to reinforce the left wing without withdrawing forces from the right. Gackenholz stated with absolute justification that the only relevant method was to compare the forces actually deployed in 1914 with these allotted in the plan of deployment for 1905, and by no means with the somewhat utopian figures of the Schlieffen memorandum of that year. According to the actual plan of 1905 the German troops should have arrayed as follows:

10 divisions in the East,
62 divisions in the West, namely
    54 divisions on the right wing between Aachen and Metz, and
    8 divisions on the left wing in Lorraine.
The ratio between the two wings was, as already mentioned, 7:1.

The formation of more units had been considered, but practical preparations had not yet started.

The younger Moltke had achieved an increase of forces: Two more active corps had been created and some reserve divisions had been enlarged and transformed into reserve corps. The drawing up of mobile Ersatz formations enabled Moltke, in 1914, to organize six and a half new Ersatz divisions. Thus Moltke could dispose of thirteen and a half additional divisions in 1914. His forces were therefore deployed in 1914 as follows:

9 divisions in the East,
70 divisions in the West,[27] namely
    54 divisions on the right wing between Aachen and Metz, and
    16 divisions on the left wing in Lorraine.
The ratio between the two wings was 7:2.

In addition to these forces were six and a half Ersatz divisions, already mentioned, available as a general reserve.

From these facts one may learn:

1. Moltke had accepted the risk of further weakening the eastern front in favor of the western. This step was absolutely in accordance with Schlieffen's intention and policy ("Austria's fate will be decided on the Seine and not on the San," Schlieffen maintained)[28];

2. Moltke has used eight of the new divisions to strengthen the left wing;

3. The number of divisions employed between Aachen and Metz remained unaltered.[29] No divisions were drawn away from the right wing. In addition, this right wing could be reinforced from the general reserve and could therefore be increased to sixty and a half divisions.

If, therefore, one wants to express the proportion between the two wings of the German western front arithmetically, it is absolutely unfair and misleading to state that the size of the right wing was reduced from seven to three, and therefore that the ratio of the two wings was "watered-down" from 7:1 (Schlieffen's ingenious design!) to 3:1 (Moltke's fainthearted compromise!). Owing to the fact that no forces were drawn away by Moltke, the strength of the right wing remained seven, as in Schlieffen's times; but on account of Moltke's general increase of the German Army, the forces of the left wing were doubled from eight divisions to sixteen. Hence the proper ratio of the two wings, one to another, was 7:2. The claim of the "watering-down" and weakening of Schlieffen's *bataillon carré* belongs to the sphere of legend!

Another point of strong criticism raised against Moltke was the seizure of Liège, immediately after the decision to mobilize.

ON THE VIOLATION OF NEUTRAL TERRITORIES

The claim is that the early violation of Belgian neutrality, caused by the *coup de main* on Liège, prevented any German political action, and put the odor of aggression on Germany instead of allowing a possible French invasion of Belgium and a German action in response.[30] But Moltke had good reasons for his step. First of all, he was firmly determined to avoid in every way any violation of Dutch neutrality. He did not share Schlieffen's illusion that Holland might come to terms with Germany and allow the Germans to use Dutch railways. In a comment on Schlieffen's memorandum he wrote:

I cannot agree that the envelopment demands the violation of Dutch neutrality in addition to Belgian. A hostile Holland at our back could have disastrous consequences for the advance of the German Army to the west, particularly if England should use the violation of Belgian neutrality as a pretext for entering the war against us. A neutral Holland secures our rear, because if England declares war on us for violating Belgian neutrality, she cannot herself violate Dutch neutrality. She cannot break the very law for whose sake she goes to war. Furthermore, it will be very important to have in Holland a country whose neutrality allows us to have imports and supplies. She must be the windpipe that enables us to breathe.

However awkward it may be, the advance through Belgium must therefore take place without violation of Dutch territory.[31]

Second, he was too anxious to prevent the destruction of the Belgian railway system. In this respect Liège was vital as an important railway junction. Without its seizure the huge German right wing, hampered by the salient of the Dutch province of Limburg, could not advance without grave difficulty. This conviction was already expressed in a marginal note to the Schlieffen memorandum of 1905: "Liège and Namur are of no importance in themselves. They may be weakly garrisoned, but they are strong places. They block the Meuse railway, whose use during the war cannot therefore be counted upon. It is of the greatest importance to take at least Liège at an early stage, in order to have the railway in one's hands."[32]

In his general observations on the Schlieffen Plan he embarked in detail on the method of accomplishing the seizure of Liège:

The fortress must therefore be taken at once. I think it possible to take it by a *coup de main*. Its salient forts are so unfavorably sited, that they do not overlook the intervening country and cannot dominate it. I have had a reconnaissance made of all roads running through them, into the center of the town, which has no ramparts. An advance with several columns is possible, without their being observed from the forts. Once our troops have entered the town, I believe that the forts will not bombard it, but will probably capitulate. Everything depends on meticulous preparation and surprise. The enterprise is only possible if the attack is made at once, before the areas between the forts are fortified. It must therefore be undertaken, by standing troops, immediately war is declared. The capture of a modern fortress by a *coup de main* would be something unprecedented in military history. But it can succeed and must be attempted, for the possession of Liège is the *sine qua non* of our advance. It is a bold venture whose accomplishment promises a great success. In any case, the heaviest artillery must be at hand, so that in case of failure we can take the fortress by storm. I believe that the absence of an inner rampart will deliver the fortress into our hands.

On the success of the *coup de main* depends our chance of making the advance through Belgium without infringing Dutch territory. The deployment and disposition of the army must be made accordingly.[33]

There is no indication or evidence of what means Schlieffen had contemplated for seizing Liège.[34] However, after reading Moltke's passages carefully one gets the impression that he was eager to secure the proper fulfillment of the German Army's right wing, wheeling through Belgium in accordance with Schlieffen's plan. The plan for the *coup de main* on Liège was no doubt inspired by a keen aspiration to carry out the plan to the letter, and not to oppose or modify it.[35]

Special attention should be drawn to the passage in which Moltke stressed that the capture of Liège "must therefore be undertaken by standing troops *immediately war was declared.*" This train of thought caused a curious chain of events: For the German offensive against France to be a success, the advance of the strong right wing through Belgium was essential; for securing this advance, the seizure of Liège was vital; this seizure was necessary at the earliest possible moment in order to ensure the railway junction intact. This, however, could not be done without a request or ultimatum, and in case of a Belgian refusal to allow the German troops to pass through that country, a declaration of war seemed unavoidable. Therefore, a strange situation had arisen on the eve of war: Owing to the departmentalization of the German governmental structure, the Chancellor, the Foreign Office, and German diplomats abroad had no knowledge of the details of the military plans for war (and in the case of the German Ambassador in Brussels, no knowledge of the pending invasion of Belgium). In order to secure the capture of Liège in due time, Moltke had himself drafted, as early as 26 July 1914(!), a proposal for an ultimatum to the Belgian government (the document later to be known as the German "Sommation" to Belgium) and forwarded it to the German Foreign Office. There, Referent Wilhelm v. Stumme made some minor modifications, Undersecretary of State Arthur Zimmermann and the Chancellor edited it, and Secretary of State Gottlieb von Jagow signed the final copy. The main alterations consisted in transforming the draft from a "Proposal for a Letter to the Belgian Government" into a decree directed to the German Minister in Brussels, who would deliver it to the Belgian government only after having received further instructions. The text of the document remained largely unaltered.[36] There is no doubt that Moltke's intention was only to present the Foreign Office with a strategic confirmation of an ultimatum to Belgium, and he had probably not thought at all that the Foreign Office would use *his* draft as such. Strangely enough, an anachronistic argument from Schlieffen's times had crept into the declared motive for the ultimatum. French violation of Belgium's neutrality was mentioned as the reason for Germany's drastic step. It will be remembered that, in accordance with Schlieffen's original plan, the *bataillon carré* should assemble in the vicinity of Aachen, an action that would take about ten to twelve days; consequently, Schlieffen hoped that the French would, in the meantime, lose their nerve and invade Belgium themselves. Now, since the seizure of Liège was planned for the third day after mobilization, there was no prospect that French troops would invade Belgian territory prior to a German invasion. However, owing to the fact that the German Chancellor had never before occupied his mind with the international and legal aspects of a pending German violation of Belgian neutrality, although he knew the general intention of the soldiers, he was caught unprepared and was apparently quite content that Moltke had seized the initiative and even invaded the domain of foreign affairs. Thus Moltke's proposal was conveyed to the German Minister in Brussels. Moltke wrote to the Foreign Office again on 3 August:

On Tuesday, 4 August, at six o'clock a.m., it must be announced to the Belgian Government that, owing to the uncooperative behavior of the Royal Belgian Government towards our well-meaning proposals, and in view of the French menace, we are compelled to carry out our unavoidable and necessary security-measures, even, if necessary, by force of arms. This proclamation is necessary because our troops will enter Belgian territory tomorrow morning. I regard this explanation as sufficient, for Belgium has declared that she will oppose every penetration by force of arms. I think a declaration of war undesirable, because I still reckon with a Belgian understanding, if the Belgian Government will realize the seriousness of the situation.[37]

The German Envoy in Brussels got instructions conforming to this letter.

It has already been demonstrated that the political gains expected by Schlieffen as a result of postponing the attack on Liège were of a doubtful manner. On the other hand the advantages of the early seizure of the town and fortress were important from a purely military viewpoint. Even W. Foerster,[38] one of Moltke's critics, was compelled to agree that from a "purely military angle, the *coup de main*, conducted surprisingly before the completion of the deployment, has brought us almost intact, the possession of the Belgian main railway line through Liège. The possession of this line is nothing less than an indispensable preliminary condition for the accomplishment of the whole Schlieffen campaign."[39] This late appreciation of the *coup de main* is confirmed by contemporary evidence: a letter of Max Hoffmann to his wife dated 13 August 1914. Hoffmann was, at that time, an officer on the staff of the Eighth Army in the East and later became Ludendorff's successor as Chief of Staff of the Eastern Command.

The successes in the West are magnificent, and promise well for the future. The capture of Liège was especially important. It had been long prepared for and the place had been thoroughly reconnoitered, so that it was very depressing to learn that the first attack had failed. We would have been weeks behindhand in the entire campaign, and as everything depends on a speedy victory in the West, our joy over the success was doubly great.[40]

On the other hand General Groener, the main beneficiary of the *coup de main*, in his capacity as Chief of the Railway Department, refused to admit that the seizure of Liège had saved the Belgian railway network for German use. He maintained that the deliverance of the "Sommation" to the Belgian government, as well as the surprise attack on Liège, had presented the Belgians with an early warning and could have led to the destruction of the railway installations. "That it nevertheless did not occur," he maintained in an afterthought, "was mainly due to their perplexity and the technical difficulty of carrying out large-scale destructions."[41] He admitted, however, that this state of perplexity, because of which prepared demolition charges in tunnels and under railway bridges had not been ignited, was a direct result of the surprise caused by the unexpectedly early capture of Liège. That, however, is quite an important reason!

Another accusation laid against Moltke is the claim that whereas Schlieffen had confined the German left wing in the West to a purely defensive task, and was even prepared to fall back under French pressure, Moltke assigned to that wing, after having strengthened it, an offensive mission. The Groener triumvirate and their followers have coined for this mission the nickname "Extratour in Lothringen" (the special tour in Lorraine).

"THE SPECIAL TOUR IN LORRAINE"

Schlieffen had believed in a French defensive attitude at the outbreak of a German-French war because of the strong eastern fortifications erected by the

French after the war of 1870–1871. It was, therefore, Schlieffen's intention to lure the French Army out into the open field by means of wheeling with a strong right outflanking wing through Belgium, and throw it back southeastward toward the Swiss border or the French's own eastern fortifications.

Moltke believed, with good reason, that the French would take the offensive. It seemed, therefore, quite possible that the main purpose of the wide-swung right wing might become superfluous: A battle of decision could be waged without carrying the assigned mission of the right wing to its final conclusion. This would mean that instead of an imperfect Cannae—or a mere Leuthen—of Schlieffen's design, a perfect one could be achieved by a combined action of both wings. (It may also be assumed that subconsciously, or even consciously, there lurked in Moltke's mind the longing for a second Sedan in the vicinity of the historic site and conducted by another Moltke!) However, despite the consequent agitation of the Schlieffen school, such a train of thought was not opposed to, but rather a logical conclusion from, Schlieffen's teaching: After all, the sweeping through Belgium was not an end in itself, but only a means. Moreover, Schlieffen himself had produced such a variant and attached it as map No. 5 to his memorandum.[42] And as a matter of fact, Schlieffen himself had presented such a solution on the staff ride of 1904. Then, the party representing the French Army was trapped in Lorraine and completely destroyed. General von Moltke attended this staff ride as one of Schlieffen's deputies (Generalquartiermeister). Why should he not have been impressed by such a prospect? In 1906, in the first staff ride that he himself conducted, Moltke decided to drop the great encirclement of Paris in favor of a participation of the right wing in the decisive battle in Lorraine, after the French main forces had advanced there. That was also in accordance with the elder Moltke's principle, so often praised by Schlieffen, of concentrating the forces from various quarters directly on the battlefield.[43]

It cannot be overlooked that, following the younger Moltke's course for the decisive battle, the time and place of battle depended on the enemy's action, whereas Schlieffen wanted to impose his will on the enemy right from the beginning. He looked for a decision on the right wing whatever his enemy's steps might be,[44] because a decision here would turn the tide in Germany's favor, even after a French success on the Upper Rhine and in southern Germany.

The disappointing results in August 1914 were not the consequence of a wrong conception,[45] but rather the result of indecisive conduct of affairs. Unfortunately for Moltke, the command of the left wing in Alsace and Lorraine had been given to the Bavarian Crown Prince, as the Commander-in-Chief (C-in-C) of the Bavarian Army. For reasons of prestige and dynastic interests, Prince Rupprecht of Bavaria (1869–1955) would not consent to a retreat of his troops, a move that was essential for the success of the whole plan in order to entice the French to advance as far as possible from the shelter of their fortress line. On the contrary, Rupprecht ordered an early attack by his Bavarians,[46] which enabled the French to slip back into the security of their defenses. Moltke was not strong enough to enforce his will over particularistic interests.[47] One may speculate whether Schlieffen, with his Byzantine attitude to royalty, would have overcome these challenges.

Moltke must be blamed, however, for not recognizing in good time that his plan in Lorraine had stranded, and that therefore the vast forces of the left wing were uselessly bogged down in front of the French eastern fortresses. These forces could and should now have been used elsewhere. It is doubtful whether they could have been transferred to the extreme right of the right wing because of the transport situation, but they could nevertheless have reinforced the left flank of the right wing and thus enabled a gradual shift of the whole wing to the right. But perhaps, even in this instance, Moltke had stuck too much to the letter of the Schlieffen Plan, which demanded that "a new army must be formed with the task of advancing on the Moselle between Belfort and Nancy."[48] Groener's assertion that "Moltke's advisors, who fostered the break-through,[49] probably did not know of the Schlieffen memorandum"[50] does not hold water. Moltke's many marginal notes and remarks on the document refute the continued claim that he had stored it, unused and disregarded, deep in the drawer of his desk.[51]

MOBILIZATION DAY, 1914

Moltke's troubles began on Mobilization Day. In 1913 he had discarded the Grosse Ostaufmarsch (deployment of the German main forces in the East), which until that year was kept up-to-date in the files of the Great General Staff, because he thought it superfluous with regard to the political situation. Now, unfortunately for Germany and Moltke, events reversed the basic assumptions of the war plan. The Austrian Archduke's assassination in Sarajevo caused the Russians to mobilize first, and not *after* France, as anticipated by the German planners. It also resulted in a diversion of large Austrian forces to the Serbian front instead of against Russia. And as if it were not difficult enough for Moltke to set his army's deployment into motion under such changed circumstances, new adversities emerged from a different quarter. On 1 August 1914 the German Chancellor conveyed to the Kaiser a note from Count Karl Lichnowsky (1860–1928), German Minister to the Court of St. James, with the information that Sir Edward Grey (1862–1933), the British Foreign Secretary, had offered to prevent French mobilization against Germany, provided that the Germans would refrain from deploying forces in the West. Moltke was urgently summoned to the Royal Palace, and the Kaiser suggested: "Let us simply deploy the whole Army in the East!" The horrified Chief of Staff explained to his royal master that there was, for the time being, only one war plan, and that any attempt to change it at this moment would invite certain disaster. The deployment of an army of millions "was not a thing to be improvised, it was the product of a whole year's hard work." To change the plan by directing the whole army to the east would be to send "a barren heap of armed men, disorganized and without supplies."[52] Wilhelm II grumbled indignantly: "Your uncle would have given me a different answer!'' At least Moltke managed to convince the Emperor not to confuse the complicated deployment schedules and let them run according to plan. He suggested that after completion of the predesigned troop movements, it might be possible to shift forces to the east, but that for the time being no alterations could be tolerated, otherwise he could not bear responsibility. This actually meant the immediate violation of Luxembourg's neutrality and the invasion of Belgium by troops allocated for the surprise raid on Liège, facts that would have, in any case, wrecked a British attempt for appeasement and mediation. "During this scene I got into rather a desperate mood," Moltke explained. "I realized the gravest dangers for the coming war, in these diplomatic actions, which threatened to interfere with our mobilization."[53] As a matter of fact, as soon as the Chancellor grasped the calamitous consequences of the 16th Division's move into Luxembourg, he insisted on its instantaneous cancellation. This time the Kaiser ordered his aide-de-camp to cable a halt order directly to the 16th Division's H.Q. in Trier, without paying attention to the presence of the Chief of Staff. "I felt as if my heart was about to break into pieces," reported Moltke afterward. "The danger rose again, that our whole deployment might be thrown into confusion. What that meant can only be fully appreciated by him who is acquainted with the complicated and detailed work of such a deployment. While every single train is regulated to the minute, every alteration must affect deployment in the most fatal manner."[54] Obviously, in that elaborate mechanism no margin was left for Clausewitz' concept of friction! After returning to his own office Moltke burst into tears. It has been suggested that these tears indicated Moltke's sudden realization that he had lost his royal master's confidence. But there may be another, much more sensible explanation, offered by Moltke's son in his argument with Walter Görlitz: The Chief of Staff suddenly realized that his eight years' efforts to prevent the Kaiser's interference in military matters had been in vain. Wilhelm II again seemed inclined to take charge of the conduct of war, a tendency that Moltke considered had been eliminated by the former's promise to abstain from active participation in Imperial Maneuvers. Hence Moltke was again compelled to expect encroachments from his impulsive Kriegsherr at any time.

THE IMPLICATIONS OF AN "HONORABLE NAME"

Even Moltke's most ardent accusers did not deny him some outstanding personal qualities. After all, he was not a complete nonentity.[55] Görlitz admitted that he was outstandingly well read and had a versatile literary interest and a deep affection for truth and beauty. He deduced, from Moltke's letters to his fiancée, a somewhat tenderhearted, brooding, and skeptical nature. But at the same time he had, especially in religious matters, a progressive outlook, very different from Schlieffen's orthodoxy and pedantry.[56] Von Kuhl recognized Moltke's comprehensive education and his thorough experience as a field commander but blamed him for lack of iron nerves. Colonel Max Bauer, a prominent figure in the German Supreme Command during the war and later involved in right-wing activities during the Weimar era, maintained that "Moltke was a highly cultured and clever man of unimpeachable character . . . a man of strong feelings, perhaps too much so . . . but was an irresolute man."[57]

General Ludendorff pointed to the fact that "General v. Moltke was less theoretical than Count Schlieffen . . . gifted with an outstanding strategic view and a very fine understanding of strategic situations. He might have been a very great soldier had he only possessed a more tough and unyielding will."[58]

There is the impression gained of Moltke's personality from his own expressions. In a letter to his fiancée of 13 October 1877 he wrote: "From day to day my feeling grows that I am in possession of the power to get on in the world, and my thought about you is the ever sparkling well from which I draw my force to move on, forward as I owe it to you and my name."

Notwithstanding, the famous name heaped a tremendous burden on his shoulders. It has been told that at the time the Kaiser offered him the office of Chief of the General Staff, Moltke asked whether he wanted to win twice in the same lottery.[59] He realized this, too, during an official mission to Moscow in 1896. When he was awarded the "Order of the Black Eagle" by the Emperor in 1909, in gratitude for a successfully conducted maneuver, he "felt a little bit ashamed. Uncle Helmuth had to win a war in order to receive this highest Prussian award. We epigones achieved it in three days of manoeuvres."[60] When announcing, on 1 September 1914, what he thought was a great German victory, he could not resist reflecting that it was achieved on the anniversary of the battle of Sedan.[61]

Even after the so-called Marne disaster, comparison with the elder Moltke was unavoidable. Karl von Einem, one-time Prussian Minister of War, and at that time commander of a corps, recalled in his memoirs a meeting with Colonel General v. Moltke in Reims. They argued hotly about the reasons for the German retreat. Von Einem criticized the G.H.Q. for remaining in Luxembourg, too far away from the battlefront. Moltke's answer, "My dear Einem, how could I move around half of France with the Kaiserr during the advance?" was replied to with a sharp "Why not? The Kaiser would probably not have objected to it. Your great uncle took upon himself the responsibility of leading his king straight on to the battlefields of Königgrätz and Sedan."[62]

Obviously, it was not easy to live up to the expectations of a great name. Even more so, as Moltke was also the successor to the office of Schlieffen, who was highly admired in many quarters of the army and particularly in the General Staff. One may imagine the tremendous psychological stress of these two features. It can be learned from various sources that right from the beginning, Moltke's appointment was strongly opposed. Schlieffen himself was not too delighted with the nomination of his successor, although, characteristically, there is no evidence of any open objection by him. However, the Chief of the Military Cabinet, General Moriz von Lyncker, particularly opposed Moltke's appointment. Although overruled by his royal master, he wrested from him a promise that in case of war, Moltke would be relieved either by General Colmar von der

Goltz or General Hans H. v. Beseler. However, when war broke out this did not happen.[63] Geyr von Schweppenburg claimed to know that there was an agreement that Moltke's term of duty in the General Staff would be restricted to two years.[64] How deep-rooted the antagonism to Moltke was is indicated in a letter of a certain G. Count Lynar, who was at that time a subaltern officer. He revealed that, in 1913, the superiors in his regiment, garrisoned at Darmstadt, far away from Berlin, had discussed in the presence of the junior officers the necessity of approaching Moltke personally and demanding his resignation because the Cabinet could not be encouraged to present the Emperor with the true facts concerning general opinion in the army against the Chief of General Staff. Later it was reported that the attempt had met with success, and that Moltke had promised to resign immediately after the Imperial Maneuvers of that year. Count Lynar learned that owing to the extraordinary success of the maneuvers, particularly on account of Moltke's brilliant final discussion and his having been congratulated by everybody present, Moltke decided to carry on "for a while."[65] That Moltke was aware of such a critical attitude is demonstrated by a letter of 21 September 1912: "With regard to the manoeuvres, I have had—as it is usual to say—a 'good press.' The newspapers have obviously given up calling me a fool."[66]

The opposition remained still after the outbreak of war and even in the closest circles of the OHL.[67] Moltke had to fight for his decisions, particularly since his Chief of Operations, Lieutenant Colonel Gerhard von Tappen, was an ardent disciple of Schlieffen and tried to make Moltke conform instantly with the original Schlieffen Plan. Moltke, however, firmly pursued his own ideas. Nevertheless, there may be no doubt that Moltke's strange position and its setting exercised a heavy strain on his conduct of the war.

MOLTKE'S CONDUCT OF WAR

Knowing about the opposition inside his own staff, and also being aware that the Minister of War, Erich von Falkenhayn (1861–1922), and the Chief of the Military Cabinet were working against him and undermining his position,[68] the Chief of General Staff did not dare to be absent from G.H.Q., fearing that during his absence the Kaiser might again interfere with the conduct of affairs. This explains, at least partly, the strange phenomenon of Lieutenant Colonel Richard Hentsch's fateful mission,[69] and that Moltke, for the first time, had visited the command posts of the armies (not yet the front line) on 11 September, viz., during the retreat from the Marne. Not only was it objected to that he did not visit his troops, but also that OHL, until 30 August, had remained in Koblenz and had then advanced only to Luxembourg, which was much too remote from the decisive right wing. At first glance those objections make sense, although Schlieffen, too, had located his "modern Alexander" far away from the battlefront.[70] However, Schlieffen had demanded that the commander should be linked with the front by a variety of communications. In peacetime, communications between armies and OHL were considered an easy task, owing to the habits of the Great General Staff's rides and the large-scale operational war games, in which the supreme leaders could issue their orders and directions unhesitatingly every night, in any minuteness of detail, even to the most remote armies. In the reality of 1914 this was not the case with regard to communications to the vital right wing. Therefore, Moltke had good reason to stay in Koblenz and, afterward, in Luxembourg: He was concerned not only with the right wing, but also with the raging battle in Lorraine and, above all, the critical and dangerous situation in East Prussia. Von Kuhl admits that safe communications with the Eighth Army in the East were a decisive consideration for the location of the Supreme Command.[71] Lieutenant Colonel Wilhelm von Dommes, Head of the Political Section of the General Staff, maintained that the desire to safeguard communications with the East, where a highly critical situation had evolved, for the time being prevented any further transfer of OHL. He stated that from Luxembourg, communications to all fronts were secured.[72] Both v. Tappen, Chief of Operations, and v. Dommes declared, in 1933, that "von Moltke had by every means kept the strings firmly in his hands."[73]

This statement has been strongly attacked since the events of 1914. It has been said that Moltke "let the reins drag on the ground."[74] Bauer's opinion was that OHL behaved in an absolutely passive manner. Yet he also mentioned the reasons for this behavior. The governing idea in G.H.Q. was that "one should interfere as little as possible with the conduct of the armies. After all, the armies maintained contact with the enemy, and therefore have a clear image of the situation and should not be hampered in their decisions."[75] This time the younger Moltke consciously acted completely in accordance with the principles of his uncle, who refrained from giving explicit orders and confined himself to issuing general directives.[76] However, the younger Moltke overlooked the fact that his uncle had been handicapped in the direct conduct of the armies by communications difficulties, which the nephew should have already overcome (although he had not!). In places where the coordination of several armies was necessary, he solved the problem by giving the command of a particular group to the senior commander on the spot. This procedure had its disadvantages, as was to be expected, because one has to realize that every army commander was, above all, concerned with the conduct of his own permanent army, and could reach an over-all impartial outlook only with difficulty.

Moltke has been strongly criticized for not installing before hand intermediate command levels, like the army group headquarters (Heeresgruppen), which were created later on. This criticism should have been made of Schlieffen, who had not foreseen the burning need for such an establishment. There is no indication in his writings, exercises, staff rides, and maneuvers that he ever considered such a solution. Why should his successor, credited with less experience, act differently?[77]

Schlieffen also failed to solve the delicate problem of a sound command structure at the highest level. There were no concerted actions between the army and naval staffs, and none between military, political, and economic agencies.[78] The Kaiser was theoretically the crowned head of all these authorities and personified the meeting point of all the different interests. But it simply did not work! Even on the purely military level the navy was not informed about the pending invasion of Belgium, although the occupation of the channel coast involved immediate naval problems, and to the same extent, the General Staff of the Army did not know that the Admiralty had long ago dropped the plan of an early naval offensive in British waters. Even in Schlieffen's time the few attempts to conduct combined army-navy maneuvers almost failed on account of petty budget quarrels between the relevant ministries.[79] Wilhelm Widenmann's suggestion, in 1912, for a grand-scale war game, embracing army, navy, Reichskanzler, Foreign Office, Colonial Office, Ministry of Economy, Ministry of Finance, Reichsbank, etc., to be directed by the Kaiser in order to investigate the over-all problems of a future war, was objected to by all concerned, including von Moltke, for fear of the Kaiser's unstable and unpredictable character.[80]

A strong refutation of the constant accusations of Moltke's feeble conduct of war, alleged to be the result of personal weakness, was his vigorous reaction to the events in eastern Prussia. Having reached the impression that General Friedrich Wilhelm von Prittwitz, C-in-C Eighth Army, might retreat further than absolutely necessary, Moltke dismissed him without a second thought and was extremely lucky in the selection of the new command structure for the East. At this instance, by no means, "did the reins drag on the ground."

The too-early transfer of two corps from the western front to the east is commonly regarded as the younger Moltke's gravest failure.

ON THE TRANSFER OF TWO CORPS FROM THE WEST TO THE EAST

On 25 August 1914 the Belgian fortress of Namur surrendered, and the two German corps that had hitherto been engaged in the siege were freed for action. In the meantime, owing to the continued advance of the German Armies, these corps had been pushed out of the front line, and therefore Colonel General von Bülow, C-in-C of the German Second Army and in charge of the armies on the extreme right wing, reported these corps to OHL "as available for other duties."[81] This announcement fitted in just too well with the tense atmosphere at G.H.Q. regarding the situation in eastern Prussia. It also accorded with Moltke's statement of 24 February 1909, contained in his correspondence with the Austrian Chief of Staff, Conrad von Hoetzendorff, in which he stated that "every unit becoming redundant in the West will be immediately thrown to the East."[82] Moltke had no reason to doubt the highly esteemed von Bülow's judgment. Consequently, the following order was issued on 26 August at 3:10 AM:

For the earliest possible transportation to the East the following formations will march:
All available units of the Guards Reserve Corps in two columns, in accordance with

their respective infantry divisions, to Aachen, and the available units of XIth Corps' infantry divisions to Malmédy and St. Vith resp. The day of arrival of advanced parties at Malmédy, St. Vith and Aachen is to be reported immediately, also the intended daily marching destinations.[83]

As a matter of fact, Moltke intended shifting six corps to the east, and a third corps, the Fifth, had already been removed from the front line. But learning that the tide in the East was stemmed, and realizing, despite the overoptimistic reports from the army commands,[84] that a decisive battle in the West was now imminent, Moltke sent only two corps. Ludendorff declared afterward that he did not need these reinforcements and had not asked for them. Moreover, he had explained in a telephone conversation with the Operational Branch of OHL that, for the time being, he did not require any late-arriving reinforcements for participation in the battle of Tannenberg, and that the two corps in question might be used elsewhere. But it cannot be denied that the situation in the East at that moment was desperate, and that the Kaiser, despite previously consenting to the stripping of the eastern front of strong defending forces, was now shocked into reality by Cossacks pillaging sacred Prussian territory.[85] Moreover, local authorities appealed to the Empress, and she in turn conveyed these appeals for help to her husband in OHL. In addition, on 25 August, Conrad von Hoetzendorff, the Austrian Chief of Staff, had cabled to Koblenz and stressed the urgency of reinforcing the German forces in the East.[86] After all, why should Moltke be confident that the new commanders in the East, Paul von Hindenburg and Erich Ludendorff, would ultimately succeed where their predecessor had been compelled to give in? Ludendorff's daily report of 24 August, for instance, could not inspire such a belief: "Our mind is resolute, but a bad end is not out of the question."[87]

Even though Moltke himself admitted in his memoirs that the transfer of these two army corps was his gravest blunder, the blame should not be put on him alone. Schlieffen's influence had a hand in it, since it was a common feature of Schlieffen's staff ride exercises to shift forces from the West to the East immediately after an initial success in the West. He had explained his viewpoint in the final discussion of his last war game in 1905 (Moltke was present and already earmarked for succession): "If we intend to wage war in France for months, we cannot, on the other hand, disregard the Russians completely. We cannot just watch them crossing the Vistula, Oder, Elbe and, in spite of it all, wage war in France. This is completely out of the question."[88]

In accordance with Schlieffen's standard procedure, four corps and four additional reserve divisions had been moved from the West to the East during the staff ride east of 1897, on the twenty-fifth day after mobilization (M + 25). Two and a half corps and two cavalry divisions were transferred on approximately the twenty-ninth day after mobilization in the exercise of 1899. In 1901 the transfer of nine (!) corps and three cavalry divisions occurred on M + 23. Finally, in 1903, the transferred forces numbered eleven (!) corps on M + 27.[89]

In the opening paper issued for this exercise, Schlieffen had outlined the following situation:

Until the 27th day after Mobilization, the battle in the western theater of war has been decided in such a way that the French Army, which invaded Alsace-Lorraine, was compelled to retreat with heavy losses behind its fortified lines on the Meuse and Moselle. That does not mean the end of the war. France, as soon as she has re-gathered forces, will sally forth and start a new struggle. Nevertheless, a short break will occur, and this will be used by Germany to turn in force against the Russian armies, which, in the meantime, have invaded Eastern Prussia. Eleven corps, i.e. as many as it is possible to carry by train from West to East in a comparatively short time, will reinforce the seven corps already on the Russian border, and thus provide the opportunity to take the offensive at least at one point.[90]

No wonder that in the final exercise in 1907, with Moltke already directing, the opening paper ran: "Three corps, made available from elsewhere, have detrained along the railway line Osterode-Korschan [i.e., places in East Prussia]. . . . Another corps is on its way."[91] In his memoirs Wilhelm Groener recollected that he had conducted an exercise of the Railway Department in 1912 and, in accordance with Schlieffen's usage, had practiced the transfer of four corps to the East in the wake of a decisive German victory over France in the Eifel on M + 30.[92]

During the actual events in 1914, Moltke, without any doubt, was in line with Schlieffen and steered a moderate middle course from among Schlieffen's various solutions: the transfer of two corps on M + 26. Even the execution of the initial intention, of transferring six corps, would still have rested comfortably inside Schlieffen's limits.[93]

One still wonders why Moltke did not extricate two corps from the left wing, and thus avoid weakening the precious right flank. All the more so, since Schlieffen had taught, in 1901, that for the transfer from the West to the East, those corps should be chosen that were the nearest to railway stations.[94] From the order of 26 August one may easily learn that the Guards Reserve Corps and Eleventh Corps had to march a great distance to the railway stations, whereas the formations of Sixth and Seventh Armies in Alsace and Lorraine were still near the railheads. Nevertheless, there were good reasons for accepting von Bülow's generous offer regarding the two corps released from the siege of Namur. First, at that time, while the reports from the armies on the right wing gave the impression that they were in unopposed pursuit of a beaten adversary, the situation in front of the left wing was tense.[95] Second, particularistic tendencies swayed the balance again. King Ludwig of Bavaria was promised that his army would be deployed only in a body, and that was actually done on the left wing. It could not be expected that Bavarians would defend eastern Prussia, maintained General Hermann von Stein, Moltke's deputy, at the staff conference presided over by the Kaiser, in which the reinforcement of the East was discussed.[96]

However, most of Moltke's critics admit that even without these two corps, in their opinion transferred prematurely, the battle of the Marne could have been won by the Germans.[97] It was a variety of circumstances, they maintained, that deprived the splendid German Army of its well-earned victory in 1914. Among those circumstances was the tremendous squandering of forces on secondary missions, such as the envelopment of Antwerp and other fortresses, which slowed the momentum of the right wing.

THE DIMINISHING STRENGTH OF THE GERMAN RIGHT WING

Forces were in fact detached for the siege of Antwerp and other Belgian and French fortresses; but even a superficial glance into the "Holy Bible" of the Schlieffen school, the memorandum of 1905, reveals that the great master himself had allotted, substantial forces to these tasks. "For the investment of Antwerp, five Reserve Corps," wrote Schlieffen, adding in brackets "perhaps not enough." Map No. 3 supplementing the plan, which shows the expected situation on M + 31, the day the German right wing would envelop Paris from west, south, and southeast, still presents these five reserve corps investing Antwerp.[98] Schlieffen also apportioned forces for the investment of a number of other smaller fortresses and realized that the rear of the army must be safeguarded. He was completely aware of Clausewitz' law of "diminishing forces during advance." The reality that faced Moltke was not different from Schlieffen's forecast and was handled according to Schlieffen's plan. It is therefore pure hypocrisy for fervent Schlieffen disciples to accuse Moltke of having squandered forces and having thus rendered victory impossible.

The climax of Moltke's short period as a general in actual combat was the Marne battle (as a matter of fact, he was never credited in the slightest for the victories in the East, although they were achieved while he was still Chief of the General Staff and he had contributed decisively to their success). Never before had a battle caused such a tremendous flood of publications as this one. It therefore seems unnecessary to describe the battle in detail; but two vital points will be considered: the reasons for the change of direction of the extreme right wing, thus deviating from the master plan, and the nightmare of gaps in the German front.

THE BATTLE OF THE MARNE—SEPTEMBER 1914

Why did the German First Army, suddenly wheeling southward and, on 4 September, even eastward, present its right flank to a sally from Paris, instead of pursuing the planned envelopment of Paris from the west? In the last days of August the Third Army was pulled to the left, owing to difficulties in front of the Fourth and Fifth Armies on the Meuse. The Second Army, in order to avoid a gap either between its left flank and the Third Army, or its right flank (in case it responded to the Third Army's pull) and the quickly advancing First Army, was compelled to stretch its line. Suddenly, it had to accept battle, being heavily attacked by the French Fifth Army on 29 and 30 August. As this assault was repulsed by the Second Army in the battle of St.-Quentin, the First Army, whose Chief of Staff was General von Kuhl, an outstanding disciple of Schlieffen, decided to exploit its success and swing from its southwestern direction of advance, southward in the direction of Compiègne.[99] Although OHL had assigned the First Army the route to the Lower Seine in its order of 27 August, in accordance with the Schlieffen Plan, it now assented to the change of direction on 30 August.[100]

What caused the First Army to spoil the master plan?

A psychological explanation is offered by Wilhelm Breucker,[101] who maintained that Ludendorff and Kuhl had been heads of the department in the General Staff and both had been regarded as "the best horses in the stable." Precisely at that time the news of the victory of Tannenberg (26–30 August 1914) had reached the western front. It was well known that Ludendorff had been a decisive figure there. Is it not too human to assume that von Kuhl wanted his own victory, at least as decisive as Tannenberg and in the grand style, by enveloping the French Fifth Army?[102] The British Expeditionary Force (B.E.F.), directly in front, was no longer regarded as a menace, for it was learned from a captured letter of Sir John French that he intended to extricate the B.E.F. from the front line. About the formation of the new French Sixth Army, which was liable to endanger the German First Army's right flank, nothing was known at that moment in First Army's H.Q.

Besides the psychological explanation, there were more concrete reasons. It was questionable whether the actual German forces on the right wing on 1 September were sufficient to act in accordance with OHL's order of 27 August. In other words: Could the Schlieffen Plan still be implemented? It seems worthwhile to follow J. Kühl[103] in a little exercise of arithmetic: The distance from the Oise–Seine junction to the coast is, as the crow flies, 125 kilometers. If a section of 15 kilometers is assumed for an army corps advancing in offensive, approximately eight corps were needed to cover this stretch of the German First Army. The First Army, at the time, was actually composed of five corps. On the other hand, at the left flank of the right wing, the Fourth Army, together with the Fifth, occupied an arc around Verdun reaching westward only as far as Châlons. That meant that the line between Châlons and the Oise–Seine junction, measuring about 150 kilometers, ought to be covered by the German Second and Third Armies. There, owing to the difficult ground and taking into account the huge fortress of Paris, corps sections of only 12 kilometers should be counted on. That would necessitate twelve corps instead of the seven actually deployed.[104] Although the outermost edges of the flanks were dictated by the enemy, the Germans had the choice of either agreeing to gaps between the armies or accepting an uncovered flank. Whereas the enemy in and around Verdun was regarded as strong, there seemed to be no adversary of any importance near the sea. It was therefore only natural that OHL took the risk of an open flank on the utmost right. Consequently, it was no longer possible for the First Army to move toward the Lower Seine. Even if Moltke had shifted forces from the left wing in Lorraine in good time (at this point, for purely speculative purposes, the transport problem involved in such a shift will not be taken into consideration) and had abstained from dispatching the two corps to the East, it still remains doubtful whether the forces would have been sufficient at that moment. After all, Schlieffen had never considered that the French might turn the tables and, efficiently supported by their excellent railway system, surround the German right flank, instead of themselves being exposed to encirclement.

However, even the eastward pull of the German armies did not prevent the opening of gaps between the armies. Von Bülow, C-in-C Second Army, was already worried about his flanks, since on 28 August both his neighbors had pulled away excentrically. Subsequently, OHL recognized that the order of 27 August no longer fitted reality. At the same time it learned about the shift of French forces from the French right wing to Paris. These forces could now threaten the open German right flank. OHL admitted that the initial aim of pushing the French forces to the southeast was no longer feasible, and therefore, new orders were issued on 5 September.[105] The First and Second Armies were ordered to hold on and secure the German front opposite Paris—the Second Army, south of the Marne, and the First, on the northern shore of that river. It had been thought in OHL that the First Army was already echeloned in depth for the protection of the right flank.[106]

But as a matter of fact, when the order reached the First Army's H.Q., its units, with the exception of one reserve corps, had already dashed forward and crossed the Marne ahead of the Second Army and in absolute defiance of OHL's explicit order. The weak reserve corps on the extreme right of the German array clashed head-on into the assembly area of the new French Sixth Army and uncovered the precarious situation into which the First, nay the whole German Army in the western theater of war, had run. While von Bülow insisted on pulling the First Army back and to the left in order to eliminate the menace of the B.E.F.'s penetrating between both German Armies, Colonel General Alexander von Kluck, C-in-C First Army, and his Chief of Staff, von Kuhl, visualized a decisive victory on the Ourcq by means of encircling, in their turn, the French Sixth Army. Regardless of von Bülow's fear and objections, all the corps of the First Army were gradually extricated from the front opposite the B.E.F. and thrown to the northwest to encircle the enveloping French left wing. A wide gap, screened only by comparatively small covering forces, split the German front open! Von Bülow's fear for his flank was reflected in G.H.Q. It was feared that in order to close these dreadful gaps, it might be necessary to withdraw the forces on the extreme right flank. That was the reason for Lieutenant Colonel Hentsch's mission and his fateful trip to the Army H.Q. of the right wing, which resulted in breaking off battle and eventually escalated into a wholesale retreat of the entire German right wing in the West.

Raging Schlieffen partisans maintained that these actions forfeited an over-whelming German victory. They drew attention to the complicated situation in which the B.E.F. would have found itself had it advanced into the gap between the German First and Second Armies. In that case it would have been exposed to a concerted German assault on both flanks. One wonders whether what happened was really the result of a loss of nerve by all concerned—von Moltke; von Bülow and his Chief of Staff, von Lauenstein; von Kluck and his famous Chief of Staff, von Kuhl; and, last but not least, the fateful emissary, Lieutenant Colonel Hentsch—or whether the hand of an already dead man, von Schlieffen, was involved. Had not Schlieffen hammered into the heads of his pupils and subordinates, time and again, the danger of gaps, and preached indefatigably the ultimate necessity of closing the ranks of the company-like front of armies of millions?

Most of his exercises[107] bear this feature. Von Mantey confessed that from the beginning of the war, everybody was worried about gaps and the danger of enemy penetration through the German lines.[108] Schlieffen's influence seems, therefore, to be far more responsible than either von Bülow (whom Groener charged in his reminiscences with having always been opposed to Schlieffen's Cannae theory and having displayed considerable preference for frontal attacks, thereby deliberately spoiling the plan[109] or the problem of various diseases, which were held responsible for the fateful decisions of the heroes involved in this drama—v. Kluck and v. Kuhl being excluded on account of their good health.[110]

Without pretending to be competent to evaluate these clinical findings, it does seem that the accumulation of ill health at the top level of the German Army is irrelevant to the actual events and some apologetic afterthought. As for the charges against Hentsch,[111] it seems purposeless to try to solve the mystery of his mission, in particular whether he was authorized to order a retreat or not, for, because both Moltke and Hentsch died during the war, no confrontation ever took place. In 1917, in response to a request of Hentsch, a committee of inquiry appointed by Ludendorff cleared the former of the charge of having acted arbitrarily.

Schlieffen must also be blamed for an additional indirect contribution to the disastrous outcome of the Marne battle: his stress on encirclement as the patent solution, and his rejection of break-through. He had preached it year after year, and at the moment the German Army was called on to resort to break-through instead of encirclement, it was unprepared for such an enterprise. For what was the gist of OHL's order of 5 September? The breaking off of the enveloping movement of the extreme right wing and the taking up there of a waiting position against the expected enemy action from Paris, shifting the main decision, hitherto planned for the right, to a break-through in front of the German center on the heights of Sezanne and at the marshes of St. Gond, supplemented by a second break-through of the German left wing. This change of plan left the German intermediate ranks completely unable to coordinate their actions with a new operational idea. Instead, they disobeyed orders, as in the case of the First Army, and stuck to the oft-exercised scheme of Old Schlieffen, namely, an outstripping, encircling pursuit on the western flank.

It is obvious that the overstretched logistic lines also had a vital share in the events of the Marne battle.

LOGISTICS IN 1914

The railway situation at the beginning of the Marne battle, as presented by the German semiofficial work,[112] was difficult indeed.

The First Army relied on the line Aachen–Liège–Brussels, which reached Cambrai on 26 August and Chaulnes, 16 kilometers south of Peronne, on 30 August.

The Second Army was supplied by a line running from Aachen through Liège, which was extended to Fourmies near Hirson on 30 August.

The Third Army depended on the line Stavelen–Liège until 31 August and on a narrow-gauge line to Trembloi, 11 kilometers south of Rocroi, commencing on 6 September.

The Fourth Army was supplied through Luxembourg, and the railhead reached Sedan on 1 September and Vousier on 8 September.

The Fifth Army had grave difficulties, caused by the demolition of important tunnels near Montmédy, which was reached on 30 August.

The railheads, in every case, were at least 125 kilometers behind the front, and in the case of the Fifth Army, as far as 160 kilometers. At that time General Hoffmann, a most competent military expert, maintained that "the advance of a German Army must come to a standstill when it reaches about 100 km. from the railway."[113] As a matter of fact, south of Namur the destruction of railway facilities—tunnels, bridges, communications and water supply for locomotives— was on an ever-increasing scale.[114] So Moltke's prophesy of 1904, that "in the enemy's country we shall suffer from want of railways, whereas the enemy will profit from abundance,"[115] proved true. The Belgian railway network, despite Schlieffen's final conclusion in 1904, was not the best link between the German and the French railway lines. In order to overcome these difficulties the armies of the right wing had been provided with all the motor transport columns then available. The size of these columns in themselves imposed clear-cut restrictions on any further increase of the right wing, as the Chief of Operations, v. Tappen, had pointed out.[116] He considered a German force of up to twelve army corps the ultimate maximum strength that could be maintained north of the Meuse in 1914. Obviously, even for purely logistic reasons, there was a limit to the unrealistic dreams of a superstrong *bataillon carré.*[117] Groener, in his role of Military Railway Director, admitted that a quick shift of forces from the left wing to the right was possible only as far as Luxembourg, owing to the continuing considerably low efficiency of the railway lines inside Belgium.[118] From Luxembourg the units would have to march on by foot.

In this context it should not be overlooked that von Moltke was much more aware of the impact of logistics than his predecessor. During his term of duty in the General Staff, in addition to staff rides for operational and tactical purposes, staff rides dealing with logistical problems were also introduced for General Staff and administration officers.[119] In 1911 a permanent Mobilization Commission was formed by Secretary of State for the Interior Clemens von Delbrück, to deal with the economic problems of mobilization. The terms of reference for this commission were the collection of statistical data regarding existing stocks and the creation of an Imperial grain reserve. The purchase of grain from neutral markets and its storage were to be begun, the provision of the industry with coal and raw materials was to be prepared, and the distribution of manpower for industry and agriculture was to be regulated. It was necessary to summon experts from all branches concerned; but the Chancellor objected to the proceedings because the discussion of such problems with a wide circle of people might be interpreted as direct preparations for an imminent war, an impression that he was determined to avoid at any cost. In 1914 the General Staff again forwarded a memorandum to the War Ministry and other offices concerned, stressing the importance of economic preparations for war and the storing of sufficient food supplies and raw materials. As the proceedings made headway only late in spring 1914, it was actually too late to influence events. It should be mentioned that even in the last week of July 1914, Secretary Kühn of the Treasury refused the allocation of money for a large-scale purchase of wheat in Rotterdam. His opinion was that there would be no war.[120]

Similarly, Colmar von der Goltz' appeal was ignored. In his book *The Nation in Arms* he demanded a thorough survey of the food situation in Germany in face of an expected British blockade. He came to the conclusion while serving for many years on military-diplomatic missions abroad, and was able to learn about the importance of British sea power. His appeal was in vain. German soldiers firmly believed in Schlieffen's concept of a quick and short war as the definitive remedy for economic strangulation.

The first attempt at planning a war economy was undertaken only in 1916. Moltke, at that time holding the degrading office of Head of the Deputy General Staff in Berlin, an organization without any real function and authority, had, until then, fought incessantly for the coordination of war efforts with the home front, despite the military ignorance of the problem.

The Marne battle and its aftermath—the "race to the sea," i.e., the last struggle for an open flank in the West, which is investigated in chapter 5—were the end of the attempt to carry out the Schlieffen Plan.

There remains the hypothetical question whether a better conduct of affairs than that displayed by the unlucky younger Moltke would have secured a German victory in 1914. Among Schlieffen's partisans there is no doubt that victory had slipped from Germany's reach solely on account of Moltke's actions. Many Anglo-Saxon writers have at one time or another held the same view.[121] Having now acquired further wisdom through the experience of the Second World War, this conclusion seems, after all, to be dubious. Far from trying to attribute to the younger Moltke qualities of superb leadership, which he apparently lacked,[122] it seems from the testimony presented so far that the dead Schlieffen bore a much heavier responsibility for the German failure than the living Moltke. Some of the more essential points need to be further emphasized.

1. Schlieffen had strengthened the tendency, apparently inherent in the German national character, to dogmatize, imposed his Cannae scheme, and at the same time blotted out any thought of other solutions, for instance, break-through. The latter was rejected as a worthless French notion. At the moment when reality demanded the renunciation of encirclement and the resort to break-through of the French center, German soldiers at all levels were unable to adopt this unusual idea.

2. Since 1871 Germany had enjoyed a lasting peace, which prevented German soldiers from practicing war under real conditions. These had to be substituted with exercises. Schlieffen had acquired his reputation from his mastery in conducting maneuvers, war games, and staff rides. In these games and exercises, fairly large hostile armies were usually quickly surrounded and forced to surrender by German troops, after a war of short duration. This was the image imprinted on German soldiers' minds. This image bore grave consequences in the opening phase of the real war, and the outcome of the Marne battle merely dispersed previous illusions.

3. Schlieffen had realized that the numerical odds were against Germany and its allies.[123] Nevertheless, he failed to draw the proper conclusions. He believed that his "patent prescription" of a quick, victorious campaign in the Cannae style would compensate for inferiority in numbers. He did not include Germany's shortcomings in the economic field in his calculations. The latter had not, of course, influenced the events on the Marne, but having there lost the golden opportunity of an early victory, the battle of the Marne marks the point from which the economic factors began to increase in importance.

4. The gigantic design of the Schlieffen Plan did not pay the homage due in real war to the factor of friction. Armies of millions of soldiers covered thousands of square miles, while advancing hundreds of miles in enemy country, but no margin was left for the surprises and uncertainties of war. Schlieffen stated in his writings that for a perfect battle of Cannae, a Hannibal on one side and a Terentius Varro on the other were needed. The latter must cooperate in his own destruction. Schlieffen and his followers had obviously assumed that the French High Command would accept *a priori* the role of Terentius Varro. Even Wilhelm Groener's studies on the Schlieffen Plan always assumed that superb leadership would reign on the German side, while on the opposite side there would be nobody to recognize the meaning of the German moves.

5. Finally, as Liddell Hart had so rightly put it:

The great scythe-sweep which Schlieffen planned was a manoeuvre that had been possible in Napoleonic times. It would again become possible in the next generation—when airpower could paralyze the defending side's attempt to switch its forces, while the development of mechanized forces greatly accelerated the speed of encircling moves and extended their range. But Schlieffen's plan had a very poor chance of decisive success at the time it was conceived.[124]

At the end of this chapter one must consider some of the issues concerning Moltke's chief accusers, General Wilhelm Groener and General von Kuhl.

One wonders how such an outstanding disciple of Schlieffen as von Kuhl could deviate from Schlieffen's master plan, as was done by the First Army, and then yield to Hentsch's retreat order at the moment he thought victory was within certain reach. No explanation is offered by Kuhl himself in his voluminous writings about the First World War.[125]

Groener's motives seem to lie in the psychological field too. Had not he, the high-ranking Würtembergian officer of common origin in the German General Staff, accepted responsibility for the events of November 1918 that led to the Kaiser's abdication? Was he not suspected in nationalistic military circles on account of his cooperation, as Deputy Chief of General Staff and Ludendorff's successor, with the Socialist Friedrich Ebert (1871–1925) and his securing in such a manner the Weimar Republic? Moreover, had he not accepted office as minister in various Republican governments? The only way not to lose the confidence of the nationalist and military group that he wanted to belong to, was by posturing as the most faithful and orthodox partisan of the worshiped Schlieffen, "the bearer of the certain secret of victory," and to find a scapegoat for Germany's misery and disaster. Running through the Groener Papers[126] one is struck by the vehemence with which he repulsed any, even the slightest, attempt to approach Moltke objectively. The suspicion arises that Groener, in his capacity as Reichswehr-Minister, has strongly influenced the official presentation of the First World War.[127]

Far from trying to turn Colonel General Helmuth von Moltke into a hero and Great Captain, it now seems that German scholars and soldiers should attempt a more objective and unbiased approach to the opening phase of the First World War. This was tried here by a foreigner. It also seems that Moltke might provide an excellent subject for a psychological case study, which would probably offer the historian some more definite clues of the fateful events of the younger Moltke era.

Now, a few words about Liddell Hart's charges concerning Clausewitz' responsibility for the events on the Marne. He maintained that the Germans had forfeited victory in the West because of their adherence to Clausewitz' law of strategy "to keep the forces concentrated." Instead of moving in a wide-stretched net formation—as Napoleon used to move, in order to distract his enemies—they closed ranks, looking at the Napoleonic system through Clausewitz' "distorted lenses," fearful of the risks they might run if not marching shoulder to shoulder. Thus the Marne became "the grave of German prospects of victory in the war," and it would be appropriate to engrave "Clausewitz' Law" on the tombstone. Moreover, "other consequences of Clausewitz' teaching manifested themselves," namely, "in their blind pursuit of 'the one means'—the destruction in battle of the enemy's armed forces, the Germans spurned the chance not only of seizing ill-defended Paris, but of occupying the unguarded Channel-Ports—ripe apples that were ready to fall into their mouths."[128]

However, if the Germans were concerned at all with Clausewitz' teaching, it was only through the "distorted lenses" of Schlieffen. But what had German commanders really perceived from Clausewitz' wealth of thought? During the First World War, six successive editions of *On War* were published.[129] From 1915 these editions were provided with prefaces from the most prominent German generals, in addition to Schlieffen's introduction of 1905.[130] One is struck by the rubbish expressed in these prefaces. The only point these soldiers had grasped from Clausewitz' theoretical edifice was the one and only point already stressed by Schlieffen in 1905: the idea of annihilation. If, however, the Marne was the grave of German prospects of victory in war and something ought to be engraved on the tombstone, then the writing should read "Cannae obsession."

NOTES

1. "Einen Namen mit gutem Klang." The Kaiser's letter to v. Schlieffen of 29 Dec. 1903. BHA—Rep. 92, GFM A. v. Schlieffen, Nr. 12, also printed in GFM Schlieffen (ed. Eberhard Kessel), *Briefe*, Göttingen, 1958, p. 303.

2. *Ibid.* "Er hat die nötigen Führereigenschaften, den nötigen Schneid und keine Sorge vor Verantwortung."

3. Wilhelm Groener, *Der Feldherr wider Willen*, Berlin, 1930.

4. Schlieffen's aide-de-camp and son-in-law, General W. v. Hahnke, tried to turn the tables on Moltke and accused him of having intrigued against Schlieffen and worked toward the latter's dismissal. The reason, Hahnke maintained, was resentment over Schlieffen's sarcastic critique of v. Moltke's performance as a leader in the Imperial Maneuvers of 1900, and Schlieffen's conspicuous ignorance of Moltke's role as Quartermaster General. This opinion was aired in Hahnke's letter to v. Freytag-Loringhoven of 5 May 1924. BHA—Rep. 92, W. v. Hahnke, Nr. 6/12. However, a private letter of Schlieffen's written to Count Ernst v. Schlieffen on 15 Sept. 1905 gives the reasons for Schlieffen's dismissal as follows: "I am almost 73 years old, nearly blind, half deaf and have now also a broken leg. It is high time to resign and I have good reasons to believe that my repeated request for resignation will be complied with in the present year." BA/MA—43/5.

5. Generaloberst Helmuth von Moltke, *Erinnerungen, Briefe, Dokumente, 1877–1916*, Stuttgart, 1922. This is an unsatisfying selection of Moltke's papers, which the German Foreign Office tried to suppress at that time because they revealed Schlieffen's intention to violate Holland's neutrality too. With regard to the unpublished Moltke papers, Mrs. E. Schotte-von Moltke, Colonel General v. Moltke's granddaughter, has informed me that her uncle, i.e., Moltke's son, destroyed his father's papers in 1945, when he fled from Berlin. No collection of original Moltke papers is therefore to be found in German archives.

6. On the night of 7 Jan. 1905; reported in Moltke's letter to his wife on 8 Jan. 1905.

7. Generaloberst H. v. Moltke, *op. cit.*, p. 296.

8. That is, Field Marshal H. v. Moltke.

9. Generaloberst H. v. Moltke, *op. cit.*, p. 325.

10. Generalmajor Friedrich von Mantey, *Der verkannte jüngere Moltke*, 1946–1948. BA/MA—HO5–6/23.

11. The term "verwässert," with regard to Moltke's alterations of the Schlieffen Plan, was apparently coined by Field Marshal v. Hindenburg. *Vide* Generalfeldmarschall Paul von Hindenburg, *Aus meinem Leben*, Leipzig, 1920, p. 118. It was subsequently used in other publications, especially pro-Schlieffen ones, concerning the First World War.

12. Moltke consequently held to this view: In his exchange of opinions with the Austrian Chief of Staff he expressed the same order of priorities (Secret Letters No. 781 of 21 Jan. 1909 and No. 793 of 24 Feb. 1909, printed in Feldmarschall Conrad, *Aus meiner Dienstzeit, 1906–1918*, Wien, 1921, vol. 1; Moltke's memorandum of Dec. 1912, printed in E. Ludendorff, *Urkunden der Obersten Heeresleitung*, Berlin, 1922, p. 54.

13. Letter written from St. Avold, in Lorraine, during a staff ride. Generaloberst H. v. Moltke, *op. cit.*, p. 292.

14. "Eine Antwort an Herrn Walter Görlitz betr. das Kapitel 'Der Krieg ohne Feldherr' in seinem Buch 'Der Deutsche Generalstab' von Hauptmann a.D. Adam v. Moltke, Sohn des Generaloberst Helmuth v. Moltke, 1958." BA/MA—HO7–1/24.

15. Hermann Gackenholz, *Entscheidung in Lothringen 1914; der Operationsplan des jüngeren Moltke und seine Durchführung auf dem linken deutschen Heeresflügel*, Berlin, 1933.

16. Moltke himself has admitted, in his memoirs, that he "took upon himself Schlieffen's deployment of the main forces for attack on France and stood to it with complete conviction." Groener wrote in a letter to his wife on 23 Aug. 1914 and in his diary on 25 Aug. that "the spirit of late Schlieffen is with us; this man, who has contrived all these ideas that we are carrying out, deserves the first monument after the campaign. It is marvellous how this great spirit was blessed by Providence, in order to foresee all of which much come. Wherever a leader frees himself from his spirit, as for instance now in the East, he faces disaster [that was a hint to v. Prittwitz' retreat in East Prussia]. General v. Moltke, too, expressed the opinion that Schlieffen's idea must prevail over the operation." Wilhelm Groener, *Lebenserinnerungen*, Göttingen, 1957, p. 161. Von Kuhl, too, maintained that Moltke "kept to Schlieffen's plan of operation with conviction, as far as the deployment of the main forces in the West was concerned." Hermann v. Kuhl, *Der Weltkrieg 1914–1918*, Berlin, 1929, vol. 1, p. 11.

17. K. Mayr, "Kriegsplan und staatsmännische Voraussicht," *Zeitschrift für Politik*, Bd. 14 (1925), H.5, pp. 298–299. (Mayr himself was an advocate of the priority for an offensive in the East and opposed to the Schlieffen school.)

18. E. Ludendorff, *Der totale Krieg*, München, 1935, p. 116. However, in an earlier publication, in 1922, he wrote that Moltke "held firmly to the execution of Schlieffen's thoughts." E. Ludendorff, *Kriegführung und Politik*, Berlin, 1922, p. 71.

19. This memorandum is printed in E. Ludendorff, *Urkunden, op. cit.*, pp. 51–60.

20. An unpublished fragmentary manuscript of Adam von Moltke, *Blätter zum Leben, Wirken und Leiden meines Vaters Generaloberst Helmuth von Moltke*. I owe much gratitude to Mrs. Eva Schotte-von Moltke, Hamburg, who gave me the opportunity to

look into this manuscript, which the Moltke family intends to publish, and allowed me to take notes and quote from it.

21. It is important here to draw attention to Moltke's marginal note to Schlieffen's opening sentence of the memorandum of 1905 ("In a war against Germany France will probably at first restrict herself to defense."), which reads: "France's offensive or defensive attitude will essentially depend on the 'casus belli': if Germany causes the war, France will probably be on the defensive. If, however, the war is desired and caused by France, she is most likely to conduct it offensively. If France wants to re-conquer the lost provinces, she has to invade them, i.e. take the offensive. I do not consider it altogether certain that France will remain on the defensive under all circumstances. However, the frontier fortresses built soon after the war of '70–'71 stress the defensive idea. But this does not accord with the offensive spirit ever inherent in the nation, nor with the doctrines and views now prevalent in the French Army." MGFA—Nachlass GFM Graf v. Schlieffen, Mappe I, Stück 2, Stück 3, printed in Gerhard Ritter, *The Schlieffen Plan*, London, 1948, p. 135.

22. It has often been hinted that the Grand Duke of Baden also influenced military planning in order to avoid a French invasion of his duchy. Groener has hinted to this fact in a letter to Colonel v. Mantey of 9 May 1926 (BA/MA—HO8–46/38:1) and twice in his letters of 13 March 1935 and 21 May 1935 to Mrs. v. Hahnke, v. Schlieffen's daughter (BHA—Rep. 92, W. v. Hahnke, Nr. 17/18 and Nr. 19/20). In the same year he also referred to it in the preliminary notice of his memorandum on the Schlieffen Plan, addressed to historian Dr. Siegfrid Mette, author of *Vom Geist deutscher Feldherren. Genie und Technik 1800–1918*, Zürich, 1938 (BA/MA—HO8–46/51). Ludendorff revealed in a letter to E. Zimmermann (published in "Um Schlieffens Plan," *Süddeutsche Monatshefte*, March 1921) that v. Moltke mentioned during a staff ride the necessity to protect Baden.

23. Ludendorff, *Der totale Krieg, op. cit.*, p. 100.

24. *Vide* Book One, chapter 2.

25. E. Ludendorff, "Der Aufmarsch 1914," *Deutsche Wochenschau*, 3. Jg., Nr. 32—8 Aug. 1926, quoted in W. Elze, *Schlieffen*, Breslau, 1928, p. 9.

26. Even W. Groener, in *Der Feldherr wider Willen, op. cit.*, p. 191, was compelled to admit that the German Army of 1914 was short of the numbers required to operate the Schlieffen Plan.

27. This number includes two divisions deployed at the beginning as the "Northern Army" in Schleswig–Holstein as a safeguard against an expected British invasion of Denmark.

28. Moltke had despatched a memorandum to the Austrian Chief of Staff, Conrad von Hoetzendorff (1852–1925), on 10 Feb. 1913, in which he stressed: "The conduct of a great war of the Triple Alliance against the Triple Entente, even against Russia and France alone, will require the effort of all forces and the exploitation of all chances for leading to a successful end. More than ever before, every dispersion of force bears danger. As Austria will need all her forces for carrying out the struggle against Russia, so Germany will need hers in the struggle against France. Hence I might have recommended that all our forces now arrayed in the East be deployed in the West, had not the considerations for Austria prevented my doing that. For in the contest between Germany and France lies, in my opinion, the center of gravity of the whole European War, and consequently the fate of Austria will not be decided on the Bug, but definitely on the Seine." BA/MA—Nachlass Bauer/Nr. 14.

29. This has also been confirmed in a letter of Ludendorff in 1921. Cf. E. Zimmermann, *op. cit.*, and again in 1922, in Ludendorff, *Kriegführung und Politik, op. cit.*, p. 72.

30. As a matter of fact, the German Chancellor, Bethmann-Hollweg, had already disclosed the German intention of marching troops through neutral Belgium, to the British Ambassador in Berlin, Sir Edward Goschen (1847–1924), in his famous conversation on the night of 29/30 July 1914. Hence, even prior to the German mobilization and declaration of war, the British had an almost official knowledge of German intentions with regard to Belgium. Cf. Fritz Fischer, *Griff nach der Weltmacht*, Düsseldorf, 1961, pp. 85–86. Much earlier but quite definite hints could be found in publications, partly translated into foreign languages, of prominent German military writers. Friedrich von Bernhardi, for instance, wrote in 1912 (published in English in the same year): "Leaving all political conditions aside, we can very well imagine a German offensive against France being conducted by the northern wing of the German Army, with its extreme right along the sea-coast, advancing with the armies echeloned forwards through Holland and Belgium, while the German forces in the south evade the blow of the enemy etc." F. v. Bernhardi, *On War of To-Day*, London, 1912, vol. 2, pp. 328–330. Von Falkenhausen had even earlier, in 1909, sketched the starting situation of an exercise that formed the background for his book, as follows: War between Germany and Austria on one side, and France, England, and Italy on the other. Belgium's neutrality was violated by France and Holland's by England, which provided the pretext for Germany to use both countries as battlefields in a movement quite similar to the Schlieffen Plan. Freiherr von Falkenhausen, *Der grosse Krieg der Jetztzeit*, Berlin, 1909, pp. 11–12.

31. MGFA—Nachlass GFM Graf v. Schlieffen, Mappe I, Stück 2, Stück 3, printed in G. Ritter, *op. cit.*, p. 166.

32. *Ibid.*, G. Ritter, p. 137. I cannot accept Correlli Barnett's assertion that Moltke "did not think operationally in terms of railways." Cf. Correlli Barnett, *The Swordbearers*, London, 1963, p. 85.

33. MGFA—Nachlass GFM Graf v. Schlieffen, Mappe I, Stück 2, Stück 3, printed in G. Ritter, *op. cit.*, pp. 166–167.

34. There is also no written evidence that Schlieffen was at all concerned with the problem of railway destructions. Groener's vague statement that "it should certainly be assumed, that when planning, he took into account the possibility of railway destructions in Belgium, even though there is no written evidence" (BA/MA—HO8–46/51) is not too convincing.

35. G. Ritter asked in an article, "Der Anteil des Militärs an der Kriegskatastrophe von 1914," *Historische Zeitschrift*, Bd. 193 (1961), the question, "Why this unbelievable hurry?" and replied: "The Chief of the General Staff was afraid that the wide-swung advance through Belgium against France might fail if the French had enough time to block it, by means of advancing their troops in good time into Luxembourg and Belgium. Moreover: the Belgians could, in face of the imminent danger of war, block the gaps between their forts around Liège and prepare demolitions of the Meuse bridges and the railway lines so necessary for the advance, without any possibility of preventing it on our part. In other words: the enterprise of the Schlieffen Plan was so hazardous that it could only succeed by a very quick, surprising German forward push, a sudden outbursting assault on Belgium." It is interesting that Colonel Bauer, at that time an officer in Operations Department, maintained in his book, *Der grosse Krieg in Feld und Heimat*, Tübingen, 1921, p. 40, that the Schlieffen Plan "pre-supposed the success of the *coup*

de main against Liège.'' So, too, held General von Moser: ''With the seizure of Liège,'' he wrote, ''the invasion gate and the deployment space on Belgian soil, necessary for the execution of the great Schlieffen field operations of the German right wing, were in German hands.'' Otto v. Moser, *Die obersten Gewalten im Weltkriege*, Stuttgart, 1931, p. 152.

36. One of the interesting omissions was the promise, besides the guarantee of the continuance of the Belgian monarchy, to compensate Belgium with territorial annexations from France in case of amicable conduct. Generaloberst v. Moltke, *op. cit.*, p. 17.

37. Deutsche Dokumente (DD) Nr. 788, quoted in Joh. Victor Bredt, *Die belgische Neutralität und der Schlieffensche Feldzugsplan*, Berlin, 1929.

38. Wolfgang Foerster, *Aus der Gedankenwerkstatt des Deutschen Generalstabes*, Berlin, 1938, pp. 15–16.

39. The same idea is also expressed in Wolfgang Foerster, *Graf Schlieffen und der Weltkrieg*, 2d rev. ed., Berlin, 1925, p. 44, and in Hermann v. Kuhl, *Der Marnefeldzug 1914*, Berlin, 1921, p. 82. The latter, as Chief of Staff of the German First Army whose advance was blocked by Liège, had admitted this fact, despite being an orthodox Schlieffen disciple. Georg Wetzell, Chief of Operations Department in the second part of the First World War, maintained that the bold *coup de main* has overcome a special weakness of the Schlieffen Plan and must be considered as ''an ingenious as well as an indispensable completion'' of the plan. Generalmajor Wetzell, ''Schlieffen—Moltke (der Jüngere)—Bülow,'' *Militär-Wochenblatt*, Jg. 109 (1925), Nr. 44, p. 1355.

40. Max Hoffman Nachlass. BA/MA—HO8–37/1. Also printed in Major-General Max Hoffmann, *War Diaries and Other Papers*, London, 1929, vol. 1, p. 38.

41. BA/MA—HO8–46/51, p. 93 (a letter of v. Kuhl to Groener, 18 Sept. 1935) and pp. 99–100 (Groener's reply of 22 Sept. 1935).

42. *Vide* G. Ritter, *op. cit.*, p. 190.

43. German military theorists tried sometimes to evolve different theories from Napoleon's and the elder Moltke's conduct of war. It has been said that both agreed on the decisive effect of an attack on the flanks and into the rear of the enemy. But whereas Napoleon concentrated his forces prior to the battle, Moltke marched with divided forces and concentrated on the battlefield only. It follows that Schlieffen's *bataillon carré* of the right wing was shaped in accordance with the Napoleonic idea, whereas the younger Moltke's design of the battle in Lorraine with participation of both wings was on the pattern of his uncle's concept.

44. Field Marshal Gottlieb v.Haeseler, probably the best brain in the German pre–First World War army, is reported to have commented on this concept in 1914: ''You cannot carry away the armed strength of a great Power like a cat in a bag.''

45. Ludendorff maintained in 1922 that ''Col. Gen. v. Moltke by taking these measures, had prevented a tension on the left wing and, what really mattered, created the possibility for a great victory.'' E. Ludendorff, *Kriegführung und Politik*, *op. cit.*, p. 73. F. v. Lossberg, an efficient staff officer and brilliant tactician, held the view that a great encirclement victory in Lorraine was feasible and the best way of freeing forces, subsequently, for the right wing. F. v. Lossberg, *Meine Tätigkeit im Weltkriege 1914–1918*, Berlin, 1939, pp. 6–9 passim.

46. Rupprecht wrote in his diary on 15 Aug. 1914: ''I must admit that the idea of alluring the enemy into the space between the Nied and Saar seems to me absolutely artificial, and difficult to carry out. Moreover, I do not believe that the enemy will favor us by advancing in that direction and entering the trap prepared for him there. If possible,

we should fulfil our mission, i.e. attracting as large an enemy as possible, in an offensive way, in order to impose the law on him instead of having it dictated by him." Two days later his entry read: "I pointed out that a continuing withdrawal will damage the offensive spirit of the troops and continual changes of orders undermine their confidence in the higher command levels." Kronprinz Rupprecht von Bayern, *Mein Kriegstagebuch*, München, 1929, vol. 1, pp. 12 and 18, respectively.

47. Immediately on the outbreak of war the Bavarian king, Ludwig III (1845–1921), had proclaimed the special war aims of his country: "Division of Alsace-Lorraine [having been called since 1871 "Reichslande" under the supervision of the German Reich], dissolution of Belgium and the taking possession by Germany of the Rhine estuary." After Rupprecht's victorious advance in Lorraine, the king declared at G.H.Q. in Koblenz on 15 Aug. 1914 that he would now insist on the wholesale incorporation of Alsace into the Bavarian kingdom. Cf. F. Fischer, *op. cit.*, p. 211.

48. That is perhaps the reason for the allotment of additional Ersatz divisions from the general reserve to the Sixth and Seventh Armies.

49. Between Toul and Epinal.

50. W. Groener, *Der Feldherr wider Willen, op. cit.*, pp. 9–19. The German Crown Prince, Wilhelm (1882–1951), C-in-C Fifth Army in 1914, admitted in his memoirs that he, like others, knew about the Schlieffen Plan. Cf. Kronprinz Wilhelm, *Meine Erinnerungen an Deutschlands Heldenkampf*, Berlin, 1923, p. 67. So did General M. Hoffmann who mentioned in his book *The War of Lost Opportunities* that the Schlieffen Plan "was quite familiar to us officers of the General Staff of Schlieffen's school; we had played it through dozens of times in war games and staff rides." M. Hoffmann, *op. cit.*, vol. 2, p. 22.

51. In this context it may be of interest that Karl Justrow, who scrutinized the First World War from the standpoint of a technician, rejected Schlieffen's opinion that the fortress line between Belfort and Verdun was almost impenetrable. He maintained that Schlieffen was too obsessed by this technical error and therefore never considered a breakthrough in this direction. K. Justrow, *Feldherr und Kriegstechnik*, Oldenburg, 1933, p. 223. The same view was held by Lieutenant Colonel A. Hauffe of the German General Staff in a lecture at the German War Academy on 14 March 1936 on the subject "Der strategische Überfall" (the strategic surprise attack): "It is nevertheless my opinion that a strategic break-through through the French eastern defenses, which were partly obsolete, could be expected of the German Army in 1914, and even as a major operation, in case the authorities wanted to avoid the violation either of Swiss or Belgian neutrality. Such an operation would have been aimed, from the operational viewpoint, favorably toward the heart of France; its grave disadvantage and danger was that a French-Belgian-British army could advance through Belgium into the rear of the German main army and thus endanger the German armament resources in the Ruhr basin." BA/MA—W10–1/22.

52. Generaloberst v. Moltke, *op. cit.*, p. 19.

53. Generalleutnant a.D. v. Zoellner, in *Schlieffens Vermächtnis*, Berlin, 1938, p. 14, maintained that owing to the delicate railway situation, even the elder Moltke could not have handled such an enterprise with any hope of success. On the other hand, rumor has it that Groener, Chief of the Military Railway Department, would have found a solution for the transport problem. As a matter of fact, the latter has outlined in his memoirs (W. Groener, *Lebenserinnerungen, op. cit.*, pp. 145–146) a possible solution. One should, however, bear in mind that he started dictating his memoirs in 1938 (*vide* D. Groener-Geyer, *General Groener*, Frankfurt am Main, 1955, p. 340). Much earlier,

in a letter of 28 Dec. 1922 to General E. Kabisch (E. Kabisch, *Streitfragen des Weltkrieges 1914–1918*, Stuttgart, 1924, p. 332), he had admitted that even he, Groener, as Chief of the Military Railway Department, could not vouch for a safely functioning railway transport in case of an improvised switch of the army deployment.

54. Generaloberst v. Moltke, *op. cit.*, p. 22.

55. On the other hand, v. Freytag-Loringhoven wrote to v. Hahnke on 9 Oct. 1920: "Well, well, all these good people were of inferior value (Minderwertigkeiten): Moltke, Stein and Co . . . " BHA—Rep. 92, W. v. Hahnke, Nr. 5.

56. On the other hand, Leo Geyr v. Schweppenburg, in an article, "Der Kriegsausbruch 1914 und der deutsche Generalstab," *Wehrwissenschaftliche Rundschau*, Jg. 13, H.3 (1963), claimed to remember that Moltke was unceasingly occupied in prayers on Mobilization Day. "He was a very respectable, but extremely religious man. Schlieffen would not have acted in such a manner in his holy wrath." He contrasted the younger Moltke's excitement on Mobilization Day with his uncle's stoic tranquility on the eve of the war declaration in 1870.

57. Oberst Bauer, *op. cit.*, p. 33.

58. However, one should bear in mind that later on, at the time Ludendorff evolved his special "Weltanschauung," Moltke was blamed, on account of his lack of willpower, for unconsciously becoming a tool of the "super-national" Powers, Rome, Juda, and their arms' bearers, the Free Masons, in their attempt to enslave the German race. *Vide* Ludendorff's works and especially *Das Marnedrame. Der Fall Moltke-Hentsch*, München, 1934. In the same year another pamphlet on the subject and in the same spirit was published: *Die Deutsche Tragödie an der Marne*, Potsdam, 1934, signed by a certain H. Graf Moltke. My investigation in the *German Dictionary of Nobility*, with the valuable help of Dr. Count v. Merveldt from the German Federal Archives in Koblenz, did not reveal any member of the Moltke family of that time with a Christian name commencing with the letter H. Mrs. E. Schotte-von Moltke, too, could not identify H. Graf Moltke as a member of the family (she thought that it might be a member of the Austrian branch, but I could not find any confirmation for this guess). It seems, therefore, that in this case the author's name and initial should be regarded as a pseudonym (or a forgery?). The same circles had already branded the unlucky Lieutenant Colonel Hentsch, who issued the retreat order on 9 Sept. 1914, as a French Free-Mason and share-holder of the Banque de France, from Jewish origin, of course, who had planned his destructive actions against Germany many years beforehand. Interesting documents on these aspects may be found in MGFA—WO1–5/127 (previous superseded number: OKW/916), Reichswehrministerium-Wehrmachtsabteilung. Geheime Akten über die "Tannenberg-Schlacht"—Ludendorffs Teilnahme und allgemeine Angelegenheiten betr. General Ludendorff (Vom Dez. 1934 bis Okt. 1938).

59. Cf. Feldmarschall Conrad, *op. cit.*, vol. 1, p. 69.

60. Letter of 19 Sept. 1909. This remark, however, is not sufficient to justify Görlitz' assertion that Moltke's admiration for his great uncle was mixed with concealed respect resulting from a feeling that he, himself, had fallen short of expectations. Groener, too, liked to hit at the younger Moltke in his publications by referring to the elder Moltke as "the great uncle."

61. Letter of 1 Sept. 1914.

62. Generaloberst Karl v. Einem, *Erinnerungen eines Soldaten, 1853–1933*, Leipzig, 1933, p. 177.

63. Cf. BA/MA—KO8–5/1, Nachlass Widenmann, Wilhelm: "Erinnerungen an und

Erlebnisse mit geschichtlichen Personen.'' This is by no means firsthand evidence from von Lyckner, but reported to Widenmann by Count Oskar von Platen, sometime Lord Chamberlain of the Imperial Court, who claimed to have heard it from v. Lyncker. This information may be regarded as some kind of court gossip, but it conveys, nevertheless, a certain attitude of mind. The document itself was written during the winter of 1945–1946, and the reflections contained should therefore be approached with some reservations.

64. Geyr von Schweppenburg, *op. cit.*, p. 152.

65. BA/MA—HO8–46/50, Groener Nachlass, a letter from G. Count Lynar to Groener of 3 Feb. 1932.

66. In the original text: Trottel.

67. OHL-Oberste Heeresleitung, Supreme Command.

68. Von Wienskowski in his book *Falkenhayn*, Berlin, 1937, p. 10, relates that already on 10 Aug. 1914, i.e., before the actual advance of the German Army had begun, v. Lyncker had asked v. Falkenhayn whether he might be prepared to take over command of the army in case of Moltke's illness or indisposition. As early as 25 Aug., i.e., before the Marne disaster, Groener wrote in his diary: "There are rumors about Moltke's successors—Lauenstein or Knobelsdorf." W. Groener, *Lebenserinnerungen, op. cit.*, p. 161.

69. *Vide* in more detail later in this chapter.

70. It was also in accordance with §17 of the "Grundzüge der höheren Truppenführung vom 1 Januar 1910" (D.V.E. Nr. 53).

71. V. Kuhl, *Der Weltkrieg, op. cit.*, vol. 1, p. 37.

72. Generalmajor a.D. von Dommes, "Angreifen so lange es geht," *Deutsche Soldatenzeitung*, 10 Sept. 1953.

73. *Berliner Lokalanzeiger*, 7 Feb. 1933.

74. "Liess die Zügel am Boden schleiffen."

75. BA/MA—Nachlass Bauer/Nr. 33, a memorandum of 10 Nov. 1926 to the "Reichsarchiv" (the editing body of the German official history of the First World War). This position was already defined by Colmar von der Goltz as a general principle that "a superior should never prescribe from a distance, what a subordinate on the spot is in a better position to determine for himself." C. v. d. Goltz, *The Nation in Arms*, London, 1906, p. 107.

76. In 1883 von der Goltz wrote: "The name Direktiven thus casually adopted is not pretty—a purely German word would have sounded better—the principle, however, is excellent. According to the definition of the work of the General Staff, Direktiven are 'communications from a higher authority to a subordinate commander, intended less to convey definite orders as to his immediate action, than to indicate leading features for general guidance. The latter should then facilitate judgement in subsequent decisions to be taken independently.' Such communications, which while allowing great latitude, ensure effective co-operation of all the forces, are singularly opportune in these modern times, when, owing to the size of armies, single objects are striven for with divided forces. They are doubly practicable for the purposes of the great general headquarters, which are usually at some distance from the main army, and can only exercise control in a general way." C. v. d. Goltz, *op. cit.*, pp. 112–113. A few pages preceding this quotation he said: "How far details may be gone into, will depend upon the position of the person commanding. The commander-in-chief at the head of great armies, composed of independent corps commanded by generals of high rank, will often have to confine himself to an expression of his wishes and intentions, leaving it to them to contribute to

their realization, according to the extent of their means." *Ibid.*, p. 110. V. Falkenhausen maintained in 1909 that "the independence to be granted to subordinate leaders, and with it the dependence on their qualities and performance, will be much greater than ever before, owing to the size and number of army units set into motion." F. v. Falkenhausen, *op. cit.*, p. 9.

77. Crown Prince Rupprecht reached the conclusion that OHL should have remained in Berlin, together with the center of the political power and, similar to the solution in the East, nominate a Supreme Commander in the West. In Berlin, OHL could concentrate on strategy and issue operational directives to the Supreme Commanders of the eastern and western theaters of war. Rupprecht, *op. cit.*, vol. 1, p. 411. The same idea was picked up by the Chief of Staff of Rupprecht's army group, v. Kuhl, in his work *Der Weltkrieg, op. cit.*, vol. 1, p. 151.

78. Bauer, *op. cit.*, p. 42, maintained that Schlieffen was only concerned with the warfare on land and "the political, naval and economic aspects were after all not his business."

79. Cf. Dr. Friedrich-Christian Stahl, "Der Grosse Generalstab, seine Beziehungen zum Admiralstab und seine Gedanken zu den Operations-plänen der Marine," *Wehrkunde*, Jg. XII, H.1 (1963).

80. BA/MA—KO8–5/1.

81. "Zu anderer Verwendung."

82. Feldmarschall Conrad, *op. cit.*, vol. 1, p. 396. Conrad gives a full quotation of a secret official letter (Nr. 793, 24 Feb. 1909) from Moltke to his Austrian counterpart.

83. Quoted in Generalfeldmarschall v. Bülow, *Mein Bericht zur Marneschlacht*, Berlin, 1919, p. 30.

84. Groener wrote in his diary on 23 Aug.: "From the reports of the army H.Q.s and all other sensations here in G.H.Q. one received the impression that the war against France is already decided, though it may still last a little longer. Perhaps there is still a great catastrophe in store for the French—Sedan lies near at hand." W. Groener, *Lebenserinnerungen, op. cit.*, p. 160.

85. Already on 21 Aug. 1914 von Prittwitz, C-in-C Eighth Army, vigorously demanded reinforcements; otherwise, he could not hold his ground in East Prussia. Cf. E. Kabisch, *op. cit.*, p. 77.

86. On 2 Sept. Conrad again begged v. Freytag-Loringhoven, German liaison officer with the Austrian G.H.Q., to bring about an urgent transfer of two German corps to Galicia. Frhr. v. Freytag-Loringhoven, *Menschen und Dinge, wie ich sie in meinem Leben sah*, Berlin, 1920, p. 146, maintained that OHL should have ignored the Russian menace, even consent to a defeat in the battle of the Masurian Lakes and carry out the offensive in the West. Then, after a certain victory on the Marne, the Russians could still be beaten and Berlin saved from siege and capture. Of course, a chain of suppositions.

87. "Stimmung entschlossen, wenn auch schlimmer Ausgang nicht ausgeschlossen."

88. Quoted in W. Foerster, *Aus der Gedankenwerkstatt, op. cit.*, p. 52, and in the same author's book *Graf Schlieffen, op. cit.*, p. 24. The full text of this final discussion is to be found in MGFA—Nachlass GFM Graf v. Schlieffen, Mappe II, Stück I/32, Schlussbesprechung Kriegsspiel, Nov.-Dez. 1905.

89. Cf. A. v. Schlieffen, *Dienstschriften*, Berlin, 1937–1938, vol. 2.

90. *Ibid.*, vol. 2, pp. 241–242.

91. BA/MA—HO8–46/111:1.

92. W. Groener, *Lebenserinnerungen, op. cit.*, p. 133.

93. With regard to the expected moment of decision in the West, Moltke was in line, too, with Schlieffen. He himself estimated in the letter of 24 Feb. 1909 to Conrad that if France adopted an offensive attitude, a decision might be reached three weeks after mobilization. If the French remained passively behind their defenses, then four weeks might be needed. Moltke reckoned that entraining in the West, traveling to the East, and detraining there would require nine to ten additional days. Conrad, *op. cit.*, vol. 1, p. 395.

94. A. v. Schlieffen, *Dienstschriften*, *op. cit.*, vol. 2, pp. 222–223.

95. Cf. E. Ludendorff, *Das Marnedrama*, *op. cit.*, p. 11.

96. Kabisch, *op. cit.*, p. 116. That such considerations really played a part may be deduced from the final phrase of Wilhelm II's Order of the Day, after the battle of Tannenberg, which read: "I am proud of My Prussian regiments" (Ich bin stolz auf Meine preussischen Regimenter). Quoted in W. Elze, *Tannenberg*, Breslau, 1928, p. 343.

97. Even Groener in *Das Testament des Grafen Schlieffen*, Berlin, 1927, p. 205.

98. It is regrettable that so distinguished a scholar as G. Ritter overlooked this vital piece of information and omitted these five corps from the reproduction of Schlieffen's maps. That particular original map, as drawn by W. v. Hahnke, Schlieffen's son-in-law and aide-de-camp, may be found in MGFA—Nachlass GFM Graf v. Schlieffen, Mappe III. (Strangely enough at the time I was working in Freiburg/Br.—in the summer of 1963—that file contained Schlieffen's memorandum of 28 Dec. 1912, together with maps No. 1, 2, 3, 5, 6, in fact, supplementing the memorandum of 1905. Other maps were contained in Mappe I—Stück 4, holding maps 4, 5a, 7, 8, 9, together with other maps not connected with the memorandum of 1905.)

99. The message of the First Army transmitted to OHL on 30 Aug. 1914, 10:30 PM read: "First Army wheeled in direction of the Oise and shall advance toward Compiègne-Noyon on 31st, in order to exploit success of Second Army." Quoted in Generaloberst A. v. Kluck, *Der Marsch auf Paris und die Marneschlacht 1914*, Berlin, 1920, p. 76. Cf. also E. Kabisch, *op. cit.*, pp. 355–356.

100. At 2:13 AM on 31 Aug., First Army's H.Q. received the wireless message: "The movements carried out by the First Army conform to the intentions of OHL." Cf. the same sources as mentioned in note 98. The text of the orders of 27 Aug. in Müller-Loebnitz, *Die Führung im Marnefeldzug 1914*, Berlin, 1939, pp. 114–116.

101. Wilhelm Breucker, *Die Tragik Ludendorffs*, Stollhamm (Old.), 1953, pp. 22–23.

102. V. Kuhl wrote in his own account of the Marne battle: "The brilliant victory of Tannenberg became known. All energy was strained in order to achieve, too, a great success on the Oise." V. Kuhl, *Der Marnefeldzug*, *op. cit.*, p. 109.

103. Johann Kühl, *Macht mir den rechten Flügel stark!*, Kiel, 1934, pp. 69–70.

104. Not to mention that the real strength of units had dwindled, owing to the great distance covered by foot-marches and by continuous engagements. Moreover, some units were in even more rearward locations.

105. The full text of these orders in Müller-Loebnitz, *op. cit.*, pp. 117–118.

106. V. Mantey reported that when Lieutenant Colonel Hentsch had passed the IVth Corps of the First Army he had exclaimed: "Children, where have you run off!? You should have followed in echelon or you might wreck Moltke's whole concept!" BA/MA—HO5–6/23.

107. *Vide* Book One, chapter 2.

108. V. Mantey, "Umfassung, Umgehung und Durchbruch. Eine Schlieffen Studie," *Wissen und Wehr*, Jg. 12 (1931), H.10.

109. Cf. Groener, *Der Feldherr, op. cit.*, p. XIV, and Groener, *Das Testament, op. cit.*, pp. 19–20.

110. Especially the Swiss Eugen Bircher, who, in his book *Die Krisis in der Marneschlacht*, Bern, 1922, pp. 264 ff., has made a great show of his medical analysis of the central personalities in the Marne battle: Moltke, Bülow, Lauenstein, and Hentsch. Crown Prince Rupprecht, too, had made observations regarding Moltke's health in his diary, and so did Groener in *Der Feldherr, op. cit.*, pp. 245–246, and in *Lebenserinnerungen, op. cit.*, p. 152. (However, in a letter of 19 Aug. 1914 he remarked that "Colonel General von Moltke is very vigorous and lively." *Lebenserinnerungen, op. cit.*, p. 157.)

111. *Vide* note 58. To give an additional impression of the stupid nature of some of these assertions, it should be mentioned that Ludendorff believed that Hentsch had deliberately delayed his departure from the Second Army's H.Q. to First Army in order to arrive there on 9 Sept., "for Free-Masons salute each other with 3 times 3 (the figure 9 being consecrated to Jahveh.)"

112. Reichsarchiv, *Der Weltkrieg 1914–1918*, Berlin, vol. 3.

113. M. Hoffmann, *op. cit.*, vol. 2, p. 62.

114. Bauer (*Der grosse Krieg, op. cit.*, pp. 56–57), who, as an officer in the Operations Department of OHL, was supposed to know, doubted whether Paris could still be seized but maintained that "anyhow the advance would have come to a standstill near Paris because the supply of replacements, communication and equipment had broken down and the repair of railway lines was slow, owing to thoroughly destroyed bridges." General v. Falkenhayn, Minister of War and v. Moltke's successor, also admitted that in mid-September 1914 the railheads were five days' march behind the troops. Cf. E. v. Falkenhayn, *Die Oberste Heeresleitung 1914–1916 in ihren wichtigsten Entschliessungen*, Berlin, 1920, pp. 9–10. The Bavarian Crown Prince, at that time C-in-C Sixth Army, mentioned in his diary on 18 Sept. 1914 that four German Armies (First, Second, Sixth, and Seventh) were relying on one single railway line through Brussels and Valenciennes. Kronprinz Rupprecht, *op. cit.*, vol. 1, p. 127.

115. "In Feindesland sind wir die Bahnarmen, der Feind der Bahnreiche."

116. G. Tappen, *Bis zur Marne, 1914*, Oldenburg, 1920, p. 8.

117. Colmar v. d. Goltz had already drawn attention to the difficulty of maintaining logistically huge hosts: "It will be seen that gigantic struggles between forces composed of from 10 to 15 army corps, under a single commander, will not be beyond the bounds of probability. Such are, however, proportions which have not yet been realized in modern times; and it is easily conceivable how greatly the questions of feeding and mobility will be affected, no less than the tactical leading." C. v. d. Goltz, *op. cit.*, p. 2.

118. Groener, *Der Feldherr, op. cit.*, pp. 187–190.

119. Used here for the German "Intendantur Beamte." BA/MA—HO5–6/23, v. Mantey. These staff rides were nicknamed "Mehlreisen" (Flour rides).

120. V. Kuhl, *Der Weltkrieg, op. cit.*, vol. 1, pp. 107–108. In his memoirs Groener recalled that he had suggested the purchase of the harvest of the River Plate in 1913, but interoffice quarrels had prevented it, and the Chancellor had been restrained from exercising his authority. *Lebenserinnerungen, op. cit.*, p. 135. It should be mentioned that economic preparations in France were in no better shape; *vide* Richard D. Challener, *The French Theory of the Nation in Arms, 1866–1939*, New York, 1955, in particular chap.

3, "1914: The Economic Consequences of a Military Theory." One should, however, keep in mind that the French alliance with Great Britain and, at a later stage, with the United States eased the French situation, desperate as it was.

121. For instance, Fuller, Liddell Hart, G. A. Craig, and others.

122. It cannot be denied that he possessed the will to win. On 7 Sept. 1914, i.e., two days before the final "Marne disaster," he released to the German press the full text of Joffre's offensive order, which had fallen into German hands, and added his own inspiring comment: "At the end of the war our Fatherland must achieve a peace proportionate to the unprecedented sacrifices which our people have so unanimously made, and which will not be liable to be disturbed for an unbounded time by any adversary." Quoted in G.Jäschke, "Zum Problem der Marne-Schlacht von 1914," *Historische Zeitschrift*, H. 190/92, April 1960, p. 338.

123. It seems that a certain underestimation of the Russian Army's qualities and an overevaluation of the virtues of the Austro-Hungarian Army was also prevalent, which distorted the actual proportion of forces even more to Germany's disadvantage.

124. Liddell Hart's foreword to G. Ritter, *The Schlieffen Plan*, *op. cit.*, p. 7.

125. That he had the feeling of having committed a grave blunder is indicated by the fact that on Sept. 10 1914 Kuhl had prepared a report of his discussion with Lieutenant Colonel Hentsch on the previous day, signed it, together with his Chief Quartermaster (Oberquartiermeister) W. v. Bergmann, had it witnessed by an officer of First Army's staff and attached it to the official War Diary of First Army. It is obvious that the document was prepared a full day after the occurrences it describes, and without having been confirmed and countersigned by Hentsch. It demonstrates, however, a sense of history (and how to shape it) and the feeling that a vindication of First Army's actions might be appropriate.

126. BA/MA, Groener Nachlass.

127. He himself mentioned in a letter to Mrs. v. Hahnke, Schlieffen's daughter, on 1 Jan. 1938, that such charges were made against him, for instance, by General Marx. BHA—Rep. 92, W. v. Hahnke, Nr. 28/31.

128. Liddell Hart, *The Ghost of Napoleon*, London, 1933, pp. 140–142 passim.

129. One in 1914, three in 1915, one in 1917, and one in 1918.

130. The prefaces are from Field Marshals Prince Leopold of Bavaria, von Bülow, and von Mackensen; Colonel Generals von Kluck, von Eichhorn, and von Woyrsch; Generals Count von Bothmer, von Beseler, von Hoetzendorff, von Scholz, and von Böhm-Ermolli; and from the Prussian Minister of War, Lieutenant General Wild von Hohenborn.

5

Case 2: The Race to the Sea

THE AFTERMATH OF THE MARNE BATTLE

On 9 September 1914 the German right wing began its retreat, commencing with von Bülow's Second Army's right flank, which was considered endangered by the B.E.F.'s advance into the gap between the First and Second Armies. Consequently, the First Army's left flank was bent to the rear too, and when von Bülow broke off the battle of his successful left wing and ordered its retreat together with the Third Army's right flank (the latter receiving its orders from von Bülow, by-passing the Third Army's C-in-C, von Hausen), then the First Army, complying with Lieutenant Colonel Hentsch's order, was compelled to withdraw its corps from the battlefield of the Ourcq. The badly shaken French troops and the cautiously advancing B.E.F. were so surprised that they only hesitatingly followed the retreating Germans, who managed to withdraw un-molested, despite low morales, in good order.

Moltke, visiting the headquarters of his armies for the first time on 11 September, intended to confine the retreat solely to the extreme right wing and only for the purpose of closing the gap between the armies. However, when receiving a misleading message from von Bülow that a hostile break-through of the Third Army's front was imminent, von Moltke ordered a retreat of the Third, Fourth, and Fifth Armies to the line Reims–St. Menehoud, north of Verdun. On the next day the Fourth and Fifth Armies were ordered to withdraw further to a straight line running from Reims to an area north of Verdun. Thus Verdun was freed from the menacing grip of encirclement, and German troops also evacuated the vital region of the Argonnes Forest.

However, in accordance with the traditional German stress of the offensive action, and following a practice exercised in many staff rides, war games, and maneuvers, the Germans regarded their retreat only as a tactical measure, in order to reorganize their formations and gain new space to maneuver for a renewed attack. For that purpose Moltke at last ordered the transfer of the bulk of the Seventh Army from the left to the right wing and finally the concentration of the Sixth Army at Metz, thus breaking off the battle in the direction of Nancy. For both armies (minus the covering forces left in Alsace and Lorraine) a process of transfer by train into Belgium now started. They should bridge the gaps and reshape the depleted *bataillon carré* of the right wing, but the period of transport actually meant a temporary paralysis of up to a quarter of the German strength in the West (in addition to the corps still committed to the siege of Antwerp). Despite the severe blow to German morale and the consequent boost to the French resulting from the unexpected German retreat from the Marne, the German Supreme Command still stuck to Schlieffen's plan and its further continuation. On 13 September the German Armies stood north of the Aisne, and all efforts of the Allies to dislodge them from their positions ended in failure.

On 14 September 1914 von Moltke was superseded by the Prussian Minister of War, General Erich von Falkenhayn.

GENERAL VON FALKENHAYN—THE SECOND OHL

Already on 10 August 1914, on the eve of the German advance into Belgium and northern France, von Falkenhayn was earmarked by the Chief of the Imperial Cabinet as the probable successor to von Moltke.[1] Von Falkenhayn was waiting for his chance to come. He had, the whole time, strongly opposed von Moltke's conduct of the war and especially the latter's actions on the left wing. From Crown Prince Rupprecht's diary it is obvious that von Falkenhayn had advocated the shift of forces from the left wing to the extreme right wing with reference to Schlieffen's master plan.[2] He had also propagated the idea of a tougher and more centralized conduct of the armies and a more forward location of OHL headquarters.[3]

For the time being, however, von Moltke remained formally in office, although stripped of all his powers. Moltke had convinced the Kaiser that, at that juncture, the announcement of changing the Chief of General Staff would confirm the Allies' claim of a German defeat at the Marne. He was therefore prepared to make the sacrifice of covering, with his name, the actual change in command of the army (or did he still hope that the Kaiser might restore him to power after realizing that the retreat from the Marne was the salvation of the German Army from certain disaster?). The unique feature of Falkenhayn's new position was that he held military power as Acting Chief of Staff (and very soon as Chief of General Staff in his own right) combined with ministerial power as Minister of War.

Was Falkenhayn qualified for his new responsibilities? The pen-men of the Schlieffen school, who judged Falkenhayn by his future actions at Verdun, his feud with the Supreme Commander East, and who, above all, blamed him for the transition to trench warfare, denied his fitness for so high an appointment. He was not considered qualified because he was not initiated into the "secrets of victory" of the great master. Wolfgang Foerster maintained that von Falkenhayn can in no sense be called a disciple of Count Schlieffen. "He did not belong to that narrow circle of General Staff officers, who surrounded Count Schlieffen, and upon whom the latter relied for direct support . . . he served only a short time in the General Staff, when headed by Count Schlieffen. On the whole he was less a man of theoretical knowledge and studies, and more a practical worker, with conspicuous organizational gifts.''[4] Even one of Falkenhayn's biographers, v. Wienskowski, admitted that the former had not undergone that thorough training to which the General Staff had been exposed under Schlieffen's direction.[5] Nevertheless, he held that v. Falkenhayn was, in the final analysis, a partisan of Schlieffen and was determined to conduct the war in accordance with the master's teaching.[6] General a. D. Marx refuted that judgment sarcastically:

It was generally asserted that the wrong dispositions were a consequence of the fact that Falkenhayn, owing to his activities in China, lacked the correct General Staff training. . . . Expressed in rude language, it means that the pupil Erich von Falkenhayn was absent from his class when the chapter "Cannae" was taught; by the time he returned from China, the teacher had already passed on, the deficiency could not be made up any more.[7]

FALKENHAYN'S FIRST OPERATIONAL PLAN

Having been appointed on 14 September 1914 to direct the German Army, von Falkenhayn reviewed the situation single-handed during that night. In his memoirs he revealed that he did not doubt that the main German effort would continue in the West, even after the battle of the Marne.[8] What then was his new plan? A new decisive battle to be fought on the extreme right wing of the western front. For that purpose more forces should be concentrated there. Moltke had already transferred the major parts of the Seventh Army and pushed them into the gap between the First and Second Armies. Now the Sixth Army, too, should be quickly assembled at Maubeuge until 21 September. In order to cover up that space of time the German right wing should undertake a further withdrawal. Falkenhayn actually had in mind a complete disengagement of the First Army from enemy contact, carried out by means of an eccentric retreat to the north, even as far as St.-Quentin. Should the enemy press on in his pursuit, the withdrawal might be continued even as far south as Cambrai. This would be all the better, for such steps would expose the enemy flank to a mortal blow. The Seventh and Second Armies were to hold a line running from Laon southward to Reims and, if pressed by the enemy, even further to the east. The new gap emerging between the First and Seventh Armies would be bridged by the Cavalry Corps of the Army (Heereskavallerie). The new general offensive was to start on 18 September, commencing from the left, near Verdun, and shifting gradually to the right.

It was a daring plan, again aimed at hitting against the enemy's open left flank during his advance. In accordance with the best German tradition, it demanded

the regaining of operational space and maneuver by means of a deliberate ret-
rogressive movement. A further essential requirement of the plan was the ultimate
possibility of transporting huge forces by train from Metz to Maubeuge, in
accordance with the timetable laid down for the offensive. Both factors imposed
leaden weights on the smooth execution of a logical plan. Economic considerations, positive as well as negative ones, prevented any further large-scale retreat.
Moreover, any further retrograde movement would expose essential lateral railway lines to the enemy's grasp.

But the railway situation was an even more important factor: For the transfer
of forces from Metz to the right wing only one double-rail line was available,
running through Aachen–Brussels–Mons–Cambrai–St.–Quentin. On this line,
too, all the supplies for the four armies of the right wing (First, Seventh, Second,
and Third) were dependent. The transport of troops would impose severe restrictions on vital provisions. There was an alternative route through Diedenhofen
and Luxembourg, but it was interrupted by a blown-up bridge near Namur.
Troops could, of course, detrain there, entrain again west of the town, and move
on by train to Charleroi, but the bulk of the troops would nevertheless be faced
with a route march from Namur to their destination. Taking into account that to
shift one single army corps 140 transport trains were required, and that under
the railway conditions in Belgium and northern France in mid-September 1914
approximately forty trains a day could run, it was obvious that the assembly of
the Sixth Army at Maubeuge could not be accomplished until 21 September.

Moreover, in the afternoon of 15 September von Falkenhayn learned that von
Bülow, now in command of First, Seventh, and Second Armies, had ordered a
new attack of his forces, west of Reims, and Colonel Tappen, Chief of Operations
in OHL, had already withdrawn one army corps from each of the Third, Fourth,
and Fifth Armies and put them at von Bülow's disposal. Falkenhayn consented
to these arrangements because he was anxious to avoid the issue of counter orders
as his first step in office, fearing that they might lead to disorder and the loss
of confidence by the troops in the High Command. Also, he was persuaded by
Tappen that the Allies were again nearing the end of their tether, and that,
therefore, any blow delivered against them might turn the tide. At least Bülow's
offensive would tie down the enemy forces in the front and prevent their shift
to the left against the German right flank.

Thus von Falkenhayn dropped his plan of the previous night and ordered the
German extreme right wing to remain in a defensive position instead of falling
back. He maintained that the arrival of the Sixth Army would enable the delivery
of a final *coup de grace* into the enemy's open left flank, after having occupied
his forces opposite Reims. However, owing to the transport difficulties von
Falkenhayn consented to a piecemeal use of the Sixth Army in battle. ''It will
remain our main aim,'' he wrote in his instruction to Rupprecht, C-in-C Sixth
Army, on 18 September, ''to achieve the decision of battle on the right wing
of the Army as soon as possible, and, with forces as strong as possible, even if
they are deployed in succession.''[9]   German experts were later divided in their

opinions about the moment when the Schlieffen Plan became unfeasible. Some maintain that, even before the battle of the Marne began, the Schlieffen Plan was already wrecked, owing to insufficient forces. Others believe that the retreat from the Marne put an end to the execution of the plan, and that there were no further expedient to restore its execution. But a few are convinced that Falkenhayn's first decision, during the night of 14–15 September, of resorting to a war of movement again, although at first in a retrograde direction, might have rescued Schlieffen's plan. In their opinion it follows that Falkenhayn's change of mind on the afternoon of 15 September delivered the death blow to the old master's design. However, the series of battles conducted by von Falkenhayn up to the end of the year, shifting gradually to the west and titled "the race to the sea," indicated that von Falkenhayn himself had not yet given up hope of a resumption of the decisive outflanking move on the German right wing.

THE "RACE TO THE SEA" AND THE BATTLE OF FLANDERS, 1914

Falkenhayn's consent to von Bülow's attack on the enemy between Reims and Soissons, called the "Battle of the Aisne," did not lead to the expected result. However, the Germans succeeded in frustrating Joffre's attempt to envelop the German right flank. Notwithstanding this move, another battle had to be fought, further to the west, in Picardy, which ended in the same way. Neither side managed to encircle and outflank its opponent.

With difficulties in transporting all of his forces from the left wing to the right, von Falkenhayn tried, in the meantime, to distract his enemy's attention from the right to the left by means of launching a new attack in the Verdun area. There, at one point, St.-Mihiel, the Germans managed to cross the Meuse and to install a bridgehead. Then, like two angry wrestlers circling around each other, the battle shifted further to the west into Artois, only to again result in a "draw." It was now already mid-October. On 16 September von Falkenhayn had ordered the final assault on Antwerp to be pressed. On 9 October, Antwerp was finally captured, after part of its garrison had escaped and reached the Allies' left flank. Three divisions released from the siege of Antwerp, and four army corps, newly levied in Germany, were now molded into a new Fourth Army under Duke Albrecht of Württemberg's command.

Now at last Falkenhayn turned his attention to the sea and realized that leaning his right flank on the coast might prevent any further encirclement of that flank. Consequently, German troops occupied Ghent on 11 October, Lille the next day, two days later Bruges, and finally Ostend on 15 October. The Allies had, in the meantime, extricated the British troops from the battlefield of the Aisne and shifted them, too, to the coast, together with the Belgian Army, which had escaped from Antwerp. The mutual "race to the sea" came to an end. Neither side had succeeded so far in turning its opponent's flank. What next?

Von Falkenhayn still had a trump hidden up his sleeve: his newly created

Fourth Army, reinforced by the bulk of the German heavy artillery now freed from the siege of Antwerp. This army was ordered to attack along the sea shore and crush the enemy positions on the Yser. At the same time Rupprecht's Sixth Army was to attack from Lille, westward to the Flemish coast. The hope was nourished that with the additional heavy artillery and the fresh troops, the hostile lines would be penetrated and the enemy's rear reached. However, enemy re-action and a number of domestic handicaps frustrated German hopes: First of all, it was not enough to have heavy guns available if they lacked ammunition. That was a direct result of Schlieffen's pre-war belief in a short war. Second, despite the bravery of the German assault troops, their advance was hampered by the sea flooding in through sluices opened by the Belgians, and inundating the ground below sea level. And last, but not least in importance, the fresh corps, mainly young volunteers from Germany's universities, attacked with vigor and enthusiasm but without adequate training and battle experience. Falkenhayn, in his memoirs, used transport difficulties as the reason for not switching the raw troops to a quiet section of the front and drawing from there experienced units. From the sad slaughter of these high-spirited volunteers one may deduce the doubtful value of utilizing newly created formations, which had played so vital a part in Schlieffen's original plan.

However, Schlieffen's disciple, von Kuhl,[10] as well as Falkenhayn's biographer, H. von Zwehl,[11] held that the battle of Ypres was the last attempt to return to Schlieffen's plan after all the previous failures. It was the restoration of Schlieffen's basic idea of seeking a decision by encircling the adversary's left flank. Von Kuhl maintained that there was no reason for condemning Falkenhayn for this enterprise. But it failed. Nobody else has defined the whole course of events better than old Schlieffen: "Everyone strives to envelop," he said in 1905, "and therefore extends his front. Everyone strives to avoid encirclement, and therefore extends his frontline likewise."[12] And so it really was! Falkenhayn, on the one hand being anxious to stick to Schlieffen's principle of encircling the enemy's left flank, despite having insufficient forces at his disposal, and on the other hand being afraid of becoming himself encircled on his right flank, was dragged into the spiral movements of the race to the sea, which ended in stalemate.

THE TRANSITION TO STATIC WARFARE

H. Rosinski considered the real turning point of the First World War to be not 9 September, the day on which the German command suffered a signal setback through the breakdown of its famous plan of campaign, but the fifteenth of that month, the day on which Falkenhayn decided against a return to mobile strategy.[13] The attempt to return to mobile warfare on the northern flank shifted the struggle gradually from the Aisne, through Picardy, into Artois, and finally bogged down in Flanders. Both sides believed that they would return to the offensive again, but both sides feared a hostile break-through. The first reason led to clinging to the ground already held, regardless of its suitability for a defensive action, whereas for the second reason, both sides dug in and erected obstacles. "That twilight situation between offensive and defensive is the actual source of position warfare," as General Walter Reinhardt put it in a lecture to officers of the Reichswehr.[14] In fact, in the last quarter of 1914 neither side had yet realized that a new era in warfare had begun. Both sides regarded themselves as still pursuing the strategic offensive. The deadlock after the first battle of Ypres (30/10–24/11/1914) was commonly considered to be only the result of mutual exhaustion.

However, German OHL regulations had already ordered the preparation of several parallel trench lines, instead of the single one customary hitherto. Furthermore, these regulations demanded the utmost defense of every line. Should the enemy, despite all preparations, capture a line, a position, or a section of a line, then it was a matter of principle to counterattack immediately and recapture the ground just lost. These rules introduced a priori a certain rigidity into the conduct of war and prevented any flexibility, hitherto regarded as an essential ingredient of German strategy and tactics.

A warning that something of this nature might happen in the near future had already been given by the Boer War in South Africa (1899–1902) and the Russian-Japanese War (1904–1905). However, Schlieffen had his panacea ready: outflanking! "This is the best manner," wrote von Falkenhausen, following Schlieffen's line, in his study on flank-movements and mass-armies, in 1911, "to obviate the justifiable concern of late, that warfare in the present time might decline into a so-called position warfare."[15] Because of this and other notions from Schlieffen's armory, Clausewitz' warning that "the line of defense may run from sea to sea or from one neutral country to another"[16] went unheeded. This prophecy, however, foreshadowed what had actually happened, from Belfort in the south to Ostend in the north, at the end of 1914. It seems too hypothetical to wonder whether Schlieffen might not also have been driven onto the defensive had he commanded the German Army in 1914; however, von Kuhl did not disregard the fact that it might have occurred to him.[17]

It remains to consider whether it might not have been wiser to shift the German effort from the west to the east after having failed at the Marne to inflict a deadly blow on the French Army.

DECISION IN THE WEST OR IN THE EAST?

Von Falkenhayn himself was not unaware that the question of the German center of gravity was a serious problem that demanded a clear-cut solution. In his memoirs he dealt elaborately with Schlieffen's reasons for an initial offensive in the West. He expressed full agreement with Schlieffen's conclusions. Nevertheless, he admitted that the situation that faced him at the time of his accession to OHL was a challenge for new considerations: Would it not be a sounder policy to break off the unsuccessful offensive in the West, adopting there a defensive posture, and exploit to the maximum the achievements of the Germans in the East, thereby keeping the promise given to the Austrian ally, that in six weeks' time, Germany's army would rush to Austria's assistance against the Russian "steam roller"?

However, von Falkenhayn held to the original plan of operation, afraid to release the pressure on the Western Allies and retreat to a line that could be better defended by smaller forces, on economic grounds. He also thought that the eastern theater of war was unsuitable for combat actions during the winter, and that, consequently, the ultimate result would be stalemate in both theaters of war: in the West for want of forces, and in the East because of the sodden ground or the severe climate. Although Max Hoffmann, senior staff officer in the East, maintained in his letters of 21 and 24 October 1914 that the new corps, deployed in the East instead of being sacrificed in the West, would have turned the tide completely in Germany's favor,[18] the Austrian Army High Command were demanding, at the same time, the transfer of no less than thirty German divisions from the West to the East.[19] Although von Falkenhayn did not deny the justification of the Austrian cries for help, he considered himself unable to denude the western front of troops before staging a promising decisive battle in Flanders. The East was, in the meantime, advised to resort to every possible makeshift. (As a matter of fact, one of the new corps was given to the East from the outset.)

One wonders whether von Falkenhayn's attitude to the problem, "major effort in the East or in the West?" was really inspired by sheer envy of the successes of Hindenburg and Ludendorff in the East, as his opponents claim, and that he therefore strove desperately for his own success in the West, or whether it was really influenced by an orthodox adherence to Schlieffen's priorities.

NOTES

1. *Vide* note 68 of chapter 4.

2. Kronprinz Rupprecht von Bayern, *Mein Kriegstagebuch*, München, 1929, vol. 1, p. 121, entry of 15 Sept. 1914.

3. Falkenhayn advanced his staff to Charleville, a 140–kilometer leap forward, on 26 Sept., and the Kaiser and his entourage followed suit on 28 Sept.

4. Wolfgang Foerster, *Graf Schlieffen und der Weitkrieg*, 2d rev. ed., Berlin, 1925, p. 86.

5. V. Wienskowski, *Falkenhayn*, Berlin, 1937, p. 12.

6. *Ibid.*, p. 111. However, as a result of the controversy between Falkenhayn and Hindenburg–Ludendorff over the question of the center of gravity of Germany's operations in the East or in the West, Max Hoffmann, at that time senior staff officer in the East, wrote in a letter on 1 Dec. 1914: "I am struck with horror at the conduct of war in the West. This man Falkenhayn is the evil angel of our Fatherland, and unfortunately he has His Majesty in the bag." BA/MA—HO8–37/1.

7. Generalleutnant a. D. Marx, *Wertleistung und Werturteil*, Potsdam, 1938, p. 20.

8. E. v. Falkenhayn, *Die Oberst Heeresleitung 1914–1916 in ihren wichtigsten Entschliessungen*, Berlin, 1920, pp. 12 ff.

9. Quoted by W. Solger, "Falkenhayn," in F. v. Cochenhausen, ed., *Heerführer des Weltkrieges*, Berlin, 1919, pp. 79–80.

10. Hermann v. Kuhl, "Graf Schlieffen und der Weltkrieg," *Wissen und Wehr*, Jg. 4 (1923), H.1, pp. 4–5.

11. H. v. Zwehl, *Erich von Falkenhayn*, Berlin, 1926, p. 81.

12. *Vide* chapter 2, under "The Cannae Concept and the Idea of Annihilation." In this context it is of interest to mention that some German military writers called this phase of the war not "the race to the sea," but "the race for the open flank."

13. H. Rosinski, *The German Army*, Washington, D.C., 1944, p. 91.

14. Walter Reinhardt, *Wehrkraft und Wehrwille*, Berlin, 1932, pp. 136–137.

15. Freiherr von Falkenhausen, *Flankenbewegung und Massenheer*, Berlin, 1911, p. 198.

16. *On War*, VI, 4, p. 367.

17. H. v. Kuhl, *op. cit.*, p. 5.

18. BA/MA—HO8–37/1, pp. 11–12.

19. V. Falkenhayn, *op. cit.*, p. 22.

6

The Attitude of Schlieffen and His Successors Toward England

"Gott strafe England!" (May the Lord punish England)—a slogan stamped
on German letters during World War I

GERMANY'S HOPE OF BRITISH NEUTRALITY

The nervousness of Germany's rulers on the night of 1 August 1914, resulting
from the misleading telegram of the German Ambassador to the Court of St.
James regarding the British attitude to the pending war,[1] sheds a sharp light on
German sensitivity to the position of Great Britain. Although there was no reason
why England should betray her allies at that particular juncture, German states-
men nonetheless deluded themselves that a miracle might happen and Great
Britain would remain neutral. That such aspirations were not confined solely to
Germany's politicians, but also had partisans among soldiers, is indicated by
Major General Wilhelm von Hahnke, von Schlieffen's son-in-law and aide-de-
camp for many years, in a memorandum, "The Military Political Attitude of
Count Schlieffen Toward England," prepared in April 1931.[2] In this document
v. Hahnke tried to demonstrate that although Schlieffen did not hold the qualities
of the British Army in great esteem, he nevertheless had a strong desire to
prevent the addition of Great Britain to the camp of Germany's potential enemies.
Moreover, he even believed, almost until the end of 1905, i.e., nearly to the
end of his term of office, that England would maintain a position of benevolent
neutrality toward Germany.

Hahnke's statements were made thirteen years after the German collapse, as
part of an attempt to show that the German defeat in the First World War was
the fault, not of Schlieffen, but of successors who had deviated from his plan.
They therefore require thorough and critical investigation, the more so, as Schlieffen frequently had taken into account a hostile belligerent Great Britain. As early
as 1896, in a final exercise for junior staff officers, there was a clear hint of the
possibility of British military intervention against Germany.

Moreover, Schlieffen's writings enumerated many good reasons for England's rancor toward Germany.

THE REASONS FOR ANGLO-GERMAN HOSTILITY

Whereas it was reasonable for the elder Moltke and Bismarck to count on English neutrality, changing political circumstances made it necessary for Schlieffen to reckon with British intervention. During Wilhelm II's reign there were too many troublesome issues that created friction between the two nations, above all, the menace of an overgrowing German Navy.[3] Of course, the German violation of Belgian territory, planned by Schlieffen, turned the possibility of a hostile England into a probability. This was explicitly expressed in the last war game conducted by Schlieffen, and in the final discussion of that game he said: "The situation upon which this war-game was based is the same as that already presented for months, by 'France Militaire,' later on by 'Matin' and now in all newspapers. That means a war against England, France and Russia."[4]

During his retirement Schlieffen continued his military and political studies, and in his famous article "On the War in Present Times" reached the conclusion that "jealous" England was the ringleader of the anti-German coalition. "Schlieffen was convinced," wrote his son-in-law to von Freytag-Loringhoven on 5 May 1924, "that the Kaiser, the Chancellor (both Bülow and Bethmann), the Ministry of State, the Foreign Office and the Reichstag, were completely struck with blindness about the danger of the English encirclement and its consequences, the near-imminent World War."[5] A letter of 13 December 1911, obviously written to Freytag-Loringhoven, sheds light on Schlieffen's train of thought with regard to England. The gist of it was that England had not only been afraid of the increased and strengthened German fleet, but also of French and Russian ambitions for colonial expansion. However, it had managed to subjugate France at Fashoda and Russia had suffered defeat in Manchuria. It became also obvious that Italy, despite being a member of the Triple Alliance, would in case of war join the anti-German Entente (because of its rivalry with Austria). There remained only the danger presented by Germany. Although the Morocco crisis had provided an opportunity to solve this problem by force of arms, this chance could not be exploited because the Royal Navy as well as the British Army was not in a state of battle-readiness. Schlieffen concluded, however, that the reshuffle in British top appointments "will soon restore the Navy to its battle-readiness." War with England seemed therefore unavoidable.[6]

This new insight concerning the Anglo-German relationship is also expressed in the 1912 version of the Schlieffen Plan:

The power and prestige of the German Army proved their worth in 1905 and 1909. Neither France nor Russia was willing to take up arms, once Germany left no doubt about her determination to fight back. This favorable state of affairs underwent a change in 1911.[7] German resolution was paralyzed by England's threat to come to the assistance of France with 100,000 men. In 1911 England would have yielded before Germany's manifest intention of using the army if necessary, as France had done in 1905 and Russia in 1909. But on this occasion it was Germany who yielded, and so the spell was broken which had so far made her army seem invincible.[8]

Thus besides the traditional archenemy France, England was ranked top among Germany's adversaries. "It is to be hoped," Schlieffen continued in his memorandum of December 1912, "that England's will may not be decisive for ever, and that Germany will one day regain the position of power necessary to her economic prosperity. Without a war this will scarcely be possible."

Since the younger Moltke adhered to the Schlieffen Plan, it is no wonder that as he consented to the violation of Belgium's neutrality, he was firmly convinced that a clash with a British Expeditionary Force was inevitable. This he laid down in his memorandum of December 1912.[9] It was his conviction that unless Great Britain joined a formal alliance with Germany, the latter could not waive the only chance of quick success in the West (by means of marching through Belgium). In a memorandum identified by German historian W. Elze as having been prepared in 1913, Moltke said:

A violation of Belgian neutrality will result in England's enmity. It is a question of life and death for England to prevent a German foothold on the opposite coast of the Channel, which would hold the possibility of the latter gaining further maritime strength and endangering the island state more, and would be liable to tie down permanently all English forces and prevent England from exercising its world domination. Germany could promise as solemnly and as convincingly as possible that she would evacuate Belgium voluntarily, even after a successful campaign over France, and in England nobody would believe in such a promise. The point whether Germany, for the sake of English neutrality, should refrain from an advance through Belgium, might have been worthy of consideration, had not England left no doubt that she will participate in the war on our enemies' side, whether we march through Belgium or not.[10]

The same idea was posited by Wilhelm Groener in his memoirs:

At the present time I have a conviction as firm as a rock, that the British, even without our violation of Belgian neutrality, would have appeared on the battlefield, albeit perhaps a few days or weeks later. It may be admitted that our step provided those cabinet-members, inclined towards the Entente—especially Sir Edward Grey—with a suitable slogan. But there is no doubt that they would have found another; at worst they would have resorted again to the threatened European balance of power.[11]

After Moltke's dismissal, following the retreat from the Marne, he surveyed, in November 1914, the events of the first month and a half of war and concluded that all previous diplomatic attempts to woo England had been a vain hope right from the beginning, owing to the latter's selfish policy of interest.[12]

Similar ideas were expressed by Grand Admiral Alfred von Tirpitz (1849–1930) in a memorandum on the conduct of war at sea, dated 25 January 1915:

"The innermost reason for the present European war, lies in England's desire to bend down her strongest competitor on the European continent, if possible by political measures and, should a favorable occasion emerge, by means of war. If one condenses that idea into a single geographical notion, then the motive for war lies in the City of London."[13] In his memoirs Tirpitz held to Schlieffen's ringleader thesis regarding England and said: "Who was the major opponent? In my opinion, doubtlessly the one who possessed the biggest resources and the most comprehensive will for war. London was always the political brain of the Entente; she now became, on an ever increasing scale, the military brain, too."[14]

Schlieffen's reasoning of England's enmity had set the fashion for all his successors. General von Falkenhayn, the so-called Second OHL, maintained in his famous "Christmas Memorandum" of 1915[15] that England's aim was "the permanent elimination of what seems to her the most dangerous rival." And Ludendorff stated in his memoirs that

England has watched our economic boom, our cheap labor and iron diligence with uneasiness. Germany was the strongest power on land in Europe as well. She also possessed a good and developing navy. That made England fear for her world domination. The Anglo-Saxons felt that their habit of mastery was endangered. The English government assembled the Navy, whose center of gravity only a little while ago was in the Mediterranean, in the North Sea, and the Channel. Lloyd George's (1863–1945) menacing speech of 21 July, 1911, threw a glaring flashlight on England's intentions, which she had otherwise so skilfully disguised.[16]

It is therefore obvious that Great Britain's apparent hostility toward Germany became an axiomatic component of the way Germany's soldiers judged the military-political situation. Consequently, they had to consider how to handle this delicate situation.

HOW TO DEAL WITH A BRITISH INTERVENTION AGAINST GERMANY ON THE CONTINENT?

In 1905, at the time Schlieffen was designing his plan, he was apparently resigned to the prospect of British adherence to the Franco-Russian cause. However, he obviously thought that Great Britain could send only a token force to the Continent. Moreover, he also assumed that the transfer of the B.E.F. would require a considerable period of time: "If in a Franco-German war, the English plan to land a force of 100,000 men or more in Antwerp, they can hardly do so in the first days of mobilization. No matter how well they prepare the assembly of their three army corps, their army organization and defense system present so many difficulties, that their sudden appearance within the great Belgian fortress is almost inconceivable."[17]

During a discussion about fortifications on 23 December 1904 with the Chief of General Staff and von Freytag-Loringhoven, at that time head of the Historical

Branch of the German General Staff, Schlieffen estimated the value of Antwerp's defenses with special reference to a possible landing there of British forces (allied with France!). However, on the same occasion he accepted v. Freytag's opinion of the low quality of the British Army, an impression based on its performance during the Boer War. Schlieffen very much enjoyed v. Freytag's suggestion of the desirability of punishing England, should it instigate the war, by driving its forces helter-skelter into the sea.[18]

In the final discussion of his last war game in December 1905 Schlieffen embarked on the possibilities for an intervention of a British force on the Continent. "It is not the most important, but the most interesting question," he said, "in which way England will participate in the war, and whether her army, as some people assume, will land in Jutland, where it may feel itself rather lonely, or, as others pretend to know, in a Channel port, in order to play the unenviable role of auxiliary troops."[19] As a matter of fact, in this particular war game the assumption was that the British would get ashore at Dunkirk and Calais.

In the memorandum of February 1906, however, the following British possibilities were surveyed: The first—an English landing at Antwerp ("a not unfounded prospect"). The second possibility credited the English with the intention of landing at Esbjerg. This possibility might be carried out at two different stages: "Sometimes the supposed plan is to appear at a very early stage on the Jutland Coast, some times it is to delay the enterprise until the German and French forces are already engaged in battle. Advantage is to be taken of Germany's completely denuded state, for a march on Berlin, possibly with the assistance of some French corps."[20]

Freiherr von Falkenhausen had openly discussed in his book *The Great War in Present Times*, published in 1909, a British invasion of Holland.[21] Von Schlieffen considered the same possibility as he labored on the alteration of his plan. At the end of 1912 he reached the conclusion that his right wing must march through Dutch territory as well. He then took into account the chance of a British landing in Holland, which would threaten the German flank.

Schlieffen intended to involve the B.E.F. in the destruction of the French Army from the very beginning. The strong and deep German right wing, the *bataillon carré*, could cope with an English landing without losing too much of its momentum. Even in 1920, after the disastrous defeat of Germany, Wilhelm Groener still believed in the possibility of this achievement: "Should, on its way, the "*bataillon carré*" of the right wing encounter the English, landed at the Flemish coast, or the French, then the wheeling will come to a temporary stop, the English will be beaten and rendered harmless,[22] and then 'quick march!' again."[23] It seems so easy that one gets the impression of a military march-past, with bands and flying colors, instead of a bloody war.

In case of a British landing in Antwerp ("a not unlikely prospect"), "they will be shut up there, together with the Belgians. They will be securely billeted in the fortress, much better than on their island, where they are a serious threat and a standing menace to the Germans."[24] This cynical remark is apparently the source of the widespread slogan, prevalent in German military circles, that a British landing corps would be "arrested by gendarmes."

There was a firm belief, neglecting, however, historical lessons, that the complete defeat of France would induce Britain to make peace. Or, as Wilhelm Groener defined it: "Were the French army decisively beaten and pushed against its eastern defenses and into the Jura, were Paris and the Channel ports in our possession, then we would have attained the military position needed to negotiate a peace with England. Should the latter decline this offer, one could regard the situation in the West with unconcern and turn, for the next decisive blow, to the East."[25] In 1938 Groener still maintained that in 1914 it had been feasible to defeat England on French soil,[26] that a B.E.F. involved in a general French defeat and a German occupation of the channel ports would have prevented any further British intervention on the Continent. A repetition of Wellington's tactics in Portugal (Torres Vedras, 1810) seemed to be out of the question, or at least, not of any decisive influence. On the other hand the possession of the channel ports was regarded as a constant and unbearable threat for Great Britain.[27] In any case Schlieffen and his disciples regarded the strict fulfillment of the Schlieffen Plan as the best answer to any English participation in the pending war.

Even after the war many distinguished German experts maintained that the swift overthrow of France would have determined England's fate, too, at a stage when it was not yet able to levy its conscription army. England would simply have missed the boat.[28] And would not the small British regular army have raised the cry of anguish, "To the ships!" after a French defeat at the Marne or the Seine, and desert its ally?[29]

The younger Moltke, who was more a man of the world than old Schlieffen— simply because of the more cosmopolitan connections of the Moltke family— tried to shift the war against "perfidious Albion" into a new dimension: undermining the empire. As early as 2 August 1914 Moltke outlined to the German Chancellor the extent of German attempts at subversion: From the Turkish base, subversive work should be started inside India, Egypt, and Persia, and the South African dominions should be stirred up. Again, on 5 August, Moltke referred to his previous suggestions of 2 August and cherished the idea of inciting the United States toward a naval action against England, hinting that Canada could serve as the reward of victory.[30] Pipe dreams, of course, whose execution could have been unpleasant for the British Empire.

However, looking back after his dismissal, Moltke blamed his failure to overrun France at the first onset on the quick assistance England rendered to France.[31] Evidently he still held to Schlieffen's opinion of 1906 that the British could not easily land a force in the first days of mobilization. Nevertheless, he differed from Schlieffen on a basic issue—again as the result of his broader political understanding: He believed that England would carry on fighting even after a French and Russian defeat.[32] That opinion was shared by Moltke's successor, von Falkenhayn, who considered as a grave mistake the widespread view among

German soldiers and politicians that a decisive defeat of Russia would persuade the Western powers to give in and come to terms with Germany.[33]

Germany's sailors, however, headed by Grand Admiral von Tirpitz, charged the General Staff of the Army with having staked everything on France's defeat, having ignored the English menace, and not having grasped what really mattered. The concept of a quick victory over France had led to the erroneous conviction that the destruction of France would bring England to terms. Admiral Tirpitz wanted interference with the British lines of communications, and the early seizure of Calais. After all, the English being deprived of access to the channel ports would be forced to shift the crossing of troops and supplies to Cherbourg and Brest, viz., instead of an easy traversing of mere inland waters, the crossing of the open Atlantic. Tirpitz claimed that neither von Moltke nor von Falkenhayn would listen to him.[34] This view is supported by an Englishman, Liddell Hart, who ridiculed the Germans for ignoring the importance of the seizure of the channel ports, which lay at their mercy during the period of the Allied armies' retreat. "A month later," he maintained, "the Germans were to sacrifice tens of thousands of their men . . . to gain what they could have secured initially without cost."[35]

However, the battle in Flanders in 1914 was aimed at the possession of the channel ports and was regarded by von Falkenhayn, at that time, as the most effective way of interfering with the British conduct of war. Nevertheless, the moves of the parties involved resulted in the stalemate of trench warfare.

On Christmas Eve, 1915, v. Falkenhayn prepared a memorandum, reviewing the war and outlining suggestions for the further conduct of it. A considerable part of this document dealt with England and the way in which it might be forced to surrender. He saw in the fact that England had introduced compulsory military service proof that it was severely shaken. But it had not yet given up hope to attain its end, the permanent elimination of its most dangerous rival—Germany. Falkenhayn examined the various ways of encountering England. One was, of course, an attempt to defeat England on land. But he ruled out any prospect of landing on the British Isles. There remained the continental theaters of war in Europe and the Middle East. Eliminating one by one he reached the conclusion that however desirable it would be to deliver a decisive blow at England on French soil, it could not be recommended. Since for England the campaign with its own troops on the European continent was but a "sideshow," Falkenhayn considered it the best course to defeat its allies, the French, Russian, and Italian Armies, and to put them out of the war. This might convince England to give up. Although even that was not sure, he concluded it "a strong probability."[36]

General Moser, on the other hand, thought it possible, even in 1915, to split open the allied front, in the section Bapaume–Arras–Lens, and to achieve a break-through right along the seam between the French and British Armies, in order to push the British, who would lack space for maneuver, into the sea, to seize the fortresses Calais, Dunkirk, and Boulogne, and to regain a war of movement against the denuded French left wing.[37] At the end of 1917 similar ideas were again under review. The idea underlying these plans was the utilization of Clausewitz' concept of selecting a thrusting line against a coalition, namely, the achievement of a political aim—in this particular case the withdrawal of England from the war—by means of physically dividing the partners of the alliance.[38]

Despite such ideas, and despite his fine political sense, Falkenhayn decided on the fateful battle of Verdun in order to drain French power.[39]

Field Marshal von Hindenburg succeeded von Falkenhayn as Chief of General Staff on 29 August 1916, at a time of high crisis: The fighting at Verdun was in a state of deadlock, the Germans had not reached any strategic objective; the remainder of the German front in the West had narrowly escaped penetration and disintegration in the desperate battle of the Somme; the Austrians were severely shaken by Brusilov's great offensive; Rumania had joined the Allies two days before, declared war on Austria-Hungary, and started an invasion of Transylvania. Hindenburg was accompanied, as in all his previous appointments, by General Ludendorff, who got the new title of First Quartermaster-General and was in fact the "strong man," the real policy- and decision-maker. However, a fortunate sequence of events—the quick conquest of Rumania (27 September 1916–8 January 1917) by v. Falkenhayn, the outbreak of the Russian Revolution (November 1917), the collapse of Italy in the twelfth battle of the Isonzo (24 October–26 December 1917)—created for the first time a situation that enabled the Germans to gain superiority in numbers on the western front. This superiority, of course, would be for a limited period only, in view of the expected arrival of American forces in France, as a result of the official American declaration of war on 6 April 1917, following the commencement of unrestricted submarine warfare by Germany on 1 February 1917.

The problem was, what should be done to fully utilize this temporary superiority? An offensive in Italy was ruled out because it would not force the main Allied powers to give up. The question was, therefore, against whom should the main blow be delivered: the French or the English? With regard to the English, it was obvious that the European continent was no longer a "sideshow," as Falkenhayn had defined it, but had turned into a major theater of war.

In November 1917 Colonel Bauer of the Operations Branch in General Headquarters prepared a memorandum, "On the Continuation of the War 1917–1918,"[40] and reached the conclusion that even if Russia and Italy should leave the war, France, England, and the United States would carry on, nourishing the hope that Germany would collapse at the home front or in the West. He therefore maintained that "from a political viewpoint, it is important to get hold of the English. Their collapse will drag down America and France, whereas that would not happen in the opposite case." "I therefore suggest, for political reasons, that the blow be delivered against the English, who are the soul of this war."[41] Bauer's actual proposal was a break-through along the seam between the French and British forces, the establishment of a defensive front against the French wing, and "rolling up"[42] the English front to the north, while aiming at the general direction of Boulogne–Calais, i.e., the channel coast. He rejected a frontal attack on the extreme right along the sea-shore because he was afraid that it might only push the English back and not defeat them decisively.

Among the German Army group commanders who were asked by OHL to forward their suggestions for future operations, Crown Prince Rupprecht suggested an offensive against the English, whereas the German Crown Prince favored an assault against the French at Verdun. At a conference of the Chiefs of Staff of the Army Groups, presided over by Ludendorff on 11 November 1917, the latter laid down as one of the guiding principles for a future operation that "we must beat the English."[43] And he became so excited about the prospect of hitting at the English that at the end of December 1917 he told Crown Prince Rupprecht that he was afraid the British might spoil the whole affair by forwarding a peace offer, which Germany could not refuse for reasons of domestic policy.[44] It is obvious that not the achievement of peace, but the delivery of a blow against Great Britain became an end in itself.[45] However, after having squandered the last hope of a German success, during the fruitless offensives in spring 1918, Ludendorff as the *ultima ratio* clung to the scanty hope that, as in Russia, a revolution in London might rush to Germany's aid.[46]

Hindenburg, Ludendorff's formal superior, was a believer in the channel-coast concept and in his memoirs expressed the opinion that had the Germans reached the channel shore, they would have directly touched on the main life artery of England.

Max Hoffmann looked at the problem on more political lines than his companions in arms, although he, too, tried to evade the ultimate consequences of a political approach. "We cannot defeat England," he wrote on 3 April 1915, "at least not yet. I shall live to see it, but not in this war [sic!]. Therefore, in my opinion, we ought to try to make terms with England. She will negotiate—she is hard hit at many points: heavy losses, especially of officers, domestic troubles (the effect of our U-boats have, incidentally, been much over-estimated), Egypt, the Sudan, India, the Dardanelles and especially Japan!" The result of a mutual agreement, after the restoration of Belgium ("for England cannot allow a German Antwerp—against that she must fight to her last penny"), according to Hoffmann would be: "England would then retain Calais and Boulogne and would have, of course, to maintain close relations with us, in order to protect herself against her former Allies. I should regard this as a possible basis for negotiations. It is, of course, possible that I am mistaken." In this case even Hoffman pinned his hopes on wishful thinking: "We may have a piece of luck, such as Turkish successes against Egypt, or a revolt in India, or else an earthquake, that may improve our situation."[47] The Bavarian Crown Prince had arguments with Ludendorff in May 1918 and was prepared to restore Belgium in order to remove the bone of contention, which was blocking an understanding with Great Britain. Ludendorff was, of course, opposed to any idea of giving Belgium away. Rupprecht then maintained that the only way to keep Belgium in German possession was the complete destruction of England, a possibility in which he hardly believed.[48]

There were, of course, other, less diplomatic suggestions on how to deal with England. Admiral von Tirpitz recommended the installation of heavy artillery on Cape Gris-Nez (for which the seizure of Calais was a *conditio sine qua non!*), and thus the interruption of traffic in the channel, the disturbance of movement on the Thames, and even the bombardment of London. A consistent bombardment of London, he held, would lead to psychological and economic consequences.[49] Less conventional was a measure suggested by Hoffmann. "Nobody will accept my radical treatment," he wrote to his wife in a letter of 3 October 1915, "of spreading plague germs over Paris and London by means of air bombs. Those chaps are just too stupid!"[50]

On the other hand, what about a German invasion of the British Isles that might have suggested itself? Liddell Hart maintained that the mere possibility of a landing, or even a feint, might have "sufficed to detain a considerable part of Britain's military strength."[51] But what was the German opinion?

ON INVASION OF THE BRITISH ISLES

First of all, it should be completely clear that Schlieffen had *never* considered any invasion of the British Isles by German forces. Not only is this solemnly confirmed by his son-in-law,[52] but also there is not the slightest hint in his voluminous writings of such an intention. On the contrary, he had once (14 December 1897) attached a marginal note to a German naval memorandum, rejecting any possibility of an invasion of England. He maintained that even after a successful landing, the German Army could never achieve any decision over "the real adversary, the British Navy." The latter could be subjugated only in the event of the British government's being forced to give up and deliver its fleet (sic!).[53]

Nor did German military publicists of the period intend an invasion. The broad-minded Colmar von der Goltz wrote in 1899 that owing to the difficulty of transporting troops by sea, they will always be limited, and therefore ill-adapted for a rapid and distant advance from the coast. Landings will never have any prospect of great success. The military organization of modern states and the network of means of communications are so developed that it will always be possible to assemble a vastly superior force against the corps landed. The only exception to this is if the landed troops at once receive reinforcements, owing to popular rising.[54]

Clausewitz had already observed that "one can only justify a landing in force if one can count on the support of the area against its government."[55] That this was not the case regarding England was stated by von Freytag-Loringhoven, Schlieffen's devoted disciple, who dealt with the problem in 1911 under the disguise of an investigation into Napoleon's attempt to invade England. When an invasion may not reckon on local support against the government, Freytag had another warning from Clausewitz' teaching ready: "Enemy forces that would otherwise be dormant are consequently in some degree brought to life. This will be very marked if the enemy's war plans have included militia and arms are available for distribution to the populace."[56] At that point von Freytag-Lor-inghoven felt compelled to provide a footnote to the quotation: "As is now the case in Great Britain in a quite extended manner." Clausewitz' warning finished as follows: "New means of resistance are created—means that border on guerilla warfare and can easily bring it about."[57] Taking up Clausewitz' idea, von Frey-tag-Loringhoven maintained that nowadays any country of culture, supported by the effect of modern weapons and improved communications, is capable of successfully repulsing an invasion from the sea. It is obvious that the number of troops that may land will always be relatively small. Even 100,000 men landed could hardly prevail over a people's war. Circumstances were quite different at Napoleon's time: There were no railways, and no lorry columns for shifting troops quickly to the endangered beachhead; nor were there quick-firing rifles and guns capable of stopping the invader. Napoleon might have succeeded in an invasion enterprise; nevertheless, he hesitated to launch his transport flotilla unsupported by an adequate battle fleet.[58] The conclusions to be drawn for Germany from this insight were obvious.[59]

However, Falkenhayn, when reporting the reasons for the "race to the sea," had in mind not only a flanking maneuver, but also the acquisition of the French channel ports in order to strangle English traffic there and, as he said in his memoirs, "to take hold of the island itself."[60] If that were not just a slip of the pen or tongue, then unfortunately for the purposes of investigation, he did not mention how he intended to tackle that task! Neither did his Imperial master, when he exclaimed pathetically on 16 September 1914: "Those chaps [i.e., the English] must be forced to their knees!"[61] Admiral Georg Alexander von Müller, who recorded this utterance in his diary, added dryly: "The Kaiser didn't say how."[62]

If the Kaiser and his military advisors abstained from a landing on British soil, then probably nobody in Germany wanted such an enterprise. But why had they created that expensive and provocative navy?

THE TASK OF THE GERMAN NAVY

Remembering Schlieffen's idea of war against England, it is no wonder that Schlieffen never allotted any task to the German Navy. "The official intercourse with the Navy was limited only to the most extreme necessities," recalled v. Hahnke. "Operative problems regarding the war were, as far as I know, never aired by v. Schlieffen with the Navy on his own initiative. . . . In none of his studies, works, exercises or measures had he ever discussed any co-operation of the Army and the Navy."[63] He had said that "Germany's fate will not be decided on the seas." Nevertheless, as early as 19 April 1898 Schlieffen, in a letter to his Supreme War Lord, Wilhelm II, had defined the functions to be performed by the German Navy, namely, protection of the coast, transport of troops over sea, and disembarkation of the heavy artillery of the army. Joint exercises in order to evolve a common technique of embarking and disembarking and of storage of various types of weapons on board, seemed to him to be more essential "than the mutual exchange of information."[64] Colonel Bauer's notorious remark that Schlieffen had designed a plan for war on land, and it was therefore not his business to deal with the political, maritime, and economic aspects[65] is unacceptable and overstresses professional perfectionism. But a maritime orientation was outside the traditional scope of the German General Staff. In any case German soldiers had written off any prospect of German major naval actions. Von Falkenhausen, in his book *The Great War in Present Times*, dealt with the situation of the "blue" (viz., German) fleet. The movement of that fleet was reduced to a minimum by the enemy's naval superiority, estimated to be at least 2:1. The "blue" navy was therefore compelled to restrict its actions to mere torpedo-boat and submarine raids. Had it, despite this, dared to attempt a major naval battle and suffered a defeat, it was liable to leave the "blue" coast open to attack and render it defenseless.[66] Freytag-Loringhoven explained the attitude of the German General Staff by saying that "a continental Power with lengthy frontiers on land, facing many neighbors, will always strive for the center of gravity of its war preparations being directed at its land forces."[67]

Such an attitude, however, was one of the reasons the German High Seas Fleet was never taken into account as a means of intercepting or harassing the British land forces, which had to cross the channel, as Rupprecht so rightly expected.[68] Both services failed to talk together or plan together. At all events, naval experts believe that such an action might have been the only chance for the German Navy to contribute on its behalf to the common war effort.[69] Any delay to the B.E.F. during August 1914 might have had serious consequences for the then hard-pressed French Army.

The other reason for holding back the German Navy also involved England. The politicians thought it vital to preserve the navy until the end of the war, for its bargaining value in future peace negotiations with England. An intact and threatening High Seas Fleet would exert a tremendous pressure on a war-weary Great Britain longing for peace, so those circles maintained.[70]

The main reason for Schlieffen's misconception of maritime problems was rooted in a complete underestimation of the meaning of sea power. He strove after a solution to the problem of war on two fronts. He took into account the participation of Great Britain, but he focused his view solely on the British Army, reinforcing the French Army in France and Belgium. The potential danger of British sea power did not enter his mind. He believed that England could be forced to give up, without endangering the British Isles and curbing the Royal Navy. After all, would the defeat of France, and with it the defeat of the B.E.F., or the latter's withdrawal across the channel, ultimately mean that Great Britain must quit the war? Would not German operations against Russia be gravely handicapped by possible naval attacks on German commerce, or merely by a constant threat of a renewed invasion in France? Now, as we have the knowledge of the Second World War, these questions cannot simply be written off. Schlieffen had not grasped the consequences of sea power opposing land power, and the special features of the Anglo-Saxon people's character that were to be deduced from these consequences. He therefore did not pay attention to what Hans Delbrück had tried to explain in connection with the Punic War, when he emphasized the fact that Carthage was basically a land power, and was therefore finally outstripped and overwhelmed by Roman sea power, despite Hannibal's victories (including Cannae!) on land. Had Schlieffen not been so mesmerized by the battle of Cannae as his prototype of a future German war plan, he would have paid some attention to the problems of sea power, as they were embodied, at his time, in the very existence of the British Isles and the British Empire.

Despite all these reasons for the strange relationship between army and navy, one is nevertheless surprised by the complete lack of cooperation during the battle of Flanders. The navy could have rendered useful service to von Falkenhayn's land forces. Von Tirpitz had at least underlined the vital importance of the German Navy for the Flemish coast by creating the Marine Corps from redundant navy personnel and having it posted there.[71] In his memorandum of 25 January 1915 von Tirpitz suggested lines of action for all branches of the German Navy: Taking into account the tremendous superiority of the Royal Navy, he saw no likelihood of success against its main body. One has therefore to be satisfied with partial successes by means of small-scale warfare (Kleinkrieg) in order to render an equalizing of forces. But even that was doubtful. However, "the effect of a partial success lies not only in the possible equalizing of forces, but particularly in England's loss of prestige." By comparing the respective possibilities of both hostile fleets, von Tirpitz sketched the different modes of action for the German Navy as a whole:

1. Attacks of aircraft exclusively on London, especially on the docks and warehouses in the city.

2. The submarine blockade.

3. The energetic execution of military submarine and torpedo-boat warfare, with mines set against the Thames from Zeebrugge and Ostend under the direction of the Commanding Admiral of the Marine Corps.

4. The immediate opening of cruiser warfare in the Atlantic.[72]

The memorandum finished with the dramatic appeal: "The present situation which faces Germany imperiously demands action by the Navy."

However, von Falkenhayn would only resort to unrestricted submarine warfare in order to weaken Britain's power. Moreover, he regarded this as a necessary complement to the operation against Verdun. He believed in the Admiralty's promise that England, by means of unrestricted submarine warfare, could be so weakened that it would give up in a few weeks' time. Thinking in terms of a quick termination of the war, he even accepted the risk of an irritated United States, who could become a belligerent nation in the Allied camp.[73]

W. Groener, despite his own opposition to unrestricted submarine war, defined this kind of warfare "as the transfer of Schlieffen's thoughts to the sea: the attack deep into the rear of the enemy. It was a logical enlargement of the Cannae-idea."[74] Even the responsibility for this new trend in brutal human mangling is laid against Schlieffen!

A consistent attitude toward England runs through every part of German military thinking, from the planning phase of the First World War right up to the last desperate offensives in spring and summer 1918. Its most striking feature is the complete lack of a maritime outlook.[75] It was, of course, the first time in centuries that German strategists had to deal with a hostile Great Britain, and were also compelled to think in terms of a major war outside the continental boundaries. Moreover, Clausewitz' basic work *On War* had not provided any guidance for such an occasion. Naval warfare was outside its scope.[76]

Clausewitz confined himself explicitly to war on land, and he had even gathered some experience of the British way of waging war. In 1809 he expected a British landing in order to assist Austria, and was surprised that the English had gone ashore at the Dutch island of Walcheren. He regarded this step as having been undertaken at the wrong spot. This was true from the viewpoint of German patriots, but it was no doubt right in the framework of a strategic concept, serving the political aims of the British Isles. Further lessons could be learned from Wellington's conduct of the war against Napoleon. The whole difference between insular and continental strategy was embodied in the personalities of Wellington and Blücher. One may find some traces of the impression Clausewitz received on that occasion in his "Plan of War Designed to Lead to the Total Defeat of the Enemy," being Chapter 9, Book VIII of *On War*. Sketching a plan for a war in case of renewed French aggression, he said that France must be extremely sensitive about its Atlantic coast and keep there forces to defend it. If England has but 20,000 to 30,000 landing troops available to threaten France, they might immobilize two or three times as many French.[77] Nevertheless, the main decision would be reached by the continental powers, and the British landing corps was regarded as fulfilling a secondary mission only and success of the main offensive would by no means depend on it.[78] There is no other advice offered by Clausewitz on this issue.

Despite the widespread assumption that the ignorance of the problems presented by Great Britain and British sea power was Schlieffen's fault—which is, in fact, true—the roots of that failure are much deeper. There can be no doubt that the full weight of responsibility must be put on Clausewitz' shoulders. Indeed, unawareness of that vital sphere of sea power in global military relations (although an explanation may be found in Germany's history) is the principle deficiency of Clausewitz' almost faultless theoretical edifice. Against this background one ought to be more lenient in judging Schlieffen on that point.

This traditional, and fundamental, German disregard of maritime problems will, however, repeat itself and reach tremendous dimensions in the Second World War.

NOTES

1. *Vide* chapter 4, under "Mobilization Day."
2. BHA—Rep. 92 W. v. Hahnke, Generalmajor-Ic-Bl., Nr. 116/26, "Die militär-politische Einstellung des Graf Schlieffen zu England."
3. *Ibid.*, pp. 5–6. Schlieffen himself, according to v. Hahnke, regarded the invitation of King Edward VII (1841–1910) and the British Fleet to the German naval demonstrations in Kiel in July 1904 as a provocative step.
4. *Ibid.*, pp. 8–9. One may also assume that it was at this time that the German intelligence branch sensed some kind of cooperation between the General Staffs of France and England.
5. BHA—Rep. 92, W. v. Hahnke, Nr. 6–12.
6. BHA—Rep. 92, GFM A. v. Schlieffen, Nr. 6. The opinions about England expressed by Schlieffen in this letter are completely identical with those of Admiral A. v. Tirpitz in his book *Erinnerungen*, Leipzig, 1919, chapter 15, "England und die deutsche Flotte."
7. That is, the "Second Morocco Crisis" (June–Nov. 1911).
8. Gerhard Ritter, *The Schlieffen Plan*, London, 1948, p. 171.
9. Printed in E. Ludendorff, *Urkunden der Obersten Heeresleitung*, Berlin, 1922, pp. 54–55.
10. Printed in W. Elze, *Tannenberg*, Breslau, 1927, pp. 157 ff. The title of this memorandum reads: "Verhalten Deutschlands in einem Dreibundkriege."
11. Wilhelm Groener, *Lebenserinnerungen*, Göttingen, 1957, pp. 148–149.
12. Generaloberst Helmuth v. Moltke, *Erinnerungen, Briefe, Dokumente, 1877–1916*, Stuttgart, 1922, pp. 10–11. This passage strongly echoes Schlieffen's conception of England in his essay "On War in Present Times": "This hatred of a formerly despised rival, can neither be tempered by assurance of sincere friendship and cordiality, nor aggravated by provocative language. It is not the emotions but questions of debit and credit which determine the level of resentment." Generalfeldmarschall Graf Alfred v. Schlieffen, *Cannae*, Berlin, 1936, p. 283.
13. The memorandum is printed in Admiral Georg Alexander von Müller (ed. Walter Görlitz), *Regierte der Kaiser?* Göttingen, 1959, pp. 84–85.
14. A. v. Tirpitz, *op. cit.*, p. 253.
15. *Vide* chapter 9.
16. E. Ludendorff, *Meine Kriegserinnerungen 1914–1918*, Berlin, 1919, p. 20.
17. G. Ritter, *op. cit.*, p. 161.
18. BHA—Rep. 92, GFM A. v. Schlieffen, Nr. 6. "Gespräche mit dem Chef des Generalstabes der Armee Exz. Graf v. Schlieffen bei Gelegenheit des Vortrages und bei sonstigen Anlässen. Briefe des Feldmarschalls und Sonstiges. Ende 1904 begonnen."
19. BHA—Rep. 92, W. v. Hahnke, Ic-Bl., Nr. 116/26, *op. cit.*, pp. 9–10.
20. G. Ritter, *op. cit.*, p. 163.
21. Freiherr von Falkenhausen, *Der grosse Krieg der Jetztzeit*, Berlin, 1909, pp. 11–12.

22. In the original text "unschädlich machen," a term that became, in the Hitler era, synonymous with physical extermination.

23. Wilhelm Groener, "Der Weltkrieg und seine Probleme, Rückschau und Ausblick," *Preussische Jahrbücher*, Schriftenreihe Nr. 1, Berlin, 1920, p. 18.

24. Quoted in G. Ritter, *op. cit.*, p. 162.

25. Wilhelm Groener, *Das Testament des Grafen Schlieffen*, Berlin, 1927, p. 217.

26. *Vide* Groener's letter of 30 Dec. 1938 to Mrs. v. Hahnke (Schlieffen's daughter). BHA—Rep. 92, W. v. Hahnke, Nr. 33/34.

27. Cf. Wolfgang Foerster, *Graf Schlieffen und der Weltkrieg*, 2d rev. ed., Berlin, 1925, pp. 19–20; W. Foerster, *Aus der Gedankenwerkstatt des Deutschen Generalstabes*, Berlin, 1938, p. 31. In this context it may be of interest that on 24 April 1936 at the Wehrmachtakademie a syndicate of three senior staff officers presented lessons derived from the First World War and reached the conclusion that "Germany in possession of the French Coast and the economic area should not be afraid of England." *Vide* BA/MA—W10–1/14, p. 68.

28. Cf. Friedrich von Bernhardi, *Vom Kriege der Zukunft*, Berlin, 1920, p. 146; E. Ludendorff, *Der totale Krieg*, München, 1935, p. 50; and Hermann v. Kuhl, *Der Weltkrieg 1914–1918*, Berlin, 1929, vol. 1, pp. 167–168.

29. Wilhelm Müller-Loebnitz, *Die Führung im Marne-Feldzug 1914*, Berlin, 1939, pp. 111–112. Müller-Loebnitz, however, had second thoughts and added a few lines later that the British sense of honor might have ruled out leaving the French in the lurch.

30. *Deutsche Dokumente*, III, Nr. 662, Moltke an Auswärtiges Amt and DD, IV, Nr. 876, Moltke an AA, quoted in Fritz Fischer, *Griff nach der Weltmacht*, Düsseldorf, 1961, pp. 93–94.

31. Generaloberst H. v. Moltke, *op. cit.*, p. 18.

32. Cf. H. v. Kuhl, *op. cit.*, vol. 1, p. 165.

33. E. v. Falkenhayn, *Die Oberste Heeresleitung 1914–1916 in ihren Wichtigsten Entschliessungen*, Berlin, 1920, p. 47.

34. A. v. Tirpitz, *op. cit.*, pp. 243, 251.

35. Liddell Hart, *A History of the World War 1914–1918*, London, 1934, pp. 89–90.

36. E. v. Falkenhayn, *op. cit.*, pp. 177 ff. For Falkenhayn's "Christmas Memorandum," *vide* chapter 9.

37. Cf. H. v. Kuhl, *op. cit.*, vol. 1, p. 123. F. v. Lossberg, the hero of all German defensive battles in the West, then being Deputy Chief of Operations, forwarded a memorandum in 1915, suggesting the same approach. F. v. Lossberg, *Meine Tätigkeit im Weltkrieg 1914–1918*, Berlin, 1939, pp. 137–139.

38. *Vide* chapter 1, under "The Center of Gravity."

39. *Vide* chapter 9.

40. BA/MA, Nachlass Bauer, Nr. 2. "Denkschrift über die Fortsetzung des Krieges 1917–1918."

41. *Ibid.*, p. 193 (p. 3 of the memorandum).

42. The German technical term is "aufrollen."

43. Hermann von Kuhl, *Enstehung, Durchführung und Zusammenbruch der Offensive von 1918*, Berlin, 1927, pp. 99–103. V. Kuhl was, at that time, Chief of Staff at "Army Group (Heeresgruppe) Crown Prince Rupprecht" and attended this conference; his account is therefore first-hand evidence.

44. Kronprinz Rupprecht von Bayern, *Mein Kriegstagebuch*, München, 1929, vol. 2, p. 303, entry of 20 Dec. 1917.

45. Rupprecht wrote in his diary on 20 May 1918 that "Ludendorff lacks any psychological understanding of foreign and domestic politics" (vol. 2, p. 399).

46. *Ibid.*, vol. 2, p. 394, entry of 4 May 1918.

47. Max Hoffmann, *War Diaries and Other Papers*, London, 1929, vol. 1, pp. 58–59.

48. Rupprecht, *op. cit.*, vol. 2, p. 399, entry of 20 May 1918.

49. A. v. Tirpitz, *op. cit.*, pp. 264–265.

50. BA/MA—HO8–37/1, p. 25.

51. B. H. Liddell Hart, *op. cit.*, pp. 73–74.

52. BHA—Rep. 92, W. v. Hahnke, Ic-Bl., Nr. 116/26, pp. 7, 11.

53. Cf. Dr. Friedrich-Christian Stahl, "Der Grosse Generalstab, seine Beziehungen zum Admiralstab und seine Gedanken zu den Operations-plänen der Marine," *Wehrkunde*, Jg. XII, H.1 (1963), p. 11.

54. Colmar Freiherr von der Goltz, *The Conduct of War*, London, 1899, pp. 281–282.

55. *On War*, VII, 20, p. 563.

56. *Ibid.*

57. *Ibid.*

58. That was Hitler's dilemma too.

59. Freiherr von Freytag-Loringhoven, *Krieg und Politik in der Neuzeit*, Berlin, 1911, pp. 119–122.

60. E. v. Falkenhayn, *op. cit.*, p. 23.

61. "Die Kerle sollen auf die Knie!"

62. Admiral von Müller (ed. W. Görlitz), *op. cit.*, p. 59.

63. BHA—Rep. 92, W. v. Hahnke, Ic-Bl., Nr. 116/26, p. 6. It seems to be obvious that this attitude was also a result of personal rivalry between Schlieffen, Chief of Staff of the Army, and Admiral v. Tirpitz, creator of the German Navy. Von Hahnke's letter of 16 April 1926 to W. Groener contains a clear indication: "Schlieffen did not like Tirpitz since the latter had diverted a considerable amount of the national income from the Army for naval purposes. Schlieffen regarded the battle fleet as needless. . . . Schlieffen blamed Tirpitz for fostering pacifism in the leading circles, and with Kaiser and Chancellor, since Tirpitz did not want war for the time being, because his Navy was not yet ready." BA/MA—HO8–46/38:1.

64. F-C. Stahl, *op. cit.*, p. 7.

65. M. Bauer, *Der Grosse Krieg in Feld und Heimat*, Tübingen, 1921, p. 42.

66. Frhr. v. Falkenhausen, *op. cit.*, pp. 172–173. It is interesting that von Falkenhayn was presented by the German Admiralty with the same reason for avoiding further combat, after the battle in Heligoland Bight. Cf. v. Falkenhayn, *op. cit.*, p. 15.

67. H. v. Freytag-Loringhoven, *op. cit.*, p. 270.

68. Rupprecht, *op. cit.*, vol. 1, p. 55, entry of 25 Aug. 1914: "Von der Tätigkeit der deutschen Flotte hören wir gar nichts. Sie sollte doch das Herüberkommen englischer Truppentransporte verhindern!"

69. An indication of this is provided by the naval engagement in Heligoland Bight, on 28 Aug. 1914, which cost the Germans the loss of three ships.

70. Cf. Kronprinz Wilhelm, *Meine Erinnerungen an Deutschlands Heldenkampf*, Berlin, 1923, pp. 93–94; Rupprecht, *op. cit.*, p. 122; Otto v. Moser, *Die obersten Gewalten im Weltkriege*, Stuttgart, 1931, p. 186; Otto v. Moser, *Das militärisch und politisch Wichtigste vom Weltkriege*, Stuttgart, 1926, pp. 36–37; and many other soldiers and

politicians in their memoirs. Of special value are v. Tirpitz' memoirs, *op. cit.*, pp. 265–266 and 398, and Admiral v. Müller (ed. W. Görlitz), *op. cit.*

71. Cf. v. Tirpitz, *op. cit.*, p. 264.

72. Printed in Admiral v. Müller (ed. W. Görlitz), *op. cit.*, pp. 84–85.

73. Cf. an entry in Hoffmann's diary on 28 Feb. 1916: "I have read a very interesting discussion of the U-boat war by v. Tirpitz. He guarantees that England will be forced to make peace in six months, if everything is torpedoed without regard to America and the Neutrals. If that is so, then he can go ahead, but we shall have to reckon with America as well." M. Hoffmann, *op. cit.*, vol. 1, p. 111.

74. W. Groener, "Der Weltkrieg und seine Probleme," *op. cit.*, p. 28.

75. As a matter of fact, German public opinion rejoiced at the victories of Leuthen, Königgrätz, Sedan, and Tannenberg as compared with Britain's remembrance of the Armada and Trafalgar.

76. There was, however, one admonisher in Germany's Paradise of Fools—Colmar von der Goltz. In 1883 he wrote in his *Nation in Arms* (p. 149): "States which, in the event of war, hold command of the sea, have greater facilities of utilizing their credit, than those whose harbors are immediately blockaded. The former are in a position to make use of foreign industry for arming and equipping new armies. . . . The command of the sea is, therefore, immediately productive of an access of strength, even though the fleets be not in a position to give direct support to the operations of the land forces." Even more explicitly, he stated: "It follows, that a State which means to be successful in defensive warfare, must have at its back, either the open frontiers of friendly powers, or a sea of which it holds command. A country not in this position can but only resist as long as its own industry is capable of supplying the needs of its country" (p. 269). In the fifth edition (1898) of the same book he remarked in the preface, with regard to the Spanish-American War of 1898: "It was only the extreme significance of maritime strength in relation to the world-power which was exemplified in a striking manner by the United States of North America, who, by one short and practically bloodless campaign, gained valuable colonial possessions after the destruction of two hostile fleets." A year later he wrote in his new book *The Conduct of War*: "The example of the American War of Secession, shows that, by blocking its communications with the sea, it is possible to absolutely starve out a large country which does not produce sufficient to feed its population, and *to render all its successes on land finally useless. The opposing forces being approximately equal, victory will in the end rest with the one which remains master of the seas*. It will exhaust the financial power of the other, by the destruction of its commerce and the stopping of all maritime traffic, and thus also undermine its military power" (p. 278, emphasis added). However, v. Freytag-Loringhoven warned in his book, *Krieg und Politik in der Neuzeit*, published in 1911, against Mahan's exaggerated importance of sea power (p. 270).

77. *On War*, VIII, p. 634.

78. *Ibid.*, p. 636.

7

Case 3: Tannenberg—A Modern Cannae?

THE MYTH

On 30 August 1914 more than 100,000 soldiers from General Samsonov's Second Russian Army marched into German P.O.W. camps. Samsonov, in desperation, shot himself on the field. Thus came to an end the battle of Tannenberg, second in fame only to its prototype, the battle of Cannae. Whereas almost every great campaign is embroidered with fantastic stories, there has rarely been a battle in which the mixture of reality and legend reached such a high degree.

For many years people inside Germany, and foreigners, have believed that the battle of Tannenberg had been planned by Hindenburg under Schlieffen's guidance some twenty-five years before.[1] As a matter of fact, this victory evolved gradually out of a grave crisis in which the Eighth German Army in East Prussia found itself.

SCHLIEFFEN'S PLAN FOR THE EAST

The genesis of this battle really begins with Schlieffen. While he was trying to solve the problem of a war on two fronts, he decided to defeat first the French (and probably the British) Army in the West, maintaining at the same time a mere defensive screen in the East. Moreover, he believed that the Austro-Hungarian Army could stem the Russian tide for a while, until the German forces, victorious in the West, were able to shift to the East.

The task Schlieffen had allotted to the small German Army was essentially a defensive one: the protection of the German eastern border. However, being the High Priest of the doctrine of annihilation, he maintained that this mission must be carried out in an offensive and aggressive manner. After studying the ground and his enemy's offensive possibilities thoroughly, he reached the conclusion that the chain of the Masurian Lakes would divide his opponents' approach into two eccentric directions, each column wheeling around the other end of the lakes' area. This separation, imposed by nature, would present the German commander with the opportunity of action on interior lines. He could strike hard and with full strength at whichever Russian Army came within reach first, and then turn against the other. Moreover, in order to strengthen the natural obstacle and make it impenetrable, all passages between the lakes had been blocked by fortifications. For fifteen years Schlieffen had taught this solution in war games, staff rides, operational studies, and exercises for staff officers.[2] If, however, for any reason, the enemy's onslaught were to be too overwhelming, then the Eighth Army would retreat temporarily beyond the Vistula until reinforcements from the West arrived. The preservation of this army for future actions was regarded as more vital than any temporary abandonment of eastern Prussia. Such situations appeared time and again in war games and staff rides. One should bear in mind that Schlieffen's assumption was based on a slow and cumbersome Russian mobilization and deployment, which would probably eliminate any real danger to East Prussian territory prior to a German victory in the West.

EAST PRUSSIA—1914

Unfortunately, here again, the reality of 1914 was very different from Schlieffen's suppositions. Not only had the Russians improved their mobilization procedures, but they had also preceded all other countries in proclaiming a state of mobilization, and had thus achieved a great advantage.[3] On the other hand a steady deterioration in fighting qualities and neglect of equipment made it more than doubtful whether the Austro-Hungarian Army would play its assigned role in the struggle to come, although v. Kuhl took comfort in the fact that Hannibal had won the battle of Cannae with auxiliaries of inferior value forming part of his army.[4]

The actual German plan of deployment in 1914 had allotted to the eastern front one division less than the number agreed on between von Moltke, the German Chief of General Staff, and General Conrad von Hoetzendorff, his Austrian counterpart, in 1909.[5] The result of this reduction was that General von Prittwitz marched out with only nine divisions (part of which were even reserve and territorial units). This caused Colonel (later General) Hoffmann, then First General Staff Officer of the Eighth Army, to exclaim in a letter to his wife that "if it should ever be made public with how few we were compelled to hold the East, it would be called the greatest impudence of history."[6]

Nevertheless, any purely defensive solution of the problem was ruled out not only by Schlieffen, but also by his successor, the younger Moltke.[7] After all, the forces at hand were too small for any efficient use in a defensive mission along the lengthy frontiers. Not only could such a thinly held position be broken through, but it could also be out-maneuvered and out-marched with great ease. However, as early as 1909 v. Moltke had reached the conclusion that the Russians would strive for an early success over the small German force, and invade German territory. In an oral conversation with Colonel-General von Prittwitz at the end of July 1914, he stressed that the Eighth Army must, at all costs, avoid being pushed by the enemy into a defensive role east of the Vistula, which would lead to complete destruction of the German force. On the other hand, when the fulfillment of its task east of the Vistula was no longer feasible, the army should avoid being cut off from its line of retreat behind this river in order to preserve at least its existence as an army. This order was completely in accordance with the opinion expressed by Schlieffen in the final exercise of 1898.

On 20 August 1914 General von Prittwitz judged that the situation required resort to Moltke's warning. On 17 August 1914 General Rennenkampf's First Russian Army had advanced into East Prussia and was encountered by von Prittwitz' forces, in the battle of Gumbinnen, on 19 and 20 August. The latter then received information that the Second Russian Army was on the move from the southeast, and fearing that he might be cut off from the Vistula, he decided to save his own army. It is hard to judge whether v. Prittwitz had momentarily lost his nerve, or whether he really thought that the moment had come to save the force under his command, a maneuver that had been continually enacted in Schlieffen's war games and staff rides. Even if the latter were the case, it nevertheless demonstrated a lack of any political judgment regarding his obligations toward his hard-pressed Austro-Hungarian ally. His decision was not only opposed inside his staff by his quartermaster, General Grünert, and by Colonel Hoffmann, but also by his corps commanders, especially by General Hermann v. François, Commanding General of the First Corps. The insubordination of the latter had already involved the Eighth Army at a too-early time, in the battle of Gumbinnen. He advocated an offensive approach at any event. After heated arguments between v. Prittwitz and Hoffmann, the latter managed to convince his commander that the best way to secure a retreat behind the Vistula was by throwing most of the German forces against the Second Russian Army. Otherwise, he argued, the latter might reach the Vistula before the Germans, since they had a much shorter route there. In the meantime, however, not having been informed of this new plan, v. Moltke, the Chief of the General Staff, reacted quickly by dismissing von Prittwitz and his Chief of Staff and replacing them respectively by Generals von Hindenburg and Ludendorff.[8]

THE BATTLE OF TANNENBERG

It is not the purpose of this chapter to describe the battle of Tannenberg in detail, but it seems important to raise the question whether this particular battle is really comparable with the classic battle of Cannae (or its glorified image), as has so often been suggested by Schlieffen's disciples.

"The picture of the Eighth Army looks like the Schlieffenian Cannae-picture: the center pushed back, both wings victorious," one German writer exclaimed excitedly.[9] On the map the closing stage of the battle indeed resembled Delbrück's reconstruction of the battle of Cannae, as it was adopted by Schlieffen. But was it so in substance? Certainly not! Cannae, as far as one knows, was a deliberately planned battle. The Carthaginians, who, on that occasion, used the stratagem of encirclement, were the assailants. The center of Hannibal's array had been weakened, with the clear intention that it should be pushed back by the Roman onslaught. The enveloping missions to both wings had been assigned beforehand. Hasdrubal's cavalry had moved into the rear of the Roman phalanx from the outset.

At Tannenberg, the Twentieth German Corps, which was to form the German center, had, from the beginning, a defensive mission. One should bear in mind that, as a matter of fact, the Germans fought, at Tannenberg, a defensive battle, carried out in an offensive manner, in accordance with Clausewitz' dictum. The aim, however, at that stage of the war, was not the conquest of Russia, but the stemming of the Russian tide. The Twentieth Corps had fallen back, not deliberately, but because it was too weak. It does not matter that this retrograde movement was, in due course, utilized for the final plan of the battle. The right wing of the German array was formed mainly by von François' First Corps, rushed there by rail in order to harass Samsonov's southern flank but with the reservation that in case of a German defeat, it could at this point still cover the German retreat to the Vistula. The participation of the left wing (actually fulfilling in part Hasdrubal's mission in the enemy's rear) was doubtful from the beginning. It depended on Rennenkampf's steps. Would he rush to Samsonov's assistance? If this were the case, the First German Reserve Corps and the Seventeenth Corps were to contain Rennenkampf's army, and the fight against Samsonov could, at best, be only an imperfect Leuthen, i.e., an action against one enemy wing. Only Rennenkampf's mysterious standstill for some days enabled the German commanders to take the risk and draw these two corps into battle, thus providing the missing sections of the Cannae picture. They could embark on such a risk for two reasons: First, a psychological one. During the Russo-Japanese War, Hoffmann had been an observer in the Far East and knew about an overt quarrel between Samsonov and Rennenkampf at Mukden railway station. Samsonov, who at that time commanded a cavalry corps, accused Rennenkampf of not having hurried to his assistance wtih his infantry. Hoffmann assumed, therefore, that the old antagonism and resentment would repeat itself.

The second reason was even more strongly decisive. The Germans intercepted the Russian wireless messages, which, being transmitted uncoded, betrayed their plans at every stage.[10]

It is therefore apparent that whereas Hannibal had dealt with only one Roman Army and, in destroying it, had no need to fear any interference from outside the field of battle, Hindenburg and Ludendorff had encircled one Russian Army, itself superior in force to the German opponents, with a second Russian Army present, which could have been brought into action at any time. Whether Tannenberg deserves the title of a "super-Cannae," as one German writer put it,[11] will not be discussed here. It is obvious that it was different from the prototype.

Furthermore, even this one Russian Army was not entirely involved in the envelopment. One of the outstanding features of the battle of Tannenberg was a sober judgment, on the part of the German command, as to what amount of enemy forces could be contained by the German troops available. The German High Command only engaged that part of the enemy force with which they could adequately deal. This was actually done by means of the First Corps' breakthrough at Usdau, which created a new and more suitable Russian southern flank and left outside the German encirclement certain parts of the Second Russian Army. Had the Germans tried to envelop the whole Russian force it remains doubtful whether they would have managed to close the ring and complete their misssion as convincingly as was in fact done. Ludendorff was quite right when he mentioned that this procedure was not entirely in accordance with Schlieffen's teaching of strategic encirclement, and that "the idea of tactical envelopment of a part of the battlefront, was seldom cultivated by the German General Staff, which preferred to practice 'strategy.' "[12]

In one respect, however, the battle of Tannenberg was analogous to the battle of Cannae. Both were striking, brilliant military victories, but neither, despite being battles of annihilation, was finally decisive.[13] They did not even create a sound basis from which a final victory could be evolved. The battle of Tannenberg corresponded with the general German image of battle, fostered by von Schlieffen and his school, and stirred up the belief that this might still be the way to conduct war. Soon the war bogged down into static trench warfare. Even the architects of the victory of Tannenberg, Hindenberg, and Lundendorff (and we might rightly add the name of Hoffmann, to whom we should perhaps allot the main share), although they tried hard to repeat themselves, could not produce another victory of the same quality.[14] They had, however, made the fullest utilization of the German Army's tradition and training by exploiting those virtues which had for years been nurtured by the elder Moltke and Schlieffen: attack, encirclement, and annihilation. Prittwitz' retreating troops could therefore be easily shifted into the new design of the battle of Tannenberg because they were in a frame of mind to which they were accustomed by their peacetime training.

Tannenberg, therefore, was not a second Cannae, deliberately planned, as so many maintain; but the circumstances made it gradually possible to evolve a double envelopment, which finally shaped this battle into a Cannae.[15] It would be ludicrous to assume that Hindenburg (or Ludendorff), already on 21 August, the day of his appointment, or on 22 August, the day of his travel to the East, had decided on encircling the Russians. The general ideas, however, and the determined execution of the gradually evolving operation were in accordance with Schlieffen's teaching. That was admitted by all who took part in the event. Ludendorff, summing up the battle in his memoirs, said: "I thought of General v. Schlieffen and returned thanks to this teacher."[16] That might, however, have been an afterthought (as was the very name given to this victory).[17] A contemporary letter of Hindenburg demonstrated beyond doubt that the men on the spot felt that they were acting under the spell of Schlieffen.[18]

Finally, these expressions may serve to refute a widespread claim that there did not exist a Schlieffen school and that Schlieffen had no disciples among the German leaders of the First World War, an opinion that is still held[19] by German scholars and writers, civilians and soldiers alike. After all, why should these personalities (and many others) confess so explicitly that they were pupils of the great master if it were not honorable to belong to this school? This important problem, however, will be examined in more detail at a later stage.[20]

NOTES

1. As early as October 1914 Ludendorff was approached by the Spanish Military Attaché in Germany, who wanted to know whether the battle of Tannenberg was conducted on the basis of a plan prepared beforehand, and was surprised that the answer was in the negative. E. Ludendorff, *Meine Kriegserinnerungen 1914–1918*, Berlin, 1919, p. 36.

2. The annual final exercises for General Staff officers in the years 1891, 1898, 1899, 1900, and 1901 were devoted to this particular problem. The problems presented in 1904 and 1905 also dealt with the East, not, however, with East Prussia, but with Silesia. These exercises were in addition to the annual staff rides East (the "Grosse Generalstabsreisen Ost"). *Vide* A. v. Schlieffen, *Dienstschriften*, Berlin, 1937–1938.

3. This meant a much earlier transfer of the Siberian Corps to the Russian western border. Parts of the Third Siberian Army Corps appeared in East Prussia as early as the end of Aug. 1914.

4. Hermann v. Kuhl, *Der Weltkrieg 1914–1918*, Berlin, 1929, vol. 1, p. 240.

5. Moltke's secret official letter No. 793 of 24 Feb. 1909, printed in Feldmarschall Conrad, *Aus meiner Dienstzeit, 1906–1918*, Wien, 1921, vol. 1, p. 394.

6. Letter of 13 Aug. 1914. BA/MA–HO8–37/1 (p. 1).

7. In 1907 von Moltke had presented final exercises ("Schlussaufgaben 1907") with a situation and forces similar to the events in 1914. Quoted in E. Kabisch, *Streitfragen des Weltkrieges 1914–1918*, Stuttgart, 1924, pp. 340–341.

8. As a matter of fact, Moltke had opposed the appointment of Colonel-General von Prittwitz und Gaffron (that was his full title). He regarded the latter as unfit for the post, which was the most independent in the German Army. At the beginning of 1914 v. Moltke demanded from the Military Cabinet and the Minister of War, v. Falkenhayn, to be allowed to relieve v. Prittwitz, a request that was refused. In order to compensate for v. Prittwitz' deficiencies, Moltke appointed his own senior advisor, Count Waldersee, as Chief of Staff of the Eighth Army in case of war. Cf. W. Elze, *Tannenberg*, Breslau, 1927, p. 93, and E. Kabisch, *op. cit.*, p. 85.

9. E. Kabisch, *op. cit.*, p. 73.

10. BA/MA—HO8–37/1 (p. 6). Hoffmann's letter of 4 Sept. 1914.

11. Wolfgang Foerster, *Graf Schlieffen und der Weltkrieg*, 2d rev. ed., Berlin, 1925, p. 232.

12. E. Ludendorff, *Tannenberg*, München, 1934, p. 25.

13. It is interesting that Ludendorff reached this conclusion with respect to the battle of Cannae, making the following statement in his book on Tannenberg: "The battle of Cannae has not brought about a transformation of universal history. Only soldiers are engaged in its study." *Ibid.*, p. 45.

14. The battle of Augustovo Forest in March 1915 probably came nearest to the ideal, but again, like its prototype, it was not war deciding.

15. This opinion was also held by General Hoffmann, in his book *Tannenberg, wie es wirklich war*, Berlin, 1926, p. 94.

16. E. Ludendorff, *Kriegserinnerungen, op. cit.*, p. 45.

17. Hoffmann had suggested that the orders issued for the final attack on the Russians be headed with the name of Tannenberg, in memory of the defeat of the Teutonic Knights by the Polish-Lithuanian Army in 1410. On 29 Aug. 1914 Hindenburg asked his Imperial master to accept this name for the battle, adding that "the damage of 1410 was thoroughly repaired in a wide area around this old battlefield." The letter is printed in W. Elze, *op. cit.*, p. 330. However, Admiral von Müller remarked in his diary on 30 Aug. 1914 about Hindenburg's letter: "Extremely dashing, but lacking political wisdom with regard to the Poles, who could now be of assistance." Admiral Georg Alexander von Müller (ed. Walter Görlitz), *Regierte der Kaiser?* Göttingen, 1959, p. 53.

18. The letter to General v. Bernhardi, dated 3 Sept. 1914, read: "That was a real Cannae á la Schlieffen." Printed in Friedrich von Bernhardi, *Denkwürdigkeiten aus meinem Leben*, Berlin, 1927, p. 397. The German Crown Prince Wilhelm, C-in-C Fifth Army and later on an army group commander in the West, wrote in his memoirs (*Meine Erinnerungen an Deutschlands Heldenkampf*, Berlin, 1923, (pp. 95–96): "There, in the Eighth Army, were leaders inspired by Schlieffen's spirit, who pursued his operative Cannae-idea unswervingly. The battle of Tannenberg would have filled the teacher of the German General Staff with proud satisfaction."

19. This view was expressed anew by Colonel Dr. H. Meier-Welcker, sometime director of the "Militärgeschichtliches Forschungsamt," Freiburg i/Br., in his contribution "Graf Alfred von Schlieffen," in W. Hahlweg, ed., *Klassiker der Kriegskunst*, Darmstadt, 1960, p. 349, and also in his private conversation with me in summer 1963.

20. *Vide* chapter 12.

8

Trench Warfare: Interlude of Stagnation

THE REASONS FOR THE STALEMATE

For almost four long years the war bogged down into the strange phenomenon of position warfare, without either belligerent having really wanted it. But it is obvious that both sides had unconsciously contributed to it. The first step in this direction was made when the German troops ceased to retreat after the Marne battle, but dug in on the Aisne in order to repel the pursuing Allies. After two days of battle General Joseph Joffre ordered his troops to dig in at the positions reached on the evening of 14 September 1914. During the night he issued a general directive that "now it is a matter of methodical attack, by means of exploiting all our available resources. That means that every position, as soon as it is occupied, must be fortified."[1] In the afternoon of 15 September General Falkenhayn, in his turn, ordered the German right-wing armies to hold their ground, dig in, and not to fall back. On 16 November 1914 von Falkenhayn wrote to Field Marshal von der Goltz: "Keep in your hand what you possess and never give up a single inch of ground that you have won!"[2] Joffre's aphorism, as well as Falkenhayn's, had sounded the knell of the war of movement and set the stage for the agonizing deadlock of trench warfare. Both sides had missed Clausewitz' warning: "Indeed any attack that does not immediately lead to peace must end on the defensive."[3] Now the penalty for this peacetime omission had to be paid.

Neither side knew how to handle the problem of defense. They simply were not adjusted to it. Suddenly the assault waves were stunned by superior firepower hailing on them from defensive positions. The overwhelming combination of automatic weapons with pre-ranged artillery fire heralded its emergence. "It is not conceivable that our right wing can master the French there," wrote General Hans von Plessen, Commander of the Imperial Headquarters, on 28 September 1914. "Five of our army corps are definitely unable to beat the French, though the latter are not superior in numbers at that spot. In the main all our forces are deployed in the lengthy front."[4] This utterance demonstrated the complete lack of understanding at the higher levels of the German Army for the situation that the fighting echelons had to envisage. The commanders in the field were at pains to make their superiors in the rear realize that the relationship of offensive and defensive had changed in the latter's favor, and that the time for quick and dashing advances was past.

Nobody can now deny that German military doctrine prior to the First World War was pre-occupied with offensive. Nobody was then bothered by the fact that war, as an entirety, consists of a variety of actions, among them defense as well as attack. Everybody was too mesmerized by Schlieffen's vision of delivering quick and decisive offensive blows in every direction. Even the short defensive spell in the East, until the early defeat of France in the West, was to be bridged by tactical offensive. When it turned out that the forces available were not sufficient to carry through the German plan of war, no new doctrine was at hand. Neither side could muster sufficient strength to counterbalance the increased power of defense. Suddenly one had to face the fact that armies of millions of soldiers could not wage a war of movement forever. Defense became an integral part of the war scenery, and on an ever-increasing scale. The ancient truth was again confirmed, that every war has some surprise in store for which tactics have to find an appropriate answer. Had the Germans tried to understand Clausewitz' teaching with regard to defense, they might have been better prepared for the new emergency. But German soldiers, inspired by the famous "furor teutonicus," would not listen to Clausewitz' flummery about defense. Colmar von der Goltz maintained in 1883 that the modern German fighting method is based on a conception of resolute offensive. "An idea of the offensive is tacitly at the bottom of all our theoretical treaties, and, for the most part of practical exercises also." Passive steps, like temporizing, waiting, and defensive, were against the German nature. The corps of officers strives always for "great decisive strokes upon the battlefield." With remarkable vision he then forecast what really happened in autumn 1914, namely, "the feeling of not being quite in one's element, and the necessity of fighting in unfamiliar circumstances and against strange difficulties, acts quite as prejudicially upon troops as upon individual men."[5] In a more advanced stage of the book von der Goltz said: "In this sketch of a battle, we have instinctively described an offensive battle. What German soldiers would do otherwise?"[6]

In fact, when confronted with the harsh reality of a nonoffensive battle, they hardly knew what to do otherwise. The guilt for this neglect of Clausewitz' theory of defense rests heavily on Schlieffen. The older Moltke, despite his tremendous offensive successes, had recognized that the defensive also had its role in war. Schlieffen's obsession with encirclement threw into complete oblivion all knowledge about defense.

General (later Field Marshal) Wilhelm Ritter von Leeb, in his treatise "The Defense," stripped the events of 1914 to their theoretical essentials, and reached the conclusion that the mutual exhaustion at the end of 1914 resulted from

not resorting to the more economical strategic, operative or tactical defense, wherever possible, and instead of applying wasteful attack everywhere. Therefore, at those points, where the strategic or operative decision should have been striven for, the overall strength of that particular front, that particular operation, was not sufficient to prevail over the material strength of the defense. Or the distribution of forces on that front was too equal, and therefore did not provide the strategic or operative center of gravity with reserves, strong enough and echeloned in depth, to continue, until a final decision against the increased power of the defensive and its countermeasures was reached.[7]

These facts, together with the already mentioned holding of captured ground, were considered by von Leeb as the main reasons for the deadlock in West and East.

Moreover, it is obvious that a certain state of equilibrium between the opposing forces occurred; otherwise, the stronger opponent would have managed to continue his movement, despite his adversary's opposition. The "race to the sea," having put an end to any further encirclement attempts, finally created two opposing parallel front lines (in the western theater of war from the Swiss border to the channel coast, and the same happened later on in the East from the Balkans to the Baltic Sea), and therefore any further belligerent action was confined to a frontal clash aimed, at best, at a break-through. This mode of action had not been cultivated in the German pre-war Army at either the operative or the tactical level. Despite Clausewitz' forecast that "the line of defense may run from sea to sea or from one neutral country to another,"[8] nobody had anticipated prolonged position warfare. Even the warning signals from the Far East were misinterpreted. Von Bernhardi wrote, in 1912, that

battles lasting for days will probably result in the future only when in the theater of war conditions arise which are similar to those of the Manchurian fields. Such a supposition is, however not at all likely to be fulfilled. Germany's European adversaries can only act on the offensive, if they wish to achieve anything at all. *The Germans are sure not to defend themselves behind ditches and ramparts. The genius of the German people will save it from that.* A railway net widely ramified in comparison with that of Manchuria, and an ample useful network of roads, afford great freedom of movement in most of the European theaters of war. All these conditions make us rather believe in a war of active operations than in a war of positions, although the spade is held in such high esteem.[9]

One can smile about such silliness, but one must keep in mind that the "widely ramified railway net" and the "ample useful network of roads" were among the major factors in the ability to rush reserves in order to shore up any spot where a break-through was likely to endanger the ultimate reign of defense. "The deadlock in the trenches," as H. Rosinski put it, "destroyed the immense advantage in training and leadership with which the German Army had entered the war and made a speedy victory in the old style impossible. It gave the Allies time to bring their overwhelming reserves of manpower and material to bear upon the German forces, exhausting them, until their last belated effort to regain, in 1918, the mobility which they had renounced in 1914 ended in their collapse."[10]

Germany's material inferiority was soon revealed. The first indication was a strangling shortage of ammunition. It certainly did not suffice for a massive offensive project. Economically utilized, it was barely enough for defensive purposes. Before long it was obvious that v. d. Goltz' prognosis was right, "that a State, which means to be successful in defensive warfare, must have at its back, either the open frontiers of friendly powers, or a sea of which it holds command. A country not in this position can only resist as long as its own industry is capable of supplying the needs of its country."[11] The friendly powers at Germany's back—Austria, Bulgaria, and Turkey—were not only unable to supply Germany with strategic materials, but were dependent on Germany for their own needs, and at sea the central powers were at the mercy of the British Navy.

Having failed to crush the combined French–Belgian–British Armies at the first onslaught, the German General had to consider whether to continue to hit at the Western Allies, or switch his blows against the Russians. Support for the latter argument came from the Austrian Chief of General Staff, Conrad von Hoetzendorff, and from the German Supreme Command East, Generals von Hindenburg and Ludendorff. Falkenhayn, however, was scared to death by the vastness of the Russian land-space and by the prospect of repeating Napoleon's mistakes.[12] However, being compelled to hasten to Austria's assistance from time to time, Falkenhayn, although reluctantly, allotted forces to the eastern theater of war, remaining convinced that even the most tremendous victory in the East would not spare him the need to gain a decisive victory in the West.[13]

This state of affairs had a dual effect: First, it created a tense antagonism between OHL and the commanders in the East, and second, it resulted in a constant movement of reserves to and from the East and West: "enough to secure success," as Liddell Hart put it, "but never in sufficient quantity or in time for decisive victory."[14] Muddling on became the main feature of Germany's conduct of the war during the ensuing years (and it was obviously the same for Germany's foes). One is shocked to discover that the Kaiser supported Falkenhayn's western policy, not because he was convinced of its soundness, but "because my son, Wilhelm, also wants once to have a success."[15] Nothing can illuminate the absence of positive ideas in Germany's war conduct better than that Imperial utterance.

Falkenhayn, however, early on came to believe that Germany could not afford to overstrain its scanty resources and would therefore have to evade any premature efforts in order not to become exhausted before its adversaries. He therefore embarked on a policy of limited aims and economizing his forces. He consciously renounced any intention of totally destroying his enemies and avoided any risk of delivering massive blows. He tried to persuade his opponents that it would not pay to aim for Germany's destruction because they themselves might in the process become mutilated, exhausted, and paralyzed beyond recovery. Falkenhayn believed that, when offered the stiffest resistance, Germany's enemies would at last prefer negotiations to any prolongation of a fruitless war. This standpoint of half-measures, interwoven with all the other reasons mentioned earlier, was a basis of that strange conglomerate generally known as trench or position warfare.

IN SEARCH OF A SOLUTION

There were, of course, still a number of battles conducted in accordance with Schlieffen's Cannae concept, in addition to the famous battle of Tannenberg. The battle of the Masurian Lakes (6–15 September 1914) was conducted by the victors of Tannenberg and intended to deal Rennenkampf's army a fate similar to Samsonov's army at Tannenberg. However, Rennenkampf was aware of the imminent danger and, although severely shaken, he managed to slip away. Another attempt at encirclement was undertaken at the winter battle in Masuria (4–22 February 1915), but although a great success, it was again not a perfect "Cannae." The famous campaign in Poland during the summer of 1915, culminating in the conquest of Vilna (19 September 1915), was planned by Hindenburg, Ludendorff, and Conrad as a large-scale pincer offensive from the Carpathian Mountains and East Prussia simultaneously. This daring scheme was, however, opposed by von Falkenhayn, who had his doubts whether the two jaws of the pincer, 600 kilometers away from each other, could exercise a reciprocal impact on the enemy in their middle. He maintained that all the advantages of acting on interior lines rested with the Russians.[16] One should keep in mind that that was exactly Schlieffen's opinion (and Clausewitz' too),[17] and only the harnessing of the internal combustion engine to military use made it a sound— although still daring—project in 1939. Falkenhayn therefore suggested a less pretentious plan, known as the "little pincer." As usual, the tug-of-war over the great scheme, or its modification by OHL, and especially the controversy over the size of reserves to be allotted, spoiled the final success of the operation. Despite an enormous advance into Russian territory, the offensive petered out indecisively. The defeat of Serbia in the autumn of 1915 and of Rumania at the end of 1916 (carried out by Falkenhayn after his removal from OHL) were shaped in accordance with the Cannae concept. There were also arguments whether the Austrian and German-Austrian offensives against Italy at the Isonzo should be accompanied by an additional thrust from the Trentino in Cannae style. However, if one investigates these battles, campaigns, and schemes, one easily discovers that, fundamentally, it was less a matter of theory and principle, and more the geographical and topographical circumstances and the actual layout of the enemy forces that dictated such a line of action. After the initial breakdown of theory in midsummer 1914, little consideration was given to action in accordance with any theoretical thinking.

What the soldiers were really looking for was the development of techniques and technical means for breaking the stalemate. Because the Germans had decided to cling to every piece of trench, farm, or unimportant village to the utmost, and had assumed that their opponents would do the same, both sides thought of dislodging the adversary and keeping him on the run by paving the way for an assault, by utilizing tremendous quantities of ammunition. For days large amounts of shells of all calibers were poured on enemy positions in order to obliterate them. this was the genesis of the "Materialschlacht" (the battle of material). The need for never-foreseen quantities of ammunition partly shifted the struggle from the actual battlefield and the soldiers to the centers of production and the labor force in the war industries. In order to develop a labor force appropriate to the increased demand for war material, it was necessary to discharge miners and skilled industrial workers from the fighting units. The demand for increased firepower was not confined to speeding up the production of ammunition, but also entailed increasing the number of guns, machine guns, and trench mortars deployed at the front. All this, of course, had its repercussion on raw material.

The impact of the increased hail of missiles on a position resulted in modification of the whole position system. Instead of the customary straight and single trench of peacetime, there emerged a complicated system of "honeycomb" trenches, arranged in depth and aimed at dispersing the occupying infantry to a maximum and eliminating the dreadful impact of the enemy barrage. The further implication of these developments was twofold: First of all, the assailant had to shift from pinpoint artillery fire to area coverage, which required additional ammunition; second, he now had to force his way through an elaborate network of honeycomb trenches, which again meant a greater amount of fire preparation.

Other technical methods tried out during the war consisted of using poison gas, explosives in underground mines, and, finally, in order to regain mobility, the development of tanks. As these devices had not been considered before the war, they were generally put into use at early stages of their development, and although promising initial successes, they soon evoked effective countermeasures and proved indecisive in the long run.

In order to break the stranglehold of the British naval blockade, or rather in order to retaliate against it, Germany resorted to intensified and unrestricted submarine warfare. Because the U-boat was not regarded as a decisive weapon before the war, Germany possessed only a limited number at its outbreak. Nevertheless, the Germans decided to launch the submarine war with an insufficient number of vessels. It failed to create the expected impact on the course of the war and soon evoked appropriate countermeasures. The political implications involved made the U-boat war a controversial issue and finally brought the United States into the Allied camp.

In the sphere of operations and tactics on land, the possibility of break-through had to be considered.

THE BREAK-THROUGH

Schlieffen had frequently argued against break-through operations. General Krafft von Dehlmensingen, in his treatise on break-through, revealed that official German military publications of the pre-war period never dealt with the problem of break-through, except perhaps in the pamphlet dealing with the conquest of fortresses. In that instance the issue was, of course, handled with regard to special circumstances.[18] Only von Bernhardi, in his works, had propagated penetration prior to the First World War.[19] But German soldiers would not, at that time, listen to him. On 11 August 1914 Georg Count Waldersee, Chief of Staff of the German Eighth Army in East Prussia, wrote to the German liaison officer with the Austrian High Command: "Please warn against a frontal approach, even in a tactical sense."[20]

However, owing to the new shape of trench systems, a strategic break through the hostile lines became a delicate task. It was not enough to achieve a tactical break-in into the enemy positions. Such a penetration could easily be sealed up by reserves. It was necessary to punch a hole through the entire depth of the defensive layout and reach the open field beyond it. In order to keep this "break-out" going, the maintenance of a secure corridor was essential. Strange as it may seem, neither belligerent party succeeded in making a successful break-in, and furthermore none achieved a break-out. Three times the Germans almost neared the ideal but every time fell short of the mark: The break-through at Gorlice-Tarnow in May 1915 had a tremendous initial success but reached deadlock again before becoming a war of movement; the spectacular penetration of the Italian front in 1917 slowed down and was finally contained on the Piave by French and British divisions rushed there from France; in the spring of 1918 the Germans succeeded in smashing the British Fifth Army and nearly approached the far edge of the defended area, but they had by then themselves already reached the end of their tether.[21]

The unfamiliarity with battles of penetration, resulting from the one-sided pre-war training of the German Army in the Schlieffen style, was so immense that General Hans von Seeckt, the designer of Gorlice, confessed that he had trouble in preventing troops and commanders alike from wheeling inward too early after the initial break-in. Troops were so much trained to "envelop the nearby front" that they lacked the understanding that what mattered this time was to keep on moving.[22]

There was, however, one expedient offered by Clausewitz for evading the deadlock of rigid defense and regaining mobility: an elastically conducted flexible defensive.

ON FLEXIBLE DEFENSE

Clausewitz had derived his concept of flexible defense from the experience he gained during Napoleon's invasion of Russia, and mainly from the Russian reaction to the invader. He considered this particular mode of defense as the most powerful one, the simple principle being to lure the enemy into pursuit by means of a retrograde movement and then, after having pulled him into the open field, to fall on him from several directions. Such an approach of sacrificing ground in order to gain operative mobility was, of course, opposed to the principle of "keep in your hand what you possess and never give up a single inch of ground." The latter might be a political challenge (although a doubtful one, too) but did not reckon with strategic necessities. He who acts on the defensive, in accordance with Clausewitz' postulate, creates for himself a new operative basis on the lines of a war of movement, and has every chance of regaining the ground voluntarily ceded. This actually entails a wide variety of operative choices. On the other hand, sticking ultimately only to the holding of ground limits the possibilities to one: the endurance of a hostile onslaught. There is, of course, the chance of turning to the counteroffensive after a successful repulse of the attack, provided that one still has the necessary forces for such a step. One must admit that even this attitude accords with Clausewitz' concept, for it contains the ingredients of his approach: the wearing down of the enemy and the gaining of time.

It is obvious that Falkenhayn's first decision on the night of 14–15 September 1914 fitted into Clausewitz' concept.[23] Had he carried it out, position warfare might have been averted. His second thoughts released the reciprocal chain reaction that led to four long and bloody years in the trenches. In 1917 Ludendorff missed another golden opportunity of breaking the spell of stagnation. In the face of French Field Marshall Robert Georges Nivelle's imminent offensive, the Germans had planned a deliberate retreat to the "Siegfried Line," thus evading the blow and simultaneously shortening their defensive line and gaining stronger reserves. This was a much admired maneuver.[24] Notwithstanding, it lacked Clausewitzian consequences: It was not used for regaining the initiative. Although brilliantly conducted, it was a simple retreat, without any intention of hitting back at the French during their advance. That the Germans did not make a more constructive use of the "Alberich" movement is a further indication of how void of any positive ideas the First World War had become.

Later in the same year Army Group Rupprecht contemplated a preliminary German retreat in Flanders, in the face of the expected British offensive there. However, the troops preferred enduring the assault in their "comfortable" positions to the "hardship" of a tactical retreat and a sudden "about turn!" against the pursuing enemy. Indeed, one is not surprised by such an attitude after three years of stalemate.

Ludendorff crowned this chain of errors, after the breakdown of his 1918 offensives in the West, by failing to order a retreat from the bulges created by the German attacks. This time he in his turn reverted to a policy of not yielding an inch of ground, and thus played into the hands of his opponents. Germany's fighting power probably could have still been preserved by ceding ground and skillfully redeploying its forces further back.

In the framework of the present study only small consideration has been given to the four terrible years of war, as they held only scanty evidence of any impact of theoretical thinking. Things just muddled on!

There was only one attempt to formulate an entirely new and unique concept: Falkenhayn's Verdun scheme.

NOTES

1. Quoted in *Der Weltkrieg 1914–1918* (*Reichsarchiv*), Berlin, 1925–1944, vol. 5, p. 126.

2. "Halte was du hast, und gib nie einen Fussbreit von dem auf, was du gewonnen hast." Quoted, *Ibid.*, p. 585.

3. *On War*, VI, 3, p. 365, emphasis added.

4. Quoted in W. Erfurth, *Die Uberraschung im Kriege*, Berlin, 1938, p. 81.

5. Colmar von der Goltz, *The Nation in Arms*, London, 1906, pp. 143–144, passim, emphasis added.

6. *Ibid.*, p. 355.

7. Wilhelm Ritter von Leeb, *Die Abwehr*, Berlin, 1938, p. 107. It was perhaps Leeb's personal tragedy that during the Second World War, when commanding Army Group North against Leningrad, he himself felt the strength of defense that he had so brilliantly analyzed in his treatise.

8. *On War*, VI, 4, p. 367.

9. Friedrich v. Berhardi, *On War of To-Day*, London, 1912, vol. 2, p. 241, emphasis added.

10. H. Rosinski, *The German Army*, Washington, D.C., 1944, pp. 90–91.

11. C. v. d. Goltz, *op. cit.*, p. 149.

12. Cf. Erich v. Falkenhayn, *Die Oberst Heeresleitung 1914–1916 in ihren wichtigsten Entschliessungen*, Berlin, 1920, p. 48.

13. *Ibid.*, p. 47.

14. Liddell Hart, *A History of the World War 1914–1918*, London, 1934, pp. 179–180.

15. "Weil mein Sohn Wilhelm doch auch einmal einen Erfolg haben will." Cf. Admiral Georg Alexander von Müller (ed. Walter Görlitz), *Regierte der Kaiser*? Götlingen, 1959, p. 97, entry of 9 April 1915. One will remember that Crown Prince Wilhelm was at that time C-in-C Fifth Army in the West.

16. E. v. Falkenhayn, *op. cit.*, pp. 45–46.

17. *Vide On War*, VIII, 9, pp. 617–618. Schlieffen, in his pragmatic manner, wrote in a memorandum of 1893, pointedly: "If Austria from Galicia, and Germany from East Prussia, want to operate from entirely opposed base-lines, 400 km. apart, then the offensive as well as the defensive are likewise rushing headlong to their ruin. As long as Russia's mobilization and deployment is slow and cumbersome, it is to be recommended that both allies fall upon the weak, just assembling, Russian troops, by the shortest routes, in order to prevent the deployment of the whole Army. Since it is no longer possible to surprise the Russians by means of a sudden attack, it is no longer advisable to attack a strong opponent *from such a distance* without any co-operation and without any possibility of mutual support." Quoted in W. Foerster, *Graf Schlieffen und der Weltkrieg*, 2d rev. ed., Berlin, 1925, p. 152.

18. Konrad Krafft von Dellmensingen, *Der Durchbruch*, Hamburg, 1937, p. 13.

19. *Vide* Book One, chapter 2. F. v. Bernhardi, *Vom Kriege der Zukunft*, Berlin, 1920, pp. 134–136.

20. Quoted in W. Elze, *Tannenberg*, Breslau, 1927, p. 205.

21. For more details, *vide* chapter 10.

22. Generaloberst Hans von Seeckt, *Gedanken eines Soldaten*, Berlin, 1929, p. 20.

23. *Vide* Book Two, chapter 5.

24. Groener in a letter to Mrs. v. Hahnke, Schlieffen's daughter, on 3 Sept. 1935, considered this maneuver as Ludendorff's finest performance. BHA—Rep. 92, W. v. Hahnke, Nr. 21/22.

9

Case 4: The Degeneration of the Art of War: Verdun 1916

FALKENHAYN'S CHRISTMAS MEMORANDUM, 1915—A NEW CONCEPT IN WARFARE

Considering Falkenhayn's famous Christmas Memorandum of 1915,[1] one is struck by the peculiarity and novelty of his military ideas. However, in fairness to Falkenhayn, one should judge his opinions against the background of general confusion created by the new and unexpected phenomenon of trench warfare. One must admit that Falkenhayn made the first attempt, although miscarrying as it did, to grapple with the problem intellectually.

On the other hand one is highly impressed by his outstanding ability to grasp the political situation that pertained at the end of the first seventeen months of war. Although Falkenhayn, like his predecessors, regarded England as the ringleader of the hostile alliance, he had ruled out any thought of a direct strike against England. But he also thought it pointless to look for a decision in the East or on the Italian front. His conclusion was, therefore, to deliver indirectly a twofold blow against England.

The first part, as Falkenhayn defined it in his memorandum, was intended to employ every weapon that is suitable for striking at England on its own ground: Submarine warfare would strike at the enemy's most sensitive spot because it aimed at severing his oversea communications. Falkenhayn could not find any justification on military ground for refusing to employ this most effective weapon.

The second part was aimed "against England's tools on the Continent." Among these, France was regarded as the most profitable target, owing to the fact that "the strain on France has almost reached the breaking-point—though it is certainly borne with the most remarkable devotion."

The conclusion of Falkenhayn's Christmas Memorandum contained his blue-print for Germany's strategy in 1916. He ruled out the uncertain method of a mass break-through, which he considered beyond the German means. However, within German reach "behind the French sector of the front *there are objectives for the retention of which the French General Staff would be compelled to throw in every man they have."* By doing so, the French forces *"will bleed to death,"* since "there can be no question of a voluntary withdrawal." And that would happen whether the Germans reached their goal or not. He reasoned that for such an operation limited to a narrow front, Germany would not be compelled to overstretch its forces. It could even repel enemy relief attacks to be expected on other fronts. The Germans would be free to accelerate or draw out their offensive, to intensify it or break it off from time to time, as suited their purpose. As objectives, Falkenhayn considered Belfort or Verdun; he gave preference to Verdun.[2]

This section of Falkenhayn's memorandum contains so many, in some ways shocking, military ideas that it seems worthwhile to examine them one by one. First of all, Falkenhayn rejected the "uncertain method of a mass break-through." This was a lesson "deduced from the failure of his enemies' mass attacks," which he had analyzed earlier in the memorandum:

Attempts at a mass break-through, even with an extreme accumulation of men and material, cannot be regarded as holding out prospects of success against a well armed enemy, whose morale is sound and who is not seriously inferior in numbers. The defender has normally succeeded in closing the gaps. This is easy enough for him if he decided to withdraw voluntarily, and it is hardly possible to stop him from doing so. The salients thus made, enormously exposed to the effects of flanking fire, threaten to become a mere slaughter-house. The technical difficulties of directing and supplying the masses bottled up in them are so great as to seem practically insurmountable.[3]

Falkenhayn, therefore, looked for a method that would make it unnecessary to resort to a mass break-through.

Because masses for such a break-through were not available. (Falkenhayn had rejected any offensive proposals of his army commanders requiring thirty divisions or so), he was in search of objectives that could be achieved with "limited resources." These "limited resources" would logically be matched with limited objectives or, as Falkenhayn had put it, "an operation limited to a narrow front" (one should remember this phrase to the letter when examining the actual design of the German assault "in the Meuse-area in the direction of Verdun"). One obvious purpose of acting in such a way was the desire to husband one's own forces. A certain moderation of aims was therefore probably the mainspring of Falkenhayn's train of thought, rather than a lack of determination, as some of his critics accused him later. He renounced voluntarily the danger of striving for a final decision by means of taking a calculated risk.[4] He believed that in this worldwide economic struggle, it was essential not to become exhausted before your opponent. One ought, therefore, to abstain from overstraining one's forces.[5] He would content himself with demonstrating to Germany's adversaries that it might not be worthwhile "to pay the price for our subjugation."[6]

In order to achieve the utmost gain from acting with limited forces on limited objectives, it seemed necessary to choose objectives that would, by their very existence, compel the enemy "to throw in every man they have." This meant that the whole game was staked on the moral issue, since by renunciation or loss of the objective, "the moral effect in France will be enormous." That was a novel adaptation of one of Schlieffen's principles. Schlieffen had once said that sometimes, in place of Hasdrubal the cavalry commander acting in the enemy's rear and cutting his line of retreat, a natural obstacle or the border of a neutral state might be substituted.[7] The French Commander-in-Chief was to be pushed, not against a physical obstacle—the sea shore, a river, a swamp or a high and impenetrable mountain range—but against a moral obstacle.[8] No French general could dare to sacrifice such an object without having tried his utmost to hold it. The battle of Verdun was proof of the correctness of Falkenhayn's guess that national pride could serve as an obstacle as much as any physical one, or even better.

Further, an atrocious idea emerged: If the French accepted that challenge, "the forces of France will bleed to death." This was a completely new concept in the history of war. Until now, generals had striven to subdue their adversaries by means of a clear-cut victory in battle or in a series of battles. As means to that end, generals had the choice of two operational offensive methods: either encircling their enemy or breaking through his line. The basic idea behind these operations was that the best way is to attack the enemy at his ill-defended flanks and in his unprotected rear, or to tear up the flanks by means of a break-through that would enable him to reach the opponent's rear and simultaneously "roll up" his front line, beginning from the break-in point. Falkenhayn departed from this method of waging war. His "bleeding white" theory was based on the assumption that the assailant, in a protracted struggle, should always inflict more casualties on the defender than he would suffer himself at the same time.[9] He did not aim at a mobile operation or a break-through in the conventional sense, but at the installation of a gigantic "suction pump" in order to "drain" the French lifeblood. Later, Falkenhayn used to call the battlefield of Verdun the "Meuse-mill".[10] It seems more than doubtful whether he ever realized that his troops were ground in that mill as much as his adversary's. Whereas Falkenhayn expected the ratio of mutual losses to be approximately five French to every two Germans, the real ratio was 362,000:336,800.[11]

In this fateful document every word and phrase counted. The sentence dealing with the assumption that "the forces of France will bleed to death—as there can be no question of a voluntary withdrawal" ends with the subordinate sentence "whether we reach our goal or not." This implied that the conquest of the objective was only of secondary importance. But on the contrary, Falkenhayn regarded it as essential that the chosen object should not collapse too quickly, for in that case it would not fulfill the function of draining blood. On 26 May 1916, i.e., three months after the commencement of the Verdun battle, Rupprecht reported Falkenhayn's statement, made at a conference of army chiefs of staff at Meziere, that "the OHL has never had the intention of capturing Verdun."[12] One may believe that it was not an afterthought, but the revelation of a preconceived design.

As sincere as his intention was to involve France in the "Meuse-mill," he nevertheless hoped to induce the British to take part in the general slaughter too. He believed, mistakenly and with grave consequences for the German cause, that the British would stage "relief attacks" on other parts of the front, and that the Germans could "hope to have sufficient troops in hand to reply to them with counter-attacks." That was Falkenhayn's trump, hidden up his sleeve.

By conducting the whole operation in such a manner, he was convinced that he would maintain his maximum freedom of action. In his words, Germany would be "perfectly free to accelerate or draw out the offensive, to intensify it or break it off from time to time, as suits the purpose." That would doubtlessly be one of the most desirable achievements a general could hope for, It would mean that he had managed to eliminate his adversary's will, and could conduct his operations regardless of his opponent's moves. As it turned out, this thought was an illusion. For German national pride became involved as soon as the French had accepted the challenge. The situation was like that in the fable about the hunter who tried to catch a bear: It was not quite clear who held whom, the hunter the bear, or vice versa.

The last point in Falkenhayn's memorandum was the selection of an objective that would stimulate all the declared intentions. He decided on Verdun, for it was also a thorn in the German flesh.[13] Some people maintained that a certain mystic remembrance of Verdun's importance in the days of the Carolingians played a part in Falkenhayn's decision. However, he was apparently much too clever and realistic a personality to allow the intrusion of such romantic and irrelevant thoughts into his military planning.[14] In any case the selection of a fortress was not, at that time, regarded as an insurmountable obstacle and would, *a priori*, meet Falkenhayn's hopes of a protracted conflict. The quick collapse of the Belgian fortresses and those of northern France under the German heavy artillery (one of Schlieffen's creations) made everybody believe that the day of the fortress was gone. The French, too, had lost their belief in fortresses and had therefore stripped even Verdun of its heavy armament. Verdun, however, despite the dismantling, was not a simple fortress, but a fortified area. It closely resembled Clausewitz' description in his chapter on the defensive battle: The defender waits for the hostile attack in a carefully chosen and prepared position. He has erected solid defenses at the most important points, fortified villages, and erected obstacles. His intention is to inflict heavy losses on the enemy at low cost to himself. He can confidently survey the battle as it smolders before his eyes. His positions are arranged in depth. At every level—from division to battalion—he has reserves. Moreover, a substantial reserve—one quarter or even one third of the whole force—is kept far in the rear, far enough to avoid casualties from enemy fire and even to remain outside any possible envelopment by the foe. This reserve will be used at the moment the enemy reveals his whole plan and has spent most of his forces.[15]

It is not known whether Falkenhayn actually had this part of Clausewitz' teaching in mind, but it corresponds with all he was looking for in the enemy's behavior in his future battle. His critics did not understand his real intentions. General Hoffmann argued, for instance, that "the attack on Verdun was right if it was successful. But when it became obvious that the French were staking everything on holding it, and when it began to call for sacrifices, not merely in men but in ammunition, it should have been given up.''[16]

For Falkenhayn's purpose it was essential that the French *should* stake everything on holding Verdun. As early as 13 January 1916, prior to the German assault, Rupprecht, in his diary, doubted whether Verdun would be a success. For "it has never been regarded as an indication of exceptional Generalship (Feldherrnkunst) to tackle the opponent at his strongest point.''[17] On 25 February, i.e., on the fifth day of the German offensive, he wrote to his father, the King of Bavaria, that "attacking at Verdun means to grapple the bull at his horns.''[18] That was exactly what Falkenhayn wanted. He was not served with a quick victory, which would forfeit his new concept of gradually wearing down the enemy. Only a slowly developing battle would enable the French to conduct their defense in accordance with Clausewitz' doctrine. Moreover, only a slowly developing battle would cause the French to accept the challenge. A quick and sudden conquest of Verdun would be just another defeat, to be added to the list of previous ones. But the possibility of defending Verdun successfully would increase the wave of French patriotic feeling, so essential for Falkenhayn's design. Hermann Ziese-Beringer derived the following formula from Falkenhayn's Verdun design: "Own modest expenditure of manpower, plus strongest employment of material on a narrow front, plus attack of a point, for the retention of which, France is compelled to throw in the last man: that, altogether, is equal to a battle of bleeding to death.''[19]

THE PLANNING PHASE OF THE VERDUN BATTLE[20]

Some special features of the conduct of Falkenhayn's attack at Verdun need illumination. He obtained the Kaiser's consent to his plans for 1916. It may be doubted whether the latter, who regarded himself as a competent strategist, understood the consequences of this monstrous design. Falkenhayn accordingly issued the first orders to Crown Prince Wilhelm's Fifth Army,[21] asking for detailed assault plans to be prepared and forwarded for approval. Immediately a series of discrepancies between these two levels—the G.H.Q. and the army command—began. Whereas the army command had prepared a plan for the quick capture of the fortress of Verdun, almost by a *coup de main*, based on the effect of heavy artillery, Falkenhayn spoke only about "attacks in the Meuse-area in the direction of Verdun.''[22] That was not accidental. For Falkenhayn's real intention was never revealed to anybody. Nobody (except probably the Kaiser) had seen his Christmas Memorandum.[23] Therefore, the Crown Prince believed that a normal combat mission had been ordered, which should be solved in a normal way.[24] Despite the discrepancy between the command level giving the order and that carrying it out, Falkenhayn approved the Fifth Army's plan of battle. He did not want to disclose his real intentions and probably believed, for psychological reasons, that the prospect of capturing Verdun would serve as an incentive for extreme efforts by the troops involved. After all, he could do that, for he had some effective regulators in order to steer the battle in the desired direction.

First of all, he limited the extent of the front to be attacked. Whereas the Fifth Army's proposal was to attack simultaneously on both banks of the Meuse, Falkenhayn ordered that it be confined to the initial assault against the right bank.[25] The reason given was that the two additional divisions required for the enlarged attack on the left bank would reduce the German general reserve below its acceptable rate. The true reason may already be found in the memorandum's phrase "for an operation limited to a narrow front, Germany will not be compelled to spend herself completely, that all other fronts are practically drained." Both ideas—the limited front and the preservation of sufficient reserves—are already inherent in this formulation. Again Rupprecht had not grasped Falkenhayn's real purpose when he wrote in his diary on 15 February 1916, six days before the assault, that the strongest point in the whole French front—Verdun— could be attacked only with considerable forces and on both banks of the Meuse simultaneously. The attack on the left bank was carried out at a later stage, in accordance with the concept "to accelerate or draw out the offensive, to intensify it or break it off from time to time, as suits the purpose." Falkenhayn's purpose was a clear-cut one.

Falkenhayn's other grip on the control lever was by means of manipulating the reserves. Falkenhayn had promised the Crown Prince that adequate reserves would be available "in time" to keep the battle going. In any case, by pretending technical difficulties, like the shortage of suitable accommodation, the reserve divisions remained under G.H.Q.'s control and were kept far away from the battlefield. Unfortunately for the poor Crown Prince, "in time" did not mean the same thing to him as it did to Falkenhayn. Wilhelm expected the reserves to be ready immediately behind the battle line, and pushed forward in order to keep up the momentum of the assault, in order to achieve the quickest and earliest capture of Verdun. Falkenhayn, on the other hand, was interested in first drawing into the battle as many French reserves as possible. A quick and too-early collapse of Verdun would not serve this purpose. As Alistair Horne has so rightly said: "Seldom in the history of war can the commander of a great army have been so cynically deceived, as was the German Crown Prince by Falkenhayn."[26]

The regulation of the flow of operations at Verdun was but one aspect of the problem. For Falkenhayn had nourished the secret hope that hostile "relief attacks" were "to be expected," and he could "indeed hope to have sufficient troops in hand to reply to them with counter-attacks." It seems that Horne's expression "the cautious Falkenhayn's fears of Allied counter-attacks"[27] is an underestimation of Falkenhayn's real intentions. Judging from the formulation of his memorandum,[28] he was not afraid of Allied counter-attacks, and indeed hoped that they would occur. He wished to inflict punishment on "perfidious Albion" at the same time he was draining the French blood. Only the method was different. First, if the British should move out into the open and attack the German trenches, only then would the German reserves strike back and exploit the success far beyond the British lines of trenches. Falkenhayn believed that the British riposte was due north of Arras. He accordingly ordered the Sixth Army to prepare the German counter-offensive and promised eight additional divisions from the general reserve. When Rupprecht recorded in his diary on 12 February 1916[29] "that General Falkenhayn was himself not clear as to what he really wanted, and waiting for a stroke of luck that would lead to a favorable solution," he was wrong with regard to the first part of the sentence. Falkenhayn wanted to inflict heavy losses on the French ("bleed them white"), and thus compel the British, by rushing to their assistance, to present him with an opportunity of hitting back and thus regain a war of movement. Because the Sixth Army's judgment regarding the complete unpreparedness of the new Kitchener armies was correct in pointing out that such an occasion was unlikely to happen, Rupprecht was therefore right in the second part of his observation. It was indeed wishful thinking to expect a British relief attack north of Arras at that time. Nevertheless, it remains doubtful whether the acceptance of this judgment would have accelerated the flow of reserves into the Verdun sector,[30] since the basic gap between the will of the Fifth Army to capture the fortress and Falkenhayn's striving after a battle of exhaustion for his adversary, was unbridgeable. The key to a solution was the reserves. These were in Falkenhayn's hands and he guarded them jealously.

An additional aspect of the reserves problem should be considered: By making the use of his reserves (with regard to the expected British riposte) dependent on various possibilities, Falkenhayn had actually lost his freedom of action to the same extent as he had lost it at the very moment that Verdun turned to be an issue of prestige for Germany.

UNEXPECTED FRICTIONS IN FALKENHAYN'S SCHEME

While Falkenhayn was conducting his extraordinary battle of attrition "in the Meuse-area in the direction of Verdun," and was waiting for the British relief attack to come, the tables were suddenly turned on him from unexpected quarters. On 4 June 1916 the Russians penetrated the Austrian front in Galicia and routed the Austro-Hungarian Army. Considerable German forces were needed to plug the breach. It was at once obvious that Falkenhayn had underestimated Russia's abilities. His prognosis, made in the Christmas Memorandum, that Russia's "offensive powers have been so shattered that she can never revive in anything like her old strength" was completely upset.

This misjudgment was not his only failure; he should have been blamed even more for the mistakes he made that led to the Austrian breakdown. The whole affair began with a controversy between the German and the Austrian Chiefs of General Staff over strategic issues. Conrad had suggested delivering a deadly blow against Italy in a joint operation, relying on the fact that the western front as well as the eastern had stabilized and could weather any storm. Alternatively, he asked for the relief of sufficient Austrian troops by Germans, on the Russian front, in order to embark with his own troops on the Italian enterprise alone. Falkenhayn mistrusted Austria's ability to carry out such an attempt. In the general atmosphere of mutual distrust, neither side had revealed its plans.

At the same time that Falkenhayn secretly prepared his Verdun campaign, Conrad withdrew his best units from the Russian front and transferred them to the Italian theater of war. The second-rate divisions that remained in Galicia did not even try to counter the Russian onslaught. Falkenhayn was taken by surprise, and his plans, as well as those of his Austrian counterpart, were thrown into confusion. Falkenhayn, in his memoirs, has put the whole blame on Conrad. As a matter of fact, as early as 20 August 1919 Colonel Bauer, this prominent figure in German headquarters, noted in a memorandum about Verdun that even though Falkenhayn had disliked the idea of an Austrian offensive in Italy, he had not made any serious effort to prevent its execution. In fact, he even knew the exact date of its execution. Bauer maintained that the fact that the offensives in the Meuse area and in Tyrol were independent of each other only stressed the necessity for concerted action between two allies.[31] In the way the operations were actually handled, all the advantages of fighting on interior lines were lost.

The English, too, refused to play their part. They could not be induced to launch premature attacks and continued with their preparations for an offensive on the Somme. This was eventually staged, together with considerable French troops, which, according to Falkenhayn's program, should already have been exhausted (''bled white''). In the long run France could claim with full justification that Verdun was a French victory—at least ''the bear got a grip on his hunter.''

THE "STRATEGY CONTROVERSY"

It remains to look into the theoretical background of the phenomenon of Verdun. After the First World War, German historian Hans Delbrück (the same man to whom Schlieffen owed the discovery of Cannae) introduced the term ''attrition-strategy.''[32] This strategy was the opposite of ''annihilation-strategy.''[33] Delbrück has based this theory of two poles of strategy, as opposed to the one-pole annihilation strategy, on Clausewitz' note of 10 July 1827, which was found together with the unfinished manuscript of *On War*. It contained the statement that the whole work needed revision:

War can be of two kinds, in the sense that either the objective is to *overthrow the enemy*— to render him politically helpless or militarily impotent, thus forcing him to sign whatever peace we please; or *merely to occupy some of his frontier-districts* so that we can annex them or use them for bargaining at the peace negotiations. Transition from one type to the other will of course recur in my treatment, but the fact that the aims of the two types are quite different must be clear at all times, and their points of irreconcilability brought out.[34]

Delbrück's interpretation of Clausewitz' note set the stage for the famous "strategy controversy" of German soldiers and scholars whom they contemptuously called "civil strategists." To embark on this controversy would not serve the purpose of this investigation.[35] What is nevertheless relevant is the fact that Falkenhayn was praised as an attrition strategist, as opposed to other generals who adhered to annihilation strategy. That Falkenhayn had conducted a strategy of attrition, either deliberately or in despair, cannot be denied. But it seems doubtful whether he had gotten his weapons from Clausewitz' armory. There is no doubt that Clausewitz was not exclusively the prophet of annihilation that the German pre–First World War generation had thought him to be. In Clausewitz' theory, annihilation comprises only one component in a vast scale of other means, which may lead toward the fullfillment of the aims of a particular war. Nowhere in his writings is the idea of draining your enemy's blood—the satanic readiness to sacrifice hundreds of thousands of your own men in order to kill or maim twice as many of your opponents—to be found. To have invented such a theory is the unique privilege of Falkenhayn.[36] It was also contrary to Schlieffen's conception (we have already called Schlieffen the High Priest of annihilation!). Schlieffen would have vigorously rejected any solution in the Falkenhayn Verdun style. For it meant, above all, the launching of a frontal attack—"grappling the bull by his horns"—and Schlieffen's negative attitude to frontal attacks is well known.

On the other hand Falkenhayn obviously never realized that he had chosen a doubtful strategic course. On 12 July 1919, shortly after the end of the war, he published an article on Verdun in the "Militärisches Wochenblatt" (*Military Weekly*) whose gist was to refute the criticism aired against his Verdun campaign. He maintained "that the operations in the Meuse-area, as long as they were kept going, fulfilled the purpose, for which they were launched, and would have achieved, had they been carried on, their final aim, i.e., to bleed the French to death." The majority of the French divisions had been knocked to pieces in the cauldron of Verdun. He put the main blame for being compelled to weaken the western front on "the lamentable collapse of the Austro-Hungarian front in Galicia." The design of the Verdun campaign "as an offensive with a limited objective, its manner of execution, which enabled us to adjust the enterprise to the necessities of the general situation, have proved its value." Falkenhayn went on that "there is every reason to believe that it was this kind of operation, which would have helped us to a successful end to the war."[37]

One doubts whether this posture was, and is, acceptable. One thing, however, remains clear: Both opposing armies were never the same again after having undergone the treatment of the "Meuse-mill." For the troops involved it was not an academic controversy over strategic concepts; for them it was plainly the "Hell of Verdun." The only difference in the long run between the fighting parties was a quantitative one. Whereas the Allies could bear their losses, human and material as well, and compensate for them out of their vast resources, the

Germans could never recover. The prime of Germany's manpower and the morale of its army lay buried in the craters of the Meuse hills.[38]

If trench warfare is to be regarded as a phenomenon of degeneracy in the art of war, the occurrences at Verdun during 1916 certainly represent its lowest ebb. In no way did they contribute toward breaking the vicious circle of static warfare, and therefore it remained a false doctrine right from the beginning.

NOTES

1. The full text of this memorandum was released for the first time in Falkenhayn's own memoirs, *Die Oberste Heeresleitung 1914–1916 in ihren wichtigsten Entschlies-sungen*, Berlin, 1920. An English translation is printed in General Erich von Falkenhayn, *General Headquarters 1914–1916 and its Critical Decisions*, London, 1919, pp. 209–218.

2. E. v. Falkenhayn, *General Headquarters, op. cit.*, pp. 183–184.

3. *Ibid.*, pp. 179–180.

4. Liddell Hart has defined this as follows: "Falkenhayn was history's latest example of the folly of half measures; the ablest and most scientific General—'penny wise, pound foolish'—who ruined his country by refusal to take calculated risks." Liddell Hart, *A History of the World War 1914–1918*, London, 1934, p. 273.

5. E. v. Falkenhayn, *General Headquarters, op. cit.*, p. 58.

6. *Ibid.*, p. 245.

7. Generalfeldmarschall Alfred v. Schlieffen, *Cannae*, Berlin, 1936, p. 262.

8. E. Kabisch, *Verdun. Wende des Weltkrieges*, Berlin, 1935, p. 9. Beside this original idea, this book does not contain as much valuable information as does, on the contrary, the scholarly work of Hermann Wendt, *Verdun 1916*, Berlin, 1931, which is a *sine qua non* for every investigation into the battle of Verdun. Alistair Horne, *The Price of Glory*, London, 1962, mainly relied on it, even though it is omitted from the bibliography of principal sources attached to the book. German Werth's book, *Verdun, Die Schlacht und der Mythos*, whose revised edition was published in Bergisch Gladbach (Federal Republic of Germany) in 1982 was received here only recently and could not yet be analyzed.

9. It is interesting that the same idea had also penetrated British military thinking. The well-known slogan that it did not matter to break through the German lines, but that what really mattered was "to kill as many Germans as possible," has obviously the same mental roots. It is hard to say whether the Germans preceded the British or *vice versa*. However, as early as 28 Jan. 1916 the Bavarian Crown Prince Rupprecht, who was at that time an army commander on the western front, referred to an article published in the *Daily Telegraph* that had propagated the idea. He added the remark that "now on the English side, too, the idea of attrition-strategy is prevailing" (cf. Kronprinz Rupprecht von Bayern, *Mein Kriegstagebuch*, München, 1929, vol. 1, p. 419). Rupprecht at that time already knew that Falkenhayn had decided on the basic concept of the future battle of Verdun. In any case the idea was not made public at the time, for the battle had not yet started. It seems, therefore, that the article Rupprecht was referring to had preceded the publication of the German conception. Whether at that time this article reflected

official British military policy, or was the private opinion of a journalist requires further investigation.

10. "Maasmühle." "Meuse-mill" is a literal translation, but perhaps it would be more appropriate to use the term "Meuse-mincer."

11. Cf. H. Wendt, *op. cit.*, p. 194.

12. Rupprecht, *op. cit.*, vol. 1, p. 472. This basic posture had already been formulated much earlier in Falkenhayn's letter of 21 July 1915 with regard to the situation in the East: "In my opinion our operations are not aimed at Warsaw or Ivangorod, but against the hostile troops, which must be beaten as quickly and thoroughly as possible." Quoted in Wolfgang Foerster, *Graf Schlieffen und der Weltkrieg*, 2d rev. ed., Berlin, 1925, p. 132.

13. For this reason Ludendorff maintained that this point for the attack was well chosen. E. Ludendorff, *Meine Kriegserinnerungen 1914–1918*, Berlin, 1919, p. 161.

14. In his memoirs there is not the slightest hint of such an idea. As a matter of fact, his memoirs are written in a dry and impersonal style, only the third person singular being used.

15. *On War*, VI, 9, pp. 390–391. That was also the French concept as expressed in H. A. Brialmont, *Les Regions Fortifees*.

16. Max Hoffmann, *War Diaries and Other Papers*, London, 1929, vol. 1, p. 144, entry of 21 Aug. 1916.

17. Rupprecht, *op. cit.*, vol. 1, p. 414.

18. *Ibid.*, vol. 3, p. 5.

19. Hermann Ziese-Beringer, *Der einsame Feldherr. Die Wahrheit über Verdun*, Berlin, 1934, vol. 1, p. 125.

20. Alistair Horne's book is recommended for the reader who wants a comprehensive and vivid picture of the battle.

21. Since one is now acquainted with the real background of the Verdun battle, Crown Prince Rupprecht's suspicion (Rupprecht, *op. cit.*, vol. 1, p. 414) that the battle had been launched for dynastic reasons, in order to glorify the Imperial Crown Prince, may be easily discarded. Nevertheless, the Kaiser himself, not understanding what his Chief of General Staff had in mind, might have held such notions.

22. "Angriffe im Maasgebiet mit Richtung auf Verdun."

23. Not even the Quartermaster General of the German Army, v. Freytag-Loringhoven, with whom Falkenhayn had discussed the problems concerning Verdun, and who was highly respected for his military knowledge and for being Schlieffen's favorite disciple. Falkenhayn had not disclosed his real plans, and hence Freytag-Loringhoven believed that a quick capture of the right bank of the Meuse, supported from the left bank, was planned. Cf. Freiherr von Freytag-Loringhoven, *Menschen und Dinge, wie ich sie in meinem Leben sah*, Berlin, 1920, pp. 291–293. General Schmidt von Knobelsdorf, Crown Prince Wilhelm's Chief of Staff and actually commanding the latter's army, wrote in a letter of 6 March 1933: "Unfortunately I never got to know Falkenhayn's memorandum. I don't even know when it came into being and whether it was made known, even to a limited circle. Even during discussions I can't remember any subsequent reference to its content, which I am only now acquainted with. That was most regrettable!" H. Ziese-Beringer, *op. cit.*, vol. 2, p. 200, note 24.

24. Schmidt von Knobelsdorf claimed that the order issued to him orally by von Falkenhayn was: "Capture of the fortress by accelerated procedure" (Fortnahme der

Festung im beschleunigten Verfahren). H. Ziese-Beringer, *op. cit..* vol. 2, p. 200, note 24.

25. It is interesting to note that during the winter of 1912–1913, Moltke had presented, as an exercise dealing with fortress warfare, the problem of an attack on Verdun. The standard solution, distributed by the Great General Staff, was an assault from the northeast on the right bank of the Meuse. Incidentally, a young captain from the staff of Metz' fortress had rejected this solution and held that, owing to the danger of hostile artillery and flanking fire from the left bank, the only solution promising success would be an offensive from the north on both banks simultaneously. General Kabisch, who was at that time Chief of Staff of Metz' fortress, ordered an expert investigation by the senior Artillery Staff Officer, who, in his turn, confirmed the captain's argument. Moltke, informed by Kabisch, did not react. It is doubtful whether this "standard solution" somehow influenced Falkenhayn's planning, as Kabisch thought it might have. E. Kabisch, *op. cit.*, p. 35.

26. A. Horne, *op. cit.*, p. 40.

27. *Ibid.*, p. 39.

28. It seems essential to quote here the original text: "Es [i.e., Germany] kann mit Zuversicht den an ihnen zu erwartenden Entlastungsunternehmen entgegensehen, *ja hoffen*, Kräfte in genügender Zahl zu erübrigen, um den Angriffen mit Gegenstössen begegnen zu können!" I have emphasized the important phrase.

29. Rupprecht, *op. cit.*, vol. 1, pp. 426–427.

30. On 6 April 1916 Rupprecht wrote that he had received information that, behind the Second and Third Armies, there were still some divisions in G.H.Q. reserve. He asked the innocent question: "Why does G.H.Q. hold back so many reserves?" and went on: "It is my impression that this is one of the reasons why the offensive at Verdun is conducted with insufficient forces." He added, however, that Falkenhayn still hoped the enemy would push further reinforcements into the sack of Verdun (the German noun "sack" is used here in the meaning of "trap") and finally bleed to death. Rupprecht, *op. cit.*, vol. 1, p. 444.

31. BA/MA, Nachlass Bauer, Nr. 2, p. 65.

32. As a matter of fact, Delbrück's term reads "Ermattungsstrategie," which should be translated "strategy of exhaustion." Nevertheless, "strategy of attrition" seems to be a more appropriate translation and expresses better the essence of Delbrück's term.

33. "Vernichtungsstrategie."

34. *On War*, p. 69.

35. Hans Delbrück himself had reviewed the controversy in Book III, chapter 6 and Book IV, chapter 3 of his *Geschichte der Kriegskunst im Rahmen der politischen Geschichte*. Cf. also H. Delbrück, *Ludendorffs Selbstporträt*, 10th ed., Berlin, 1922, pp. 12–13, and G. A. Craig's contribution, "Delbrück: The Military Historian," in E. M. Earle, ed., *Makers of Modern Strategy*, Princeton, 1952. H. Delbrück's most systematic exposition of his concept of two forms of strategy is in his work *Die Strategie des Perikles, Erläutert durch die Strategie Friedrich des Grossen*, Berlin, 1890.

36. He had overlooked (or disregarded) Clausewitz' warning that "two decisions, and therefore two kinds of reaction, are possible on the defending side, depending on whether the attacker is to *perish by the sword* or *by his own exertions*" (*On War*, VI, 8, p. 384.). Falkenhayn had rather unconsciously drawn on himself a combination of both possibilities by choosing the role of the assailant at Verdun.

37. Quoted in H. Wendt, *op. cit.*, pp. 187–188.

38. Curiously enough, one German writer—H. Ziese-Beringer, in his book *Der einsame Feldherr. Die Wahrheit über Verdun*—reached the conclusion that Falkenhayn should gain the credit for the mutinies in the French Army in 1917 because they were the aftermath of the Verdun battle. This seems to be a rather doubtful argument.

10

Case 5: The "Great Offensive" of Spring 1918: Ludendorff's Last Bid for Victory

AT LAST, WAR ON ONE FRONT ONLY

By the middle of 1917 it became clear that Russia would drop out of the war under the effects of the revolution. For the first time since those remote days of the Wars of the German Unification, the direct menace of war on two fronts was almost over. After Russia had concluded peace at Brest–Litovsk on 3 March 1918, Germany was able to concentrate nearly all its forces in the West. For the first time since the opening phase of the war, German forces would outnumber the British and French in the western theater of war. As a matter of fact, far more divisions, artillery, and war material were available in 1918 than in 1914.

Although German hopes rose high in view of the renewed prospect for a victorious termination to the war, there were no illusions over the fact that the present superiority in numbers would be for a short period only. In order to retaliate against the stranglehold of the British naval blockade, and because of the belief in the possibility of forcing Great Britain to its knees, German U-boats had, on 1 February 1917, begun to sink Allied and neutral shipping on sight. On 2 April 1917 the United States declared war on Germany. Even as unprepared for war as the former was, it was obvious that the immense potential of manpower and war material would make itself felt on the Allied side before long.

If the German leaders—since 29 August 1916 Field Marshal von Hindenburg as Chief of General Staff and General Ludendorff as his First Quartermaster-General—wanted to stake Germany's fate on offensive action again, it had to be done as soon as possible, before the United States could actively interfere. They were again haunted by Schlieffen's old problems: How to gain a swift and decisive victory in the West? But there was no point in resorting to Schlieffen's plan. This time two frozen front lines were opposing each other. All efforts to penetrate them in either direction had failed so far. Moreover, time was in the Allies' favor. There was no reason why the latter should not just sit down and wait for the U.S. reinforcement to come. That was exactly what the German High Command was anxious to avoid.

What were the means of action open to Germany?

GERMANY'S ALTERNATIVES FOR ACTION

There was a logical possibility for the Germans to stay on the defensive in the West, while consolidating their gains in the East. Based on defensive experience it was feasible indeed that Germany, with the additional reserves released from the eastern front, strengthened by the economic advantages of occupying the Ukrainian granary and Rumania's oil fields, might weather the expected onslaught of the Western Allies, despite the U.S. reinforcements. By wearing down their strength, Germany's enemies might, in the long run, become inclined to accept a peace of mutual understanding. Militarily, this defensive could be reinforced by an increased submarine war against Allied shipping; in the political field, Germany could offer a complete withdrawal from the West, including Belgium, in return for keeping its gains, wholly or partly, in the East.

However, the influence of the stranglehold of the British naval blockade fell heavily into the scale. In November 1917 Colonel Bauer prepared a memorandum about the continuation of the war in 1917–1918,[1] in which Part III dealt explicitly with the condition of the country and the army (Zustand von Heimat und Heer). He stated that "the condition of the country has gone from bad to worse. There is a shortage of manpower for the army and the war industry. Industrial output is declining. . . . Food supply and clothing becomes more and more difficult. Domestic affairs are in an extraordinarily bad tangle and gnaw at the nation's power." Bauer partly blamed the indolent government but admitted that the situation was mainly the result of limited resources and of being shut off from the world. He made it clear that the state of deterioration would go from bad to worse: The manpower situation was nearing a catastrophe, where it was difficult to decide whether the scarce resources should be directed into the armed forces or into mining and industry; exploitation of prisoners of war, women, and adolescents could no longer compensate for the losses on the front; the transport situation in the armed forces and inside Germany had reached a critical stage, and on that account a definite breakdown of Germany's agriculture was to be feared for the coming year; the wear and tear of war material, including ammunition, could hardly be covered, and no increase in the production of war material was to be expected.

On account of such considerations the defensive solution was ruled out and regarded as leading toward certain defeat. An offensive effort was preferred. Wolfgang Foerster thought it possible to observe in Ludendorff's decision for an offensive, an action in the spirit of Schlieffen, namely, "not the wish not to be beaten, but the burning desire to beat the enemy . . . must determine the decision."[2] Nevertheless, after the breakdown of the German spring offensives, Field Marshal Hindenburg stated at the war council of 14 August 1918 that he hoped to hold his ground on French soil. Ludendorff afterward obliterated the word "hope" from the record of the meeting, which now read that the Field Marshal "stated that we will hold our ground on French soil and thereby impose our will on the enemy." Hans Delbrück quoted this occurrence in his testimony before the subcommittee of inquiry of the German Reichstag, which investigated the reasons for the German collapse, as an indication that if in August 1918, after the setback of the offensives, such ideas could be nourished by the German generals, it might be assumed that with the fresh forces at hand before the offensive, a purely defensive attitude might have been even more promising.[3]

There was, of course, a possibility of staying on the defensive in France and of delivering the hostile coalition an offensive blow elsewhere. At least three areas could be considered: in the Middle East, in the Balkans, and in Italy. The Middle Eastern situation had deteriorated for the German Alliance to such a degree that the idea of a major action there had to be dropped. That was the case, too, with regard to the Macedonian theater of war. On the other hand Italy might have been knocked out of the war, and considerable French and British forces might have become involved there in an Italian defeat. Rupprecht wrote in his diary on 21 January 1918:

Since I am not expecting a striking success from a German offensive in the West, I consider it more correct to employ all the forces freed from Russia for a renewed offensive in Italy, in the course of which we may certainly expect to beat the Italians decisively, and at the same time also considerable parts of the British and French armies. Having achieved that—and that can be done very soon—I would turn to the offensive in France with all the forces freed in the meantime from Italy.[4]

Ludendorff, however, was not fond of that idea, although it was suggested in strong terms by his Austrian allies. He regarded an enterprise in Italy as indecisive and a waste of effort, in face of the expected U.S. intervention. In his opinion a decisive step had to be undertaken as soon and as directly as possible, without the detour through Italy. Otherwise, it might be too late to stem the U.S. tide.

Professor Delbrück, contemptuously labeled "civil strategist" by the German soldiers, suggested in his testimony before the committee of inquiry an additional solution—the adoption of a defensive posture in the West, and a march on Petersburg and Moscow, aimed at the overthrow of the Soviet regime. A bourgeois government should be installed there, and a treaty of friendship concluded between Germany and the new Russian State. Such line of action, held Delbrück, would have changed Germany's constellation completely and forced the West to come to terms.[5]

The German OHL, however, settled on a decision in the West. That meant a break-through, or a series of break-through attacks, against the hostile trench system somewhere between Belfort and the channel. Although all attempts of break-through by either side hitherto did not encourage further break-through offensives, the Bavarian Crown Prince, as early as 1916, maintained, nevertheless, that the more superior qualities of German leadership would finally lead to success, even in such a complicated endeavor.[6] Ludendorff reported in his memoirs that three possible localities had been under consideration: the first in Flanders, between Ypres and Lens; the second, between Arras and St.-Quentin or La Fere; the third, on both sides of Verdun simultaneously, without a direct attack on the fortress itself.[7]

These sections of the front were not under review for geographical or topographical reasons only; the main question was, against whom should the major blow be delivered: the English or the French? Or should the initial thrust be aimed at splitting the partners at their points of contact, while taking into account Clausewitz' considerations for the selection of a center of gravity? This was so obvious a reason that Swiss officer E. Bircher had forecast such a German line of action at the end of 1917.[8]

The action in Flanders against the British Army had the support of Army Group Crown Prince Rupprecht, whereas Army Group Command German Crown Prince (Wilhelm) supported the attack in the neighborhood of Verdun against the French. For the offensive proposal in Flanders, F. v. Lossberg, at that time Chief of Staff of the Fourth Army and highly esteemed in OHL, had also prepared his own study and forwarded it to Ludendorff.[9] On the other hand Ludendorff's own Chief of Operations, Lieutenant Colonel Wetzell, had prepared a memorandum in favor of the Verdun offensive.[10] The offensive in the St.-Quentin section, along the seam of the French and British Armies, was suggested by Colonel Bauer, a member of Operations Staff, in his memorandum of November 1917, which has already been mentioned.

There were many pros and cons regarding each of the proposals. From the point of view of enemy strength to be expected at any spot, the strongest enemy concentrations were to be anticipated in Flanders, where the last British offensive had just petered out, and in the vicinity of Verdun. It was also assumed that since the battle of Cambrai, stronger hostile forces might be near that locality. The neighborhood of St.-Quentin was considered the weakest point in the enemy's array.

Other considerations were concerned with the conditions of the ground at various periods of the year. OHL had assumed that the Lys valley, which had to be crossed for the Flanders offensive, would not dry up sufficiently before mid-April. Ludendorff, with an eye on the Americans, regarded that as too late a date for commencing the general offensive. Von Lossberg, on the other hand, not completely ruling out a German setback, considered the late start—he had mid-May in mind—as an advantage. The Germans would, in that case, return to the defensive in late autumn, and thus an enemy counteroffensive would be quite unlikely before the spring of 1919. He also held the opinion that the delay would allow the transfer of more divisions from the East and a longer training period for all the troops concerned. The latter idea was not so unreasonable. After all, the troops had to be taught the new practices of offensive in a static war, after four years of mainly defensive action.[11] The central assault could be launched quite early in the year—approximately in February or early March 1918—but would lead into that artificial desert deliberately created by the German "Alberich" movement of the 1917 retreat. The southern attack was handicapped by rather rough country but could be let off at any time.

Ludendorff faced a dilemma. From a strategic point of view the northernmost offensive had to be regarded as the most hopeful. There was a clearly defined objective: the seizure of the channel ports Calais and Boulogne, a substantial blow to Great Britain and, consequently, much shorter front lines for the Germans, which meant more reserves and better chances of continuing the war. Tactically, it involved the disadvantages of tricky ground and of starting at a strong point in the adversary's defenses. The southernmost offensive near Verdun, if successful, would also shorten the German front line, but its advantages were mainly in the tactical field, and hardly any strategical aims could be attributed to it. The offensive in the St.-Quentin section was the most promising from a purely tactical standpoint. It would obviously meet the weakest spot in the enemy's line, it could be launched early in the year, and, despite touching at the cratered field of the Somme battle, the ground seemed to present no special difficulties. On the other hand the strategic objective was not clear-cut. Ludendorff himself admitted that "the central offensive had the appearance of a pipe dream."[12] He thought of counterbalancing this shortcoming by directing the center of gravity of the operation from between Arras and Peronne toward the coast. If, however, this thrust met with success, it might have great consequences: the separation of the British from the French Army[13] and the pushing of the English to the sea-shore.

Ludendorff had to reach a decision. He decided on an offensive in the center. He probably felt that this particular decision was somewhat unbalanced: Too much consideration was given to the problem of achieving an initial tactical success. It is hard to say whether his explanation that "tactics were preferable to pure strategy. Without a tactical success the latter could not be set in motion"[14] was an attempt to reason an opportunistic approach, or whether he really thought he had reached a new insight. In any case this "tactics-before-and-above strategy" idea was different from Clausewitz' definition of the relationship of strategy and tactics, and opposed to Schlieffen's approach, which stressed operational considerations above the tactical. It presented a departure from the traditional German position.[15] Ludendorff claimed to have deduced this approach from the failure of Allied offensives during the three previous years. If one strips Ludendorff's attitude to its essentials, it simply means resort to brute force without acting on any operational idea.[16] That it was really so is illuminated by the following scene: Toward the second phase of the spring offensives in 1918, Crown Prince Rupprecht, C-in-C of an army group, asked an officer on his staff to find out at OHL what the operational idea for the next phase of the operations was. Ludendorff snapped back through the telephone: "I won't suffer that word 'Operation.' We are going to pierce a hole. For the rest we shall live to see. That was the way we used to do it in Russia, too."[17] After the war he explained that sometimes one is lucky, and the favorable strategic and tactical directions of a thrust converge; but sometimes they diverge, as, for instance, in France in the spring of 1918. In the latter case tactical considerations should carry the decisive weight.[18]

But that was not the only dilemma to confront Ludendorff.

THE PROBLEM: ONE SINGLE BLOW OR SUCCESSIVE SHOCKS?

On 11 November 1917 Ludendorff presided over a conference of chiefs of staff of the German army groups, which was held at Army Group Rupprecht's H.Q. in Mons. Ludendorff summarized his conclusions as follows:

The situation in Russia and Italy will apparently make it possible to deliver a blow in the western theater of war in the next year. A reciprocal equilibrium of forces is about to be expected. About 35 divisions and 1,000 heavy guns will be available. That will suffice for *one* offensive; a second great simultaneous offensive, for instance as a diversion, is out of the question. On the whole our situation demands that we strike as soon as possible, and if possible at the end of February or the beginning of March, before the Americans can throw strong forces into the balance. *We must beat the English.* These are the basic guidelines of the operation.

The operation, suggested by Army Group Crown Prince Rupprecht, towards Hasebrouck—code-named "St. George"—against the flank and rear of the English main forces, is doubtless very effective, but, after all, the difficulties of the ground are tremendous. Above all, the attacks depend on the weather and cannot be launched so soon. In order to gain time, one could first tie down the French, by means of a diversionary attack, for instance near Verdun, in this manner cutting off the bulge there, and then turn against the English. But the forces and ammunition are not sufficient for that purpose.

It remains to examine whether there exist better preliminary conditions for an operation more towards the south. An attack on St.-Quentin in particular, seems to offer success. After having reached the Somme-line Peronne-Ham the attack might be advanced in a north-westerly direction, while leaning the left flank on the Somme, and lead to a "rolling up" of the British front.[19]

Ludendorff stressed the need to destroy railway stations by long-range fire and air bombardment, which would hamper the transfer of enemy operative reserves, as being extremely important for the success of the operation.

However, much earlier, in a conversation with General Hoffmann on 17 April 1917, Ludendorff had said that a break-through in the West was much more difficult than in the East. One had to try at various points in order to find out where the enemy was weakest and at which point an attack should be made with all the strength.[20]

He finally adapted a method of successive blows at various places, intended to so shake enemy resistance that it might finally crumble, rather than achieving and nourishing a forceful break-through. The same attitude was suggested by von Lossberg and Wetzell in their respective memoranda.

It is obvious that Ludendorff was quite aware that he had violated one of Clausewitz' maxims, namely, that "it is one of the most important and effective principles of strategy: *a success gained somewhere must be exploited on the spot as far as the circumstances permit it*; for all efforts made whilst the enemy is involved in that crisis have a much greater effect, and it is a bad economy of force to let this opportunity slip away."[21] In order to meet his critics, Ludendorff later supported his decision by referring to Friedrich the Great, who was supposed to have said that "it is easier to squeeze to death 15,000 men than to defeat 80,000. It has, however, the same effect whilst risking less. Gaining many little successes means the gradual accumulation of a treasure. In the course of time one grows rich without even knowing it."[22]

Von Kuhl explained that Ludendorff was afraid of becoming involved in a "Materialschlacht," which might exhaust his resources, and therefore preferred to break off the battle and try his luck in a new direction.[23] Such an attitude was, however, opposed by von Kuhl's chief, Crown Prince Rupprecht, who wrote to his father, the King of Bavaria, on 19 April 1918:

The results of the first offensive thrust were of such a kind, that only a little more was needed to completely rout the English; then, on 27 March,[24] OHL, in view of their own not inconsiderable losses, decided to give up the attacks on the British and to turn with strong forces against the approaching French, instead of staying on the defensive against the latter. The English, in consequence, were presented with the opportunity of being able to fortify their front anew.[25]

That was exactly what Clausewitz had predicted!

Ludendorff, afraid of putting all his eggs in one basket, launched a series of offensives, switching efforts from place to place[26]: from the St.-Quentin area (21/3/–5/4/1918) to Lys (9/–29/4/1918) and then to the Aisne (27/5–6/6/1918). Having intended to return and hit at the British in Flanders again, Ludendorff was overpowered by the unexpected success in Champagne, and after four years German troops again crossed the Marne (15/7–7/8/1918). In fact, nowhere had a final break-through been achieved. The most successful offensive, and that which came the nearest to a complete break-through, was the initial onslaught against the British Fifth Army in the March offensive. But gradually Germany's reserves were worn down. Once an offensive petered out a new run could hardly be expected.[27] Clausewitz' students should not be surprised by that discovery.

While longing for the annihilation of his adversaries, Ludendorff nevertheless resorted essentially to a strategy of attrition not so different from Falkenhayn's position, which he had so fiercely opposed. What other name could be given to a strategy that expected that—in Hindenburg's words—"by the repetition of small strokes (Teilschläge) the hostile edifice might one day 'on occasion' collapse"?

COMMAND ARRANGEMENTS FOR THE OFFENSIVE

No less curious than the whole design of the offensive were the command arrangements made for it. The whole section to come under the German attack was under the command of Army Group Rupprecht. So were the three armies—Second, Seventeenth, and Eighteenth—that would participate in the offensive. Rupprecht wrote in his diary on 21 January 1918 that the Eighteenth Army was to be transferred to Army Group German Crown Prince:

OHL was polite enough to ask me whether I would agree with this. Of course, I said "yes." From a military point of view, the separation of 18th Army from my Army Group is a great mistake. . . . For political reasons, especially after the fiasco at Verdun, it is desirable to give the German Crown Prince a chance to repair the damage (which incidentally should be entered against Falkenhayn's huge account), by means of taking part in an offensive. In my opinion he should have been given a much earlier opportunity, and that in the eastern theater of war, where it was much easier to gain laurels.[28]

By stressing the dynastic considerations for the division of command, Rupprecht had touched on only one aspect of the problem, and even in that case had only partly revealed its real significance. Ludendorff, in his memoirs, gives an additional reason, namely, his intention to direct the battle himself. He considered it a difficult undertaking for OHL to interfere in a battle conducted by one single army group. On the other hand he held the opinion that if the other army group was also involved in the battle, it would more readily throw in its own resources without objecting to it.[29] Ludendorff, like Schlieffen, believed in a company-like drill of armies and in their strictest conduct by the highest level.

With regard to the dynastic aspects of the problem, Ludendorff expressed his and Field Marshal Hindenburg's personal pleasure at giving His Imperial Highness Crown Prince Wilhelm a fair share in the coming offensive. Despite this apparently loyal attitude, it emerges from Delbrück's evidence before the parliamentary committee that Ludendorff's real intention was not so loyal. Young Wilhelm was but a pawn in Ludendorff's political game. He had previously been used by Ludendorff for the overthrow of Chancellor Bethmann-Hollweg, and had an active finger in the pie in deposing the Kaiser's Privy Councellor, Rudolph v. Valentini, who was disliked by OHL. At that time, at the beginning of 1918, Ludendorff thought of getting rid of the Kaiser, and Colonel Bauer, on Ludendorff's behalf, had already approached Crown Prince Wilhelm and suggested his accession to the throne. Without the change in the command structure of the "Great Spring Offensive," the Bavarian Crown Prince might have become the sole victor of the battle, and the German Crown Prince would have commanded a quiet front. Strategically, that would have had no consequence at all; but for Ludendorff's domestic policy it was of the greatest importance that his candidate for the throne should become a war hero.[30]

Both considerations—his desire to maintain the direct conduct of the battle in his own hands, and the elevation of Crown Prince Wilhelm—led to the odd spectacle of three armies taking part in an operation aimed at the same objective—on a narrow front of 75 kilometers—being split up under two army groups. Coordination of units fighting shoulder to shoulder had to travel all the way from one army to the army group, through OHL to the other army group, and down to the neighboring army. No wonder such an arrangement produced constant frictions and, far from creating a company-like army front, resulted in a series of missed opportunities.

However, that was not the only deficiency of the German spring offensives.

THE REASONS FOR FAILURE

Some of the roots of failure have already been touched on: The economic breakdown, aggravated by the British naval blockade, attached leaden weights to the military operations. There was shortage of ammunition and transport facilities (shortage of horses and of fuel and rubber for mechanized transport), a lack of spare parts, and lack of replacement weapons. As a consequence, the German Army had long before been divided into two kinds of divisions: "assault divisions" (Angriffsdivisionen), which had been provided with adequate transport facilities, and "static divisions" (Stellungsdivisionen), which had only to hold their ground in rigid defense. One could not assign any active missions to the latter type of divisions, and the High Command was therefore limited to its freedom of disposition.

No less hampering was the manpower situation. It led to a serious shortage of reserves. Once units had suffered heavy losses they could not be replenished. The strength of units dwindled steadily. Finally, there was no choice other than the dissolution of divisions in order to reinforce others with their remains. A lack of sufficient reserves, among other factors, prevented the full operative exploitation of initial successes.

The shortage of reserves ruled out from the beginning any thought of conducting diversionary attacks on secondary fronts in order to tie down enemy reserves and prevent their interference on the main battlefield. Despite difficult command arrangements on the Allied side, too, reserves were hastened to the endangered sections much earlier than was anticipated by the German planners. Air bombardment of railway installations, as ordered by Ludendorff, proved ineffective at this premature stage of military aviation.

The selection of the battlefield of the previous Somme battle, and the scene of the "Alberich" retreat, imposed brakes on a swift advance. The inadequacy of German transport capabilities, combined with the difficulty of the ground to be traversed, hampered the advance of artillery, ammunition, and supplies in the wake of the assault troops.

The command chaos created by Ludendorff has already been dealt with. Against the background of scanty reserves, and the burning need to utilize them to the utmost, the command structure tended to add to the confusion and held no advantages whatsoever. Lack of a strong central reserve, which should have been exclusively at the disposal of the commander of the offensive, forestalled the exploitation of the unique, but unexpected, opportunity presented by the crumbling away of British General Sir Hubert Gough's Fifth Army. Once the *coup d'oeil* was missed the redirection of forces toward the breach had no chance.

Even worse, from the German point of view, is the impression of irresolution in the conduct of the whole affair that one gets from switching from objective to objective. This lack of consistency in pursuing a selected goal was apparent. Instead of concentrating on a certain achievable objective, other tempting directions were followed. The offensive "fanned out"[31] without any recognizable center of gravity. Rupprecht wrote on 5 April 1918, the day the St.-Quentin offensive was given up: "It is obvious that one cannot discern a proper purpose in all OHL's directives. They always mention certain landmarks, which should be reached, and one gets the impression that OHL, as it were, lives from hand to mouth, without acknowledging a fixed purpose."[32] A further criticism made by Rupprecht of the conduct of affairs was the overhasty renewal of a new offensive thrust in a new direction, without allowing the necessary time for preparations. All the subsequent steps bore the mark of unjustifiable haste in face of still-organized hostile fronts. Ammunition was running short, the regrouping of artillery and assault troops was inadequate, but nevertheless, new attacks were frenziedly pressed forward. One gets the impression that somebody in G.H.Q. was running berserk.

In 1944 Wolfgang Foerster prepared a study of Ludendorff's strategy for the period of April to October 1918, and drew attention to the fact that Ludendorff had lacked in understanding the great importance of the tank, especially as a means of overcoming the stalemate of trench warfare. One should not regard that remark as some kind of afterthought on Foerster's behalf. The idea of a tracked armored combat vehicle had been forwarded to the German High Command. Allied trials, although still infected by infantile diseases, had set the stage for the development of that weapon. It remains Ludendorff's fault for not having provided the German Army with this offensive weapon and for neglecting the creation of effective countermeasures against enemy tanks.[33]

"Ludendorff's strategy in the East, had been so forceful and so far-sighted, that his indecision and short-sight in the West is difficult to explain," wrote Liddell Hart. He thought that Ludendorff was unable to overcome the strain generated by the direction of too many vast operations or that he missed the assistance that Hoffmann had rendered throughout the 1914–1916 campaigns in the East. Liddell Hart concluded: "In any case the campaign leaves the impression that Ludendorff had neither his former clearness as to the goal, nor the same grip on the changing situation."[34] That is an attempt to explain psychologically the blunders of the leading figure in the drama. There is no doubt that psychological reasons were part of the complete picture. However, General von Moser, Ludendorff's wartime colleague, offered a different psychological interpretation of Ludendorff's wavering attitude. Moser criticized Ludendorff's compromise between the operative break-through in the direction of Boulogne and the tactical break-in at St.-Quentin, toward Amiens. He maintained that Ludendorff was never a man of compromise and half-measures. Why then did he adopt a middle course? "The reason was that he, like the majority of German leaders and General Staff officers, being ardent pupils of Schlieffen, doubted at the bottom of their hearts either the certain feasibility or the decisive effectiveness of a great operative break-through."[35] It seems, however, that Ludendorff's cardinal sin, leading to the ultimate collapse of the German Army, was that he trod in Falkenhayn's footsteps.

"NEVER YIELD A SINGLE INCH OF GROUND YOU HAVE WON!"

It is a strange thing that Ludendorff had designed the spring offensives of 1918 in order to break the stalemate of static warfare and to regain a war of movement, and finished by clinging stubbornly to every piece of ground. The latter attitude demonstrated a complete change of opinion on his behalf. Paragraph 6 of his new regulations, "The Attack in Position Warfare," issued on 1 January 1918, read: "Objective, purpose and conduct of the attack vary according to scale and depth. . . . Should it be intended to hold the objective permanently, it must offer more favorable conditions for defense than the line from which the attack was orginally launched. However, one will frequently achieve the aim of the attack even by withdrawing sooner or later to the line of departure."

That was a logical approach. Notwithstanding, Ludendorff decided to depart from his own regulations and ordered the troops to hold the ground where their advance stopped. The result was deep German salients into the enemy line, which by no means presented "more favorable conditions for defense," but rather invited hostile concentric counterattacks. Despite the convincing success of the German retreat in 1917, Ludendorff this time refused to adopt a flexible conduct of operation in face of the expected enemy onslaught. Overstressed and fatigued as the German troops now were, their overstretched line was penetrated at many places, and only with the utmost difficulty could the breaches be plugged. Ludendorff was at his wits' end and panicked. There was no obvious reason why the German High Command should not have resorted much earlier to a flexible defense, utilizing existing positions in the rear and commanding them with counterattacks into the advancing enemy's flanks. That was one of the lessons to be learned from Clausewitz. And the Germans could have afforded it, for they were still on French and Belgian soil.

NOTES

1. BA/MA, Nachlass Bauer/2. "Denkschrift über die Fortsetzung des Krieges 1917–1918." The memorandum does not bear the date of the day in November 1917.

2. Wolfgang Foerster, *Graf Schlieffen und der Weltkrieg*, 2d rev. ed., Berlin, 1925,

p. 272. The quotation from Schlieffen is from *Dienstschriften*. Berlin, 1937–1938, vol. 1, p. 87. *Vide* also Book One Chapter 2, under "The Cannae Concept and the Idea of Annihilation."

3. Korreferat des Sachverständigen Geheimrat Prof. Dr. Hans Delbrück zu den Gutachten des Generals a.D. von Kuhl und des Obersten a. D. Schwertfeger," in *Das Werk des Untersuchungsausschusses der Deutschen Verfassungsgebenden Nationalversammlung und des Deutschen Reichstages 1919–1926*, Berlin, 1925, Vierte Reihe, 3. Band, pp. 280–281.

4. Kronprinz Rupprecht von Bayern, *Mein Kriegstagebuch*. München, 1929, vol. 2, pp. 323–324.

5. *Untersuchungsausschuss, op. cit.*, 4. Reihe, 3. Band, pp. 253–254.

6. Rupprecht, *op. cit.*, vol. 1, pp. 444–445.

7. E. Ludendorff, *Meine Kriegserinnerungen 1914–1918*, Berlin, 1919, p. 473.

8. E. Bircher, *Die Schlacht an der Marne*, Bern, 1918, p. 247. The book went to print at the end of 1917.

9. The full text is quoted in F. v. Lossberg, *Meine Tätigkeit im Weltkriege 1914–1918*, Berlin, 1939, pp. 315–320.

10. Printed in Hermann v. Kuhl, *Entstehung, Durchführung und Zusammenbruch der Offensive von 1918*, Berlin, 1927, pp. 107–112. Kuhl's book is a special edition of his expert evidence delivered to the parliamentary committee of inquiry and also published in *Untersuchungsausschuss, op. cit.*, 4. Reihe, 3. Band, I. Teil.

11. On 1 Jan. 1918 Ludendorff issued a new pamphlet in the series, "Vorschriften für den Stellungskrieg" (Regulations for Position Warfare), which read: "Teil 14: Der Angriff im Stellungskrieg" (Part 14: The Attack in Position Warfare).

12. "Der mittlere Angriff ging scheinbar sehr ins Weite." Ludendorff, *op. cit.*, p. 474.

13. It is of interest that Ludendorff, in his memoirs, did not mention at all that a thrust along the "seam" of the British and French forces could create a critical command situation in the Allied camp, as was in fact the case.

14. "Die Taktik war über die reine Strategie zu stellen. Ohne taktischen Erfolg war eine solche nicht zu treiben." Ludendorff, *op. cit.*, p. 474.

15. H. Rosinski maintained: "A further consequence . . . is the deep-rooted German conviction that the *Whole determines the Part*, not otherwise and that in consequence a superior grasp of the situation and conduct of the action as a whole will compensate for any errors made in detail by subordinate commanders. The logical conclusion should have been a marked predilection for strategic or operational over tactical action in the German Army, but although this tendency is not entirely absent, hard, practical common sense has, on the whole, tended to preserve its leaders from abberations in this respect. On the contrary, the Scharnhorst school, Clausewitz not excepted, tends, if at all, to place the basic tactical above the strategic factor. With Moltke the two are almost equally balanced and it is only with Schlieffen that we arrive at a distinct tendency towards a one-sided over-emphasis upon the operational factor as a result of his 'Strategy of the Absolute.' When Ludendorff, in March 1918, therefore rightly decided that in the particular conditions of the "war in the trenches," the tactical factor would have to be placed above the strategic, he was strongly taken to task by many of Schlieffen's pupils." H. Rosinski, *The German Army*, Washington, D.C., 1944, pp. 188–189.

16. On 6 June 1936, in the famous Mittwochgesellschaft (Wednesday Society), Wilhelm Groener talked about the "Persönlichkeit und Strategie Ludendorff's" (Cf. BA/MA, Kl. Erw. 179–2–Sitzung 942). In connection with the conclusions from this speech

he wrote on 13 May 1938 to Mrs. v. Hahnke: "At present I am dealing with Ludendorff's strategy in 1918, which, as a matter of fact, was not a strategy at all, for the so-called Great Offensive of that year was not based on operative considerations, as Ludendorff himself admitted in his memoirs. It was a last attempt to extort victory by applying brute force." BHA—Rep. 92, W. v. Hahnke, Nr. 31/32.

17. Rupprecht, *op. cit.*, vol. 2, p. 372, entry of 3 April 1918.

18. E. Ludendorff, *Kriegführung und Politik*, Berlin, 1922, p. 214.

19. Quoted in H. v. Kuhl, *op. cit.*, pp. 102–103.

20. Max Hoffmann, *War Diaries and Other Papers*, London, 1929, vol. 2, p. 173.

21. *Hinterlassene Werke des Generals Carl von Clausewitz über Krieg und Kriegführung*, vol. 8: *Der Feldzug von 1815 in Frankreich*, Berlin, 1862, pp. 149–150.

22. E. Ludendorff, *Kriegführung und Politik, op. cit.*. p. 22.

23. H. v. Kuhl, *op. cit.*, p. 113.

24. The offensive was launched on 21 March 1918.

25. Rupprecht, *op. cit.*, vol. 3, p. 23.

26. On 13 Feb. 1918 he reported to the Kaiser: "One should not expect an offensive as in Galicia or Italy; it will be a gigantic struggle, commencing at one point, proceeding to another, and requiring a prolonged period of time."

27. Rupprecht wrote in his diary on 12 April 1918, i.e., three days after the commencement of the Lys offensive: "What now counts above all is to wear down the British, in order to make their defeat certain. This opinion is also supported by Major Wetzell, Chief of Operations, but Ludendorff seems to prefer a series of smaller attacks. However, with smaller attacks, one achieves but smaller results than with great ones, and retains proportionally higher losses; moreover, they use up relatively more ammunition, on account of the necessary flank protection; in addition the continued regrouping of artillery requires a lot of work and tires troops andd horses to a high degree. No doubt Ludendorff is a splendid organizer, but he is not a great strategist." Rupprecht, *op. cit.*, vol. 2, pp. 379–380.

28. *Ibid.*, pp. 322–323.

29. Ludendorff, *Kriegserinnerungen, op. cit.*, p. 475.

30. *Untersuchungsausschuss, op. cit.*, 4. Reihe, 3. Band, p. 294.

31. German critics used the term "zerflattern."

32. Rupprecht, *op. cit.*, vol. 2, p. 372.

33. BAl/MA—H80–1/14. Wolfgang Foerster, *Ludendorffs Strategie von April bis Oktober 1918*, Herbst, 1944.

34. Liddell Hart, *A History of the World War 1914–1918*, London, 1934, pp. 72–73.

35. Otto v. Moser, *Das militärisch und politisch Wichtigste vom Weltkrieg*, Stuttgart, 1926, pp. 47–48.

The Relationship of War and Policy During the First World War

> "Politik hält im Krieg den Mund, bis Strategie ihr das Reden wieder ge-
> stattet!" (Policy keeps its mouth shut during war, until strategy permits it
> to speak again)
> —Wilhelm II's marginal remark, to an article in the "Frankfurter Zeitung"

It has already been stated that Clausewitz' postulate of the primacy of policy
over war should be considered as the central pillar of his theoretical edifice.[1]
How crucial many Germans considered this problem to be is indicated by the
vast number of post-war publications entitled "War and Politics" or with similar
titles. It therefore seems appropriate to conclude the investigation of the First
World War with a survey of the relationship of policy and war during its course.

GERMAN SOLDIERS' PERCEPTION OF CLAUSEWITZ' POSTULATE

It is obvious that even though Clausewitz was formally held in high esteem
by the German pre-war Army, little consideration was actually given to the gist
of his teaching. The younger Moltke had urged his son to study Schlieffen's
Cannae in order to prepare himself for attendance at the War Academy,[2] whereas
one might rather have expected that he should have been referred to Clausewitz'
work. That this attitude was not accidental is also indicated by Wilhelm Groener,
who recalled that "in my military reading, I was more occupied with books of
the practical service, than with works on high strategy. I procured Clausewitz'
'On War' only in later years."[3]

However, Clausewitz' concept of the primacy of policy over war was rejected
by the soldiers. How strong this opposition really was is illuminated by the
falsifications of the original text.[4] German soldiers were not in favor of Clausewitz' definition regarding the defense, either. Nevertheless, that particular part
of his writing was never altered in subsequent editions of his work. It is obvious
that they just could not stand the idea of the political agency dominating the

war, and were anxious to prevent the discussion of this subject, which, on the other hand, they did not evade with regard to the concept of defense. The forgery (which it essentially was!) of Clausewitz' conception of war and policy is all the more surprising, since the three wars of German unification were conducted in accordance with Clausewitz' ideas. Although reluctantly, the elder Moltke had accepted Bismarck's leading role in shaping the objective of the war and interfering in its course with political demands. In those cases where the military and the political agencies were at loggerheads, the Prussian King had always sided with the political function. However, as a result of the spectacular military successes of those wars, the military establishment had managed to achieve its independence, and the elder Moltke's formula, which he himself failed to impose at his time—that policy "acts with decisive influence at the opening and at the end of the war" but that war "serves policy best; when completely independent of policy in its action"—became the standard opinion. Finally, this posture was firmly entrenched by Schlieffen and never doubted by his successors.

Colmar von der Goltz, despite his personal experience in military-diplomatic missions, wrote in 1883: "It behoves us, therefore, to have a sharp eye for, and to guard against . . . the interference of political considerations with the strategic and tactical decisions."[5] That was, of course, the standard opinion of the German officer. However, Friedrich von Bernhardi, writing before the First World War, was more in line with Clausewitz' original idea: "The deeper we penetrate into the nature of war, the more we recognize how intimately war is interwoven with the political state of affairs which directly affects the conduct of war, so that we cannot disregard this influence of politics without becoming arbitrary."[6] Yet after the war v. Bernhardi changed his mind completely. He, surprisingly, held that diplomacy's task is completely different as soon as war has really broken out. There remained diplomacy's job of preventing other states from participating in the war, but even that may be done only by agreement of the Army High Command. Diplomacy must completely yield to the wishes of the Army High Command and abstain from taking any steps without consulting the latter. In war, political mistake is followed immediately by military punishment. Therefore, statecraft must restrict itself to paving the way for military success or its exploitation, but in accordance with orders given by the military. The statesman has to yield to the latter unconditionally. The military requirements stipulate the political. As long as war is waged, only military success should be striven for. If there seems to be any prospect of peace, the soldier alone will decide whether it might be achieved by increasing the military effort or by means of diplomacy, i.e., concessions. Only the soldier is in a position to judge that.[7]

This long-winded statement clearly explains what actually happened in the German camp during the First World War. It is strange that despite the collapse, German soldiers still had not found their way back to Clausewitz' concept.[8] No wonder General von Kuhl, when being asked by the parliamentary committee of inquiry about Ludendorff's discordant relations with the politicians in 1918, replied, with regard to Clausewitz' concept to which the questioners in that context referred, that "in spite of the high esteem in which the work "On War" is held after one hundred years, not everything contained in it is still unconditionally applicable."[9] That was, of course, a conscience break with Clausewitz. Field Marshal von Hindenburg, despite serving for a certain period as teacher at the War Academy, seemed simply to have misread the work when he wrote in his memoirs: "Clausewitz . . . knew war. . . . If we followed him we would be successful. The reverse meant mischief. He warned against encroachments of politics upon the conduct of war."[10] Even more extravagant is what Austrian General Alfred Kraus thought he had learned: "Theory teaches us: Policy must not interfere with the conduct of war: wherever, during a war, political and military requirements oppose each other, the military have the precedence."[11]

No wonder that Ludendorff, even prior to the final definition of his "Total War" theory, felt himself compelled to alter Clausewitz' concept of the war-policy relationship. In his book on the conduct of war and politics, the following aphorisms deserve attention: "The passage: 'War is a mere continuation of policy by other means' ought to run: 'War is foreign politics by other means,' and must be complemented by the passage, which will yet be proved to be true: 'As for the rest, overall politics must serve the war.' " Although OHL considered the problem of peace as a concern of politics, it had to keep an eye open, lest the peace policy of the Reichskanzler should harm the conduct of war, and above all, it had to strive for a formulation of frontiers, which should provide favorable military and economic conditions for the next war.[12]

One ought not be surprised that there was a wide range of opinion among German officers as with W. Groener's opinion, who denied the statesman the role of a strategic supreme controller. "Yet one should concede him the right, or rather the obligation, of checking whether the presumed results of an operation are compatible with the intentions and objections of policy."[13] Groener's posture should, however, be judged by the fact that at the time he wrote the quoted passages (in 1930), he had already changed over to the camp of the politicians, as Minister of Transport and Minister of the Reichswehr in the Weimar Republic.

THE RELATIONSHIP BETWEEN THE GERMAN GENERAL STAFF AND THE POLITICIANS

One may be puzzled by the fact that German statesmen did not know of Clausewitz and the rights that he had granted to them. Bismarck, who in fact took full advantage of his prerogative as the leading statesman, is said to have admitted "his shame at never having read Clausewitz, and of not knowing anything about him, except that he was a very deserving general." From Bethmann-Hollweg's apologetic memoirs one receives the impression that he did not know Clausewitz either.

Indeed, Bethmann-Hollweg had unconditionally surrendered his legitimate position as Chancellor and yielded to the dictate of the General Staff. "As with the opening of the war, political measures had to be shaped in accordance with the needs of the campaign plan, which was declared to be unalterable,'' wrote von Bethmann-Hollweg in his memoirs. This was also the case during the war. The political establishment did not take part in the drawing up of the campaign plan, neither in the alterations of the Schlieffen Plan, nor in the deviations from the plan by its execution in practice. He admitted that during his whole term of office, he was never consulted and that there was never anything like a war council. What Bethmann subsequently stated can be regarded only as the fateful resignation of his high office to play instead a subordinate and indecisive role during the course of war:

The position which war conceded to the political leadership, vis-à-vis military operations on land and sea, was decided by the things themselves. By no means could the military layman pretend to judge military possibilities, let alone military necessities. I received the impression that it was military necessities that guided the conduct of war. Behind even the most brilliant initiative displayed by the General Staff, was military compulsion. How to solve that compulsion, could only be decided by the military, even on occasions where military and political requirements went hand in hand.[14]

The Chancellor's submission to the soldiers may partly be explained by an utterance of Schlieffen regarding the position of the Prussian Chief of General Staff, "which 40 years ago was certainly nothing, but since 3 July, 1866,[15] is the most honorable position in the world.''[16] A further contribution to the odd situation may be found in the attitude of Kaiser Wilhelm II, who considered himself, above all, to be a soldier, was full of prejudices against the "silly civilians,'' and did not grasp that the war he was waging was primarily a political affair.[17] No wonder the General Staff was full of self-esteem for the over-all importance of its role. Wilhelm Groener wrote, at the outbreak of the war: "We of the General Staff strive with all our deeds to do a good job, so that—should it depend on us—the German people will live in peace for the next hundred years. Herr Reichskanzler and his chaps seem to regard the war as a philosophical idea, and are not disinclined to conclude a dubious peace as early as possible! That is out of question, we shall not only cope with the French but also with Mr. Bethmann and his Foreign Office.''[18]

The antagonism between the General Staff and the civil government came to a head during Ludendorff's term of office at OHL. Colonel B. Schwertfeger, who gave expert evidence before the parliamentary committee of inquiry, admitted that

Ludendorff considered the conduct of war, and politics, to be two separate entities, fighting each other with hostility. The conduct of war was full of hope, intending a victorious solution to the bloody conflict, whereas politics and their executives always had the feeling of disaster, if not even a downright malicious will. There was barely a word of appreciation for the fact that the politicians were also faithful sons of the fatherland, and strove with all their efforts, according to their position, for a successful termination of the war.[19]

For that delicate state of affairs the soldiers mainly blamed the lack of a strong and trustworthy personality among the civil leaders. In General v. Moser's opinion the dissonance accrued from a misunderstanding of their reciprocal functions. The statesmen lacked any strategic education, and the military experts were not trained in politics. The result was a total absence of a joint approach to the common cause, which in the long run contributed heavily to the final German disaster.[20]

Because the Kaiser, rather than occupying a neutral position above the antagonists, was, instead, part of the power struggle, one does not wonder that the military establishment dominated the politicians in every respect.

MILITARY DOMINATION

In Clausewitz' theory one can clearly tell the difference between a plan of war, which is a political act and therefore decided by policy, and the plan for a campaign, which is instrumental to the military-technical achievement of the objective. The Schlieffen Plan (the original as well as the modified version) was designed in secrecy by the General Staff without any consultation with political agencies, and was therefore only a plan for the campaign. Strange as it may now seem, Germany went to war in 1914 without a comprehensive plan for war. The German statesmen had renounced, *a priori*, their proper share in the proceedings and accepted the military plan as the ultimate oracle. Nobody heeded the fact that modern wars are a complex combination of political, economic, and military problems. By taking this course Germany turned the General Staff's position from being that of a servant into one of supremacy.

The events of July and August 1914 illuminated the limitations imposed on the freedom of political maneuver by the rigid patterns of the military plan. To make things even worse, German mobilization procedures could not separate mobilization proper from the opening of hostilities. The plan presumed violation of foreign frontiers shortly after mobilization. Therefore, as long as there was any intention of political maneuvers, mobilization had to be deferred. Yet a basic feature of the military plan was that Germany must have a time advantage in mobilizing. This explains Moltke's hysteria when the early Russian mobilization became known, and his pressure on Austria, independently of the German Foreign Office, to mobilize at once and adopt a tough political line. General Conrad von Hoetzendorff, the Austrian Chief of General Staff, exclaimed on realizing the discrepancy between notes received from different German agencies: "Who rules in Germany, the Government or the General Staff?" Moltke, afraid of disturbing the smooth running of his deployment, panicked and insisted on the declaration of mobilization as soon as Russia had begun its mobilization. This in fact prevented any further diplomatic moves aimed at solving the crisis at the conference table. Mars ruled the hour! Even worse was the fact that the General Staff had only prepared one plan for war, and therefore no alternative lines of action were possible. The war had to be conducted in accordance with a pre-arranged military plan, whether it suited the actual political situation or not.[21]

The whole problem of the violation of Belgian neutrality, already dealt with elsewhere,[22] was only one symptom of the curious relations between statesmen and soldiers and the former's submission to the latter.

It was therefore only too natural that German soldiers and sailors refused to admit that the question of unrestricted submarine warfare was, above all, a political problem.[23] Falkenhayn linked the U-boat war with his Verdun scheme and deliberately disregarded its political consequences, especially the entry of the United States into the war on the hostile side. Contemporary diary entries of German officers revealed that it was mainly the military effects of this action that were taken into consideration. Ludendorff simply maintained that "the unrestricted U-boat war, was the last means of quickly terminating the war in victory." If this were really true, as the navy said, then Ludendorff held "its conduct was our duty to the German people in the pertaining war situation."[24]

It was a strange phenomenon of the German war scenery that the more the situation went from bad to worse, the less agreement between the civil government and OHL could be established—until Ludendorff finally overthrew von Bethmann-Hollweg and became, in fact, although not by title, the dictatorial ruler of Germany.

GERMANY'S RELATIONS WITH ITS ALLIES

Symptomatic of the unsound political atmosphere were the disastrous connections between the Allies in the German coalition. It was an axiom of German pre-war policy that Germany and Austria would wage war together. Nevertheless, no joint planning for the common future war ever took place. Moreover, the German General Staff concealed its plans not only from the politicians, but also from the General Staff of its ally. Schlieffen regarded discussion with the Austrians as a security risk.[25] Although the younger Moltke cultivated more friendly relations with his counterpart Conrad, he never put his cards on the table. However, Falkenhayn's contact with the Austrians became extremely strained, and concerted actions became almost impossible. Because the performance of the Austrian troops deteriorated steadily, and more and more German troops were required for "fire-brigade actions," Austria's dependence on Germany increased. On the other hand Germany was at pains to prevent its ally from dropping out of the war. This should have called for diplomatic efforts but none was made. To the same extent that everything in Germany was handled by military orders, it was also done in relation to the Austrian ally. This strange association between the two nations in the heart of Europe prevented any sound military utilization of the advantage of acting on interior lines. Concerted actions could not be conducted in such a climate of mistrust and mutual isolation.

ON GERMANY'S WAR AIMS

The full range of the question of war aims is outside the scope of this study.[26] However, some reflections on the part played by the soldiers seem to be worthwhile.

The definition of war aims is doubtlessly a political act. Nevertheless, one will not wonder that in Germany at this time the initiative came from military quarters. Moltke's suggestions to the Chancellor and the Foreign Office in early August 1914 for subversive actions all over the globe have already been mentioned.[27] These proposals also contained suggestions on how to neutralize certain areas, and what kind of offers should be made to certain states—for instance, to Japan and the United States—in order to gain an amicable attitude toward Germany. That the Chief of Staff really took the lead in the definition of future war aims is indicated by his proclamation of 7 September 1914, published in the German press: "At the end of the war our Fatherland must achieve a peace, proportionate to the unprecedented sacrifices, which our people have so unanimously made, and which will not be liable to be disturbed for an unbounded time by any adversary." Only five days later, on 12 September 1914, the Reichskanzler echoed Moltke's opinion when he announced his formula for a future peace in almost identical terms.

The policy advocated by the soldiers, of territorial annexations in West and East, was influenced by the desire to create more strategically advantageous frontiers in regard to a future war. The most extreme supporter of such acquisitions was Ludendorff. He believed that the proclamation of high-flown political objectives would urge the German troops to increased exertions. In 1917 he pressed the government for the publication of the German terms for peace. The terms he had in mind were an overt provocation for futher enemy efforts to subjugate Germany. Rupprecht, who was more moderate—and therefore in fact more realistic—wrote in his diary: "Ludendorff is the 'strong man' and his violent nature is opposed to any compromise. He is nothing but a soldier, and not a statesman."[28] At about the same time, Ludendorff would still not agree to give back Belgium, despite Germany's desperate situation. He maintained that it was Germany's misfortune that before the war Belgium was left to Germany's foes.[29]

With regard to the Polish question, too, military and political agencies did not see eye to eye. It is generally assumed that the soldiers were opposed to the proclamation of an independent Poland on 5 November 1916, and considered that step particularly as blocking any possibility of reaching a separate agreement with Russia. It has been claimed that the soldiers were not consulted, and that the proclamation was a German gesture in Austria's favor. However, a small selection of documents, written by Ludendorff and forwarded to the German Foreign Office, give the lie to these claims. As early as 27 August 1915 Ludendorff wrote to Under Secretary of State Zimmermann: "We shall neither obtain a separate peace with Russia, nor even need it, because we are strong." On 2 September 1915, in a memorandum forwarded to Secretary of State v.

Jagow, Ludendorff predicted a revolution in Russia, which might result in the fall of the empire. "Should Poland become independent then, the new order would be carried out without us, whereas, now we can decide it." Six weeks later (20 October 1915) Ludendorff again wrote to Zimmermann and stressed the importance of not returning Poland to Russia, or ceding it to Austria either. Poland should be established as an independent State but firmly exposed to German domination. It might be a stroke of luck for Germany, Ludendorff maintained, if Austria were to be satisfied with the annexation of Serbia and would renounce its claim on Poland. On 17 July 1916, in a letter to Zimmermann written when influenced by the poor performance of Austrian troops, Ludendorff urged the creation of a Polish Grand Duchy, including Warsaw and Lublin, and the levy of a Polish Army under German command. "A Polish Army will emerge, anyhow; now we need it. It might, in practice, be inconvenient," he went on. "That is, however, secondary to the importance of this measure for victory, which we are determined to achieve and must achieve. Let us act now, it is high time."[30] These documents, chosen at random, illuminate how German generals played with the creation and abolition of states, moved frontiers to and fro, and did not confine themselves to their proper military function.

When it became obvious that Germany would by no means be in the position of strength that would enable it to dictate peace at will, the soldiers played with the illusion of achieving a "draw." Friedrich the Great's prolonged struggle against overwhelming odds was always part of the German martial myth. Now, all of a sudden, the Treaty of Hubertusburg (15 February 1763) became the longed-for ideal. This treaty was the result, as it were, of general exhaustion and mutual agreement to terminate a fruitless war. But now German soldiers overlooked the fact that time and resources were running rather low on the German side alone. This notion, however, indicated that they were at last prepared to consent to the despised strategy of attrition instead of the traditional stress on absolute annihilation.

SHIFTING THE BLAME TO THE POLITICIANS

At the time Germany was finally forced to give up the war, its soldiers played their dirtiest trick: They simply claimed that Germany was militarily undefeated; it was the politicians who had lost the war. This meant not only the breaking up of the basic war-policy partnership, but also an artificial dissolution of war into different facets, by which the soldiers were able to reap the glory and leave the responsibility for the unpleasant end to the too-obedient and submissive politicians. Probably no one will claim that the German statesmen of the pre-war and war periods were outstandingly qualified for their jobs; it is, however, obvious that their shortcomings and failures were due mainly to the unhealthy and traditional setting of the German highest administration.

This dishonesty of the soldiers was matched by another: the shifting of the blame to the homefront—the legend of the "stab in the back."

This survey of the German conduct of the First World War comes to its end. Two questions ought to be answered:

1. Did theory, consciously or unconsciously, have any impact on the conduct of that war?
2. If the answer is in the affirmative, what kind of theoretical influence was it?

By looking at the events as seen by the chief actors, it seems that the German Army went into the field accompanied by a certain theoretical ballast. This is indicated mostly by the great amount of discussion shortly after the various events of the war took place and later on. The prolonged period of helplessness and confusion in face of a new phenomenon—the static war—and the efforts toward the formulation of new doctrines are further indicators.

It is, however, obvious that despite the high esteem in which Clausewitz was formally held by the German Army, he was neither thoroughly studied nor properly understood. It was the German Army's misfortune that it had been presented with Clausewitz' teaching through Schlieffen's distorting lenses, and with the latter's oversimplified and craftsman-like interpretation. The true spirit of Clausewitz' theory was superseded by the new virtue of technical perfectionism. Had the Germans heeded Clausewitz' concept of the relationship of policy and war and understood it, and had they derived from it the proper conclusions for German's political situation, the First World War might never have been unleashed. Indeed, although Clausewitz' impact on that particular war was mainly a negative one, namely, the disregarding of his theory, Schlieffen's "shadow hung over the first World War and his influence on German military thought can hardly be over-estimated."[31] This has emerged from the preceding investigation of that war time and again.

NOTES

1. *Vide* chapter 1, under "War and Politics." We would like to draw attention to the stimulating chapter "Krieg und Politik im militärischen Schrifttum der letzten Friedensjahrzehnte," in Gerhard Ritter, *Staatskunst und Kriegshandwerk*, München, 1954, vol. 2.

2. *Vide* chapter 4, under "Moltke II and the Schlieffen Plan."

3. Wilhelm Groener, *Lebenserinnerungen*, Göttingen, 1957, p. 46. After the Second World War Field Marshal v. Kleist confessed to Liddell Hart that "Clausewitz' teaching had fallen into neglect in this generation—even at the time when I was at the War Academy, and on the General Staff. His phrases were quoted, but his books were not closely studied." Liddell Hart, *The Other Side of the Hill*, London, 1956 (paperback ed.), p. 214.

4. *Vide* chapter 1, under "War and Politics."

5. Colmar Freiherr von der Goltz, *Jena to Eylau*, London, 1913 (1st German ed. 1883), pp. 75–76.

6. Friedrich von Bernhardi, *On War of To-Day*, London, 1912, vol. 1, p. 6.

7. Friedrich von Bernhardi, *Vom Kriege der Zukunft*, Berlin, 1920, pp. 168–170 passim.

8. It is hard to say whether Bernhardi was a forerunner of Ludendorff's "Total War" theory or whether he was already propagating Ludendorff's ideas.

9. *Das Werk des Untersuchungsausschuss der Deutschen Verfassungsgebenden Nationalversammlung und des Deutschen Reichstages 1919–1926*, Berlin, 1925, 4. Reihe, 3, Band, p. 224.

10. Generalfeldmarschall Paul von Hindenburg, *Aus meinem Leben*, Leipzig, 1920, p. 101.

11. Alfred Krauss, *Theorie und Praxis in der Kriegskunst*, München, 1936, p. 44.

12. E. Ludendorff, *Kriegführung und Politik*, Berlin, 1922, pp. 23, 104–105.

13. Wilhelm Groener, *Der Feldherr wider Willen*, Berlin, 1930, p. 164.

14. Th. v. Bethmann-Hollweg, *Betrachtungen zum Weltkriege*, Berlin, 1919, 1921, vol. 2, pp. 7–9.

15. The battle of Königgrätz (Sadowa).

16. Schlieffen's farewell speech to the officers of the General Staff on 30 Dec. 1905. Generalfeldmarschall Graf Alfred von Schlieffen, *Cannae*, Berlin, 1936, pp. 388–389.

17. Cf. Admiral Georg Alexander von Müller, (ed. Walter Görlitz), *Regierte der Kaiser?* Göttingen, 1959, p. 57.

18. Wilhelm Groener, *Lebenserinnerungen*, Göttingen, 1957, p. 160.

19. Oberst a. D. Bernhard Schwertfeger, "Die politischen und militärischen Verant-wortlichkeiten im Verlaufe der Offensive von 1918," in *Untersuchungsausschuss, op. cit.*, 4. Reihe, 2. Band, p. 79.

20. Cf. Otto v. Moser,, *Das militärisch und politisch Wichtigste vom Weltkrieg*, Stuttgart, 1926, p. 8.

21. *Vide* Chapter 2, under "War and Politics," and Chapter 4, under "Mobilization Day, 1914."

22. *Vide* Chapter 2, under "War and Politics," and Chapter 4, under "On the Violation of Neutral Territories."

23. Admiral v. Müller wrote in his diary in June 1915 that "the Navy refuses to admit that the U-boat warfare—especially in our present situation—is an eminent political question." V. Müller, *op. cit.*, p. 106.

24. E. Ludendorff, *Meine Kriegserinnerungen 1914–1918*, Berlin, 1919, pp. 245–246.

25. Cf. *Ibid.*, p. 46.

26. The most comprehensive historical research in this subject is Fritz Fischer's work, *Griff nach der Weltmacht*, Düsseldorf, 1961.

27. *Vide* Chapter 6, under "How to Deal with a British Intervention Against Germany on the Continent?"

28. Kronprinz Rupprecht von Bayern, *Mein Kriegstagebuch*, München, 1929, vol. 2, p. 406, entry of 2 June 1918.

29. *Ibid.*, p. 399, entry of 20 May 1918.

30. *Untersuchungsausschuss, op. cit.*, 4. Reihe, 3. Band, p. 65.

31. Hajo Holborn, "Moltke and Schlieffen," in Edward Mead Earle, ed., *Makers of Modern Strategy*, Princeton, N.J., 1952, p. 188.

Part II

The Inter-War Period: A Theoretical Entr'Acte

The inter-war years were of importance for the formulation of a verdict on the First World War, and at the same time were the "formative years" (to borrow an expression from Alan Bullock, *Hitler: A Study in Tyranny*, Harmondsworth, Middlesex, 1962) with regard to the Second World War. Although hardly a shot was fired in anger in central Europe during these years, at least not on a major international scale, this period deserves its position as the important practical link between two great wars.

12

The Heyday of the Schlieffen School and the Reichswehr

Colonel Dr. Hans Meier-Welcker stated in his essay "Graf Alfred von Schlieffen"[1] that "in fact, Schlieffen's basic idea, looked at on the whole, has not produced a school in the reality of war."[2] Such a statement, made by the Head of the Militärgeschichtliche Forschungsamt of the Bundeswehr in Freiburg im Breisgau, and as a contribution to a scholarly work, edited by a famous historian like Professor W. Hahlweg, should be taken seriously. Moreover, Colonel Meier-Welcker repeated the same opinion in a conversation with me in the summer of 1963, and even enlarged its scope by doubting whether there was a theoretical impact of any kind on the German Army, guiding it in its conduct of war. Professor Gotthard Jäschke of Münster University, who published a survey of the Marne battle,[3] held the same view in his study, has confirmed it orally to me, and in his correspondence with me[4] has expressed surprise at my contrary view. Furthermore, in a critique of Robert Asprey's book, *The First Battle of the Marne*,[5] Professor Jäschke supported Colonel Meier-Welcker's opinion.[6] Wilhelm Groener had much earlier held a similar view: He admitted that Schlieffen had created a school of thought but maintained that the German generals, despite having been acquainted with Schlieffen's ideas, did not act in accordance with the master's doctrine because they had not really absorbed it.[7]

I do not share Colonel Meier-Welcker's view. Schlieffen had, after all, created a body of theory in his various essays, having wide publicity in his time, and through his service papers (*Dienstschriften*) being well known to the German General Staff officers and commanding generals. The purpose of the following pages is to trace Schlieffen's influence on the leading soldiers through the First World War and beyond it.

WAS A SCHLIEFFEN SCHOOL IN EXISTENCE DURING THE FIRST WORLD WAR?

As early as 1915 a certain Dr. Hans Kania used the term "Schlieffen school,"[8] which "has produced an important part of our higher leaders in the great war.

They have spread Schlieffen's ideas in the widest circles of the Army, as even his critics must admit.'' Historian Sigfrid Mette, after having studied the war game of 1905 and the operational studies of 1911–1912, gained the impression that "the Schlieffen disciples of the General Staff behaved in a more Schlieffenian manner than Schlieffen himself."[9] The younger Moltke himself began the war as an ardent partisan of his predecessor. This was confirmed by two of his closest assistants: Generals Tappen and von Dommes.[10] And in the military hierarchy, from the Chief of the General Staff downward, most of the important appointments were held by Schlieffen's former pupils. General Ludendorff was declared by Wolfgang Foerster, one of the central pillars of the post-war Schlieffen myth, as "having come forth from the Schlieffen's school" and deserving "in the fullest sense, the title disciple."[11] Even W. Groener, one of the most outspoken partisans of the great master, admitted that Ludendorff had acted in the East in accordance with Schlieffen's doctrine.[12] Only recently has Colonel General Franz Halder posited the view that "General Erich Ludendorff was a pupil of Schlieffen."[13]

However, a friend of Groener, General A. Wild, in a letter to Groener dated 23 February 1926, put forward a view similar to Colonel Meier-Welcker's opinion, namely, that "unfortunately, Schlieffen had failed to groom successors."[14] Yet that view was refuted in 1935 by H. Müller-Brandenburg in a letter to Groener's daughter. He maintained that Schlieffen "had trained a generation of General Staff officers never seen before or since, either in Germany or elsewhere." He revealed that

personalities, qualified for Schlieffen's succession, like Beseler, Eichhorn, Kluck and later on Kuhl and Freytag-Loringhoven, were never considered by the Military Cabinet to be serious contenders for Schlieffen's post. Yet next in line stood those of the younger generation, Ludendorff, Groener, Lossberg, Hoffmann, Kabisch, Tappen, Seeckt, finally Wetzell, Schwertfeger, v. Haeften etc., really an abundance of talent, all from Schlieffen's school and moulded by him.[15]

This list of German soldiers who became prominent during the war is, of course, incomplete. F. v. Cochenhausen, another pillar of the post-war Schlieffen myth, added von Hindenburg, who had served as a colonel in the General Staff under Schlieffen's direction. He also considered Field Marshal August von Mackensen, Colmar von der Goltz, and General Max von Gallwitz as Schlieffen disciples.[16] H. v. Kuhl, a prominent figure in the post-war pro-Schlieffen movement, whom Schlieffen held in high esteem at the time he served as a major on the Great General Staff,[17] wrote in 1924 that "Count Schlieffen was the teacher of the entire older generation of General Staff officers, who went afield in 1914, and that the younger General Staff officers, too, were trained in his spirit."[18] He reached the conclusion that "during the World War, Schlieffen's doctrine was in force to the fullest extent. He had trained we General Staff officers correctly."[19] General W. Erfurth, in his book *Der Vernichtungssieg*, which in

1939 still breathed forth Schlieffen's ideas, and was edited similarly to Schlieffen's work and to the General Staff's study of the Schlieffen era on the same subject, maintained that "the conduct of a battle, as at Tannenberg,[20] Komarow,[21] Lodz,[22] Limanova-Laponow,[23] in the Winter Battle in Masuria,[24] at Vilna,[25] Schaulen,[26] Hermannstadt,[27] and on the Arges[28] would have been absolutely unthinkable, without the preparation of the leaders by Schlieffen's doctrine. The Cannae-theory has, in the reality of war, proved its worth, and borne plenty of fruit, even though perfect battles of annihilation rarely occurred."[29]

One may add, without hesitation, to the roll of Schlieffen-trained staff officers the large number of commanding officers of high rank who proudly proclaimed in their memoirs that they wished to be regarded as Schlieffen's disciples, among them even commanders of royal blood like the German Crown Prince Wilhelm.

Only recently W. Foerster believed that Schlieffen's impact could be traced as running from his term of office in the Great General Staff through the First World War and beyond it, right into the Second World War. He considered Field Marshal Erich von Manstein's struggle for the campaign plan in the West in 1940[30] as having been inspired by Schlieffen's principles. Schlieffen's staff officers, Foerster stressed, "regarded and admired him rightly, as the typical representative of the doctrine of annihilation strategy. This doctrine was not only valid at the time he was holding office, as Chief of the General Staff, but kept its validity far beyond it into the Second World War, and has achieved great successes in the practice of war, as long as military leaders could maintain their sovereignty in face of amateurish interference from the third parties."[31]

It seems that there is sufficient evidence to carry the point that a Schlieffen school existed during the First World War, and that it embraced the most important part of Germany's officer corps.

THE POST-WAR SCHLIEFFEN SCHOOL

No sooner was the war over than a huge flood of German publications tried to uncover the reasons for defeat. One approach, adopted by soldiers, was of washing their hands of all responsibility for failure, and shifting the blame onto the shoulders of the politicians. It was, however, unavoidable to admit that blunders had been committed in the purely military sphere. Gradually, some kind of psychological defense mechanism was evolved that enabled the largest part of the military to save its face and to transfer responsibility to a small group of scapegoats. The common denominator of this latter group was their "sins against Schlieffen's spirit," thereby forfeiting the "certain victory." In this way the instigation against Moltke II, Falkenhayn, and others emerged.

Those in the front rank fighting this struggle did not confine themselves to publishing their own memoirs, but embarked on writing operational studies of how things went wrong and why, and how the war should have been conducted in accordance with Schlieffen's teaching. They left no doubt that if (those terrible "ifs" in history!) the war had in fact been conducted in line with Schlieffen, its outcome could only have been victory for Germany. In the forefront of this movement Generals Groener and von Kuhl, and Lieutenant Colonel Foerster ranked highest. The titles of their books and articles disclosed the general trend of their approach.

Nor was the continuation of the publications over decades an accident. It deliberately kept the issue alive by harping on the same string again and again. The second rank of the pro-Schlieffen phalanx was formed by such writers as Generals von Freytag-Loringhoven and Kabisch. Subsequently, others followed in their footsteps, among them Generals Boetticher, v. Cochenhausen, v. Zoellner, and Erfurth.[32] More behind the scene was von Schlieffen's son-in-law, General Wilhelm von Hahnke, but the correspondence filed in his own, Schlieffen's, and Groener's papers in the archives disclosed that he was heavily engaged in pulling wires.[33] From a letter of Hahnke to Freytag-Loringhoven dated 5 May 1924 one may learn that in Hugo Roch's biography of Schlieffen, chapters 4 and 5 were actually written by von Hahnke, and that the latter had contributed military and political material to all the other chapters. Moreover, he took pains to discuss his contribution to Roch's book ''word by word'' with Lieutenant Colonel Foerster of the Reichsarchiv, and forwarded the book to General von Haeften, Head of the Reichsarchiv, before sending it to the printing press. He also obtained the approval of General von Seeckt, then Commander-in-Chief of the Reichswehr. This publication seemed of such importance to von Hahnke that he himself paid for the maps, drawn by himself and attached to the book, because the publisher would not print them on his own account. Furthermore, he constantly pressed for a new publication of Schlieffen's writings. ''A new edition of Schlieffen's work shall be published, not for his reverence's sake,'' Hahnke explained,

but because, in our present misery, every educated German has the right to know what a great intellect, who was not understood by his contemporaries, thought about the war, its spiritual and material preparation and its execution. The German people has the right to know how this great strategist tried in vain to warn his contemporaries, to teach them and to convert them. The German people has the right to know what the elder Moltke's successor, who was trained for his job a whole age, thought, when the best army in the world was given into the hands of a greenhorn-strategist, right in the hour of destiny.[34]

One should not minimize the importance of this group that in modern sociological terms might rightly be labeled as a pressure group. After all, Groener soon became a minister in the Republican government and was finally appointed Minister of the Reichswehr. Foerster, von Kuhl, and von Freytag-Loringhoven achieved considerable influence, not only in their military environment, but also in German academic circles, Foerster being eventually elected a Professor of History. Other members of the Schlieffen school reached fairly high ranks in the small Reichswehr and in Hitler's new German Army. This process ought not to be overlooked.

Another line of action was the foundation of the Schlieffen-Verein (Schlieffen Society) in 1922. Field Marshal von Mackensen accepted the chairmanship of this society, Field Marshal von Hindenburg sent a congratulatory telegram,[35] Ludendorff attended the first meeting on 28 February 1922. General von Seeckt was, for tactical-political reasons, prevented from taking part in the gathering (he was, as Commander of the Reichswehr, anxious to avoid the suspicion of the Republican government toward what was considered a royalist society) but sympathized with it. Later on, officers of the new Reichswehr were permitted to attend meetings of the Schlieffen-Verein, after Mackensen's agreement to drop the "hurrah" for the Kaiser from the meetings of the society. This assured the traditional link between the old and the new armies.

The inter-war Schlieffen school, whose existence cannot be denied, exercised its influence in two main streams: in the presentation of the First World War and by shaping a theory for future war.

THE IMPACT OF THE SCHLIEFFEN SCHOOL ON THE PRESENTATION OF WORLD WAR I

Besides the publication of memoirs and operational studies, a clever expedient was used that indicates that these people had a sense for history and how historical research is carried out: They prepared memoranda and filed them in the archives (*ad acta*). These documents had an air of authenticity. With what amount of reservation they should be handled may be learned from the already quoted Hahnke memorandum on Schlieffen's attitude toward England.[36] Hahnke tried to associate Schlieffen with an amicable posture toward Great Britain, thereby shielding him against the accusation that he had underestimated England's part in the future struggle. Yet, unfortunately for Hahnke, he did not realize that the meticulous investigator could also find in the files Schlieffen's letter to Freytag-Loringhoven, whose authenticity is undoubted, which gives the lie to Hahnke's memorandum.[37] Many other examples of this kind of historical distortion may be found in German archives (for instance, Colonel Bauer's memorandum on the Marne battle).[38]

Another trick was to instigate questionnaires and requests for information by the Reichsarchiv and reply with detailed memoranda, giving them the air of documentary evidence. The archives are packed with stuff of this kind.

The major achievement of the Schlieffen school, however, was its overwhelming influence on the official presentation of the First World War by the Reichsarchiv.[39] The creed of the Schlieffen disciples forms the framework of this publication: Schlieffen's plan for war was excellent, nay, ingenious, the infallable panacea for victory. Yet the incapable younger Moltke spoiled the victory by "watering-down" the design and, finally, forfeiting it at the Marne. Falkenhayn also failed because he too sinned against the spirit of the great master. Even Ludendorff, despite conducting the battle of Tannenberg with the master's inspiration, finally, in 1918, sinned too, and therefore lost the "Great Battle in

France'' in the spring of that year. The moral is a simple one: All German successes were due to adherence to Schlieffen's teaching, but the villains who departed from the master's doctrine faced disaster. There can be no doubt that this line was imposed by the authority of Groener and by the very fact that the staff of the Reichsarchiv was mainly manned by members of the Schlieffen school.[40]

Groener, however, tried to waive his responsibility for this form of presentation. After having been charged by General Marx with having exercised one-sided pressure on the Reichsarchiv, Groener defended himself in a letter of 1 January 1938 to Schlieffen's daughter, Mrs. v. Hahnke.[41] Having nothing better to offer than the vague explanation that Generals v. Merz, v. Haeften, and Dr. Foerster, all on the staff of Reichsarchiv, had reached their point of view independently, he in his turn charged General Marx with being a technician, on account of his being a gunner, void of any deeper operative thinking, and bitterly disappointed at not having been made a divisional commander. Judging Marx by his clever and sarcastic books and essays, one tends to look at the things the other way round.

How widespread and deep-rooted the train of thought of the Schlieffen school really became may be learned from the fact that the respectable German Brockhaus Lexicon (under the entry "Marneschlacht") echoes the chain of events as given by the Reichsarchiv.

However, the Schlieffen school did not confine itself solely to influencing scholarly works, like the Reichsarchiv. They seized every opportunity for propagating its view. Dozens of books were written by members of this group throughout the years. In all kinds of newspapers, magazines, and periodicals, articles conforming to their opinion were published. Even the radio was utilized, whether in order to commemorate the anniversary of Schlieffen's birthday, or in memento of the Marne battle or any other more or less suitable occasion. Many drafts for such purposes may be found among Groener's papers.[42]

Schlieffen's disciples were not satisfied with propagating the late master's ideas; they were also a belligerent group. They kept a close eye on every publication dealing with the war and smelled heresy in every quarter. Hence the slightest deviation from their own opinion was vigorously attacked. One of the first acts of the Reichsarchiv was the preparation and circulation of a memorandum, "Die Entwicklung des operativen Gedankens im Zweifrontenkrieg von 1871 bis 1914" (The Development of the Operative Idea upon the War on Two Fronts from 1871 to 1914). Groener immediately seized the opportunity, by means of submitting his reflections, to castigate the younger Moltke for his alterations of the Schlieffen Plan of 1905.[43] When Colonel Mantey, sometime aide-de-camp to the younger Moltke, dared to defend his former chief he was immediately taken to task by Groener in a sharp and cynical letter.[44] In 1929 Professor J. V. Bredt published a book, *Die belgische Neutralität und der Schlieffensche Feldzugplan* (Belgian Neutrality and Schlieffen's Campaign Plan), in which Groener found some remarks that did not fit his own concept; for instance,

Bredt considered the Schlieffen Plan as a "basic idea" for the campaign, whereas Groener regarded it as "a plan of operation fully elaborated in all its essential points." No sooner had Bredt's book appeared than Groener filed a memorandum, "Reflections on Prof. Dr. Bredt's Work."[45] Historian Sigfrid Mette accused Schlieffen of having adopted a mechanical instead of a dynamic approach to warfare. Groener not only discussed this subject with him,[46] but also prepared a memorandum of thirteen typewritten pages in order to dismiss the charge.[47]

In the early thirties certain officers, among them Mantey, Wetzell, and Marx, discussed in military periodicals the shortcomings of the Schlieffen Plan and found justification for Moltke's alterations. Von Kuhl was especially irritated by Wetzell, who used the terms "Schlieffenfanatiker und Umfassungsdogmatiker."[48] Moreover, he was worried about a point made by Schlieffen's critics that the Schlieffen Plan had not reckoned with the possible destruction of the Belgian railway net, and that on that account the whole campaign might have become a failure. He immediately related this information to Groener on 18 September 1935.[49] Groener answered with a letter of six typewritten pages on 22 September.[50] There are, however, two additional points of interest: First, both generals were disgusted by the prospect of being compelled to discuss the matter publicly with former "inferiors" and left that task, as usual, to Lieutenant Colonel Foerster. Second, copies of the correspondence were sent to von Hahnke.[51] It could almost certainly be established that by means of such teamwork, every article either critical of Schlieffen or in favor of the younger Moltke was answered on a tit-for-tat basis.

What was the reason for all this? Groener wrote to Mrs. v. Hahnke: "In all my work, I have the intention of not only criticizing personalities, but rather of illuminating the strategy of the World War, and by way of comparison with your late father's doctrine, of proving strategic errors. This is also of importance for the future, for I am afraid that the leaders of our future Army are bound to commit the same errors as those made in the World War."[52]

Groener was pleased that General von Fritsch, Commander-in-Chief of the new German Army, was to provide a foreword to the new edition of Schlieffen's *Cannae*.[53] He considered this step to be an overt recognition of Schlieffen's teaching by Fritsch and the latter's break with Schlieffen's opponents.[54]

There were, of course, some military writers who were critical of Schlieffen's negative influence on the First World War and even more critical about the image building of Groener and his collaborators, as, for instance, Karl Justrow[55] or General Marx.[56] But these voices were drowned beneath the flourish of trumpets from the Schlieffen camp. Even Field Marshal General von Rundstedt, that excellent and sober strategist, "regarded the battle of the Marne in 1914, as having been lost by Germany, because Schlieffen's plan of a strong right flank had been watered down; the Army Command Staff, far to the rear, had not led with sufficient firmness, and the right-wing army (General von Kluck's First Army), owing to very obstinate leadership, had brought the entire right flank into a situation which could hardly be retrieved."[57]

THE IMPACT OF THE SCHLIEFFEN SCHOOL ON SHAPING
A THEORY FOR FUTURE WAR

It is interesting that F. v. Bernhardi, who, before the First World War, was strongly opposed to most of Schlieffen's principles,[58] returned from the war converted to Schlieffen's doctrine. His book *On the War of the Future*, published in 1920, exudes Schlieffen's ideas. Before the war Bernhardi preached the breakthrough rather than Schlieffen's encirclement. He had found his opinion confirmed by the actual events of the war. Nevertheless, he held the view that future wars would again dissociate from linear strategy and tactics, again strive for mobility, and therefore restore the importance of single-flanking or double-flanking encirclement on the strategic and tactical level.[59] F. v. Bernhardi absolutely rejected the idea of attrition strategy[60] and stressed anew Schlieffen's postulate that a decision is possible only in a war of movement and mobility, combined with outflanking the enemy and pressing on his rear.[61]

General von Bernhardi's renewed siding with Schlieffen's ideas was a great boon to the movement of Schlieffen's disciples. His prominence in the theoretical field of war added weight to the post-war Schlieffen school.

No less favorable was the fact that the new field manual of the Reichswehr, "Führung und Gefecht der verbundenen Waffen"[62] (Conduct and Battle of Combined Arms), published in 1921, stuck to the pre-war regulations of the Schlieffen era. The new manual stressed the importance of the offensive, especially the attack on the enemy's flanks and rear, which provides the best way for the latter's annihilation. Pursuit secures the fruits of victory and should also be directed against the enemy's flanks and rear. Defense is justified only in face of an overwhelmingly superior opponent and in order to facilitate an offensive elsewhere or at a later moment. The paragraph that read that "for a too dispersed array looms the danger of an hostile break-through, while a too narrow array invites hostile envelopment, or the turning of the flank by the foe" is Schliefenian in essence. So are the following ideas: Encirclement combined with frontal action assures the best results; the troops assigned to the encirclement should be directed toward the flanks and rear from their assembly areas beforehand and should not be shifted laterally in the front line or carried out by held-back reserves. The impact of Schlieffen's teaching is obvious.

So was Schlieffen's influence on the exercises conducted by the Reichswehr. An operative war game code-named "Elbe," conducted in the neighborhood of Berlin in 1926–1927, dealt with war on two fronts. All the standard solutions of the problems presented featured attacks encircling one or both flanks.[63] The final discussion of the exercise for General Staff officers (disguised, in accordance with the restrictions of the Treaty of Versailles, as "Führerstabsoffiziere"), in 1931, strongly resembled similar occasions of Schlieffen's times. One such aphorism stated that "the concentration of forces for the operation does not mean the pressing together at one point." The exercise dealt with a war against Czechoslovakia and suggested the solution of attacking the foe in flank and rear. In order to shift the center of gravity of the operation to the encircling wings, all secondary fronts should be weakened as far as possible. The deployment of the encircling troops should be on a wide front. The decision is looked for on the strong wing, which aims for the adversary's rear. The conclusions of the first stage of that exercise are completely imbued with Schlieffen's spirit:

The problem demanded the achievement of a victorious decision by an inferior party against a superior one. . . . The assault against the enemy's front, even if it is conducted in depth and forcefully, will not lead to success. The hostile flank and rear must be the objective. One should not hesitate, circumstances permitting, to hold back one wing completely, or to denude one's own front as far as possible, in order to make sure of striking at the hostile flank with overwhelming superiority.

The result of this exercise bore Schlieffenian features too: Seven days after the outbreak of hostilities 20,000 foes were taken prisoner and sixty guns and 350 M.G.s were captured. The next part of the exercise was staged as a war against Poland and presented the problem of operation on interior lines. One is again reminded of Schlieffen as one reads the following passage from the final discussion: "A big army cannot turn around to a new direction, as quickly as an army corps or a division."[64]

The most striking example of Schlieffenian influence was an exercise presented to the General Staff officers of the Reichswehr Ministry during the winter of 1934–1935. The theater of war was France. The exercise was simply one prepared by Schlieffen in 1893, for junior officers commissioned to the Great General Staff. This fact was, however, concealed from the officers in 1934–1935, and only revealed at the final discussion on 15 March 1935 with the additional remark that "the problem remained on the whole unaltered. . . . Even today, one may draw many-sided stimulation from Count Schlieffen's papers and exercises." Then followed the full original text of Schlieffen's final discussion, which was duly concluded: "This discussion of the problem tells its own tale. It is beyond any doubt, the basic ideas are still absolutely valid today."[65]

In fact, in 1936 a new edition of Schlieffen's *Cannae* was published with an introduction by the Commander-in-Chief of the Army, General von Fritsch (as already mentioned). This introduction stressed the theoretical importance of Schlieffen's teaching. After asking the rhetorical question whether in view of the last war Schlieffen's doctrine was wrong, von Fritsch said:

The voices raised after the war, doubting the correctness of Schlieffen's theory, have grown more and more silent. It is commonly recognized today, that it was not the annihilation idea in itself that was erroneous, but that the inadequate manner of its utilization was the reason for failure. . . . Many a critic believes that one should find fault with Schlieffen's dogmatic one-sidedness in the conduct of operations. The slogan "mania of encirclement"[66] was coined on this account. He, who charges Schlieffen with one-sidedness, has only superficially penetrated his world of ideas.[67]

To the delight of the Schlieffen school the last part was directed at that small number of writers who were not captivated by Schlieffen's ideas.

In due course the first volume of Schlieffen's service papers was published in 1937, and the second in 1938. The outbreak of the Second World War prevented the publication of further volumes. Nevertheless, a considerable body of Schlieffen's teaching was now accessible.

This break-in of Schlieffen's theory into the Reichswehr unleashed a flood of official and semiofficial publications connected with his doctrine. In 1928 Günther Frantz, by order of the Army Inspectorate for Education and Culture of the Reichswehr, published a book entitled *Die Vernichtungsschlacht in kriegsgeschichtlichen Beispielen* (The Battle of Annihilation Exemplified by the History of War).[68] This was but another of those boring compilations of its kind, but the point was that its table of contents was almost identical with Schlieffen's collection of battles in his Cannae studies and with the work of the Historical Branch of the Great General Staff, ordered by Schlieffen and published in 1903.[69]

Lieutenant General von Cochenhausen wrote in 1933: "It is an incontestable fact that Schlieffen's opinions were attacked more in his time than nowadays, since the harsh realities of the lost war have proved the correctness of his thoughts."[70] Major General F. v. Boetticher maintained at the same time that "the war has not refuted any of the opinions which he had taught."[71] Cochenhausen's biography of August von Gneisenau (1760–1831) projected into the latter's realm of thought and action terms and ideas direct from Schlieffen's armory. This deliberate anachronism was no doubt used in order to make use of Gneisenau's reputation with the German Army for Schlieffen's sake.[72]

F. v. Rabenau, Colonel General von Seeckt's biographer and Head of the Army Archives until the middle of the Second World War, published, in 1935, a book on operative decisions in face of an adversary superior in numbers, in which he preached a return to encirclement by utilizing modern means of mobility, of reconnaissance, and airpower.[73] "Those who disapprove of encirclement," he wrote,

because it will again lead to a frontal struggle, or because they hold that there are no locations which could be turned, recommend break-through operations. This is, in fact contrary to every war experience. None of our opponents' break-through attempts succeeded. Our great break-through at Gorlice-Tarnow, in May 1915, was indecisive in its final consequence. The break-through operations on the Italian front had met surprisingly weak spots, but notwithstanding, got bogged down.[74]

In 1938 General W. Erfurth published a book on surprise[75] in line with Schlieffen's teaching, and a year later, a book on the victory of annihilation[76] that matches all other Schlieffen-type compilations of that kind. He rightly maintained that modern technical means facilitated an operation on interior lines. He repeated Schlieffen's postulate of a short war on account of economic reasons, and held the view that the increased dependence of modern warfare on material calls even more for a quick decision.[77] *Der Vernichtungssieg* praised the Cannae concept. Published during the first phase of the campaign in Poland, in 1939, Erfurth, in his introduction, seized the opportunity of linking modern Cannae battles, like Tannenberg, the campaign in Serbia in 1915, and the campaign in Rumania in 1916, with the most modern mechanized Cannae in Poland.

On the official scene the new field regulations, issued by the Reichswehr in 1933–1934,[78] are again similar to the pre-war regulations and those issued in 1921. The frontal attack is analyzed but is, however, considered as leading to an obstinate, prolonged struggle. The attack in the backhand, viz., leaving the initiative for the initial assault to the foe and then hitting back, is included in the manual, but "there looms the danger that one may not reach the decision for the attack at the right moment, or not decide it at all." Transferred from Schlieffen's essay on war in modern times is the stress on mobile reserves of ammunition and especially their massing on the decisive encircling wing.

In fairness to Groener one should mention that he was skeptical of Germany's prospects in a future war. In a lecture given to the select circle of the Mittwoch-gesellschaft on 5 November 1930 he warned against Germany's becoming involved in a war. Germany should restrict itself to the most essential defense of its eastern frontier and realize that it is powerless against France. He prophesied that the so-called war of liberation, striven for by the National-Socialists, would in all certainty lead to the ruin of the Reich.[79] In a letter of 13 May 1938 he nonetheless considered that any future conduct of war by Germany ought to be based on Schlieffen's encirclement concept. Should the ground in the western theater of war become too cramped for maneuver, then one should strive for airborne encirclement. "The break-through fanatics are today, as in the past, on the wrong track. Even tanks are of no avail, because there is no insurmountable difficulty in fighting against them, with well-developed means of defense."[80] At the end of the same year he again expressed scruples about whether Germany could afford to become involved in a new world war. He stressed England's naval superiority and the necessity to hit at England through the air. Furthermore, he had no doubts that the United States would again side with England, and that the former, together with Canada, would back the British war effort with their industrial potential.[81]

THE GERMAN ARMY IN THE HITLER ERA BEFORE THE SECOND WORLD WAR

On 16 March 1935 Hitler denounced the clauses of the Versailles Treaty providing for German disarmament, restored universal conscription, and started a huge program of rearmament. The Reichswehr, shaped by General von Seeckt as a Führerheer (Leader Army),[82] provided a sound basis for the new fast-increasing army. New services, previously prohibited by the Treaty of Versailles, were added. Soon a War Academy was reinstalled, for the first time embracing all three services, as the Wehrmachtakademie. The General Staff officers studying at the academy were kept busy in researching the First World War and drawing conclusions for the future.

As early as 29 November 1935 Lieutenant Colonel of the General Staff Matzky presented his critical comment on the theories of Douhet, Fuller, Hart, and Seeckt[83] and drew conclusions for Germany's future war. Among other features he reinstated Schlieffen's concept of the necessity of a short war: "Germany's future war must be a swift war of decision, owing to cogent military-political, military-geographical and military-economic reasons. . . . The quick enforcement of a war decision is still possible today." Furthermore, in line with Schlieffen's stressing of masses, Matzky maintained that "the Army should be as large as possible; unfortunately enough, armies become decreased in war, especially the fighting units."

Some months later Lieutenant Colonel of the General Staff Willi Schneck-enburger lectured on the development of mobile formations.[84] The gist of his conclusions was the resurrection of Schlieffen's Cannae strategy of encirclement and annihilation by means of combining armored forces and airpower. Yet he was aware that situations might emerge in the future, similar to those that had led in the past to compact fronts. The new combination of mobile striking power would at last facilitate a successful break-through of the hostile front and render possible the encirclement of the adversary by expanding the break-through right into the enemy's rear.

In May 1936 a working group of three General Staff officers presented the results of their investigation into the mistakes committed by Germany in the preparation and execution of the Great War. They also made suggestions for the future.[85] The outbreak of the war and the events that eventually led to the stagnation of position warfare were reviewed fairly critically. Doubts were raised whether a Schlieffen-type encirclement operation would have offered any degree of success when put to use against vast army fronts. It was deplored that the relationship of strategy and tactics had been turned upside down, viz., tactics had to pave the way for the execution of strategy. Because tactics had failed to achieve a real break-through, strategy had been rendered useless. However, the working group warned against committing the mistake of judging a future war by what had happened in the previous one. Hence they believed, as did all the other lecturers preceding them, that the new exploitation of mechanical propul-sion on the ground and in the air would restore to power the old concept of encirclement and annihilation.

A few days later another working group had to deliver suggestions for the proper utilization of surprise in war.[86] The German field regulations prevalent at the outbreak of war in 1914 had actually been issued in 1905 and were criticized as too old-fashioned because they had not recognized the invention of motor transport, aircraft, wireless communications, and the machine gun. There was no reciprocity between German military thought and the new technical circum-stances. The Schlieffen Plan was taken to task for lacking the essential element of surprise. The distance to be covered by the foot-marching right wing was too great to keep that move secret, despite the brilliant marching performance of the troops. Fast-moving troops were nonexistent at that time.[87]

In January 1938 the War Academy circulated a draft of a pamphlet on the conduct of war ("Kriegführung").[88] This was the first attempt to lay down regulations for the combined conduct of war by all three services in a single Supreme Command. Part I dealt with the legal organizational basis and the general principles for the conduct of war. Part II discussed authority and the coordination of command. This was a serious enterprise in which much attention was paid to the relationship of policy and war, and the primacy of the former over the latter was made clear. The whole command structure, from the Head of the State downward, in no way resembled the arbitrary confusion created by Hitler during the war. On the military side of this manual, Schlieffenian ideas were predominant: The offensive was the strongest form of battle; the enemy must be annihilated after the initial victory by means of ruthless pursuit. On the whole, however, it was a quite comprehensive attempt to outline the conduct of a future war. Useful conclusions were drawn from the experience of the First World War, and full attention was given to the exploitation of modern equipment and new arms. However, the early outbreak of the Second World War prevented the completion of this enterprise.

The actual planning of war initially bore many similarities to Schlieffen's planning. The "Directive for the Unified Preparation of War of the Armed Forces"[89] of 24 June 1937—the "Blomberg Directive"—provided for two eventualities. Concentration "Red" was identical with the Schlieffen Plan of 1905, the nonviolation of neutral territories excepted: "It is the task of the German armed forces to make their preparations, in such a manner that the bulk of the armed forces can be employed against France, and that our action in the east is at first limited to defense—and that, with the employment of the smallest possible force." The opening phrase of the directive for concentration "Green," i.e., war on two fronts, with the focal point in the Southeast, echoed Schlieffen's old complaint about a Germany encircled by hostile and evil seeking foes: "To parry the iminent attack of a superior enemy coalition etc. . . . "

Finally, just before the outbreak of the Second World War, H. Foertsch published a book entitled *The Art of War Today and Tomorrow*.[90] Schlieffen's partisans were probably delighted by this work. It radiated Schlieffen spirit: The strategic offensive was the stronger form of war, the strategic defensive, the weaker one; one should strive for annihilation; attrition strategy can evade defeat but never win victory. Taking into account the advantages that the defensive had gained by utilizing motor transport for the shifting of reserves in order to counter an enveloping assault, Foertsch put special stress on Schlieffen's demand for engaging the foe in force on his front: "Only when the opponent's front is so strongly tied down by an attack, that he faces the danger of a break-through, in addition to becoming encircled, does this action appear to be adequate. Only this peril will make him indecisive in the employment of his reserves, and render certain the assailant's superiority on the enveloping wing."[91]

THE INFLUENCE OF CLAUSEWITZ

F. v. Bernhardi, who in his pre-war works had rejected Clausewitz' concept of defense, believed now that the emergence of the tank, coupled with massed artillery, would in the future make the offensive definitively superior to defensive.[92]

Leinveber, in his critical analysis of the First World War, perceived Clausewitz' theoretical edifice in the same way as Schlieffen and his partisans had considered it. According to this approach, Schlieffen's image of the war of annihilation harmonized with that of Clausewitz.[93] This view was also held by another writer closer to the outbreak of the Second World War: "The maxims of "On War," above all the annihilation idea considered as the nature of the war, became the spiritual equipment, that constituted the superiority of our leadership in the last great war."[94]

General W. Reinhardt, the last Prussian Minister of War and afterward holding many high-ranking appointments in the Reichswehr, lectured on Clausewitz.[95] He, too, overlooked the importance attached by Clausewitz to the relationship of policy and war and mainly recognized his emphasis on annihilation. Comparing the doctrines of Clausewitz and Foch, he credited Foch with striving for the shaking of the enemy's morale, whereas Clausewitz' more sober and realistic thoughts were directed at killing or capturing the foe. A morally shaken and discouraged warrior may regain his courage and carry on the fight, whereas a dead one remains dead. This was Reinhardt's interpretation of Clausewitz' teaching. On the whole he considered Clausewitz' theory to be obsolete for the following reasons:

The impact of modern firepower and the importance of the spade had completely changed the image of battle.

The ever-increasing importance of logistics requires more organizational qualities in the leaders.

The clash between the hostile parties tends to be frontal.

The division between strategy and tactics had become blurred, and the classic definition of Clausewitz did not meet the demands of the present.

Experience has proved the moral advantage of the offensive over the defensive, and therefore changed the relationship between the two, contrary to Clausewitz' formulation. Because of improved modern armament it is nowadays easier to attack than to defend, but modern means of transport support the defense.[96] However, from his experience in the war Reinhardt gained confirmation for Clausewitz' concept of the diminishing force of the attack, which presents the defense with some advantages.

On one point General Reinhardt agreed with Clausewitz: A deliberate retreat may serve as a means of resistance, provided that it does not turn into a rout. Indeed, the "Hinhaltender Widerstand" (delaying resistance) was one of the operative innovations introduced by the Reichswehr.[97]

In order to complete the picture it should be mentioned that General Beck,

Chief of the General Staff of the Army until close to the outbreak of the Second World War, considered the relationship of policy and war as Clausewitz wanted it to be understood: "The political purpose of the war must be obvious, and must also include in its calculation the final act of every war, the achievement of peace. Only a clearly defined purpose renders it possible to derive from it, and from available means, a military objective."[98] This was perhaps the reason he so staunchly opposed Hitler's plans for war.

APPENDIX B

A short selection of publications of the Schlieffen school between the two world wars in chronological order (memoirs of commander in chiefs not included).

1920

F. v. Bernhardi, *Vom Kriege der Zukunft.*
W. Groener, *Politik und Kriegführung.*
W. Groener, *Der Weltkrieg und seine Probleme. Rückschau und Ausblick.*
V. Freytag-Loringhoven, *Generalfeldmarschall Graf von Schlieffen.*
V. Freytag-Loringhoven, *Heerführer im Weltkriege*, 2 vols. (2d vol. in 1921).
V. Kuhl, *Der deutsche Generalstab in Vorbereitung und Durchführung des Weltkrieges.*

1921

Bauer, *Der grosse Krieg in Feld und Heimat.*
W. Foerster, *Graf Schlieffen und der Weltkrieg.*
V. Kuhl, *Der Marnefeldzug.*

1922

Rüdt von Collenberg, "Graf Schlieffen und die Kriegsformation der deutschen Armee."

1923

V. Kuhl, "Graf Schlieffen und der Weltkrieg."
V. Kuhl, "Ost- oder Westaufmarsch 1914?"

1924

E. Kabisch, *Streitfragen des Weltkrieges 1914–1918.*
V. Kuhl, "Graf Schlieffens 'Cannae.' "
H. Rochs, *Schlieffen.*

1925

W. Foerster, "Wollte Graf Schlieffen Holland im Ernstfall vergewaltigen?"
Krafft v. Delhmensingen, "Schlieffen—Moltke der Jüngere—Bülow."
H. Müller-Brandenburg, *Von Schlieffen bis Ludendorff.*

1927

W. Groener, *Das Testament des Grafen Schlieffen.*

1928

G. Frantz, *Die Vernichtungsschlacht in kriegsgeschichtlichen Beispielen.*

1929

V. Kuhl, *Der Weltkrieg 1914–1918.*

1930

W. Groener, *Der Feldherr wider Willen.*

1931

W. Foerster, *Aus der Gedankenwerkstatt des deutschen Generalstabs.*

1933

F. v. Boetticher, *Graf Schlieffen: sein Werden und Wirken.*
V. Cochenhausen, ed., *Von Scharnhorst zu Schlieffen.*
W. Groener, "Zum 100. Geburtstag des Grafen Schlieffen."

1934

E. Kabisch, *Die Marneschlacht: eine deutsche Tragödie.*
J. Kühl, *"Macht mir den rechten Flügel stark!"*

1935

E. Kabisch, *Verdun. Wende des Weltkrieges.*
F. v. Rabenau, *Operative Entschlüsse gegen einen an Zahl überlegenen Gegner.*

1937

V. Cochenhausen, ed., *Führertum.*

1938

E. Buchfink, "Moltke und Schlieffen."
W. Erfurth, *Die Überraschung im Kriege.*
V. Zoellner, *Schlieffens Vermächtnis.*

1939

V. Cochenhausen, ed., *Heerführer des Weltkrieges.*
W. Erfurth, *Der Vernichtungssieg.*
W. Müller-Loebnitz, *Die Führung im Marne-Feldzug.*

NOTES

1. In W. Hahlweg, ed., *Klassiker der Kriegskunst*, Darmstadt, 1960.
2. "In der Tat hat Schlieffens Grundidee im ganzen gesehen in der Kriegswirklichkeit keine Schule gemacht." *Ibid.*, p. 349.
3. Gotthard Jäschke, "Zum Problem der Marne-Schlacht von 1914," *Historische Zeitschrift*, Heft 190/92, April 1960.
4. 22 July 1964.
5. Robert Asprey, *The First Battle of the Marne*, London, 1962.
6. In *Historische Zeitschrift*, 198. Band, p. 411.
7. W. Groener, *Der Feldherr wider Willen*, Berlin, 1930, pp. XIII, 3.
8. Dr. Hans Kania, *Graf Schlieffen der Chef des Grossen Generalstabes als Vorbereiter des Grossen Krieges*, Potsdam, 1915, p. 22.
9. Sigfrid Mette, *Vom Geist deutscher Feldherren. Genie und Technik 1800–1918*, Zürich, 1938, p. 261.
10. *Berliner Lokalanzeiger*, 7 Feb. 1933.
11. Wolfgang Foerster, *Graf Schlieffen und der Weltkrieg*, 2d rev. ed., Berlin, 1925, p. 232.
12. BHA—Rep. 92, W. v. Hahnke, Nr. 17/18. Groener's letter to Mrs. v. Hahnke, 13/3/1935.
13. P. Bor, *Gespräche mit Halder*, Wiesbaden, 1950, p. 69.
14. "Ausserdem hat es Schlieffen leider versäumt sich Nachfolger zu erziehen." D. Groener-Geyer, *General Groener*, Frankfurt/Main, 1955, p. 357, note 3.
15. *Ibid.*
16. F. v. Cochenhausen, ed., *Von Scharnhorst zu Schlieffen 1806–1906*, Berlin, 1933, pp. 317–319 passim.
17. Cf. *Ibid.*
18. Hermann v. Kuhl, "Graff Schlieffens 'Cannae,' " *Militär-Wochenblatt*, Jg. 109 (1924), Nr. 16, p. 418.
19. *Ibid.*, p. 419.
20. 26–30 Sept. 1914.
21. 24 Aug.–Sept. 1914.
22. 16–25 Nov. 1914.
23. 5–17 Dec. 1914.
24. 4–22 Feb. 1915.

25. 19 Sept. 1915.

26. Autumn 1915.

27. 27–29 Sept. 1916.

28. 1–5 Dec. 1916.

29. W. Erfurth, *Der Vernichtungssieg*, Berlin, 1939, p. 104.

30. *Vide* chapter 15.

31. W. Foerster, "Einige Bemerkungen zu Gerhard Ritters Buch 'Der Schlieffen Plan,' " *Wehrwissenschaftliche Rundschau*, Jg. 7, H. 1 (Jan. 1957), p. 41.

32. A short list of the more important publications, is given in chronological order in Appendix B.

33. Cf. BA/MA—HO8–43 Schlieffen Nachlass; BA/MA—HO8–46 Groener Nachlass; BHA—Rep. 92, Nachlass W. v. Hahnke, Generalmajor; BHA—Rep. 92, Nachlass Generalfeldmarschall A. v. Schlieffen.

34. BHA—Rep. 92, W. v. Hahnke, Nr. 6/12.

35. "In Dankbarkeit und Verehrung für meinen grossen Lehrmeister" (In gratitude and veneration of my great teacher). Quoted in H. Rochs, *Schlieffen*, Berlin, 1926, p. 82–83.

36. *Vide* Book Two, chapter 6.

37. *Vide* chapter 6, under "The Reasons for Anglo-German Hostility."

38. BA/MA, Nachlass Bauer, Nr. 9.

39. *Der Weltkrieg 1914–1918 (Reichsarchiv)*, Berlin, 1925–1944, 14 vols. Formally it was only a semiofficial publication, but while an official work is still lacking, the Reichsarchivwerk is considered in Germany, and all over the world, to be the official German presentation of the war.

40. Cf. also Gerhard Ritter, *Staatskunst und Kriegshandwerk*, München, 1954, vol. 2, p. 248, and Gerhard Ritter, *Der Erste Weltkrieg*, Schriftenreihe der Bundeszentrale für politische Bildung, Bonn, 1964, p. 12. General W. Marx, *Die Marne—Deutschlands Schicksal?*, Berlin, 1932, hinted in the same direction.

41. BHA—Rep. 92, W. v. Hahnke, Nr. 28/31.

42. Cf. BA/MA—HO8–46/81.

43. BA/MA—HO8–46/41:5. The document is dated 15 Nov. 1919 in Groener's handwriting. It contains the following interesting passage, which soon became the leitmotif of his literary work: "If one reads Schlieffen's memorandum of 1905, one might howl with rage and shame about our stupidity in 1914. One had only to put this gospel of victory into one's pocket, if one did not know it by heart, and read it again!"

44. BA/MA—HO8–46/38:1. Letter of 9 May 1926.

45. BA/MA—HO8–46/40:4.

46. Cf. BHA—Rep. 92, W. v. Hahnke, Nr. 21/22. Groener's letter of 3 Sept. 1935 to Mrs. v. Hahnke.

47. BA/MA—HO8–46/51, pp. 79–91.

48. "Schlieffen fanatics and dogmatists of encirclement."

49. BA/MA—HO8–46/51, p. 93.

50. *Ibid.*, pp. 98–103.

51. They are to be found in BHA—Rep. 92, W. v. Hahnke, la, pp. 35–40.

52. BHA—Rep. 92, W. v. Hahnke, Nr. 19/20. Letter of 21 May 1935.

53. That was the edition of 1936.

54. BHA—Rep. 92, W. v. Hahnke, Nr. 23/24. Letter of 2 Dec. 1935 to Mrs. v. Hahnke.

55. Karl Justrow, *Feldherr und Kriegstechnik*, Oldenburg, 1933, pp. 35–36, 246.

56. W. Marx, *op. cit.*, p. 12.

57. Günther Blumentritt, *Von Rundstedt. The Soldier and the Man*, London, 1952, p. 22.

58. *Vide* Book One, chapter 2.

59. F. v. Bernhardi, *Vom Kriege der Zukunft*, Berlin, 1920, pp. 10–12.

60. *Ibid.*, pp. 136–137.

61. *Ibid.*, p. 195.

62. D. V. Pl. Nr. 487. "Führung und Gefecht der verbundenen Waffen (F. und G.)" (1921).

63. BA/MA—W10–1/4. Ubungsreise "Elbe." The chief umpire of the game was Colonel Werner v. Blomberg, Hitler's first Field Marshal and Minister of War.

64. BA/MA—W10–1/25. "Weiterbildung der Führerstabsoffiziere 1931/32."

65. BA/MA—W10–1/27. "Winterausbildung 1934/35 der Gen. St. Off. d. Rw. Min."

66. "Umfassungssucht."

67. Generalfeldmarschall Graf Alfred von Schlieffen, *Cannae*, Berlin, 1936, pp. V/VI.

68. G. Frantz, *Die Vernichtungsschlacht in kriegsgeschichtlichen Beispielen*, Berlin, 1928.

69. Grosser Generalstab, *Der Schlachterfolg, mit welchen Mitteln wurde er erstrebt*, Berlin, 1903.

70. Generalleutnant v. Cochenhausen, ed., *op. cit.*, p. 317.

71. *Ibid.*, p. 299.

72. *Ibid.*, pp. 98–99.

73. F. v. Rabenau, *Operative Entschlüsse gegen einen an Zahl überlegenen Gegner*, Berlin, 1935, pp. 8–11.

74. *Ibid.*, p. 14.

75. W. Erfurth, *Die Überraschung im Kriege*, Berlin, 1938.

76. W. Erfurth, *Der Vernichtungssieg, op. cit.*

77. W. Erfurth, *Die Überraschung, op. cit.*, p. 147.

78. H. Dv. 300/1. Truppenführung (T.F.), I. Teil (Abschnitt I-XIII), 1933; II. Teil (Abschnitt XIV-XXII), 1934.

79. BA/MA—Kl. Erw. 179–1. Protokolle der Mittwochgesellschaft: Sitzung 860 vom 5/11/1930: Groener, Die Kriegführung der Zukunft.

80. BHA—Rep. 92, W. v. Hahnke, Nr. 31/32. Groener's letter to Mrs. v. Hahnke.

81. BHA—Rep. 92, W. v. Hahnke, Nr. 33/34. Groener's letter to Mrs. v. Hahnke dated 30 Dec. 1938.

82. *Vide* chapter 13.

83. BA/MA—W10–1/9. "Kritische Untersuchung der Lehren von Douhet, Fuller, Hart und Seeckt." Vortrag gehalten am 29/11/1935 an der Wehrmachtakademie von Oberstleutnant des Generalstabs Matzky.

84. BA/MA—W10–1/12. "Führung, operative und taktische Verwendung schneller Verbände, wie müssen sie organisiert sein." Vortrag gehalten am 21/2/36 an der Wehrmachtakademie von Oberstleutnant des Generalstabs Schneckenburger.

85. BA/MA—W10–1/15. "Unsere hauptsächlichsten militär-politischen, strategischen, kriegswirtschaftlichen und psychologischen Fehler in der Vorbereitung des Weltkrieges und im Weltkrieg selbst. Welche allgemeinen Erkenntnisse ergeben sich daraus für die Kriegführung?" Vortrag gehalten am 5 Mai 1936 an der Wehrmachtakademie

von der Arbeitsgemeinschaft II: Oberst d. Generalstabs v. Rintelen, Oberstleutnant d. Generalstabs Schneckenburger, Korvettenkapitän Wagner.

86. BA/MA—W10–1/16. "Die Überraschung ist ein Produkt aus Geheimnis und Schnelligkeit. Die Wirkung der Überraschung und ihrer Faktoren auf allen Gebieten der Kriegführung ist zu untersuchen. Es sind Vorschläge zu machen, wie durch Organisation, Erziehung und Führung 'Geheimnis' und 'Schnelligkeit' zur höchsten Wirkung gebracht werden können. Täuschung und List als Mittel der Kriegführung." Vortrag gehalten am 8 Mai 1936 an der Wehrmachtakademie von der Arbeitsgemeinschaft III: Oberstleutnant d. Generalstabs Hauffe, Korvettenkapitän Meendsen-Bohlken, Major d. Generalstabs Korten.

87. Compare this view with Liddell Hart's opinion in the foreword of Gerhard Ritter's *The Schlieffen Plan*, London, 1948.

88. BA/MA—W10–1/1. "Kriegführung (3/1/1938)."

89. "Weisung für die einheitliche Kriegsvorbereitung der Wehrmacht," printed in Peter de Mendelsohn, *The Nuremberg Documents*, London, 1946, pp. 21 ff.

90. Hermann Foertsch, *Kriegskunst heute und morgen*. Berlin, 1939.

91. *Ibid.*, pp. 203–204.

92. F. v. Bernhardi, *op. cit.*, pp. 131–132.

93. Leinveber, *op. cit.*, p. 169.

94. Generalmajor a. D. v. Schickfus und Neudorff, "Clausewitz," in F. v. Cochenhausen, ed., *Führertum*, Berlin, 1937, p. 346.

95. "Clausewitz," printed in W. Reinhardt, *Wehrkraft und Wehrwille*, Berlin, 1932, pp. 110–174.

96. This statement indicates how deeply Reinhardt's perceptions were still anchored in the experience of trench warfare, hence he did not grasp the implications of mobile warfare, facilitated by the modern means of transport and communication.

97. *Vide* chapter 13.

98. L. Beck, *Studien*, Stuttgart, 1955, pp. 60, 63.

13

Hans von Seeckt: A New Approach to the Art of War in the Era of Mass-Armies

Another feature of the German military inter-war scene was presented by Colonel General Hans von Seeckt (1866–1936), the architect of the Reichswehr. Seeckt is generally considered as a mere man of action.[1] Yet he added his own individualistic contribution to the German theory of war. His biographer, General v. Rabenau, who was closely acquainted with Seeckt, maintained: "Seeckt recognized that art, as well as science, cannot dispense with theory. It is true that operative leadership is neither art nor science, but, indeed, both at the same time; this is apparently a contradiction, but only apparently. The indispensability of theory becomes evident when one considers that every war brings forth, and must bring forth, new theories."[2]

THE IMAGE OF A SMALL PROFESSIONAL ARMY

It is commonly known that von Seeckt advocated a small professional army of picked troops instead of indulging in a mass-army. Some people maintain that he instead made a virtue of necessity simply because the Treaty of Versailles permitted a German Army of only 100,000 men. Perhaps, to a certain degree, that was so. Yet it seems that Seeckt's ideas should be considered as the antithesis (or anticlimax) to the concept of mass-armies introduced by the French Revolution, investigated and analyzed by Clausewitz, and hailed by Schlieffen. It was the closure of the circle, which in modern times began with the small mercenary armies of the Cabinet Wars, continued through the wars of the nineteenth century and the First World War, and ended in the search for a way out of the carnage of prolonged trench warfare.

The idea was not entirely new, even in Germany. As early as 1883 Colmar von der Goltz had maintained:

Looking forward into the future, we seem to feel the coming of a time when the armed millions of the present will have played out their part. A new Alexander will arise, who, with a small body of well-equipped and skilled warriors, will drive the impotent hordes before him, when, in their eagerness to multiply, they shall have overstepped all proper bounds, have lost internal cohesion, and, like the greenbanner army of China, have become transformed into a numberless, but effete, host of Philistines.[3]

Daring, straightforward thoughts at a time when Schlieffen reveled in armies of millions! In 1909 von Falkenhausen wrote: "The idea has already been aired, that in the course of time, circumstances might lead to the return of small armies, especially highly-trained in long-term peace-time service. This does not seem to be out of the question, and would implement a retrograde movement which quite often occurs in Nature. Yet it seems that, for the time being, the path for such a 'volte-face' is still blocked."[4] Soon after the First World War, at a time when von Seeckt was already laboring on his new concept, von Kuhl, in an essay on Schlieffen's Cannae concept, maintained that "the war of the future will display new patterns. . . . Perhaps, as many believe likely, instead of armies of millions, small armies, like Hannibal's 50,000 Carthaginians, will again wage the battles of the future, whilst mechanical tools of war will take the place of the elephants."[5]

One should keep in mind that after the First World War, General Fuller and Captain Liddell Hart had evolved the concept of mechanized forces and propagated the idea of small professional armies. There is no doubt that their thoughts, too, had a considerable impact on German military thinking in general and on Seeckt in particular.

After his dismissal from the post of Chef der Heeresleitung of the Reichswehr, in his book *Thoughts of a Soldier*, written in his characteristic and polished style, Seeckt expressed what he had in mind. "Is it really necessary," he asked,

that each time a belligerent conflict becomes inevitable, entire nations should fall one upon the other? The soldier ought to ask himself the question, whether such mammoth armies can be conducted in terms of a strategy aiming at a decision, and whether or not every war between these masses is again doomed to torpidity. It may be that the principle of mass armies, the peoples' levy, has already overshot itself, the *fureur de nombre* is at an end. Mass becomes immobile; it cannot manoeuvre and therefore cannot win victories, it can only crush by sheer weight.[6]

What was Seeckt's vision of the future war? It will begin with a reciprocal attack of the air fleets, which are always ready for action. The targets are the hostile air force, and only after its overthrow will the attack be directed against other targets. All great troop concentrations provide for valuable and easy assault targets. Interference with the mobilization of manpower and material is one of the major tasks of air attacks. The offensive will then be taken over at the utmost speed by troops ready for action, i.e., the peacetime army. The more high class the army is, the more mobile, the more determined and qualified its leaders are, the greater are its prospects of beating the opposing forces quickly and even rendering the foe prepared to conclude peace. At the time that both professional armies struggle for the first decision, the home defense forces commence their deployment. The party that was victorious in the first act of the war will strive to hinder the formation of compact material fronts. The whole future of warfare appears to lie in the employment of mobile armies, relatively small but of high quality and rendered distinctly more effective by the addition of aircraft, and the simultaneous mobilization of the total forces, either to feed the attack or for the home defense.[7]

What were the organizational patterns of such a modern army, as suggested by Seeckt? "The peace-time army, which might also be termed the covering or operating army, should consist of professional, long-term soldiers, volunteers as far as possible."[8] The length of the term of service depends mainly on the task assigned to the individual soldier. The number of soldiers in that army will conform to the material means of the State, its military-geographical constellation, and its size but should at least provide protection against a hostile surprise attack. Three factors are essential for the maintenance of such an army: a high degree of mobility, the most effective armaments, and a permanent flow of replacements. This operating army should not require any replenishments for its first engagement, or as little as possible. Therefore, mobilization becomes superfluous.

Side by side with that army stands a nucleus of officers, noncommissioned officers, and troops, forming training formations and schools, providing for a brief period of compulsory military training to be given to all fit youngsters in the country and for periodical refresher courses.

In this way a military mass is constituted which . . . is well able to fulfill the duty of home defense, and at the same time, to provide from its best elements, a continuous reinforcement of the regular, combatant army in the field. In order to make that period of training tolerable, it must be preceded by a training of the youth, which lays less emphasis on the military aspects than on general physical and mental discipline, but that can be carried out effectively, only by governmental compulsion.[9]

With regard to armament, Seeckt maintained that "the smaller an army is, the easier it will be to arm it with modern equipment, whereas to keep modern weapons permanently ready for an army of millions is an impossibility." Therefore, the operating army would be armed with high-class equipment. The only possible solution for the bulk of the defense army appeared to be the continual establishment of prototypes of desirable weapons, their current testing in research institutes and on the firing range, and the necessary arrangements with industry for securing quick mass production, in case of need. By means of renouncing refinements in the cause of simplicity, production time might be shortened. In any case the necessary period from the production order to delivery would be covered by the operating army.

However, Seeckt was in a dilemma about what the final mission of his tiny Reichswehr should be. Three solutions were open to him:

1. The creation of an Eliteheer (an elite army);

2. using the Reichswehr as a basis for a conventional mass-army; or

3. the formation of a Führerheer (a leader's army).[10]

Seeckt settled on the third possibility. According to von Rabenau, he had in mind an army of approximately 5 million soldiers, compared with Germany's 10–million-man army after 1917.[11] It is hard to say whether this was really Seeckt's intention, or whether it was an afterthought of Rabenau in order to close the gulf between Seeckt's conception and Hitler's new conscript army. Seeckt's own writing, and what others have derived from it, hardly supports Rabenau's view.

After Hitler's rearmament in 1935 the Wehrmachtakademie embarked on an examination of various domestic and foreign ideas regarding an efficient future army. The already-mentioned lecture of Lieutenant Colonel Matzky on 29 November 1935 surveyed the theories of Douhet, Fuller, Hart, and Seeckt.[12] The principal consideration presented by this lecturer was the peril of war on several fronts, which, in Germany's geographical position, appeared to be unavoidable. This was one of the reasons for the rejection of Douhet's theory of airpower for solving all military problems of the future.

As to Fuller's doctrine of a fully armored army, Matzky held that Germany ostensibly had already carried out this concept to a high degree: A number of Panzerdivisionen, similar to Fuller's ideal division, were to be created. The German short-term conscription army might be considered as constituting Fuller's "occupation army," as some young and overenthusiastic Panzer soldiers would have liked to regard it too. But this superficial similarity is illusory (as our Matzky put it: Thank Heaven, it deceives!). Despite the Panzer fanatics, Fuller's theory was definitely unsuitable for Germany. Why? Not only was the terrain on Germany's frontiers unsuitable for armored divisions, thereby making the latter incapable of carrying the burden of combat alone, but there was also no point in deploying Panzer units against well-defended enemy positions. The break-through had to be undertaken by the infantry, with adequate support. But these forces can by no means be "occupation soldiers" of the Fuller type. For such an enterprise real warriors with offensive spirit and offensive power are required. Furthermore, the lecturer had his doubts how a Panzer army could, single-handed, prevail after having penetrated deep into enemy territory. It would be surrounded in no time and destroyed, as the Britain Army maneuvers of the previous year had clearly shown. Lieutenant Colonel Matzky's final verdict on Fuller's theory of war was: "Unfit for German circumstances!"[13]

For almost identical reasons, Seeckt's concept was rejected. With reference to the fact that the makeshift "assault-battalions" and "assault-divisions" formed of picked troops during the later part of the First World War had been of no avail, Matzky pointed out that it would be utopian to believe that an elite army of 200,000 men could be a match for the eighty to ninety French divisions that could be expected in a fortnight. The small Seeckt-type army, efficient as it might be, would be worn out and crying for reinforcements before the point of decision would have been reached. It was not the masses that should be blamed for the failures of 1914, but the mental inability to shape and conduct them properly. With that perception the ostensible need of the "small" army became null and void.[14]

Liddell Hart survived Matzky's scrutiny far better than the others. Liddell Hart's approach of considering surprise mainly as a psychological problem and only secondly as a technical one, and maintaining, therefore, that increased mobility should, above all, serve the achievement of psychological surprise, appealed to Matzky. So did Liddell Hart's tactical opinions: "Hart's tactical views are throughout at bottom reasonable. He allocates the armor to the right objectives, and does not forget that it is the *infantry*, which, in co-operation with tanks and artillery, is compelled to strive for a decision."[15]

To cut a long story short the recommended solution was, after all, a return to Schlieffen's mass-army, improved by mechanized means, better communication facilities, and the demand for a better mental understanding in conducting such a host.

Before turning to another part of Seeckt's work it seems appropriate to quote the opinion of one of Germany's most distinguished soldiers of the Second World War, General Frido von Senger und Etterlin, famous for his defense of Monte Cassino. Summing up the campaign in France in 1940 he wrote:

If one thinks over the war up to now, one will recollect the vision of the clever General von Seeckt, which was rejected as wrong by the military at his time. Seeckt conceived the future form of war as a struggle between small professional armies, to which the elite of a combatant nation would rally: Stukas (divebombers), Panzer troops, parachutists. By the side of this force, the popular army—comprising the bulk of infantry—played only a subordinate role. In view of the present course of the war, Seeckt was right. Nobody could forsee that a skilful combination of modern weapons, untested as yet by the experience of war, would yield such swift results.[16]

FLEXIBILITY

Seeckt gave the new Reichswehr, to use an expression of Liddell Hart, "a gospel of mobility, based on the view that a quick-moving, quick-hitting army of picked troops could, under modern conditions, make rings round an old-fashioned mass-army."[17] The field manuals of that period stressed the importance of surprise and flexibility in exploiting success. Above all, contrary to Schlieffen's "modern Alexander" concept and despite much better means of communication, Seeckt insisted on commanders being further forward than in the previous war. The reasons for this attitude were the shortening of the lines of communications, exerting more direct influence on the troops in battle, and getting acquainted with the ground on which the troops were fighting and its peculiarities.[18] It is typical of Seeckt that his regulations did not provide for position warfare, whereas the regulations of other armies were still under the spell of the experience of the past war. He put Schlieffen's postulate "operation is movement" at the top of the training orders for the Reichswehr. This spirit gave the German Army, during the initial phase of the Second World War, its superior quality despite material inferiority.[19] Nevertheless, under Seeckt's command the defensive was not neglected.[20] Yet his concept of the defensive was much more flexible than that unintentionally practiced during the Great War. This even emerges from merely looking at the terminology created for the purpose. The regulation "Truppenführung (T.F.)" (the Conduct of Troops) divided the term "Abwehr" (Defensive),[21] which covers the whole spectrum of that form of battle, into two main streams: "Verteidigung" (defense),[22] in which the defender is determined to wage a decisive battle, and "hinhaltendes Gefecht" (delaying engagement) or "hinhaltender Widerstand" (delaying resistance), by means of which the defender is not prepared to accept a decisive battle.[23] The latter form meant a return to Clausewitz' concept of the flexible defense, a step that none of the German war leaders had dared to endeavor on a large scale during four years of trench warfare.[24] It was Seeckt's privilege to have given the German Army a lead in the sphere of the defensive as well. While others remained under the spell of trench warfare and looked for a remedy in concrete and steel (the "Maginot spirit"), Seeckt introduced flexibility even in this apparently rigid sphere. W. v. Leeb, the German defensive expert of the inter-war period, stressed the importance of a flexible defensive, supported by mechanized troops, the air force, and a high degree of improvisational skill in erecting obstacles and tank traps, as the only measure of freeing troops from the traditional imaginary fear of open flanks and gaps (which, it may be added, was inherited from Schlieffen!).

That it was not Hitler alone who abandoned flexible defense in the Second World War, but the military themselves who also had a finger in the pie, is indicated by a remark in Halder's war diary: " 'Delaying resistance' to be killed at once!" In an explanatory footnote to the printed edition, he added: "This form of combat, widely practised in the 100,000 men Army, should be abolished, because the circumstances have changed, and during the Polish campaign, the toughness of our defensive ("Abwehr") suffered on its account."[25]

In one sphere, however, von Seeckt remained the product of his own generation. Despite his grasp of mobile warfare he did not realize the important role of armored mobility. It was not the fetters of Versailles that prevented him from doing so, but rather the fact that it was completely outside the scope of his thoughts. He wrote about the future importance of cavalry, and when he said cavalry he meant it, and did not use it as a disguise for armor, as some of his interpreters have tried to maintain.

ON RUSSIA

Clausewitz' experience, against the background of Napoleon's debacle in 1812, set the fashion for the attitude of the German military toward Russia. The elder Moltke, Schlieffen, the younger Moltke, and Falkenhayn all were afraid of becoming lured into the vast Russian spaces. After the war, however, different opinions emerged. General Hoffmann, until the end of the war Chief of Staff of the Supreme Commander East, wrote: "It is a strange thing that, even now, comparisons with 1812 often appear in German periodicals and newspapers. The people who write them do not realize that the difficulties that Napoleon had, at that time in his campaigns, have been overcome by modern means of communications and transport. If Napoleon had had railways, telephones, motors, the telegraph and an air force, he would have been in Moscow today."[26] General Reinhardt, in his lecture on Clausewitz, was even more fundamentally opposed to Clausewitz:

Clausewitz establishes that Russia, by her campaign of 1812, has taught that an empire of great dimensions cannot be conquered; "which might just as easily have been known before." But in fact, in the course of World history, vast spaces had been conquered by Huns, Mongols, also by Persians, Hellenes, Spaniards and others, *inter alia* Russia by the Mongols, because the conquerors' armies were cut out for such conquest. Had Napoleon's strategy in 1812 begun with the organization of a mobile army, instead of with the shaping of a campaign plan, he might perhaps have mastered the space, which his cumbrous and pretentious Western-European divisions could not overcome.[27]

When I asked whether these were isolated personal opinions, or whether they heralded a new German approach to the problem of Russian space,[28] Colonel Dr. Meier-Welcker replied:

The military thinking, regarding the situation of the Reich in the East, was dominated by the very existence of Poland. One had always to face the permanent menace that Poland might seize East Prussia, especially, for instance, in 1932. The Reichswehr leaders doubted, and even denied at that time, that the Reichswehr could hold its ground against the Polish armed forces. In such circumstances, any hostile action against Russia had to be ruled out at all. On the contrary! There was indeed the co-operation with Russia as a counterpoise against Poland. I have never heard from military quarters, any thought that Germany could attack Russia, either during the Reichswehr period or afterwards, until the autumn of 1940.[29]

This view entirely coincides with what Seeckt himself had written and with what had been written about him. Seeckt was appalled by the Russian space, which he knew too well from his own experience. "Russia's defensive power and her evading-space are great, and the experience of 1812 frightened," he wrote.[30] In a letter of 31 January 1920 Seeckt outlined his attitude to the eastern question: Neither Germany nor the Entente could exercise any influence on the domestic development of Russia. Seeckt regarded a political and economic agreement with Russia as an irrefutable objective of German policy. By no means should Russia become a foe. Therefore, no support should be rendered to Poland, even should it be swallowed up. To the contrary, Seeckt longed for this to happen.[31]

In September 1922 Seeckt stated his approach to the eastern problem, and to Poland in particular, on similar lines, in a memorandum to the Chancellor of the Reich. He stressed that Poland's very existence was intolerable and incompatible with Germany's conditions of life. It will disappear by way of its own domestic weakness and by Russia—with German aid. "Poland is even more unbearable for Russia than for us; Russia will never come to terms with Poland. Poland can never offer Germany any advantages." Russia and Germany restored to the frontiers of 1914, might provide the basis for a mutual agreement. Therefore, this German attitude toward Poland should not be kept anxiously as a secret. Germany cannot overestimate the advantage arising from Poland's becoming convinced that, in case of its participation in a war on France's side against Germany, it will have Russia on its neck.[32]

Another expression of Seeckt confirms that he was convinced that by pursuing a pro-Russian policy he had solved the ancient problem of war on two fronts. In his essay "Germany Between East and West" he wrote: "It has been said that Count Schlieffen even in the hour of his death uttered: strengthen the right wing! Let us now appeal to German politics: keep the back clear!"[33] Seeckt had realized that the two-front dilemma could not be solved on the military level alone, without policy contributing to its solution.

POLICY AND WAR

From the above-mentioned conclusion one might have gotten the impression that at least Seeckt had found the way back to Clausewitz. He had, in fact, contemplated the problem of the relationship of policy and war a great deal. In a memorandum prepared as early as 17 February 1919 he said:

A State which claims worldwide influence, i.e. wants to conduct foreign politics, needs a reliable, that means a well-trained and well-equipped army . . . this seems to be almost commonplace and taken for granted. . . . The objection of the present day, that a strong army induces to a policy of conquest, is untenable. The use of the army is decided by the policy of the State. If the latter is at fault, then it will make wrong use of the army; a sound policy will use it in a right way. . . . Domestic executive power depends on power. That power is only provided by a reliable, disciplined, army, ready for action at any time. . . . If our policy is conducted by men who prefer action, and will not just remain passive, then none of them will consider a strong army as detrimental to his policy.[34]

Nevertheless, in his essay "On Catchwords" Seeckt stated that he had reservations whether Clausewitz' postulate of "war as a mere continuation of policy by other means" was still applicable to the present situation.[35] Seeckt's dilemma actually sprang from his negative attitude toward the rulers of the Weimar Republic, whom he agreed to serve only for the sake of Germany's unity, in order to prevent the very real danger of the country becoming split by particularistic tendencies. Hence, not identifying himself with the Republican regime, Seeckt was anxious to keep the Reichswehr out of domestic politics. It has been said that ancient Prussia was not a State with an army, but an army that had adopted a State. The Reichswehr of the Weimar Republic was obviously something different from that. It was a State inside a State. Or, in Seeckt's own words: " 'Keep your hands off the Army!' I call to all parties. The Army serves the State and the State alone; for it is itself the State."[36]

During the final discussion of the leaders-ride (Führerreise) of 1923 Seeckt put before the officers his opinion on the policy-war relationship. Because the conduct of war and the ability to wage war are the decisive factors in the policy of a major power, policy influences the conduct of war. He regarded as a grave mistake to believe that wars are waged in a space void of politics, and "that it could some day be put behind lock and key, in order to cede the field entirely to pure politics." The differences in appearance between the two have been stressed too much, and the homogenity of policy and war has been ignored. Both correspond with nature, which is based on the struggle for existence. "Struggle means aspiring to the enemy's annihilation, peace means the short enjoyment of power."[37] Of course, from such a statement to Hitler's Darwinistic approach is only a small step!

Finally, in 1924, at the time of the French occupation of the Ruhr basin, Seeckt played with the idea of unleashing a popular uprising if it proved necessary.[38] This was similar to Clausewitz' fostering such a movement between 1809 and 1812. However, Seeckt was too much a professional soldier to believe in the effectiveness of such a movement. In his opinion, armies could be beaten only by armies. Moreover, he was also too much a Prussian aristocrat not to fear the social consequences of such an endeavor, especially after the Revolution of 1918 and the still-persisting social unrest in Germany. No doubt this idea arose on the spur of the moment and was nothing but making a virtue of necessity.

SEECKT AND SCHLIEFFEN

In his *History of the German General Staff from 1918 to 1945* General Erfurth held the opinion that Seeckt desired the reinstatement of a German General Staff as it had been before the war.[39] In fact he tried to carve himself a more important position than that held by Schlieffen. Seeckt explained why he had not confined the exercise of 1923 to General Staff officers, as was the practice in the past, but had also ordered the participation of commanding generals.

Contrary to previous practice, according to which the purpose of staff rides was the training of General Staff officers, I have regarded it as my duty to base the rides conducted by me on the training of leaders. Even the so-called Great General Staff rides, which were conducted by the Chief of the General Staff, and dealt with matters at the highest level, were attended by Generals, only in their capacity as Quartermaster Generals (Oberquartiermeister), or a small number of Chiefs of Staff, and they were taken care of in the most tender manner. The Chief of General Staff had no right, whatsoever, to direct influence upon the instruction of leaders. Few of the Commanding Generals had a desire to occupy themselves with the instruction of the Generals under their command. Beyond the final discussions of manoeuvres, and the notion that a Commanding General, himself, could still learn something new, it seemed to be out of place. As a result the General Staff was uniformly trained, but, on the other hand, the operative ideas, even of such outstanding personalities as Counts Moltke and Schlieffen, had not penetrated fully into the circle of the real leaders. That I have dared to bring into being new methods, contrary to the past, is due to my conscious attempt to shape, from this small army, the leader army of the future.[40]

Whereas in Schlieffen's time the Chief of the General Staff could press for uniformity of thought at the level of General Staff officers only and had to yield a certain degree of intellectual independence to commanding officers, Seeckt strove to impose a uniform pattern at all levels and ranks.

On several occasions Seeckt had to announce publicly his attitude toward Schlieffen and the latter's doctrine. Although the general tone of his utterances was in line with the powerful Schlieffen school of his time, one can read between the lines a certain degree of criticism of his former teacher. In a foreword prepared for a new edition of Schlieffen's "Friedrich the Great" Seeckt wrote: "Friedrich's pupils led at Jena; Schlieffen's pupils led before and at the Marne. Battles are decided, not by theories of war, but by leaders. Victory is reached not by knowledge, but by being. Not intellect, but character, makes a General."[41] In his essay "On Catchwords" Seeckt was highly critical of Schlieffen's over-emphasis of the Cannae concept and even more condemnatory of the distorted application of the encirclement principle by Schlieffen's disciples.

What happened to Schlieffen's theory? If one gives the "Cannae" idea the right meaninng, he will find the demand for a conduct of battle, that will lead to the enemy's annihilation. This may, at best, be achieved by strongly enveloping both hostile flanks—see Cannae. This ideal solution requires one's own superiority at the decisive spot, and an enemy, who allows himself to become encircled on both flanks. . . . In order to prove the effectiveness of the encirclement, there was no need to go back to Cannae. Should, however, the encirclement become an impossibility . . . then the leader cannot declare, that he is at his wits' end. He will still act in accordance with Schlieffen, if he consciously deploys the bulk of his forces at the most effective spot, even against a frontal attack, for which Schlieffen coined the sarcastic slogan of "ordinary" victory.—Let us be honest! How many . . . manoeuvres, or map-battles have been conducted, without . . . encirclement, if possible on both flanks? One should always assume that the director of the exercise was aiming at encirclement. Did any attempt at breakthrough ever have the slightest prospect of success in those exercises?[42]

Seeckt then complained how lasting this impact had been on the German military mind so that, even after the experience of the war, he had to fight in the Reichswehr against the same stereotyped tendencies. It is of interest that, with regard to the events in summer 1914, Seeckt thought that Moltke was so fascinated by the prospect of waging a tactical "Cannae" in Lorraine, that he eventually lost sight of the strategic objective—the winning of the war.

NOTES

1. Colonel Meier-Welcker, sometime Chief of the Militärgeschichtlichte Forschungsamt of the Bundeswehr, wrote in a letter to me on 28 Sept. 1964: "Among the officers' corps of the Reichswehr, theoretical thinking was but little developed. Seeckt, for instance, was anything but a theorist." Colonel Meier-Welcker had himself served in the Reichswehr. He published in 1967 the most authoritative biography of Seeckt.

2. F. v. Rabenau, *Seeckt. Aus seinem Leben, 1918–1936*, Leipzig, 1940, p. 499. It is a pity that Rabenau had to pay a lot of lip-service to Hitler's genius in this book in order to render possible the publication of Seeckt's biography, since it was von Seeckt who crushed the Hitler Putsch in 1923. However, one may find many hidden attacks aimed at Hitler; for instance: "In the most concrete sphere, namely war, the abstract is indispensable. In order to work with abstract things an intellectually trained personality is essential. . . . It has occasionally been said that sound common-sense may suffice. One must admit that this is indeed a prerequisite. Yet the avoidance of an unsound knowledge, as a prerequisite of strategic success, seems perhaps to be too primitive an approach." V. Rabenau was eventually murdered by the Nazis in the Flossenbrügg concentration camp on 12 April 1945, barely a fortnight before the final German collapse.

3. Colmar von der Goltz, *The Nation in Arms*, London, 1906, p. 5.

4. Freiherr von Falkenhausen, *Der Grosse Krieg der Jetztzeit*, Berlin, 1909, pp. 7–8.

5. Hermann von Kuhl, "Graf Schlieffens 'Cannae,' " *Militär-Wochenblatt,* Jg. 109 (1924), Nr. 16, p. 419.

6. Generaloberst Hans von Seeckt, *Gedanken eines Soldaten*, Berlin, 1929, p. 86. Attention should be called to the fact that Seeckt's approach is absolutely contrary to Ludendorff's concept of "Total War," which will be dealt with in chapter 14.

7. *Ibid.*, pp. 93–100.

8. *Ibid.*

9. *Ibid.*

10. V. Rabenau, *op. cit.*, pp. 461–462.

11. *Ibid.*, p. 618.

12. *Vide* chapter 12, under "The German Army in the Hitler Era Before the Second World War." BA/MA—W10–1/9.

13. BA/MA—W10–1/9, pp. 50–54.

14. *Ibid.*, pp. 56–58.

15. *Ibid.*

16. Frido von Senger und Etterlin, *Krieg in Europa*, Köln, 1960, p. 27.

17. Liddell Hart, *The Other Side of the Hill*, London, 1956, p. 19.

18. D.V.Pl. Nr. 487. Führung und Gefecht der verbundenen Waffen (F.u.G.), 1921, 61.

19. P. Bor, *Gespräche mit Halder*, Wiesbaden, 1950, p. 87.

20. After Hitler's rearmament, however, the traditional assault spirit—the *furor teutonicus*—was reinstated and the defensive dropped.

21. "Abwehr" should simply be translated as "warding off."

22. I am quite aware that it is an arbitrary attempt in trying to distinguish in English between "defensive" and "defense," but I could not think of a better way of presenting the German distinction between "Abwehr" and "Verteidigung."

23. These terms are explained in Wilhelm Ritter von Leeb, *Die Abwehr*, Berlin, 1938, p. 1, footnote 1.

24. W. Erfurth wrote in 1938: "The World War proved that Clausewitz' theory of flexible defense is valid even under the circumstances of position warfare." W. Erfurth, *Die Überraschung im Kriege*, Berlin, 1938, p. 131. It should be remembered that the German "Infantry Training Regulations" of 1906 referred briefly to delaying combat.

25. "Hinhaltender Widerstand töten." Generaloberst Halder, *Kriegstagebuch*, Stuttgart, 1962, vol. 1, p. 75.

26. Max Hoffmann, *War Diaries and Other Papers*, London, 1929, vol. 2, "The War of Lost Opportunities."

27. Walter Reinhardt, *Wehrkraft und Wehrwille*, Berlin, 1932, p. 161.

28. In connection with the Second World War, one should also ask whether these views exercised any influence on Hitler's decision to start a war with Russia. This problem is dealt with in more detail in chapter 16.

29. Colonel Dr. Meier-Welcker's letter to me of 28 Sept. 1964.

30. Generaloberst von Seeckt, *op. cit.*, p. 61.

31. Quoted in F. v. Rabenau, *Seeckt*, p. 252.

32. *Ibid.*, pp. 316–317.

33. *Ibid.*, pp. 308–309.

34. *Ibid.*, p. 463.

35. Generaloberst von Seeckt, *op. cit.*, pp. 16–17.

36. *Ibid.*, p. 116.

37. Quoted in F. v. Rabenau, *op. cit.*, pp. 521–522.

38. *Ibid.*, p. 522.

39. W. Erfurth, *Die Geschichte des deutschen Generalstabes, von 1918 bis 1945*, Göttingen, 1957, p. 281.

40. Quoted in *ibid.*, pp. 130–131. Also in F. v. Rabenau, *op. cit.*, pp. 520–522.

41. BHA—Rep. 92, GFM v. Schlieffen, Nr. 67. Written in Rome on 20 Feb. 1927.

42. Generaloberst von Seeckt, *op. cit.*, pp. 17–20.

14

Ludendorff's "Total War"

Ludendorff's theory of "total war" might have been left outside the scope of this study had it not become so widely confused with Clausewitz' concept of the "absolute war" and, on the other hand, exercised great influence on Hitler's conduct of war. Therefore, it appears appropriate to touch briefly on this subject in order to round off the picture of the inter-war period.

One should keep in mind, however, that Clausewitz' conception of the "absolute war" was a philosophical exercise designed to reduce war to its abstraction and to strip it, for the purpose of theoretical contemplation, of all influences imposed by reality.[1] Ludendorff's "total war" has nothing in common with Clausewitz' notion, and is far from being a philosophical concept. Ludendorff's intellect was not fit for philosophy of Clausewitz' kind, although during the last two decades of his life he published many racialist books and edited a periodical with philosophical pretensions. This aspect of Ludendorff's life, and many other features of his personality, interesting as they are, will not be dealt with here. However, he was the first German who dared to attempt an overt and definite break with Clausewitz' teaching. "All theories of Clausewitz," he said, "have to be thrown overboard."[2] "His work belongs to a past period of World History, and is mostly out of date. One may even get confused by studying it."[3]

WAR AND POLITICS

According to Ludendorff, the image of war has changed since Clausewitz' days. At the latter's time the Cabinet Wars that had been waged by governments and their armies, without the participation of their people, were already over. The French Revolution, witnessed by Clausewitz, had released popular forces. Ludendorff, ignoring Clausewitz' real intention, maintained that these forces were far away from the violence of "absolute war." The wars of 1866 and 1870–1871 did not approach it either, despite the last phase of Gambetta's war against the German invaders, which had displayed a popular energy and passion hitherto unknown. The Germans, who at that time still regarded war as the exclusive business of the army, were confused by this novel phenomenon. The First World War, however, already had a different character. Not only armies were involved in war, but whole nations. Not only the soldiers in the front suffered, but also the homefront. As the nature of the war had changed, so, too, had the relationship of policy and war. It was politics in particular that had to undergo changes. Ludendorff charged Clausewitz with having narrowed the meaning of policy to the notion of foreign or external policy only, and with having tried to subordinate the conduct of war to foreign policy. Ludendorff, on the other hand, coined the term of "Gesamtpolitik" (over-all policy) as distinct from foreign politics, which led him to the following acrobatic manipulation: "War is foreign politics by other means. As for the rest, overall policy must serve the war."[4]

Modern war tends to be "total" because it involves the whole population of a country and not only the armed forces. The improvement of aircraft, their extended range and bombing capacity, carry the war deep behind the front line, into the enemy country. The population is exposed not only to the impact of bombing, but also to the influence of hostile propaganda media like leaflets and wireless messages. It is also likely to suffer from economic measures, like enemy blockade, or from self-imposed deprivations in order to divert vital materials to the war effort. All these different fields, which were somehow connected with the war, must be properly coordinated in order to support the struggle for existence of the nation. They must, therefore, all become subordinated to the war, including politics. In Ludendorff's definition, "war and politics serve the survival of the people, but war is the highest expression of the racial will to live. Therefore politics has to serve the conduct of war."[5] The leader of the total war has, therefore, the right to demand from the leader of "total politics"[6] the unity of the nation as "the national duty of total politics."[7] This does not mean simply the inspiring of national enthusiasm, but, above all, the suppression of any potential discontent by means of imposing the most extreme censorship on newspapers and radio, severe laws against treason, closure of the frontiers to neutral countries, prohibition of meetings, shadowing of railway traffic, and, of course, protective custody for malcontents and potential saboteurs. The latter should be handled rigorously, for they are likely to undermine the unified effort of the national community.

However, the total conduct of war and total policy should not only prevent the shattering of national unity, but also take positive steps to inspire national enthusiasm by means of exploiting propaganda media to the utmost. Close touch with the problems of mass psychology will help politics in selecting the means to be employed for the strengthening of the national morale.

Indeed, protective actions, as well as propaganda, should be put into use not only at the outbreak of war, but should become permanent features of the peacetime scenery, meaning in fact the creation of a "Police State" *par excellence*. Psychological warfare aimed against other nations should also be waged permanently in peacetime.

All these activities might easily blur the boundaries between peace and war. Some people rightly had doubts whether, under such circumstances, war is still a continuation of policy by other means, or whether peace becomes a continuation of war without actual shooting.

In order to achieve a coordinated and effective war effort, total war must be directed by one central authority. Ludendorff had no doubt whatsoever that this authority must rest with the commander-in-chief. The latter should already be appointed to his high office in peacetime in order to exert control over the preparations for war in every field. Thus he would assure that all the resources of the nation would be at the army's disposal. The commander-in-chief would not only command the armed forces and watch the military preparations for war, but would also direct and coordinate finance, commerce, production, national education—in particular propaganda—in short, he would exercise dictatorial authority.[8]

An essential point in Ludendorff's concept is the question of the declaration of war. He chastised Germany's politicians for having played into the enemy's hands in August 1914. He rationalized: "People show no understanding for wars of aggression, but I daresay they will understand a struggle for existence. They too easily consider a declaration of war as the expression of aggression. . . . A nation, and every individual in it, will support the conduct of war with the fullest effort, only if they are firmly convinced that life and existence are at stake."[9]

TOTAL WAR AND MILITARY PLANNING

In this sphere, Ludendorff departed from Schlieffen's usage and returned to the conception of the elder Moltke.

I remain convinced that deployment orders should settle the deployment only. They should take into consideration future operations, by way of grouping the troops in the deployment area, but should never fix plans for the course of operations, which will exceed the very first information about the adversary. This is the limit of paper considerations, the seriousness of the reality of war starts here, and it does not allow the execution of plans, but demands the exploitation of the opponent's obvious weaknesses.[10]

In retrospect, Ludendorff maintained that the Schlieffen Plan against France was excellent for the circumstances of 1904–1905, but unfit in 1914. Ludendorff was in favor of operational studies in peacetime in order to check deployment measures and polish up the technique of reaching decisions, but he was strongly opposed to considering these studies as theoretical experience and, above all, rejected the pursuing of a "prefixed plan" in face of the enemy.

The military plan embraces not only military measures, but also the financial and economic spheres, as well as the material and moral welfare of the population. The supreme coordinator of all these functions, Ludendorff left no doubt, was the commander-in-chief.

WAR ON SEVERAL FRONTS

Total war strives for a decision. This demands from the leader of the total war that he press an offensive at the most decisive spot. The selection of that spot is vital because in a war on many fronts, one cannot attack everywhere without violating the principle of concentration of force and the center of gravity. The question which enemy should first be attacked in order to reach an early decision by way of his defeat should be answered as follows: that opponent which is considered to be the most dangerous. The art of conducting war demands the creation of a center of gravity at the decisive point and the unhesitant denuding of less essential fronts, even if it should mean a temporary exposure of a province or provinces to hostile invasion. In this case all able-bodied men and all potential war material should be evacuated in accordance with the basic plan of deployment. If guerrilla warfare against the invader is intended in those districts, it should be planned and organized beforehand.

Sometimes the commander-in-chief will hold back reserves near central railway junctions in order to throw them into battle in the most promising direction after the situation has cleared up sufficiently. One has, indeed, to consider whether such a line of action will not offend against the principle of utilizing all available forces right from the beginning.

ON SUPERIORITY IN NUMBERS

Ludendorff was in fact a believer in the slogan that "God is on the side of the stronger battalions." Because the leader of the total war will strive to terminate the war as quickly as possible, taking into consideration that a prolonged war might undermine the unity of the nation and create economic difficulties, he must insist on having at his disposal, from the beginning, the whole manpower of the nation, well trained, well equipped, and properly organized. It is true that in history instances were known when "weak battalions" had carried the day. However, in the long run Germany was crushed in 1918 by the sheer weight of enemy numbers. Therefore, one can never be too strong for the first decisive clash. "Superiority in numbers is too often the vital factor in war. It is a mistake to forget that, and to make a virtue of necessity. The importance of numbers must be recognized with inexorable clearness."[11]

DEFENSIVE AND OFFENSIVE

As early as 1922 Ludendorff said that he was unable "to share the opinion, expressed in 'On War,' that the defensive form of war is stronger than the offensive."[12] That is a somewhat strange utterance from Ludendorff's mouth after he learned this truth the hard way. In his book on total war he maintained that it is useless talk, to discuss the question, as has so often been done in the past, even by Clausewitz, and as perhaps theorists still do today, whether the offensive or the defensive is the stronger form of war, and whether it is not the highest art of conducting war, to let the enemy run against the defenses, and only after the collapse of his assault, to take to the counter-offensive. These are dangerous artificialities which obscure the seriousness and simplicity of the total war. . . . When attacking, one dwells upon the proud feeling of superior power, those imponderables, that give force to a properly conducted attack, even against an enemy, superior in numbers. . . . The offensive is always the decisive form of battle.[13]

With regard to fortifications, Ludendorff admitted their importance for the war on land as well as for the conduct of naval warfare. They render possible the concentration of force for the creation of a center of gravity in the decisive direction.

ON ENCIRCLEMENT

A burnt child dreads fire. Since the failures in 1918 Ludendorff never got rid of his dislike of the break-through. He warned that "frontal attacks will always lead to one's own considerable losses."[14] Modern means will, however, render possible a concerted assault in front, flanks, and rear: Infantry divisions will attack in front and in the flanks, mechanized formations will strive for the rear of the enemy's array, and aircraft will add a new dimension to the picture. This new dimension will indeed seriously influence the image of naval combat. The battle on land and sea will be the more decisive if preceded by a successful contest in the air. Mobile forces, penetrating deep behind the hostile front, will block the enemy's lines of retreat and cut him off. "Similar circumstances will arise from a gap in the hostile front, through which the assailant can push forth, as I did at Tannenberg.[15] In such a case, one should first envelop in a purely tactical fashion the existing inner wings of the enemy by fire, then try to split those wings more and more, in order to widen the hole in the hostile front permanently, and through this hole continue the encirclement further and further."[16]

ON AERIAL WARFARE

Besides the task of combating the hostile air force, acting against the rear installations of the opposing front and against the enemy's line of communications, a new factor was to emerge from the deployment of the air force. This would be the terrorizing of the adversary's country. The bombing of the opponent's war industry would inflict punishment not only on the workers in the plants, but also involve large parts of the civil population. Should anti-aircraft measures be properly organized, and the people be inspired by an obstinate spirit, then a lot of time and effort might be required in order to break the popular will to resist. However, "at the moment that air superiority is reached, and the hostile armed forces are hit, then the territory of the enemy will become the target of the air force."[17]

No sooner had Ludendorff written down his ideas on total war than they were immediately put to the test in the Abyssinian War (1935) and the Civil War in Spain (1936). More trials were still to come!

NOTES

1. *Vide* chapter 1, under "War and Politics."

2. "Alle Theorien von Clausewitz sind über den Haufen zu werfen." E. Ludendorff, *Der totale Krieg*, München, 1935, p. 10.

3. *Ibid.*, p. 3.

4. E. Ludendorff, *Kriegführung und Politik*, Berlin, 1922, p. 23.

5. E. Ludendorff, *Der totale Krieg, op. cit.*, p. 10.

6. Since Ludendorff had discovered the totality of war, he got enchanted by that term and everything became "total."

7. E. Ludendorff, *Der totale Krieg, op. cit.*, p. 16.

8. One may assume that Ludendorff projected into the image of his general all the personal aspirations and desires that he himself had since his accession to OHL in 1916, and that his biting attacks on the "politicians" no doubt reflect his frustration at not having reached his final goal of dictator of Germany.

9. E. Ludendorff, *Der totale Krieg, op. cit.*, pp. 87–88 passim.

10. *Ibid.*, p. 93.

11. *Ibid.*, p. 49.

12. E. Ludendorff, *Kriegführung und Politik, op. cit.*, p. 10, footnote.

13. E. Ludendorff, *Der totale Krieg, op. cit.*, pp. 77–79.

14. *Ibid.*, p. 74.

15. Ludendorff never missed an opportunity to stress his exclusive responsibility for the battle of Tannenberg. In a letter of 21 May 1935 to Mrs. v. Hahnke, Groener recalled that a short time after the battle of Tannenberg, at the dinner table, Ludendorff murmured to himself, but loud enough to be heard by his dinner companions: "One more victory like Tannenberg, and I shall be immortal." BHA—Rep. 92, W. v. Hahnke, Nr. 19/20.

16. E. Ludendorff, *Der totale Krieg, op. cit.*, p. 73.

17. *Ibid.*, pp. 82–83.

Part III ————————————————
Hitler's War: Traditional Theories in a Changed Environment

Since the German generals and staff officers have been released from the prisoner-of-war camps and the German archives thrown open to general access, a torrent of memoirs, collections of documents, campaign studies, and comprehensive works concerning the German side of the Second World War has flooded the student of this war on an ever-increasing scale. Never before has a war been illuminated so thoroughly in all its aspects as this one. However, one should keep in mind that the even more outspoken technical perfectionism of German soldiers of that era, in comparison with previous periods, coupled with the more extreme divorce of this generation from the political circumstances, renders it more difficult to trace any direct influence of theory; and one is forced to resort instead to "circumstantial evidence."

15

Case 6: The "Blitzkrieg"– Campaigns of 1939–1940: Mechanized "Cannae" Battles

The early breakdown of mobile operations in the First World War demonstrated the fact that the inadequate technical means of Schlieffen and the younger Moltke had prevented the application of the Cannae concept at the levels of operation and strategy. However, the harnessing of motor-power to military action in the inter-war period permitted the execution of large-scale encirclement movement at all levels of warfare in the Second World War. Provided that sufficient mobile forces were at hand for a certain operation, great dimensions in themselves no longer imposed restrictions on the conduct of "Cannae"-style battles. Nevertheless, one should keep in mind that the ratio between space, time, and the forces deployed in them imposed, and are most likely to impose in the future, certain limitations, as may be learned from the war in Russia.[1] However, the initial phase of the Second World War produced some striking German victories based on the Cannae concept. The most spectacular of that kind were the quick overthrow of Poland in 1939 and the lightning defeat of France in 1940.[2]

THE "BLITZKRIEG" IN POLAND

German General Günther Blumentritt has outlined the opening situation of the German campaign in Poland strikingly: A glance at the map reveals that Poland was conquered strategically before a shot was fired or a soldier had crossed the border. Poland was embraced from three sides and crushed between two mighty arms. Poland's situation was hopeless.[3]

This seems to be simple, but one will remember that in 1893 Schlieffen warned against a coordinated operation launched simultaneously from Galicia and from East Prussia, on account of the great distance between the two arms, which would not be able to render assistance to each other. Since Schlieffen's days, however, something had basically changed the military situation. Geography remained the same, and the distance between the two arms was still approximately 400 kilometers, but the introduction of motor transport and, above all, the utilization of tanks as independent fighting vehicles, organized in large units and geared to air support, made the geographical distance less frightening and haz-ardous. In sharp contrast to their adversaries, past and present, whose concept of war had remained captivated by the phenomenon of static warfare, and who had even employed their tank force for position warfare, the Germans had revived Schlieffen's maxim of "operation means movement."

Furthermore, the operative considerations of the German General Staff as-sumed that the bulk of the Polish troops would assemble in a forward position, in the great bend of the Vistula between Bromberg and Krakow. A battle of annihilation, fought against hostile forces deployed on the left shore of the Vistula, was a recurring feature in the ideas of the Prussian General Staff under the elder Moltke and Schlieffen. One will also remember that similar consid-erations of the Supreme Commander East and the Austrian Command lay at the bottom of the controversy between these authorities and General von Falken-hayn.[4] In 1939, however, owing to the favorable geographical situation and the existence of fast-moving and hard-hitting mobile forces, the German General Staff could dare to carry out, almost simultaneously, two great pincer movements: the first in order to destroy the Polish forces west of the Vistula; the second, penetrating much deeper into hostile territory, moving from East Prussia along the Narew and the Bug in order to close up Warsaw from the hinterland as early as possible, and to trap all Polish forces that might have escaped from the jaws of the first pincer. This was, however, a bold scheme, because the German forces in isolated East Prussia—the Third Army—were not considered strong enough to carry out such an enterprise single-handedly; the first thought of OHL, there-fore, was to employ them first in a movement toward the Fourth Army sallying forth from Pomerania, and then, with joined forces, to approach Warsaw from the north. Hitler, however, insisted on the large-scale "Cannae" maneuver by means of deploying the Third Army, right from the beginning, along Narew and Bug deep into the rear of the Polish Army, and to strive to join hands there with Army Group South moving from Slovakia.[5]

. However, even the Germans did not anticipate that the whole campaign would be finished in less than three weeks from the outbreak of hostilities. Such a period of time had previously been needed solely for the purposes of mobilization and the deployment of forces. In strict accordance with Ludendorff's concept of "total war," there was, this time, neither a public proclamation of mobilization nor an official declaration of war.

Field Marshal Erich von Manstein quoted an utterance of Schlieffen to the effect that the vanquished had contributed to his adversary's victory.[6] Indeed, the Poles had adopted the French Maginot concept and had prepared a linear defense along the frontier with Germany. Once the German armored wedges had penetrated this insufficiently prepared line and broken out into the open and empty rear of the Polish defenses, they had only to turn about and press on the Polish troops from their undefended rear.[7] Manstein also noted that Poland's allies in the West failed to come to its rescue by means of an offensive against

Germany in the West, aimed at forcing the Germans to break off the Polish campaign and presenting them once more with a war on two fronts.

As it was, the German plan of the campaign aimed at a huge operation of encirclement, carried out by two army groups (Heeresgruppen). Their mission, as defined by Hitler at the Obersalzberg on 22 August 1939, was strictly in accordance with Schlieffen's teaching, namely, not the reaching of a certain line of advance or a new frontier, but the *annihilation* of Poland, i.e., the destruction of its fighting force.[8] Speed was considered essential for the achievement of a decisive victory.

Pursuing these lines of action, mechanized forces rendered possible the execution of encirclement movements at the operative, as well as at the strategic, level, a feat that was not feasible at the time of Schlieffen's foot-marching armies. Between 7 and 11 September two motorized corps, together with a third corps, closed the cauldron of Radom, called by N. von Vormann "a modern Cannae in the classic style."[9] From the Polish front the two advancing mechanized corps broke off a block, believed to contain the main Polish forces, dashed forward, covering 200 kilometers in two days, regardless of their own exposed flanks, and closed the encircling ring before the Poles could even think of any countermeasures.

The success was even greater than expected by the Germans. Already on 9 September OKH (Oberkommando Heer—Supreme Command of the Army) issued new orders for a double-flank encirclement of the enemy east of the Vistula. The purpose of the advance of Army Group North was to support the crossing of the Vistula by Army Group South. Army Group North had also to send forward a strong easterly wing in order to cooperate, at a later stage, with forces of Army Group South, who would then be east even of the Bug. This was, in fact, the launching of the second, deeper pincer movement. Cutting for a second time deep into Polish territory, these actions threw any command measures of the Polish High Command out of gear from the beginning. No further Polish concerted actions were feasible.[10]

On 16 September the vanguards of Army Group North, coming from East Prussia, and of Army Group South, from Slovakia, met at Brest–Litovsk. Inside this gigantic encirclement of the Polish Army several smaller cauldrons were created, as, for instance, the cauldrons on the Bzura near Kutno, the cauldron around Warsaw, at Radom, and northwest of Lemberg. In the encirclement on the Bzura about a quarter of the Polish Army was destroyed.[11] These cauldron battles were, in fact, the forerunners of the huge battles of that type still to come in the Russian campaign. In contrast to the encirclement battles of the Schlieffen type that were planned beforehand, these encirclements developed out of quick-moving battles by exploiting situations created by the enemy's reactions.

Halder, who, as Chief of the General Staff of the Army, actually conducted the whole operation, defined as the two principal features of the campaign in Poland the pushing forward of quick-moving armored troops in order to force the foe to wage a battle with "reverted front," which in fact meant a battle in a state of encirclement, and the efficient coordination of aerial action with the fight on the ground.[12]

THE IMPACT OF THE THIRD DIMENSION

One should regard the large-scale deployment of the air force as contributing a new dimension to the Cannae picture. It fulfilled, to a certain degree, the paralyzing function of Hasdrubal's cavalry in the rear of the Roman phalanx. This became truer with the employment of airborne troops in the campaign of the West.

In fact, most of the 405 planes of the Polish Air Force were destroyed on the ground, before they could take off.[13] F. W. von Mellenthin, an outstanding German Panzer expert, has observed that "the Polish mobilization was gravely affected by the attacks of the Luftwaffe, and even those formations which did mobilize found their power of movement seriously restricted and their supply breaking down."[14] The mission assigned to the German Luftwaffe was, in fact, to fall on the Polish Air Force like a bolt from the blue, destroy the latter at its airfields on the ground, and wipe it out, on the first day of war. That task accomplished, the Luftwaffe had to create centers of gravity of close air support on the extreme wings of the encircling pincer jaws.[15] Owing to the fact that there was no clearly recognizable German mobilization and no declaration of war, the Luftwaffe caught the Polish planes on the ground as an easy prey. Furthermore, without any previous battle experience the cooperation between the German Air Force, especially the dive-bombers (Stukas), and the quick-moving Panzer columns was perfect and confirmed all the theoretical concepts evolved by the Englishmen Fuller and Liddell Hart and adopted and put into practice by the German General Guderian. In striking contrast to the First World War, which knew only the utilization of aircraft and tanks on the tactical level, the developments of the inter-war period enabled a large air force and armored formations to be employed on the operational level and to advance into the depth of the hostile territory, thus rendering large-scale encirclements possible. There is no doubt that this new way of waging war contributed to the swift termination of the war in Poland, as it did also eight months later in France.

REPETITION OF THE SCHLIEFFEN PLAN IN THE WEST?

Hitler considered France as England's "continental sword"[16] that had to be knocked out of the latter's hand in order to force it to surrender. That was, of course, not an original idea on Hitler's behalf. One will recognize that this argument was borrowed from Schlieffen's armory.[17] Hitler considered any delay of action in the West as bearing dangerous consequences. For Britain could, in the meantime, increase the number of its divisions on the Continent. He held the British troops in higher esteem than he did the French (which was the opposite of Schlieffen's attitude). He did not share his generals' awe of the French soldier. He thought the latter to be inferior to his counterpart of the First World War, mainly because of the "Maginot spirit," which had eliminated the traditional French élan. The German Panzer divisions and their tactics, and the Luftwaffe, especially the dive-bombers (Stukas), had no equivalent in the French Army. However, Hitler, like Schlieffen thirty-five years earlier, was anxious to evade a head-on attack against the strong French fortified line (this time the famous "Maginot Line"). The only way to do this was by violating the neutrality of Belgium and Holland, Belgian neutrality thus being infringed for the second time in this century. He reasoned, as Schlieffen had done, that these countries could by no means preserve their neutrality in a clash of major powers on account of their geographical situation. The war in the air would, in any case, be waged in their air space, and in case of German passivity, it might only be a question of time before the foe occupied them.[18]

On 27 September 1939, the day of the announcement of the unconditional surrender of Warsaw, Hitler revealed to his surprised generals that he had decided to take the initiative in the West in 1939. The reasons given for this unexpected move—unexpected because so far no plans had been prepared for such an enterprise—echoed Schlieffen's arguments: The vital industrial area of the Ruhr basin was too exposed to enemy access; Belgium's neutrality was scarcely a *de facto* one, if one considered that the defenses of that country faced only the frontier with Germany, whereas the border with France was open and undefended. Furthermore, Hitler was in possession of clear evidence that the Belgian General Staff was actively working together with the French General Staff, and that Brussels had been offered the deployment of French troops in Belgium and had accepted it. As in the First World War, the invasion of Belgium was therefore unavoidable.

This move would involve, as in Schlieffen's original plan, the crossing of the Maastrich Salient, viz., Dutch territory. Like Schlieffen, Hitler believed that the traversing of southern Holland could be handled as a political problem of diplomacy. He had no intention, he said, of attacking the Netherlands. He made it clear that he would not repeat the Schlieffen Plan and wheel the German right wing southward around the pivot of Diedenhofen. He would advance in a northwesterly direction, straight on to the channel coast, while shielding his southern flank by considerable forces during the advance. In order to exploit the present German military superiority, the start of the offensive could not take place too early. The Commander-in-Chief of the Army was ordered to inform Hitler as to the earliest possible date for the offensive. Hitler himself had in mind a day somewhere between 20 and 25 October 1939 for the initial assault.[19]

In one respect the situation on 27 September 1939 was completely different from the pre-First World War scenery. While, on the eve of the First World War, it was the General Staff that strongly demanded the invasion of Belgium and did not consult the political agencies, which were forced to consent, now, in the autumn of 1939, despite the successful "Blitzkrieg" in Poland, the Commander-in-Chief of the Army and his General Staff, as well as the commanders-in-chief of the Army Groups, were strongly opposed to the violation of Belgian and Dutch neutrality. They pointed to the fateful consequences of the violation in 1914.

Hitler raged in fury and settled down to prepare his own "Memorandum and Guide-lines for the Conduct of War in the West." This lengthy document was a strange mixture of historical lessons, political and strategical considerations, and an examination of tactical and psychological details. The objective of the campaign, as defined by Hitler, was the *annihilation* of the Western enemies and not the conquest of their territory. The latter was considered important only when judged in connection with its contribution toward the physical annihilation of the hostile forces. The time factor was considered as acting in the Western powers' favor. Among the reasons for acting immediately, the fact that Germany, for the first time in decades, would wage war on one front only, on account of its agreement with Russia (one will bear in mind that Schlieffen, in 1905, considered the time for action against France opportune because of the Russian domestic difficulties) ranked top. Nobody could, however, forecast how long that Russian posture would last. Hitler's opinion was that it might change in eight months, a year, or in several years. The attitude of the United States was regarded for the time being, not as absolutely anti-German, but that it might also change. (One will remember that, in 1914, too, illusions were nourished that a quick victory over France would not draw any American repercussions.)

On the other hand a prolonged war might bear many dangers for Germany: Potential friends among the neutrals might desert; the food and raw material situation was likely to deteriorate. Above all, the vital area of the Ruhr basin, for which Germany had no other alternatives as a production center, was permanently endangered by its proximity to Belgium and Holland. It was especially vulnerable to hostile air attacks. Retaliatory attacks on enemy production centers would not compensate for the actual loss in output. Should the war drag on, then the only effective means in Germany's hands were, as in the First World War, the U-boats and the new Luftwaffe. The latter would require short approach routes, namely, through Belgium and Holland, or even better, starting grounds in these countries.

Hitler considered Germany's military strength, for the present, greater and the ammunition situation much better than in 1914. France was superior only in heavy artillery, but that was an unimportant factor in a mobile war, which Germany intended to wage. Hitler, siding with the traditional German military opposition to Clausewitz' concept of the defense, explicitly stressed *the offensive as superior to the defensive*.

The sector selected by the Führer for the attack was between Luxembourg and Nijmwegen, without involving the fortress of Liège. Deployment should be in breadth rather than in depth, as was old Schlieffen's concept too. Panzers should rush forward and evade built up areas. "They are not to be lost among the endless rows of houses in Belgian towns. It is not necessary for them to attack towns at all . . . but to maintain the flow of the army's advance, to prevent fronts from becoming stable by massed drives through weakly held positions."[20] Antwerp, in particular, should not be attacked directly, but merely by-passed and invested by troops of second or third class quality, as Schlieffen had planned thirty-five years before. It is obvious that the "lessons of World War I" played an important part in Hitler's considerations.

Halder called this document, in retrospect, "an unimaginative replica of the Schlieffen plan, the weaknesses of which had been shown by the First World War."[21] Historian H. A. Jacobsen considered it as "an improvisation, void of ideas."[22]

The memorandum was followed the same day (9 October 1939) by "Directive No. 6 for the Conduct of the War," which was in fact a précis of Hitler's long-winded memorandum. The staffs of the three services were ordered to prepare their respective plans in detail. On 19 October 1939 OKH issued the "Deployment Order 'Yellow.' "[23] Because the French Maginot Line blocked a German advance across the Upper Rhine, as the fortress line of Belford–Verdun had done before in the First World War, the German army group deployed there on the left wing of the German array was to remain on the defensive inside the German West Wall. Schlieffen's plan had provided for a strong right wing, deployed from Metz to Wesel. In contrast to that plan the directive of 19 October had provided only for a strong uppermost northern wing, formed by Army Group B, which would deploy between Prüm and Wesel, while a weaker Army Group A was to cover the southern flank of Army Group B during the latter's advance to the northwest. The main center of gravity of this advance was north of Liège. It was obvious that the plan was void of any clear operational concept, and one gains the impression that it had been issued in obedience to Hitler's order, rather than to provide a plan of an operation that should be carried out. Apparently Brauchitsch and Halder, together with other Generals, still believed that the clash with the Western Powers could be avoided. The only slightly revised "Deployment Order" of 29 October 1939[24] bore the same features of vagueness.

How strongly, this time, the German military were opposed to any violation of neutral territories may be learned from a memorandum prepared by Colonel General von Leeb, C-in-C Army Group C, and forwarded to the Commander-in-Chief of the Army, von Brauchitsch, and the Chief of Staff of the Army, Halder. The memorandum was entitled "Memorandum about the prospects and effects of an offensive against France and England, by means of violation of Dutch, Belgian, and Luxembourgian neutrality" and was dated 11 October 1939.[25] Von Leeb doubted whether Germany could annihilate the military power of England and France.

The danger of a repetition of trench warfare was looming. It was doubtful whether the utilization of Panzer thrusts would be as successful in France as in Poland. After all, the French Army was not as inferior to the German Army as was the army of Poland. The violation of neutral territories would play politically into the hands of the Western powers, as was the case in 1914. The economic consequences of another static war would be disastrous for Germany. Consequently, von Leeb suggested the adoption of a defensive attitude. If the Western powers should attack Germany, the latter would benefit morally from the common feeling of defending the Fatherland. It was obvious that von Leeb, who had only recently published a treatise on defense,[26] was more impressed by Clausewitz' concept of the defensive than his warlord and, above all, took into account the political consequences of military acts.

However, in the meantime, events moved in a direction opposite to Leeb's suggestions. The Luftwaffe was eager to advance its air defense screen as far westward as possible and demanded, therefore, the occupation of Holland by the army. The Chief of Staff of the Luftwaffe succeeded in convincing Hitler of the necessity of such a line of action. Again, as in the case of the Schlieffen Plan, military-technical demands prevailed over political considerations. As a result, Hitler ordered the full-scale invasion of Holland.

The actual execution of "Case Yellow" in 1939 was prevented by the weather, which would not allow the necessary participation of the German Luftwaffe in the campaign. On 23 November 1939 Hitler called a further conference of commanding officers in order to press home his point. He returned to the problem of the violation of Belgian and Dutch neutrality. He stressed the same argument that was held by the inter-war Schlieffen school, with respect to Schlieffen's intention to violate Belgium's neutrality; namely, that it was insignificant. Nobody would care about it after a German victory. However, Hitler would not give such idiotic reasons for the violation of neutrality as had been given in 1914.[27] If Germany were to desist from entering Belgium and Holland, England and France would not. Hitler again stressed the importance of the Ruhr basin for the German war effort—the same argument that Schlieffen's disciples had always used during and after the First World War—and its vulnerability, should the British and French enter the Low Countries.[28]

If one crystallizes the main features of the first version of the plan for an offensive against France, one will soon discover that it held many similarities to the Schlieffen Plan. The right wing of the German Army in the West would have overthrown Holland and Belgium, beaten the Franco-British Armies of the northern wing, turned southward and exercised such a heavy pressure on the northern flank of the whole hostile front, that the German Armies in the south could have advanced despite the barrier of the Maginot Wall. Owing to the French fortifications, the German left wing would remain on the defensive, but was ordered to tie down the French forces that would occupy the Maginot Line by means of feinting a major offensive. Liège, with its surrounding forts, especially Eben Emael, was considered so strong that it was to be by-passed at the first instance. The main thrust of the assault would, in consequence, have been launched north of Liège. The whole plan drawn out on the map resembled in its main features the Schlieffen Plan. Yet one should keep in mind that this time, on account of the mobile forces and airpower, its execution had a better chance of success than at the time of the Schlieffen foot-marching armies.

In the wake of the postponement of the operation, owing to bad weather, new ideas were put forward and a feverish activity started behind the scenes.

THE STRUGGLE FOR A MODIFIED PLAN

The structure of the hostile front, the Maginot Wall as well as the Belgian and the Dutch defenses north of it, at this time prevented an execution of a simple encirclement movement as Schlieffen had designed it. An initial break-through was now necessary in order to make the best use of the mobile Panzer forces. Germany's opponents were, no doubt, aware that this would be the course of events. Therefore, the only way of achieving any surprise was in the selection of the break-through point and in the exploitation of the initial penetration with the utmost speed and force. It is now well known that the final plan, which was eventually carried out in May 1940, was initiated by General von Manstein. One may therefore dispense with a detailed description of the fierce controversy between von Manstein and his immediate superior, von Rundstedt, on one side, and the reluctant OKH on the other, as well as with the various backstage intrigues designed to draw Hitler's attention to the new ideas.[29] Only a few points that are connected with the subject of the present study will be illuminated here.

Manstein's principle objection to the plan, contained in OKH's orders of 19 and 29 October 1939, was that it was aimed only at a partial decision, i.e., the destruction of those enemy forces that would advance into Belgium, and the gaining of the channel coast, viz., a territorial acquisition. Schlieffen's plan was directed at the annihilation of the whole hostile force by means of a gigantic Cannae. Schlieffen was prepared to risk initial setbacks in Lorraine in order to achieve his objective of total annihilation. Manstein criticized the obvious lack of determination on the part of OKH in striving for "an absolute decision on the ground."[30] He was aware of OKH's negative attitude toward the war in the West. While being an outspoken military perfectionist, he was absolutely free from the moral scruples that the heads of the OKH still had at that time. He was therefore much more in line with Schlieffen's attitude, with regard to the general idea of the campaign, although for tactical and technical reasons he rejected a mere repetition of the Schlieffen Plan.

Manstein was aware that Schlieffen's striving for a final decision in one single move was no more feasible in the circumstances of 1939 than in 1914. He therefore suggested a two-stage campaign. Phase I: the break through the enemy front and the cutting off of those hostile forces that might have advanced into Belgium; Phase II: the final encirclement of the remaining enemy forces south of the Somme. The basic assumption was that the French High Command would anticipate a repetition of the Schlieffen Plan, and would therefore strive to encounter the Germans in Belgium as far to the East as possible. The bulk of the French mobile forces, together with the B.E.F. would therefore have been rushed into Belgium at an early date.

In order to cut off and destroy these forces the German center of gravity was to be shifted from Army Group B in the north to Army Group A in the south. To the latter the bulk of armored groups would be allotted. The Panzer corps would traverse the Ardennes, considered unsuitable ground for armored units, in the direction of Sedan, cross the Meuse, and head for the channel coast near Abbeville. The southern flank of that thrust would be covered by infantry units moving in the wake of the Panzer units. The hostile forces in Belgium would become trapped between the two army groups and finally crushed by Army Group A as the "hammer" against Army Group B's "anvil."[31] This phase accomplished, both army groups would turn to the south, and by advancing with emphasis on the right wing, between the coast and east of Paris, they would endanger the rear of the Maginot Line. This would be the opportune moment for Army Group C, hitherto on the defensive opposite the Maginot Wall, to take the offensive in its turn, and thus complete the absolute encirclement of the enemy. This particular phase strongly resembles Schlieffen's image of the final stage of his plan.

Whereas Schlieffen's plan soon lost the effect of surprise regarding the direction of his advance, mainly because of the slow foot-marching movement of the troops at his time, and only kept the impact of surprise on account of the mass of troops employed there, the Manstein plan, if properly executed, was likely to utilize surprise in respect to the direction of the thrust, the speed of the advance, and the forces deployed. Had the Germans carried out the initial plan it would have led, no doubt, to a head-on clash of the main forces of both antagonists in Belgium. Had the Germans even carried the day, they would have merely achieved an "ordinary victory," to use Schlieffen's language.

It is of interest that Manstein's suggestions were not only rejected by the more conservative OKH, but at first also by General Jodl of OKW, who was, throughout the whole Second World War, Hitler's chief military advisor. General Alfred Jodl wrote in a memorandum to Hitler: "I invite his attention to the fact that the thrust at Sedan is an operational 'secret passage,' in which one may be caught by the gods of war."[32] On the other hand the plan was enthusiastically supported by General Heinz Guderian, the Panzer expert.

In February 1940 Manstein's plan was at last tested in a series of war games, in the traditional method of the German General Staff. Guderian had suggested the crossing of the Meuse with strong Panzer and motorized forces on the fifth day of the campaign, the forcing of a break-through, and a quick advance in the direction of Amiens. Such an idea was so novel that General Halder, Chief of the General Staff of the Army, considered it to be "senseless." He was in favor of reaching the Meuse, perhaps establishing some bridgeheads, should the circumstances permit it, awaiting the arrival of the infantry armies, and then launching a concerted attack approximately on the ninth or tenth day of the campaign. He called it an "arranged general attack."[33] The unconventional idea of a quick advance of mobile wedges deep into enemy territory without worrying about the exposed flanks in order to shake the enemy's cohesion and morale was still an unusual thought for most German soldiers at that time, who were brought up in

Schlieffen's belief for the necessity of closed ranks and company drill-like advance of armies.

Another problem raised by the war game of tha period was the question whether the mobile forces should move in front of the infantry armies or be held in reserve for the exploitation of favorable situations created by the latter. Although Guderian succeeded in the long run in pressing his opinion of "mobile forces in front,"[34] the higher ranks were nevertheless kept in a permanent anxiety lest the precious Panzers might become worn down while advancing unsupported ahead of the army. This fear was, from time to time, to apply checks on the armored units that were dashing forward.

The revised version of the directive for "Case Yellow" was issued by OKH on 24 February 1940.[35] It was now vital for the success of the operation that the enemy should believe in a repetition of the Schlieffen Plan. The "Incident of Mechelen"—the crash-landing of a German aircraft on Belgian territory on 10 January 1940 with two officers of the Luftwaffe on board, who carried with them secret orders of the old version of the plan—could now be utilized for deception measures, after the adoption of the "Sichelschnitt" plan.[36]

A special feature of the final plan for the conquest of France was the employment of airborne troops for the seizure of Rotterdam and vital bridges in Holland and Belgium, and for the *coup de main* on the fortress of Eben Emael in the Liège area. Hitler himself attached much attention to the detailed planning of this raid, and one cannot resist a certain feeling that he wanted his own equivalent to the *coup de main* on Liège in August 1914.

On 10 May 1940 the German Armies invaded the Netherlands, Belgium, and Luxembourg. Ten days later Guderian's Panzers reached the coast at Abbeville. According to Schlieffen's plan of 1905, German troops would have reached Abbeville on M + 31 by a sweep from the north.

THE REVIVAL OF SCHLIEFFEN'S FEAR OF GAPS

The roots of this psychosis, which eventually contributed to the check on the German Panzers short of Dunkirk, dated back to the first week of the campaign. As early as 17 May Hitler was worried about the southern flank of his far-advanced armored corps and demanded a halt until the Twelfth Army, which was following closely behind, could close the gap. This was the first head-on clash between the Führer and OKH, which was actually conducting the campaign. Only after a whole day's arguments did Hitler consent to the further advance of von Kleist's Panzer group. No harm was done because the Führer's order had not gone through to the troops in the van.[37] The conflict was revealed in Halder's diary:

The Führer emphasized, that he sees the main danger in the south. For the time being, I cannot see any danger at all! . . . A very unpleasant day. The Führer is terribly nervous. Frightened by his own success, he is afraid to take any chance and would therefore rather pull reins on us. The pretext: anxiety for the left flank! . . . One cannot understand why. He rages and screams, that we are on the way to ruining the whole campaign and are exposed to the danger of defeat. He won't have any part in continuing the operation in a westward direction.[38]

In the relaxed and purely theoretical atmosphere of a conference, on 9 September 1938, Hitler had then known that "it is fatal for tanks to have to stop and wait for infantry." He added then: "This contradicts all laws of logic."[39] However, under the stress of war and real combat action Hitler reverted to the traditional German aversion for gaps, of the pre-armored period, which had already influenced the fate of the Marne battle in September 1914. Gaps simply appalled him. On 22 May the Führer drew the attention of the C-in-C of the Army "to the gap in the German line in the vicinity of Valencienne."[40] On 23 May, owing to the British riposte at Arras, General Hans von Kluge, C-in-C Fourth Army, was in favor of stopping the motorized units and closing the ranks.[41] Schlieffen's spirit hovered over the scene!

"CANNAE" IN THE WEST

It seems that Hitler was not confident enough to carry out the possibility of encircling the B.E.F. between the pincers provided by Army Groups A and B to its ultimate conclusion. Thus, to quote H. A. Jacobsen, "the first phase of the campaign in the West in 1940 ["Case Yellow"] ended in an 'ordinary victory,' though by the plan of the offensive and the enemies' reaction, a victory of annihilation [Cannae] would have been feasible."[42]

However, the second and final phase of the campaign in France, code named "Case Red," was Schlieffenian in essence. If one draws on the map the German routes of advance for the encirclement of the remainder of the French forces inside the triangle Paris–Belfort–Metz, one sees the picture that was in Schlieffen's mind for the total annihilation of the French Army. No wonder that Halder wrote in his diary: "Cannae steps well to the fore."[43] The German forces advancing from the north pushed the already demoralized French troops to the south and then eastward against their own eastern defenses, as Schlieffen had planned in 1905. Finally, the advance of Army Group C on 14 June and its break through the Maginot Line, as Schlieffen had foreseen for his left wing in Alsace and Lorraine, delivered the *coup de grace* to the tottering French resistance.

A battle of encirclement and annihilation on the highest strategic level had reached its victorious end. The German Army had partly emancipated itself from the one-sided Schlieffen obsession with encirclement, although only for the time being.

CONTEMPORARY GERMAN EVALUATION OF THE "BLITZKRIEG" CAMPAIGNS

Despite the obvious adherence to Schlieffen's principles, Hitler would not admit it frankly, the more so since Joseph Goebbels had proclaimed him "the greatest strategist of all times.'' On 19 July 1940, in his Reichstag speech, Hitler therefore seized the opportunity to make it clear that his plan was different from Schlieffen's plan.

Unlike the Schlieffen Plan of 1914, I ordered the shifting of the center of gravity of the operation to the left wing of the break-through front, while at the same time attempting to give the impression that I was doing the opposite. . . . As a second operation I had provided for the gaining of the Seine as far as Le Havre, as well as the securing of a starting position on the Somme and Aisne for the third assault, which should sally forth in strength through the plateau of Langres to the Swiss frontier. The reaching of the coast up to south of Bordeaux was provided as the closing of the operation. Inside that framework and in that order the operations were actually carried out.[44]

Somewhat different views were aired by Lieutenant General von Rabenau, Chief of the Army Archives, immediately after the first stage of the campaign, at the beginning of June 1940, in an article, ''The Revolution of the Conduct of War,'' prepared for the weekly *Das Reich*.[45] Referring to a friendly foreign newspaper commentary expressing the view that the war in the West was ''the overcoming of classical strategy,''[46] Rabenau considered such a conclusion to be premature. He raised the question, what ''classical strategy'' means? He maintained that the Germans understand it as Field Marshal von Schlieffen had transmitted it in his ''Cannae Studies.'' These are the external axioms of the art of war and ''will be valid as long as generals conduct armies and will keep their validity.'' Schlieffen had advocated the decision by means of annihilation of the hostile fighting force. For this purpose concentration of forces at the decisive spots was necessary, even at the cost of dangerous weaknesses at indecisive spots. This is the classical strategy that had led from Leuthen through Waterloo, Sedan, Tannenberg, and so on. ''It was the heritage of the Great General Staff.''

Although every war must produce something new, the axioms remain constant. The genius always displays innovations, breaks fetters, but does not destroy the classic principles of the art of leadership. He always builds up, never destroys. It is true that new technical means have led to a change of the strategical consequences. The leaders do not face new problems of leadership, Rabenau maintained, but are nevertheless presented with completely different demands on their abilities: The crises of decision occur with much speed.

However, von Rabenau credited not only Schlieffen for the German successes so far in Poland and in the West, but also von Seeckt's foresight into the problems of modern mobile warfare.

This essay presents a remarkable early analysis of the ''Blitzkrieg'' campaigns by a soldier of high intelligence. Yet even more interesting was the controversy over the release of the article for publication. On 4 June 1940 the Propaganda Department of OKW asked Jodl to act for the release of the essay. The minutes of the report bears Keitel's crimson pencil remark: ''I am against release! The Führer, who always reads such articles, might consider it inopportune at the present time! Perhaps later on!'' Jodl added: ''One should let those things ripen before writing about them.'' On 14 August 1940, owing to a certain relaxation in censorship measures, a further request for the release of the article was made. Jodl's remark on the minutes reveals the real reasons for the rejection: ''The relaxation of censorship measures does not apply to this article. The objection against it consists in the fact that the article rather applauds Schlieffen and Seeckt,[47] which appears to me unsuitable for the time being. I am absolutely sure that we have won not only because we have found our way back to Schlieffen and Seeckt.'' And Keitel added: ''Exactly my opinion! I am prepared to sign every word! Therefore rejection!'' That was the end of Rabenau's attempt to present the campaign in France in a historical framework. Nobody was allowed to minimize the genius of ''the greatest strategist of all times.''

It will therefore cause no surprise that on the first anniversary of the opening of the French campaign, the *Völkischer Beobachter*, the official organ of the Nazi party, published an article entitled ''The German High Command During the Campaign in the West and the Schlieffen Plan,'' written by Konstantin Hierl.[48] The latter was a high-ranking officer in the party hierarchy, who served, prior to the First World War, as a teacher of military history and tactics at the Bavarian War Academy. One can summarize the gist of that essay by quoting the final passage. ''Neither by adherence to the 'Schlieffen Plan' nor to the Cannae-doctrine nor to any other rigid theory, but by way of free artistic creation, resulting from the inspiration of his martial genius, has the Führer led the German Wehrmacht to the most glorious victory of its laudable history.''

NOTES

1. *Vide* chapters 16 and 18.

2. Other cases of Cannae-type campaigns were the conquest of Yugoslavia and Greece in 1941.

3. Günther Blumentritt, *Von Rundstedt. The Soldier and the Man*, London, 1952, pp. 42–43.

4. *Vide* chapter 8.

5. Nikolaus von Vormann, *Der Feldzug 1939 in Polen*, Weissenberg, 1958, pp. 60–61.

6. Erich von Manstein, *Verlorene Siege*, Bonn, 1955, p. 56.

7. A further handicap for the Poles was the fact that the frontier areas inside Poland had a considerable population of German stock.

8. Franz Halder, *Kriegstagebuch*, Stuttgart, 1962, vol. 1, p. 25; Helmuth Greiner, *Die Oberste Wehrmachtführung 1939–1943*, Wiesbaden, 1951, pp. 38–43.

9. N. v. Vorman, *op. cit.*, p. 108.

10. *Ibid.*, p. 104. One should keep in mind that such a movement also meant a further advance of the German main forces to the East, which might have invited French and British offensive steps on the Rhine.

11. Alfred Stenger, *Umfassungs—und Durchbruchsschlachten der deutschen Ges-*

chichte, Münster (Westf.), 1941, p. 97. This is yet another compilation in the Schlieffen school style, published during the Second World War (cf. with chapter 12).

12. P. Bor, *Gespräche mit Halder*, Wiesbaden, 1950, pp. 144–145.

13. *Ibid.*

14. Major General F. W. von Mellenthin, *Panzer Battles*, Oklahoma, 1958 (3d printing), p. 3.

15. B. v. Lossberg, *Im Wehrmachtsführungsstab*, Hamburg, 1949, pp. 27–28.

16. "Festlanddegen."

17. It was also used by von Falkenhayn in his Christmas Memorandum of 1915.

18. B. v. Lossberg, *op. cit.*, p. 45.

19. For the conference of 27 Sept. 1939, cf. H. A. Jacobsen, *Fall Gelb*, Wiesbaden, 1957, pp. 8–9; H. Greiner, *op. cit.*, pp. 55–57; Halder, *op. cit.*, vol. 1, p. 91.

20. "Denkschrift und Richtlinien über die Führung des Krieges im Westen," vom 9/10/1939. The full text of that memorandum is printed in H. A. Jacobsen, *Dokumente zur Vorgeschichte des Westfeldzuges 1939–1940*, Göttingen, 1956, pp. 4–21.

21. Franz Halder, *Hitler as War Lord*, London, 1950, p. 28.

22. H. A. Jacobsen, *Fall Gelb, op. cit.*, p. 32.

23. "Aufmarschanweisung 'Gelb,' " printed in H. A. Jacobsen, *Dokumente zur Vorgeschichte, op. cit.*, pp. 41–46. "Case Yellow" was the code name given to the campaign.

24. *Ibid.*, pp. 46–51.

25. *Ibid.*, pp. 79–85.

26. *Vide* chapter 8, under "The Reasons for the Stalemate."

27. If one reads carefully the memorandum of 9 May 1940 forwarded by the German Foreign Minister Joachim von Ribbentrop to the governments of Belgium and Holland, one cannot resist feeling that it was quite similar to Moltke's "Sommation" of 1914. The memorandum is printed in H. A. Jacobsen, *Dokumente zur Vorgeschichte, op. cit.*, pp. 215–219.

28. For the conference of 23 Nov. 1939, cf. H. A. Jacobsen, *Fall Gelb, op. cit.*, pp. 61–64 and H. A. Jacobsen, *1939–1945. Der zweite Weltkrieg in Chronik und Dokumenten*, Darmstadt, 1961 (5th rev. ed.), p. 138.

29. The whole struggle for the "Manstein- or Sichelschnitt-Plan" may be found in Manstein's memoirs, *op. cit.*, as well as in Liddell Hart's *The Other Side of the Hill*, London, 1956, and in H. A. Jacobsen, *Fall Gelb, op. cit.*; H. A. Jacobsen has investigated Hitler's share in the shaping of the final plan in a separate article. Cf. H. A. Jacobsen, "Hitlers Gedanken zur Kriegführung im Westen," *Wehrwissenschaftliche Rundschau*, Jg. 5, H. 10 (Oct. 1955), pp. 433–446. The memoranda of Manstein and the correspondence of Army Group A with OKH are printed in H. A. Jacobsen, *Dokumente zur Vorgeschichte, op. cit.*, pp. 119–156.

30. "Die volle Entscheidung auf dem Lande."

31. This was, in fact, a more modern definition of the interaction between Hannibal's various parts in the "Cannae" scheme as Schlieffen had perceived it: Hasdrubal's cavalry having been the "hammer," the slowly advancing center of Hannibal's foot-soldiers providing the "anvil."

32. "Ein operativer Schleichweg auf dem man von dem Kriegsgott erwischt werden kann." Cf. H. A. Jacobsen, *Fall Gelb, op. cit.*, p. 114.

33. "Einen rangierten Gesamtangriff." For a report of the war game, cf. H. Guderian, *Erinnerungen eines Soldaten*, Heidelberg, 1951, p. 80.

34. "Mot. Verbände voraus!" For the arguments about this problem, cf. a letter of

Blumentritt to von Manstein of 16 Feb. 1940, printed in H. A. Jacobsen, *Dokumente zur Vorgeschichte, op. cit.*, pp. 153–155.

35. "Neufassung der Aufmarschanweisung 'Gelb.' " *Ibid.*, pp. 64–68.

36. For the Mechelen incident, cf. H. A. Jacobsen, *Dokumente zur Vorgeschichte, op. cit.*, pp. 161–185. For special deception measures, cf. B. v. Lossberg, *op. cit.*, pp. 74–75.

37. Cf. H. Greiner, *op. cit.*, p. 103.

38. Halder, *Kriegstagebuch, op. cit.*, vol. 1, pp. 300–303 passim.

39. Cf. Peter de Mendelssohn, *The Nuremberg Documents*, London, 1946, p. 77.

40. Cf. H. A. Jacobsen, *Dünkirchen*, Neckargemünd, 1958, p. 73.

41. *Ibid.*, p. 82.

42. H. A. Jacobsen, *Dokumente zum Westfeldzug 1940*, Göttingen, 1960, p. 1. The events of Dunkirk and the reasons for the narrow escape of the B.E.F. are outside the scope of this study.

43. Halder, *Kriegstagebuch, op. cit.*, vol. 1, p. 346.

44. Adolf Hitler, *Der grossdeutsche Freiheitskampf. Reden Adolf Hitlers*, München, 1943, vol. 2, p. 244.

45. MGFA—WO1-6/485. Gen. Lt. von Rabenau, "Revolution der Kriegführung."

46. "Die Überwindung der klassischen Strategie."

47. "Dass der Artikel mehr das 'hohe Lied' Schlieffens und von Seeckts singt."

48. Konstantin Hierl, "Die deutsche Oberste Führung im Westfeldzug und der Schlieffen-Plan," in Wilhelm Weiss, ed., *Triumph der Kriegskunst*, 2d ed., München, 1942, pp. 67–74.

16

Case 7: "Barbarossa": In the Steps of Charles XII and Napoleon

THE RUSSIAN SPACE

The problem of Russian space has already been touched on in this study.[1] In order to evaluate, in its proper proportions, Hitler's decision to attack the Soviet Union, it seems appropriate to summarize the issue.

For generations Clausewitz' opinion about the Russian space, and about war in Russia, dominated German military thinking. He considered his conclusions, laid down in his study of the Russian campaign of 1812,[2] as being of such importance that he included them in his theoretical work *On War*. He stated that

the Russian campaign of 1812 demonstrated in the first place that a country of such size could not be conquered (which might well have been foreseen) and in the second that the prospect of eventual success does not always decrease in proportion to lost battles, captured capitals, and occupied provinces, which is something that diplomats used to regard as dogma, and make them always ready to conclude a peace however bad. On the contrary, the Russians showed us that one often attains one's greatest strength in the heart of one's own country, when the enemy's offensive power is exhausted, and the defensive can then switch with enormous energy to the offensive.[3]

Field Marshal Moltke, despite giving preference in his deployment plans to attacking Russia first, in the event of a war on two fronts, was competely daunted by the difficulties presented by the Russian space and had no conquest of Russian territory in mind. He would only consent to minor alterations of the German-Russian frontier in Germany's favor.[4]

Count von Schlieffen rejected the "Great Eastern Deployment Plan" ("Grosser Ostaufmarsch") because he considered the Russian space, i.e., its vastness and its communication difficulties, as unsuitable for the achievement of a quick and decisive victory. His successor, the younger Moltke, dropped any further work on the "Grosse Ostaufmarsch."

Colmar von der Goltz maintained, in 1883, that "a war in the East would certainly not be decided by a single struggle, but would entail a succession of campaigns."[5]

Von Freytag-Loringhoven investigated Napoleon's Russian campaign and published his conclusions in 1911. He said that Napoleon's plan of war and his actions met with the demands of the situation. But he did not succeed in beating the Russian Armies close to the frontier, and found a new adversary in the tremendous space of this barren theater of war.[6]

F. v. Bernhardi wrote in 1912 that owing to the spatial extent of the Russian Empire, a complete subjection, or even conquest, of Russia cannot be thought of at all. His judgment of the Russian space was in line with the traditional German outlook. However, he considered possible a certain reduction of Russian power by pushing Russia off the Baltic Sea.[7]

In 1913 the German Great General Staff promulgated a secret memorandum about Russian tactics. Section IV of this document, entitled "Hints for the conduct of German troops in a Russian theater of war," stressed the special difficulties of that territory: for example, bad road conditions, lack of building materials for modern roads and bridges, great distances between dwelling places, vast swamps, difficult climate conditions, lack of correct maps.[8]

When Falkenhayn was appointed to the post of Chief of the German General Staff, he, too, shrank at the prospect of becoming involved in the vast Russian territory.[9]

General Groener, in his works, stood firmly on Clausewitz' ground regarding the Russian space. He wrote in 1927 that in the gateway of the huge plain between the Vistula and the Ural stands the admonishing figure of Napoleon I. His fate ought to inspire a dismal fear of the mysterious country in any would-be attacker of Russia. He enumerated the changes that had taken place in Russia owing to the technical development there, but concluded that the essential feature of that theater of war has remained unchanged during the hundred years since Napoleon: the depth of the space. However, owing to the danger in the West the German High Command could not allow itself to become engaged in a protracted operation in these depths.[10]

Seeckt's attitude to the same problem has been dealt with in detail elsewhere.[11]

General Erfurth, in his *History of the German General Staff*, mentioned that General Wilhelm Keitel had prepared a memorandum in 1940, warning against a campaign in Russia, mainly for historic reasons.[12] Alfred Jodl, Hitler's principal military advisor, in a lecture delivered to the Gauleiters of the National Socialist Party on 7 November 1943, pointed to the dangers that accompanied the penetration into the huge Russian space.[13]

General Blumentritt summarized Field Marshal Gerd von Rundstedt's attitude as bitterly opposed to the Russian campaign from the beginning. From the First World War he had obtained considerable knowledge of the East. He therefore asked Hitler whether he realized what risks he was taking on himself by attacking Russia. Like Rundstedt, the Commander-in-Chief of the Army, Walther von Brauchitsch, and the Chief of the General Staff, Franz Halder, also had grave doubts. Rundstedt was of the opinion that had the Russians intended to attack Germany, they would have done so at the moment when the entire German Army was engaged in the campaign in the West. He therefore believed that the best security lay in strengthening the frontier defenses and leaving the Russians alone to attack or not as they pleased.[14]

In March 1943 Dr. W. Tomberg, who was responsible for the war diary of the *Wehrwirtschaftsstab* (Staff for Defense Economy), concluded a memorandum, "The most important perceptions of the World War 1914–1918 for the present war."[15] He wrote then about the military situation of the First World War (probably already with an eye on the situation at the time he was writing): "It appears once again, that Russia, owing to the largeness of her space and because of it, the many possibilities for evasion, is invincible."

It has already been mentioned that after the First World War some different ideas about the Russian space had been aired by Generals Hoffmann and Reinhardt.[16] However, it is obvious that these were only sporadic and individual opinions. They did not present a basic change in the traditional attitude of German soldiers from Clausewitz to the Second World War. We do not know whether Hitler had read Hoffmann's and Reinhardt's books or was in any way influenced by their ideas. It is important to try to understand why he deviated from the view handed down to him by generations of German military thinkers and experts.

HITLER'S DECISION TO WAGE WAR AGAINST RUSSIA

As a matter of fact, by invading the Soviet Union on 22 June 1941 Hitler had not only deviated from German military tradition, but he had also violated his own principle of avoiding a war on two fronts at any price. What were the reasons for departing from this position, which had proved its worth from the *Anschluss* with Austria onward? It seems that on account of his continental outlook, he did not fear any more danger in the West after the defeat of France and the eviction of the B.E.F. from the European mainland. From a military point of view he considered England to be defeated. Accustomed to Blitzkrieg campaigns and Blitzkrieg victories, he firmly believed that the same process could be repeated in Russia. A quick defeat of the Soviet Union would free Germany's rear from any menace if Great Britain should renew the war in the West. Moreover, Hitler meditated on the reasons why Great Britain, despite its desperate situation, would not come to terms. He deduced that England was still expecting increasing support from the United States and hoped that Russo-German relations would deteriorate. From his intelligence reports Hitler concluded that British obstinacy was mainly due to England's hope that the Soviet Union would sooner or later take the British side against Germany. He therefore resorted to Schlieffen's old solution: depriving England of its "continental sword." This meant smashing the Soviet Union. That having been achieved, England would beg for peace.[17]

However, an even more weighty reason for the attack on the Soviet Union was that Hitler's basic aims had always been expansion in the East, the famous slogan of "Drang nach Osten," as formulated in *Mein Kampf*. Of late, there is a trend to minimize the importance of that impetus for Hitler's decision. Nevertheless, one should not overlook the evidence at hand from the publication of *Mein Kampf* onward. As early as 4 September 1936 Hermann Göring read to his economic staff a memorandum prepared by Hitler. He commented that the memorandum was based on the assumption that a conflict with the USSR was inevitable.[18]

The Ribbentrop–Molotov Pact was only a temporary act for the isolation of Poland and the overthrow of France. Its purpose was to render possible the conduct of war in one direction at a time. The temporary character of the agreement had already been stressed in Hitler's memorandum of 9 October 1939[19] by a remark that "no treaty and no agreement will safeguard positively the lasting neutrality in Russia. For the time being the odds are against a Russian departure from neutrality. By eight months, a year or after some years, it might be different." A week later Halder wrote in his diary that the Führer considered Poland as a future deployment area for the German Army.[20] At a conference on 23 November 1939 the dictator explained to his generals that treaties are respected only as long as they fulfill a definite purpose. Soviet Russia, too, would keep the Non-Aggression Pact only as long as it regarded it as advantageous to its interests. He, Hitler, had no illusions about Russia's far-reaching power-political aspirations, as clearly indicated by the most recent occurrences in the Baltic and the Balkans.[21]

Hitler's thoughts took concrete shape toward a decision to attack Russia at a time when everybody was expecting him to lead his army against England. Field Marshal von Manstein held that Hitler decided on launching a *preventive war* against Russia, as long as in the West no actual enemy was within sight on the Continent.[22]

It is obvious that Hitler did not think, at this juncture, that he might become involved in a prolonged war in Russia. He was inclined to believe that he could launch a Blitzkrieg against Russia as some kind of *entr'acte* during his contest with the West. He reckoned with a Blitz campaign of three to four months. He, as well as his military advisors, considered the German Armed Forces superior to the Red Army in organization, equipment, and leadership. The Red Army was regarded as possessing a low capability for battle at this time.[23] Once shaken, the Russian Army would collapse so suddenly that it would overshadow the breakdown of the French Army in 1940. The Russian forces should not be pushed back, but broken through and encircled piece by piece. The campaign would probably terminate at the Volga River. Germany could apparently hold the conquered territory with approximately sixty divisions.[24]

The first written official hint of Hitler's intentions regarding Russia was contained in Directive No. 18 of 12 November 1940. This directive dealt with the conquest of Gibraltar and the war in the Mediterranean. However, the penultimate paragraph ran: "Political discussions for the purpose of clarifying Russia's attitude in the immediate future have already begun. Regardless of the outcome of these conversations, all preparations for the East, for which verbal orders have already been given, will be continued. Further directives will follow on this subject, as soon as the basic operational plan of the Army has been submitted to me and approved.''

On 18 December 1940 Hitler signed "Directive No. 21—'Case Barbarossa.' '' The provisional date for the commencement of the offensive, on account of which "Europe will hold its breath,"[25] was fixed for 15 May 1941.

THE STRUGGLE FOR A CAMPAIGN PLAN

Similar to the opening phase of the campaign in France, the Russian campaign had to be begun with a break through a defended hostile front. In the West the German planners could reckon with a specific reaction of the enemy, namely, the advance of the bulk of its mobile forces into Belgium. In the East no particular reaction of the Russian Army could be expected. Moreover, whereas in the West the enemy's space for maneuver was limited by the coast, the Red Army was virtually unlimited in its freedom of maneuver. If the Germans strove for a decisive action as near to the border as possible, the only way to achieve this was by driving through the Russian line two armored wedges, sufficiently distant from each other, and then, by turning inward, closing the encircling ring around the foe in their middle. This was the basic idea for the opening phase of "Operation Barbarossa."[26]

In addition to the destruction of the Russian forces in western Russia, Hitler had defined as the major operational objectives of the campaign:

1. The conquest of Leningrad, Moscow, the Ukraine, and the Caucasian oil fields;

2. the reaching of a line "from which the Russian Air Force can no longer attack German territory," and the erection of a "barrier against Asiatic Russia on the general line Volga-Archangel." From there "the last surviving industrial area of Russia in the Urals can then, if necessary, be eliminated by the Luftwaffe."

Consequently, General Halder ordered a war game to be held by the General Staff of the Army.[27] The assumption was that 130 to 140 German divisions would be available for the campaign.[28]

Based on the conclusions of that war game, Halder reported the proposed operation plan of the army to Hitler. The former pointed to the fact that the Pripet Marshes divided the theater of war into two separated sectors. The center of gravity of the whole operation would be north of the marshes. The strongest concentration of German forces would advance from Warsaw to Moscow by way of Minsk and Smolensk. A northern army group would move toward Leningrad and a southern army group, toward Kiev. Hitler agreed in principle but stressed some points that were to bear grave consequences for the future. The first point was his emphasis on encircling the enemy forces in the Baltic areas. For this purpose the central army group should be strong enough to render considerable assistance to the northern group. Hitler also considered a possibility of encircling strong enemy forces in the Ukraine. Even more portentous was his remark that it could not yet be decided whether, after the annihilation of the enemy in the north and in the south, Moscow should be attacked, or whether the thrust might be aimed east of Moscow.[29] When, on 17 December 1940, General Jodl forwarded a draft of the OKW directive to be published,[30] this document was based mainly on the proposals of OKH, which provided for a strong armored spearhead in the direction of Moscow. Hitler felt that his remarks had remained unobserved. In the meantime he became even more strongly convinced that prior to any advance toward Moscow, the hostile forces in the Baltics must be annihilated and Leningrad and Kronstadt be seized, in order to eliminate the Russian Navy from the Baltic and to reopen there German naval communications with Sweden. Hitler therefore ordered the draft to be changed and made it clear that he would consider the offensive on Moscow only after the Baltic had been cleared up. He maintained that then a concerted attack on Moscow from the north and the west would be even more advantageous.[31]

It is obvious that at this stage, as von Manstein had observed, Hitler's strategic objectives bore a preponderantly political and economic character. Hitler considered Leningrad as an important goal, as a link to the allied Finns, for the mastery over the Baltic Sea, and as the "Cradle of Bolshevism." The occupation of the Ukraine was vital for its raw materials. So was the Donetz basin on account of its industries and ores, and the Caucasus for its oil. By acquiring these areas Hitler hoped to paralyze the war economy of the Soviet Union. On the other hand OKH held the classic strategic opinion that although the conquest and maintenance of these areas were important, the prior annihilation of the Red Army was a necessary supposition. The mass of the Russian forces would be met and encountered on the way to Moscow. Moscow was the hub of Soviet power, and the Russian rulers could not risk its loss. The situation was this time totally different from 1812. Moreover, Moscow was the vital center of war production, which could not be abandoned lightly. It was also the central junction of the Russian railway network. From a strategic point of view, this cleavage of opinion meant that Hitler strove for a military decision on both wings, whereas OKH wanted it in the center of the over-all front.[32] Manstein maintained that the German Army was not strong enough for an operation on both wings on account of the proportion of opposing forces and the vastness of the operation space.[33] B. v. Lossberg, army representative on OKW Operations Staff, drew attention to the fact that the theater of operations, from the Russo-German demarcation line in Poland to the east, widened in a funnel-shaped manner. The problem of creating a clear center of gravity was of utmost importance. Despite attractive goals in the North and especially in the South—the granary of the Ukraine, the industrial wealth of the Donetz basin, and the oil of the Caucasus—

one should, von Lossberg maintained, stick to the thrust toward Moscow as the only direction promising a victorious decision in the war against Russia.[34]

If one reads Directive No. 21 carefully, one gets the impression that this particular document, issued by the High Command of the Armed Forces and signed by the Supreme Commander and Head of State, bears the same weaknesses as the Schlieffen Plan of 1905. Instead of outlining a strategic concept, it deals merely with operational or rather tactical advice. The real strategic issues remain untouched and undiscussed. One will remember that Manstein, when designing his "Sichelschnitt-plan," drew the proper conclusions from the failure of the Schlieffen Plan and prepared a two-stage plan for the defeat of France instead of Schlieffen's single-stroke design. One will also remember that, as early as 1883, Colmar von der Goltz held the opinion that "a war in the East would certainly not be decided by a single struggle, but would entail a succession of campaigns."[35] Despite the vastness of the territory to be seized and the strength of the Red Army, no consideration for a series of campaigns was contained in Directive No. 21. Everything was staked on the Schlieffenian belief in a quick campaign.[36]

From Hitler's explanation of the campaign plan at a conference on 3 February 1941 it is obvious that he had a Schlieffenian super-Cannae in mind. "It is essential," he said, "to annihilate the greatest part of the enemy rather than keep him on the run. This will be achieved if we occupy the flank areas in strength, while holding back in the center, in order to outmanoeuvre the enemy in the middle, from the flanks."[37] At the same occasion Hitler adhered to another Schlieffenian principle: the fear of gaps. He stressed that the encirclement of the Russian Army would meet with success only if the envelopment was carried out without gaps (= lückenlos).[38]

However, the direct result of the discrepancy of opinion between the dictator and his military staff was a continuing tug-of-war affecting the actual conduct of the campaign. As it was, the German center was kept too strong to carry out Hitler's design on the wings, but the latter were kept in such a strength that it prevented the execution of OKH's intention. It was simply a dispersal of effort.

After the striking successes of the central thrust during the first month of the Russian campaign, OKH was shocked by Directive No. 33, by which Hitler ordered the diversion of the mechanized formations from Army Group Center to the north and south. These units should cut off communications between Leningrad and Moscow and support Army Group North in its southern flank in the seizure of Leningrad, as well as render assistance to Army Group South. Hitler had obviously returned to his strategic super-Cannae scheme. In order to leave no doubt about his intention, this feature was strongly emphasized again in the the "Supplement to Directive No. 33" issued on 23 July. Halder, who tried in vain the same day to press on Hitler the need for a clear decision about the final objectives of the campaign, noted in his diary in despair: "von Bock [Army Group Center] is compelled to give up his armored groups and will advance towards Moscow with infantry only. He [Hitler] is not interested at all in Moscow for the moment, but only in Leningrad." Under the topic "Hitler's ideal plan" Halder wrote that "infantry divisions will close the ranks in the center, armored units will diverge."[39] Liddell Hart, as a result of his interrogation of the German generals, put it thus: "He [Hitler] seems to have visualized a Cannae-like operation of super-large dimensions, in which the already created threat to Moscow would draw the Russian reserves to that sector of the front, thus making it easier for the German wings to gain their flank objectives, Leningrad and the Ukraine. And from these flank positions his forces could then converge on Moscow, which might fall like a ripe plum into their Hands."[40]

At the same time Hitler had reached an insight identical with Ludendorff's concept in 1918.[41] He refuted the utility of operative conduct. The Russians could not be beaten by operative success because they simply would not recognize it. Hence they must be broken up piece by piece by tactical encirclements. Halder doubted whether, by adopting the concept of "tactics-before-and-above-operational-conduct," there would really re-emerge an opportunity for operations. He considered this train of thought as the beginning of "silting up"[42] the hitherto roaring operation. The result was that Hitler made the armored forces turn in each time and forge a ring round the enemy forces they had by-passed. Thus superb encirclement victories were achieved, but also a lot of precious time was lost.

The discussions over the selection of a clear center of gravity for the German operations continued from the middle of July right into the second half of August. Finally, Halder prepared a memorandum in order to stress the advantages, and the necessity, of a major thrust in the center. Hitler, raging with anger, prepared his own countermemorandum and subsequently an explicit directive (WFSt. L Nr. 441412/41 of 21/8/1941). The directive opened with the declaration that "the Army's proposal of 18 August for the further conduct of operations in the East is not in accordance with my intentions." Hitler ordered that "the most important aim to be achieved before the onset of winter, is not the capture of Moscow but to seize the Crimea and the industrial and coal region of the Donetz, and to cut off the Russian oil supply from the Caucasus area. In the north, the aim is to cut off Leningrad and to join hands with the Finns."[43]

Heinz Guderian, who was not completely in agreement with OKH because his modern Panzer concept was free from the orthodox encirclement strategy, sided strongly with the plan for reaching Moscow instead of the detour through Kiev. He wanted to drive as fast as possible straight on to Moscow and leave the encircling of enemy forces that might remain in his flanks and rear to the infantry armies. He believed that Russia's resistance would be paralyzed by a decisive blow to its center of power. He considered the diversion of his armor group for the battle of Kiev as a waste of time in face of the approaching Russian winter, which would be preceded by a mud period. However, Hitler had overruled all objections. The battle of Kiev was a smashing German encirclement victory. Yet it was almost the end of September when it was over. What next?

One possible course was to select a favorable defense line for the approaching winter that would save as much manpower as possible, to consolidate the gains, to reorganize the forces, and to prepare a renewed campaign for late spring or early summer of 1942. The main partisan of such a solution was Field Marshal von Rundstedt, C-in-C Army Group South. However, suddenly a new factor crept in: the memory of the Marne battle of 1914 and its disastrous consequences! Nobody would dare to forfeit now a chance for success at the last moment, as occurred then. Therefore, OKH, Army Group Center, Guderian, and Hitler all agreed that an attempt should be made to capture Moscow at that late juncture of the year. The undertaking was launched and failed against the combined opposition of the Red Army and nature.

At the time the German advance came to a standstill, despite the fact that millions of Russian soldiers were prisoners of war. None of the German objectives had been reached—neither Moscow, nor Leningrad, nor the Caucasus.

NEW ENCIRCLEMENT TECHNIQUES

However, the first phase of that belated push toward Moscow was an overwhelming German victory in the battle of encirclement around Vyasma and Bryansk, in which 600,000 Russians were taken prisoner. "It was a modern Cannae," said General Blumentritt to Captain Liddell Hart after the war, "on a greater scale. The Panzer groups played a big part in this victory."[44] This battle was only a further link in a chain of large-scale encirclement operations, rendered possible by the utilization of mobile forces.

What really characterized these battles—the most important being the "cauldrons" of Bialystok–Minsk, Kiev, Vyasma–Bryansk—was their being true, i.e., two-sided, Cannae-type operations. Moreover, the exploitation of the highly mobile Panzer groups enabled their utilization on the classic role of Hasdrubal, viz., closing the encircling ring in the enemy's rear and forcing the latter into a battle with reversed front.

A completely novel feature in the encirclement technique was that the envelopment was composed of two rings, the inner being formed by infantry divisions and the outer by armored forces.[45] Furthermore, mobility enabled the encirclement of "cauldrons" of, up to that time, unheard-of dimensions. The sides of the enveloping triangle created by Army Group Center and South at Kiev were 500 kilometers long. It was a theater of war rather than a battlefield. No wonder the liquidation of such "cauldrons" required a long time.

Despite this increase in the size of encirclement operations, it still remained doubtful, as in Schlieffen's time, whether the Cannae concept was applicable to strategy. After all, the pretentious design of Hitler, the super-Cannae carried out in one stroke by all three army groups from the shores of the Baltic to the Ukraine had misfired.

THE MYSTERY OF THE SIEGE OF LENINGRAD

In Directive No. 21 Hitler had ordered the capture of Leningrad by Army Group North. This was a deviation from German practice.

Clausewitz had taught that "while a decision is still in the balance a siege will be undertaken only where it cannot be avoided. Once the decision has been made, the crisis is past . . . then the occupation of fortresses will serve as a consolidation of the conquest. . . . During the crisis itself, besieging a fortress increases the problems of the attacker."[46]

The elder Moltke, a student of Clausewitz, was averse to siege warfare. As early as 1844, in his history of the Russo-Turkish campaign, he wrote that "cities of a half million population will certainly not be taken by force of arms, but must fall by themselves."[47] His aversion probably grew after his own unhappy experience with the siege and capture of Paris.

However, early on, something of the conception that a big city "must fall by itself" crept into German considerations. On 31 August 1941 Halder reported in his diary a conference concerned with Leningrad. "The question is still open," he wrote. "The basic assumption in Keitel's letter to C-in-C Army, that the population of this city cannot be fed and must therefore be driven away, is practically unfeasible and therefore worthless."[48]

However, why had Hitler, after ordering the conquest of Leningrad, apparently changed his mind and prevented von Leeb from doing so by withdrawing the armored units from Army Group North? Bernhard von Lossberg revealed the frightful truth behind these events. Hitler was no longer interested in taking the city by force of arms. He wanted the city to be enveloped and starved to death. Hitler liked to browse through documents of the First World War; he had come across a memorandum of Ludendorff dealing with the occupation of St. Petersburg. Ludendorff had stressed the difficulty of feeding the huge population of the city after its conquest. He then contemplated a solution of the problem. Hitler, by following up that train of thought, reached his own dreadful conclusion. The 2 million people living in Leningrad, instead of having to be fed, would disappear. Since in any case he intended to give the area of Leningrad to Finland, no German soldier would enter the city. It would instead become hermetically sealed off. Nobody would enter or leave the city during the winter. Starvation and Göring's Luftwaffe would do the job, and German pioneers would afterward destroy the town.[49] That this really was Hitler's train of thought was confirmed by himself in his speech at the annual gathering of the "Old Guard" in Munich on 8 November 1941. Elaborating the course of the Russian campaign he explained the situation at Leningrad:

It has recently been said that we are on the defensive at Leningrad. We were on the offensive at Leningrad only as long as it was necessary for the envelopment of Leningrad. Now we behave defensively. The other side is now compelled to break out. They will starve to death in Leningrad or they will capitulate! I shall certainly not sacrifice one single man more than will be absolutely necessary. If today somebody could relieve Leningrad, I would issue the order to storm it and we would have it broken to pieces. For he, who has marched from the frontier of East Prussia to within 10 km. of Leningrad, is also able to march these 10 km. from outside Leningrad into the city. One may believe that. But it is unnecessary. The town is surrounded. Nobody will relieve it and it will fall into our hands. If one says: "Only as a heap of rubble," I shall answer, that I have no interest in some city of Leningrad, but only in the destruction of the industrial center of Leningrad.[50]

However, the Clausewitzian principle of the culminating point of attack proved more decisive than Hitler's boasting. "From the moment when the siege of fortresses compels us to suspend the advance," wrote Clausewitz, "the offensive has as a rule reached its culminating point."[51] The 10 kilometers' distance into the city was never recovered by German troops.

THE REASONS FOR THE FAILURE OF "BARBAROSSA"

Taking into account the vastness of space and the size of the Russian forces to be annihilated, the termination of the war in one lightning campaign was doubtful. Clausewitz held that "the earlier [the] victory can be sought—that is the nearer to our frontiers—the easier it will be."[52] This Hitler tried to achieve. However, once it became obvious that the Red Army had not been destroyed in the first encounters, he should have changed his strategy and thought of a prolonged war of two or more summer campaigns. Colmar von der Goltz had taught that it might often be better to divide the operations into several successive phases. The extent of each phase must be carefully calculated, according to the means at disposal. He criticized Napoleon for the continuation of the offensive movement from Smolensk to Moscow in the second half of August 1812. This last decisive phase of his operation ought to have been another special campaign in the spring of 1813. The winter should have been used for preparations. He argued that Napoleon had failed to realize the constitution of his forces when he endeavored to finish the whole business in one single campaign.[53]

One may simply substitute 1941 for 1812 and Hitler for Napoleon, and no further comment seems to be necesary. However, one is struck by the fact that Hitler had succeeded in infecting his military experts, who should have had better knowledge, with his belief in the possibility of a short campaign. On the twelfth day of the Russian campaign Halder wrote in his diary that "it is no exaggeration to say *that the campaign against Russia was won in a fortnight.*"[54]

This illusion bore two fateful consequences. First of all, no provision for adequate reserves and sufficient replacement of manpower and war material was considered in advance. The result was the complete exhaustion of combat troops and the wearing down of the formations. The second consequence was even more dreadful. Because everything was based on the idea of a decisive victory before autumn, no precautions for providing winter equipment were undertaken. The German soldiers paid a terrific price for that when winter came.

The problem of selecting a clear center of gravity for the operation has already been mentioned. This issue can be summarized with Alan Bullock's words, that

with forces which were numerically inferior to the Russians, throughout the campaign of 1941 Hitler swung between a number of objectives, losing time in switching from one to another, stretching his resources to the limit and fanning out his armies across a thousand-mile front, while always falling short of the decisive blow which would knock Russia out of the war. He had fallen into the trap against which he had warned his generals before the invasion began, that of allowing the Russians to retreat and draw the Germans farther and farther into the illimitable depths of their hinterland.[55]

Hitler's irresolution over which course to pursue led to his frequent meddling in matters of command. His obsession with encirclement, Schlieffen's legacy to German conduct of war, led to the use of considerable forces for wiping out local points of resistance that were doomed anyway, instead of for pushing forward. Combined with this state of affairs was another vice, inherited from Schlieffen: the fear of gaps. The Supreme Commander and the Supreme Command were, as a consequence, engaged in tactics instead of conducting strategy. A striking example of this was Directive No. 41 of 5 April 1942, which dealt mainly with tactical advice: "It is therefore of decisive importance that, as in the double battle of Vyasma–Bryansk, individual breaches of the front should take the form of close pincer movements." or, "We must avoid closing the pincers too late, thus giving the enemy the possibility of avoiding destruction," or, "it must not happen that, by advancing too quickly and too far, armored and motorized formations lose connection with the infantry following them." It may be that in such a way Hitler eliminated tactical risks and managed to close gaps between his armies, but it resulted in increasing forces in the front that grew wider at the expense of its depth. That was a conclusion reached by von Brauchitsch and Halder as early as 25 July 1941, at a conference of Chiefs of Staff of the Army Groups.[56]

The climax of Hitler's peculiar and continual change of objective was reached with the Führer's decision to embark on the battle of Kiev. It resulted in postponing the attack on Moscow until 2 October 1941. Rudolf Hofmann maintained that the opening phase of the final battle of Moscow, the double battle of Vyasma–Bryansk, could have been launched five weeks earlier and the pursuit in the direction of Moscow would then have been undertaken under favorable weather conditions. Moreover, the Russian reserves would not have arrived near Moscow at that time.[57]

Despite the Blitzkrieg psychosis, which had at that time spread not only in Germany, but over the whole world, it is now clear that Germany's mobile forces were not adequate to master the Russian space. Or, as General Blumentritt put it, "1812 and 1941 proved that, with old-fashioned means of transportation, that is to say with horses and marching men, it is not possible to conquer areas of the dimensions that exist in Russia within a limited time. Neither Napoleon's strong forces of cavalry, nor Hitler's motorized formations were numerically sufficient to seize and maintain control of the countryside."[58] F. Steiner, one of Hitler's Waffen-SS generals, held the opinion that by exploiting the European industry under Germany's rule after the French campaign, the number of mobile divisions (although not all being armored divisions) could have been increased to sixty before the launching of "Barbarossa." He maintained that the lack of such a number of mobile divisions slowed down the momentum of the Russian campaign. The pace of operations was still decided by foot-marching infantry.[59] Since the final closure of the various cauldrons had to be done by infantry divisions, the advance of which was not faster than the retreat of the Russian troop, German armor formations had to stop frequently at Hitler's order and rush to the assistance of the infantry. This was the reason for the novel phenomenon of "wandering cauldrons."[60] Gradually the armored units, composing only a small part of each army group, became more and more geared to the infantry armies and were again handled as a supporting arm, rather than as a decisive weapon of warfare.

Even more surprising is the fact that the German Army was not only short of mobile forces, but also suffered from the beginning from fuel difficulties. The Chief of OKW, Field Marshal Keitel, had to impose the strictest control over fuel consumption from the autumn of 1940 in order to accumulate the necessary quantities of fuel for the planned short campaign against Russia.[61] No wonder that the prolongation of the campaign threw the whole logistic planning out of gear.

Another result of the belief in a quick termination of the war in Russia was Hitler's illusion that the enemy was beaten. The day after the start of the final push toward Moscow, in the Winterhilfe speech of 3 October 1941, Hitler announced dramatically that "the enemy is already destroyed and will never recover."[62] This prognosis was shattered by the Russian counteroffensive, as was the case with Falkenhayn's similar prognosis in his Christmas Memorandum of 1915,[63] which was shattered by Brussilov's counteroffensive. Hitler was so convinced by his belief that he ordered the stopping of ammunition production "because I know, that there is no more enemy in existence, which could not be overthrown by the quantity of ammunition at hand." On 1 December 1941 Field Marshal Fedor von Bock, C-in-C Army Group Center, cabled to OKH: "The idea, that the enemy in front of the Army Group will break down, was a hallucination, as shown by the battle of the last fortnight."[64] Despite this experience of the commanders on the spot, Hitler argued that the Russians were "dead" and that their winter counteroffensive had finally consumed all their strength. He simply closed his eyes to any facts opposed to his wishful thinking.

Having managed to weather the Russian onslaught during the winter of 1941–1942, Hitler completely departed from the plan on which the whole campaign had been hitherto based in 1942, and pursued mainly economic goals in southern Russia, while still trying at the same time to join hands with the Finns by means of seizing Leningrad. The conquest of Moscow was no longer attempted or even considered. Strategically, the German efforts split asunder in two opposed directions. The "greatest strategist of all times" did not heed the simple fact that his means were hopelessly inadequate for the simultaneous execution of such ambitious plans.

Before concluding this chapter it seems to be of interest that, as late as 1953, a certain German Captain (ret.) Ulrich Lade prepared a study entitled "The Operation Plan Against the Soviet Union (1940/41), judged by the Schlieffen Strategy."[65] While criticizing the plan of 1941 as deviating from Schlieffen's principles, Herr Lade suggested a plan that might have led to a German victory. This plan is not only in accordance with Schlieffen's teaching, as Lade maintained, but it is rather a replica of the Schlieffen Plan of 1905, transplanted to the East. As the German front was directed in this case to the east, the strong wing, Schlieffen's *bataillon carré*, was now the left one. Whereas on all other parts of the Russian front the German forces would merely remain on the defensive or pretend offensive actions, a superstrong left wing would advance into the Baltic area and seize the ports of Libau, Reval, Narva, and Leningrad. Then, following the Schlieffen drill, the left wing would wheel to the right and, by advancing from the north southward, destroy the Russian Army in a tremendous strategic Cannae.[66]

It is amazing how Schlieffen, after two lost world wars, still haunts German minds!

If, since 1812, the admonishing figure of Napoleon I has stood in the gateway to the Russian plain, then in 1941 he found in Hitler a partner for his vigil. Hitler had reached this position mainly by not heeding Clausewitz' warning and by adhering strategically to Schlieffen's legacy and the latter's Cannae obsession.

NOTES

1. *Vide*, especially Book One, chapter 1, under "On War in Russia," and Book Two, chapter 13, under "On Russia."

2. Cf. *Hinterlassene Werke des Generals Carl von Clausewitz über Krieg und Kriegführung*, Berlin, 1858, vol. 7.

3. *On War*, III, 17, p. 220.

4. Cf. H.K.B. v. Moltke (ed. F. v. Schmerfeld), *Die Deutschen Aufmarschpläne 1871–1890*, Berlin, 1929.

5. Colmar Freiherr von der Goltz, *The Nation in Arms*, London, 1906, p. 155.

6. Freiherr von Freytag-Loringhoven, *Krieg und Politik in der Neuzeit*, Berlin, 1911, p. 162.

7. F. v. Bernhardi, *On War of To-Day*, London, 1912, vol. 2, p. 261.

8. "Geheime Denkschrift des Grossen Generalstabes aus dem Jahre 1913: Mitteilung über russische Taktik." Printed in W. Elze, *Tannenberg*, Breslau, 1927, pp. 181–182.

9. E. v. Falkenhayn, *Die Oberste Heeresleitung 1914–1916 in ihren wichtigsten Entschliessungen*, Berlin, 1920, pp. 47–48.

10. Wilhelm Groener, *Das Testament des Grafen Schlieffen*, Berlin, 1927, pp. 103–104.

11. *Vide* Book Two, chapter 13.

12. W. Erfurth, *Die Geschichte des deutschen Generalstabes von 1918 bis 1945*, Göttingen, 1957, p. 265.

13. "Unterlagen für einen Vortrag des Gen.-Obersten Jodl, des Chefs WFStab, vor den Reichs- und Gauleitern über die militärische Lage (München, 7 November 1943)," printed in *Kriegstagebuch des Oberkommandos der Wehrmacht*, vol. 4, 1961, p. 1540.

14. Günther Blumentritt, *Von Rundstedt. The Soldier and the Man*, London, 1952, pp. 98–99.

15. BA/MA—WO1–8/5. Dr. W. Tomberg, "Die wichtigsten Erkenntnisse des Weltkrieges 1914/18 für den gegenwärtigen Krieg."

16. *Vide* chapter 13, under "On Russia."

17. Klee's argument (cf. K. Klee, *Das Unternehmen "Seelöwe,"* Göttingen, 1959, p. 194) that England's obstinacy should be blamed for Hitler's decision to attack Russia is sheer nonsense. Had England come to terms with Germany, Russia would have been attacked immediately. The offensive against Russia had been postponed only so far because Hitler had not yet consented to the idea of waging war in the East with an undefeated England at his back.

18. Cf. E. M. Robertson, *Hitler's Pre-War Policy and Military Plans 1933–1939*, London, 1963, pp. 87–88.

19. *Vide* chapter 15.

20. Franz Halder, *Kriegstagebuch*, Stuttgart, 1962, vol. 1, p. 107.

21. From a moral point of view, Hitler had never any scruples to breach agreements.

22. Erich von Manstein, *Verlorene Siege*, Bonn, 1955, p. 171.

23. Cf. H. Greiner, *Die Oberste Wehrmachtführung 1939–1943*, Wiesbaden, 1951, p. 290.

24. *Ibid.*, p. 326. At the conference on 9 Jan. 1941 Hitler even considered forty to fifty divisions as sufficient for the task. *Ibid.*, p. 344.

25. The final phrase of Hitler's exposition at the commanders' conference of 9 Jan. 1941 was: "Wenn der Ostfeldzug durchgeführt werde, dann werde Europa den Atem anhalten." This is quoted by H. Greiner (p. 345) from the war diary of Abt.L. (Defense Dep.).

26. The opening phrases of the "General Intention" in Directive No. 21 read: "The bulk of the Russian Army stationed in Western Russia will be destroyed by daring operations, led by deeply penetrating armored spearheads. Russian forces still capable of giving battle will be prevented from withdrawing into the depths of Russia."

27. The war game was conducted by Lieutenant General Paulus, who was, at that time, Oberquartiermeister I at OKH, a post in fact amounting to Deputy Chief of General Staff. He was later to reach tragic fame at Stalingrad.

28. Cf. H. Greiner, *op. cit.*, p. 295.

29. *Ibid.*, pp. 327–328.

30. Up to that date the operation was code named "Fritz," but the code name was changed to "Barbarossa" by Hitler's order.

31. H. Greiner, *op. cit.*, pp. 330–331.

32. Theoretically it boiled down to a clash between Schlieffenian encirclement and Clausewitzian selection of a center of gravity aimed at the enemy's main forces or a vital point, as, for instance, the capital.

33. Cf. E. v. Manstein, *op. cit.*, pp. 173–174.

34. B. v. Lossberg, *Im Wehrmachtsführungsstab*, Hamburg, 1949, pp. 114–115.

35. *Vide* beginning of chapter.
36. At a conference between the C-in-C of the Army and the Chief of Defense Dep., the former estimated that in four weeks' time the frontier battles (Grenzschlachten) would be over, and that no further serious resistance of the enemy was to be expected afterward. MGFA—III W 59/1—OKW/WFSt/L IV: Chefsachen "Barbarossa," p. 105: "Besprechung bei Chef L—30.4.1941."
37. MGFA—III W 59/1—OKW/WFSt/L IV: Chefsachen "Barbarossa," p. 4: "Besprechung über "Fall Barbarossa" und "Sonnenblume"—3/2/41. Also quoted in H. Greiner, *op. cit.*, pp. 356–357.
38. In fact, on the third day of the campaign (24 June 1941) the war diary of OKH revealed that Hitler wanted to stop the armor groups in order to plug gaps. MGFA—III-H402—Gen.St.d.H/Op.Abt.Ia: KTB-Beiträge, p. 17. On 3 July Halder mentioned that the Führer was worried about the flanks of the advancing wedge of the armored group of Army Group South. Halder, *op. cit.*, vol. 3, p. 39.
39. Halder, *op. cit.*, vol. 3, pp. 107–108.
40. Liddell Hart, *The Other Side of the Hill*, London, 1956, p. 198.
41. *Vide* chapter 10.
42. "Versanden."
43. Cf. Halder, *op. cit.*, vol. 3, pp. 192–193.
44. B. H. Liddell Hart, *op. cit.*, p. 206.
45. Cf. Halder, *op. cit.*, vol. 3, p. 13, entry of 25 June 1941.
46. *On War*, VII, 17, p. 551.
47. Quoted in Gordon A. Craig, *The Politics of the Prussian Army, 1640–1945*, Oxford, 1955, p. 209.
48. Halder, *op. cit.*, vol. 3, p. 209.
49. Cf. B. v. Lossberg, *op. cit.*, pp. 132–133.
50. Adolf Hitler, *Der grossdeutsche Freibeitsk-kampf. Reden Adolf Hitlers*, München, 1943, vol. 3, p. 97.
51. *On War*, VIII, 9, p. 625.
52. *Ibid.*, p. 624.
53. C. v. d. Goltz, *op. cit.*, pp. 265–266.
54. Halder, *op. cit.*, vol. 3, p. 38, emphasis added.
55. Alan Bullock, *Hitler. A Study in Tyranny*, Harmondsworth, Middlesex, 1962, p. 655.
56. Cf. Halder, *op. cit.*, vol. 3, pp. 118, 121.
57. Cf. H. A. Jacobsen and J. Rohwer, *Entscheidungsschlachten des zweiten Weltkrieges*, Frankfurt/Main, 1960, p. 180.
58. G. Blumentritt, "Moscow," in S. Westphal, ed., *The Fatal Decisions*, London, 1956, p. 72.
59. Cf. Felix Steiner, *Die Armee der Geächteten*, Göttingen, 1963, pp. 143–145 passim, 147.
60. Cf. Edgar Röhricht, *Probleme der Kesselschlacht*, Karlsruhe, 1958, p. 34.
61. Cf. H. Greiner, *op. cit.*, pp. 337–338.
62. A. Hitler, *op. cit.*, vol. 3, p. 79.
63. *Vide* chapter 9.
64. H. A. Jacobsen and J. Rohwer, *op. cit.*, p. 163.
65. BA/MA—H91–3/5. Ulrich Lade, Studienrat i.R., Hptm.d.R.a.D. "Der Operationsplan gegen die Sowjetunion (1940/41) im Lichte der Schlieffen-Strategie."

66. Herr Lade probably did not know that F. v. Bernhardi had already suggested a German move into the Baltics, but with less ambitious aims. Bernhardi had in mind only the cutting off of the Russians from the communications provided by the Baltic Sea. *Vide* beginning of chapter.

Case 8: Rommel in North Africa: A Modern Hannibal

THE MEDITERRANEAN THEATER OF WAR

"To Hitler, until he was about to lose it for good, North Africa remained a sideshow by comparison with the real war in the east," wrote Alan Bullock. "He never grasped its importance in the total picture of war, as Churchill had done even when Britain's power was reduced to its lowest ebb."[1] Despite the tremendous efforts of Germany's sailors to stress the importance of hitting at England in the Mediterranean, Hitler had laid down the principle that "the Alps divide the theaters of war" and had therefore left this area to Mussolini's conduct of the war.[2] Italy's inadequately equipped and trained army could not compete with the British Navy, Army, and Air Force in the region. Although reluctantly, Hitler was soon compelled to give support to his stumbling ally. However, being too much occupied with the war on the European continent, the forces despatched to Mussolini's aid were confined to a minimum.[3]

However, for the development of the art of war, this particular theater of war was important. Rommel wrote in his memoirs that

of all theaters of operations, it was probably in North Africa that the war took on its most advanced form. The protagonists on both sides were fully motorized formations, for whose employment the flat and obstruction-free desert offered hitherto undreamed-of possibilities. It was the only theater where the principles of motorized and tank warfare, as they had been taught theoretically before the war, could be applied to the full—and further developed. Even though the struggle may have occasionally hardened into static warfare, it remained—at any rate, in its most important stages (i.e. in 1941–42 during the Cunningham-Ritchie offensive, and in the summer of 1942—Marmarica battles, capture of Tobruk)—based on the principle of complete mobility.

Comparing the conduct of war in the campaigns waged by Germany during the Second World War up to that time, Rommel maintained that "in military practice, this was entirely new, for our offensives in Poland and the West had been against opponents who, in all their operations, had still had to take account of their non-motorized infantry divisions and had thus had to suffer the disastrous limitations in their freedom of tactical decision which this imposes, especially in retreat.''[4] Indeed, Rommel had had a unique opportunity of executing the novel conception of armored warfare in an almost independent theater of operations, at least in the sphere of operational conduct. The creator of the German Panzer doctrine, General Guderian, had never been given such a chance.

ROMMEL'S CONDUCT OF OPERATIONS

One does not exactly know whether Rommel was much concerned with Schlieffen's teaching. In his writings no direct reference to Schlieffen's theory can be found. However, it should be clear that he was far from being merely a practitioner and daredevil, as some people tend to believe. He combined daring leadership on the battlefield with the penetrating mind of a military thinker and writer. In his works[5] he had not confined himself to a mere description of events, but had always drawn conclusions and even formulated them as theoretical rules.

However, in practice most of his offensive moves bore obvious features of the famous Cannae maneuver. There is no doubt that he was quite aware of that fact. In a letter to his wife dated 8 April 1941, on the eve of the battle at Mechili, he wrote: ''It's going to be a 'Cannae,' modern style.''[6] He had given a lot of consideration to the problem of encirclement, as far as mobile forces were concerned. He concluded that

the envelopment of a fully-motorized enemy in the flat and good-driving terrain of the desert has the following results:

a) For a fully-motorized formation, encirclement is the worst tactical situation imaginable, since the hostile fire can be brought to bear on it from all sides; even envelopment on only three sides is a tactically untenable situation.

b) The enemy becomes forced, because of the bad tactical situation in which the encirclement has placed him, to evacuate the area he is holding.[7]

He deviated somewhat from Schlieffen's classic postulate, by concluding that

the encirclement of the enemy and his subsequent destruction in the pocket can seldom be the direct aim of an operation; more often it is only indirect, for any fully-motorized force, whose organizational structure remains intact will normally, and in suitable country, be able to break out at will through an improvised defensive ring. Thanks to his motorization, the commander of the encircled force is in a position to concentrate his weight unexpectedly against any likely point in the ring and burst through it. This fact was repeatedly demonstrated in the desert.[8]

It seems that this statement—which was rejected by Liddell Hart, who maintained that ''a break-out can be made very difficult, if the commanders in the encircling force really understand the defensive side of modern mobile warfare''—was influenced by Rommel's own experience of the break-out of General Koenig's Free French troops from Bir-Hakim and the break-out of the New Zealanders from Mersa Matruh. Rommel concluded

that an encircled enemy force can only be destroyed

   a) when it is non-motorized or has been rendered immobile by lack of petrol, or when it includes non-mobile elements which have to be considered;

   b) when it is badly led or its command has decided to sacrifice one formation in order to save another;[9]

   c) when its fighting strength has already been broken, and disintegration and disorganization have set in.

Except for cases a) and b), which occurred very frequently in other theaters of war, encirclement of the enemy and his subsequent destruction in the pocket can only be attempted, if he has first been so heavily battered in open battle that the organic cohesion of his forces has been destroyed.[10]

It is significant that Rommel has given a new meaning to the term "battle of attrition" by stating: "I shall term all actions which have as their aim the wearing down of the enemy's power of resistance 'battles of attrition.' "[11] His reason was that "in motorized warfare, material attrition and the destruction of the organic cohesion of the opposing army must be the immediate aim of all planning." However, while probably remembering the perception of attrition in the First World War and the "strategy controversy" over that concept,[12] he added explicitly that "tactically, the battle of attrition is fought with the highest possible degree of mobility."

Also deviating from Schlieffen and, on the other hand, drawing from Clausewitz' teaching was Rommel's approach to the defensive. "Like most dynamic soldiers, he was inclined to despise defense," wrote Liddell Hart, "but when circumstances compelled him to adopt it he showed an instinctive grasp of its subtle technique, and in that lay the foundations of his victories."[13] From his own mastery of mobile warfare Rommel had simply drawn the proper conclusions for the defensive counter to it. In such a way he had many times blunted the enemy assaults prior to turning himself to the offensive again. By his utilization of the defense in mobile operations, as, for example, in the battle of Sollum in 1941 and the battle of the "Cauldron" in 1942, he probably reached the highest degree of Clausewitzian flexible defense, as taught by von Seeckt's Reichswehr[14] and as ignored and opposed by Hitler.[15]

Rommel also reverted to Moltke's command technique. He regarded the detailed and pre-planned orders of the Schlieffen era as useless in the quick-changing situation of mobile warfare. He resorted instead to assigning missions in general directives and left it to his subordinate commanders to accomplish them in accordance with the circumstances. However, he exercised a firm grip on the situation by utilizing modern signal techniques to the fullest extent and, above all, by carrying to the utmost the maxim of von Seeckt and Guderian of "commanders in the front."

NOTES

1. Alan Bullock, *Hitler. A Study in Tyranny*, Harmondsworth, Middlesex, 1962, p. 680.

2. Cf. B. v. Lossberg, *Im Wehrmachtführungsstab*, Hamburg, 1949, p. 95.

3. Cf. Halder's diary entry of 3 July 1941 about future plans: "Preparation for an offensive against the isthmus between Nile and Euphrates, from the Cyrenaica as well as from Anatolia and perhaps also from the Caucasus against Iran. The former, which will always depend on supplies over sea, and therefore suffer from ups and downs, will be a secondary theater of war and will mainly be left to the Italian forces. We shall have to give up only two German panzer divisions (5th 'Light' and 15th), brought up to full strength, and various attachments." Franz Halder, *Kriegstagebuch*, Stuttgart, 1962, vol. 3, pp. 38–39.

4. *The Rommel Papers* (ed. Liddell Hart), New York, 1953, pp. 197–198.

5. His book *Infantrie greift an* summed up his experience during the First World War and his memoirs *Krieg ohne Hass* summarized the campaign in North Africa.

6. *The Rommel Papers, op. cit.*, p. 116.

7. *Ibid.*, pp. 198–199.

8. *Ibid.*

9. The latter had actually been done by Rommel with regard to the Sollum garrison during the winter of 1941–1942.

10. *The Rommel Papers, op. cit.*, p. 199.

11. *Ibid.*

12. *Vide* chapter 9.

13. *The Rommel Papers, op. cit.*, p. 208, footnote.

14. *Vide* chapter 13.

15. *Vide* chapter 18.

18

Hitler's "Hold On" Orders: Decline of the Art of War for a Second Time

Where the German soldier sets foot, there he remains.

Hitler in October, 1942

At the moment the German advance in Russia ground to a halt and the army had to resort to the defensive, the problem arose whether to conduct a flexible or a rigid defensive. The issue of flexible defense has already been investigated in chapters 8 and 13. It therefore remains only to look at the problem as handled by Hitler and his Supreme Command.

RIGID OR FLEXIBLE DEFENSE?

After the breakdown of his belated attack on Moscow in 1941, Hitler had to decide where and how to conduct the defensive. Whereas the majority of the German generals suggested the selection of a suitable "Winter-line" and a flexible conduct of the defensive, Hitler prohibited even the slightest retreat and ordered the holding of ground wherever it was. On 20 December he briefed the Chief of General Staff of the Army and the next day issued the same explanations as an explicit order. It read: "Holding on and fighting to the utmost limit. Not yielding a single step voluntarily. Mobile parts of the enemy which have broken in must be annihilated in the rear."[1] A week later the Führer again ordered that

in the defensive one must fight to the last for every inch of ground. This is the only way of inflicting bloody losses upon the enemy, weakening his morale and demonstrating the superiority of the German soldier. The yielding of even improvised positions to the enemy without fighting, results, under the present weather conditions, in irrecoverable losses of material and ammunition, and thereby reduces one's own fighting power and allows the enemy to avail himself of increased freedom of action.[2]

The same attitude of stubborn resistance and clinging to the ground was stressed by Hitler in a conference with Field Marshal von Kluge on 11 January 1942.

Hitler believed that by fighting for every inch of ground the enemy would bleed to death. One will remember that twenty-five years earlier von Falkenhayn had fostered the same belief at Verdun.

The consequences of such a conduct of war for the fighting troops in the front line were disastrous. However, many German generals who were opposed to Hitler's handling of the defense at that time thought in retrospect that Hitler's decision was right in the circumstances. General Kurt von Tippelskirch told Captain Liddell Hart after the war that "it was his [Hitler's] one great achievement. At that critical moment, the troops were remembering what they had heard about Napoleon's retreat from Moscow, and living under the shadow of it. If they had once begun a retreat, it might have turned into a panic flight." However, Liddell Hart also quoted Field Marshal von Rundstedt's caustic remark that "it was Hitler's decision for rigid resistance that caused the danger in the first place. It would not have arisen if he had permitted a timely withdrawal."[3] That Rundstedt was right in his opinion, and the other generals had exaggerated the danger of a retreat, which would have led to panic and disintegration, was confirmed by the German retrograde movements in the East, the South, and the West during 1943 and 1944. After all, the generals should have known from Clausewitz' teaching that the flexible defense, executed by morally intact troops, has all the advantages on its side. By approving Hitler's stubborn decision in retrospect, they in fact expressed doubts about the moral integrity of the German Army at that time, which appear to be unjustified.

There is no doubt that it was not theoretical considerations, or any considerations connected with the art of war, that guided Hitler. It was, rather, prestige that influenced the issues. The "greatest strategist of all times" could not yield captured ground to the enemy. That was not a unique feature of Hitler's conduct of war. It happened the same way with Ludendorff in 1918, when he could not decide to renounce ground previously seized. The explanations of Hitler and Ludendorff were identical, that a retreat would sacrifice valuable material behind the initial front line, which could not be removed in good time before the withdrawal.

It was portentous for the future German conduct of war that Hitler had worked up the belief that his "hold on" orders had stemmed the tide. What might have been regarded as a temporary expedient was now considered as a panacea in any circumstances. From now onward the flexible operational conduct of war was replaced by fanatical orders to the army "to fight to the last man" where it stood, even in positions that were tactically impossible to hold. These orders, issued by Hitler from his headquarters, sometimes thousands of miles away from the battlefield and without any real knowledge of the actual conditions, became the rule from the winter of 1941 onward. It resulted, naturally, in an eventual German retreat, pressed on Hitler by the overwhelming power of the adversary. While undertaken under hostile pressure instead of being planned beforehand, the German losses in material and manpower were generally heavier in such circumstances than those to be expected in a deliberate operational withdrawal.

The ample space of the eastern theater of war would have allowed a flexible conduct of affairs.

However, Hitler was completely under the spell of his own war experience during the First World War. He indulged in the concept of coherent and connected front lines. He never understood the necessity for concentrating troops that were insufficient for covering the vast spaces into strong points, and the art of overcoming gaps by means of flexible maneuvers. How strong, in fact, Hitler's reminiscences of the Great War were was not only displayed by his many references to them during his daily conferences (Lagebesprechungen), but they even crept into his written orders and directives. On 8 September 1942, in his capacity as C-in-C of the Army, he issued a ''Führer Order About the Principal Task of Defense.''[4] In this strange document, which was a mixture of an instruction leaflet and personal reminiscences rather than an order, Hitler stressed that ''the meaning of defending a position is not in bringing the enemy's assault to a halt, in a more or less deep inlet, but in breaking his attacking force to pieces by concentrating all suitable weapons upon it, if possible before its departure, but in any case during the course of the defensive battle. At the end of that battle, the original Main Line of Resistance (HKL = Hauptkampflinie) must remain in our possession.'' Hitler regarded a flexible conduct of defense as ''almost always basically wrong.'' He again repeated his definition that ''*the Main Line of Resistance is that line which must be held in all circumstances. It must therefore remain in our hands after the termination of the battle. Troops which are not fulfilling that demand, must consider themselves disgraced.*'' Stressing his old-fashioned outlook, as opposed to a more progressive conception, Hitler wrote:

In many cases it was hardly possible to create a HKL . . . it was necessary to hold certain sectors by means of a system of points of support (Stützpunktsystem). That was, however, a stopgap, which, by the way, bore often enough grave consequences. However, in the present situation I must demand the creation of a HKL that is connected throughout, even if it should be only thinly manned. . . . In this opinion I am reverting consciously to that kind of defense which was applied with success during the serious defense battles of the World War, in particular up to the end of 1916.

At the end of the lengthy document Hitler refuted the flexible conduct of defense. In an obvious tone of contempt he wrote:

The so-called *operational evasive movements* (operative Ausweichbewegungen), if not leading into better rearward positions, prepared long beforehand, will not change the general situation, but rather worsen it, because the opponent's force will not be reduced by it, nor will our own increase. . . . But should the rearward position be even shorter, it will benefit the enemy to the same extent as our own troops; the ratio of forces will always remain the same, but the offensive momentum of the enemy will increase. . . . There . . . is, therefore, . . . only one remedy for the defender, inferior in numbers, for the improvement of his situation; he must, by holding a well-constructed position, inflict losses upon the assailant, to such a degree, that the latter will gradually bleed to death.

About that kind of waging war the SS General Steiner remarked that "one could not design military operations in the era of general motorization by methods which were in fact already obsolete in 1917."[5] It is obvious that Hitler had reinstituted a conception of linear defense. The successful defender of Cassino, General von Senger und Etterlin maintained from his own experience that the demand of always restoring the forward edge of a defended locality, after termination of battle, could not be achieved by that party which was pushed into the defensive on account of its personnel and material inferiority. "In these battles, after serious break-ins, the forward line will never be regained," von Senger und Etterlin held. "In comparison with it, in the depth of the zone resistance is very often offered in lines where nobody would have expected it."[6]

However, Hitler imposed his will of rigid defense and resistance in the East, in North Africa, in Italy, and, consequently, at the French coast and so on until the final collapse of the German Army. Giving the German side of the Allied invasion in Normandy, General Blumentritt told Liddell Hart that he and Field Marshal von Rundstedt had already in the second week of the landing realized that the invading forces could not be driven back into the sea. However Hitler still believed that it was possible. Therefore, the troops had to continue clinging on to their cracking line.[7] In fact, on 3 July 1944 Hitler had held a principal discussion about rigid or flexible resistance. He pointed to the fact that a flexible resistance could not be risked, owing to the disparity in the air.[8] Therefore, he stood to his unrealizable maxim of not yielding ground.

HITLER'S CHANGE IN THE TECHNIQUE OF COMMAND

The elder Moltke had conducted his wars by issuing general directives to his subordinate commanders and leaving to them the details of execution. This same attitude was also formulated by Colmar von der Goltz in 1883, who wrote that in "a system like our own, it may be practicable to formulate a few general principles, one of them being that a superior should never prescribe from a distance, what a subordinate on the spot is in a better position to determine for himself. In that way orders were simplified, while the subordinate enjoys the necessary scope for the exercise of his discretion." He stressed the dangers of the opposite course, by saying that "once troops are accustomed to having every petty detail prescribed from above, they are apt to remain absolutely inactive, if, by chance, orders are not forthcoming."[9]

Count Schlieffen, had he had the oportunity to command on the battlefield, would have kept a closer grip on the affairs by issuing explicit and detailed orders. His successor, the younger Moltke, who had the chance, reverted to the usage of his uncle. Ludendorff, however, not only issued detailed orders, but also interfered with the execution by keeping control by telephone through the hierarchy of Chiefs of Staff of Army Groups, Armies, and Corps. During the Reichswehr era the "mission-tactics" (Auftragstaktik) had been reintroduced and were adhered to during the initial phase of the Second World War. This changed in direct relationship to Hitler's gradual usurpation of military power—in 1938 after the removal of von Blomberg he became Supreme Commander of the Armed Forces (Oberbefehlshaber der Wehrmacht); in December 1941, after the dismissal of von Brauchitsch, he assumed direct command over the Army, as C-in-C Army (Oberbefehlshaber des Heeres); and for some time he also held simultaneously command of an army group in southern Russia and the Caucasus. Therefore, Hitler and his OKW embarked more and more on issuing detailed orders and on interfering with their execution. As early as 26 July 1941 General Halder noted in his diary the shifting of the center of gravity from the operational to the tactical level. "If striking a small enemy concentration becomes our sole objective," he wrote, "the campaign will resolve itself into a series of minor successes, which will advance our front only by inches."[10] It is significant that the already quoted order, which dealt with the conduct of defense, contained the following phrase: "On principle no leader of an Army Group or even of an Army has the right to undertake on his own a so-called tactical evasive movement without explicit authorization."[11]

However, that was but a forerunner to Directive No. 68, issued after the failure of the Ardennes counteroffensive[12] in January 1945. It ran:

I order as follows:
1. Commanders-in-Chief, Commanding Generals and Divisional commanders are personally responsible to me for reporting in good time:
   (a) Every decision to carry out an operational movement. . . .
   (d) Every plan for disengaging or withdrawing forces.
   (e) Every plan for surrendering a position, a local strongpoint, or a fortress.
They must ensure that I have time to intervene in this decision, if I think fit, and that my counter-orders can reach the frontline troops in time.

That state of affairs was referred to by General Gotthard Heinrici, when he told Captain Liddell Hart that battalion commanders were afraid "to move a sentry from the window to the door."[13] No wonder that an atmosphere was created in which commanders tried to evade Hitler's orders, and Hitler felt it necessary to order[14] that commanders-in-chief, commanding generals, and divisional commanders, the Chiefs of the General Staffs, and each individual officer of the General Staff, or officers employed on General Staffs were responsible to him that reports made either directly or through the normal channels should contain nothing but the unvarnished truth. He threatened to impose draconic punishment on any attempt at concealment. In such a mental climate the art of war ceased to exist.

THE "CAULDRON OF DEMYANSK"

Hitler's "no withdrawal" policy bore many odd features. One such unique thing was the "cauldron of Demyansk." It is the only case in history of an isolated and encircled pocket located in front of the defensive front and maintained for twelve months (1942–1943). It was finally evacuated, only after a basic change in the situation of the whole front had taken place. It was Hitler's thesis that a "cauldron" before the front, or a salient in the front, annoys the enemy, and that it is therefore worthwhile to maintain it in order to tie down considerable hostile forces. From Demyansk, Hitler had eventually evolved his principle of fortresses and "fortified localities" ("Feste Plätze"). In fact, at Demyansk a large number of enemy formations were engaged. Notwithstanding, it remained doubtful whether Hitler's assumption was justified. The Germans had themselves tied down six divisions in the pocket and its vicinity, and this number had increased to twelve during the period of establishing a corridor. In view of Germany's total force deployed in the East, this was quite a considerable number of divisions. Yet even more important was the impact of that policy on the German Air Force. For more than three winter months the corps enclosed in the "Demyansk cauldron" had to be supplied by air. General Tippelskirch maintained that

that winter ruined the Luftwaffe—because it had to be used for flying supplies to the garrisons of the "hedgehogs." . . . The Second Corps [which held the "Demyansk cauldron"] required 200 tons of supplies a day, which called for a daily average of 100 transport aircraft. But as bad weather often intervened the actual number had had to be considerably larger, so as to make full use of an interval of passable weather—on one day as many as 350 aircraft were used to reprovision this single Corps. Many aircraft crashed as flying conditions were bad. The overall strain of keeping up supplies by air . . . was fatal to the future development of the Luftwaffe.[15]

Hitler's theory that encircled formations supplied by air exercise a tremendous pressure on the enemy, seems to be a miscalculation, judged by the events of Demyansk and, above all, after the German disaster in Stalingrad.

STALINGRAD

It was Schlieffen who had established that, for the decisive victory of Cannae, the contribution of the vanquished was as vital as that of the victor. Hitler's fundamental tribute to the defeat of his own forces at Stalingrad cannot be overestimated. It began by repeating his basic failure of the first year of the Russian campaign, of overestimating his own strength and embarking simultaneously on reaching the Volga and the Caucasian oil fields. By dividing his forces he neither captured Stalingrad on the Volga nor seized the Caucasus.

It seems, however, that the main reason for Hitler's obstinacy at Stalingrad was a psychological one. For purely military considerations, Halder had already tried to convince his warlord that the city's capture was not worth the effort and risk. However, "the city's name and its historical association with Stalin during the Civil War, made the Russians eager to defend it, as Hitler was to take it," wrote Alan Bullock. He went on: "A battle of prestige was thus joined between the two regimes."[16] The German historian at one time in charge of the war diary of OKW, Professor Percy Ernst Schramm, said in a lecture that "military action, conducted by reason of and under the spell of propaganda, leads finally to strategy ceasing to be strategy. After all, a strategy of prestige is the worst strategy of all."[17] As early as 1905 Schlieffen explained in a final discussion of a staff ride that

it has hitherto been the custom, that an army, feeling itself endangered by encirclement and not, otherwise, finding means to achieve a victory, would extricate itself from the envelopment as quickly as possible, in order to renew the battle elsewhere at a more favorable spot. Nowadays, that is no longer the fashion, as exemplified in the Far East, for even the conduct of wars is decided by fashions. Now, one holds on, even though one is surrounded. . . . It is a standpoint of the honor of arms (Waffenehre). One will not run away and nevertheless suffer great losses, one prefers to be killed instead.[18]

It was not only the "honor of arms" that was at stake, but also Hitler's premature boasting that enforced the holding on to Stalingrad. In October 1942 Hitler had announced in a speech that "where the German soldier sets foot, there he remains,"and "You may rest assured that nobody will ever drive us away from Stalingrad."[19] To make things even worse he boasted at the annual gathering of the "Old Guard," at Munich on 9 November:

I wished to reach the Volga at a certain point, near a certain city. That city happens to bear the name of Stalin himself. . . . I wished to take that city: we do not make exaggerated claims, and I can now tell you that we have captured it. Only a few small parts of it are not yet in our hands. Now people may ask: "Why does the army not advance faster?" But I do not wish to see a second Verdun, I prefer to reach my objectives by means of limited assaults. Time is of no importance.[20]

In fact, there are many people who believe, despite that statement, that for quite a long time Hitler considered Stalingrad to be his own equivalent of Falkenhayn's Verdun. His menace to the "City of Stalin" would compel the Russian leader to throw in every man he had, and thus the Russian blood would be drained. It is of interest that at the conference on 9 September 1938 at Nuremberg, when he had had the right insight about the conduct of armored thrusts,[21] he had also uttered something that should have guided him at Stalingrad. "Besides, one knows from experience that it is hard to abandon an action which has achieved only partial success," Hitler said at that occasion. "More and more units are thrown into breaches, and the bleeding-to-death, which one wanted to avoid, sets in."[22]

However, the bleeding-to-death could be avoided. There was a time when the retreat of Paulus' Sixth Army was still feasible, even after its final encirclement. Hitler, who always made a show of his knowledge of Clausewitz, could have read in the latter's work that "as for an army's retreat being cut off, the thread of narrowed or endangered lines of retreat should . . . not be overrated. Recent experience has made it plain that where the troops are good and their commanders bold they are more likely to break through than be trapped."[23]

Instead, Hitler invented another expedient. As soon as the Russian ring around Paulus' troops was closed, he issued the following order: "The forces of the Sixth Army encircled at Stalingrad will be known as the troops of Fortress Stalingrad." General K. Zeitzler, Halder's successor as Chief of the General Staff of the Army, maintained sarcastically that "thus by a stroke of the pen an encirclement became a fortress, at least as far as Hitler was concerned."[24] Furthermore, he reported that Hitler was delighted with his invention. Zeitzler argued with Hitler, but Hitler would not listen and indulged in the fantastic illusion that Göring's Luftwaffe would supply "Fortress Stalingrad" with its garrison of approximately a quarter million men.

The agony and the end of the brave Sixth Army is well known.[25]

THE MAKESHIFT OF "HEDGEHOGS" AND "FORTRESSES"

Having reached his wits' end, while being driven back on all fronts, Hitler tried to delude himself and others that by declaring certain localities to be "fortified areas" (Feste Plätze) or "local strong-points" (Ortsstützpunkte), he could stem the tide. He believed that they would act as a breakwater, split up the advancing hostile forces, and render successful counterattacks possible, which would at least inflict defeat on his enemies. However, for this purpose strong mobile reserves were necessary. These reserves were nonexistent. On the contrary, the holding of these imaginary "fortresses," on the whole, absorbed more forces than their defense was worth. Moreover, while troops conducting flexible defense retreat gradually and are always capable of turning about and of fighting successively, as Clausewitz has taught, in these "fortresses," garrisons were immobile and were therefore sooner or later overpowered and taken prisoner. It was simply a dreadful waste of manpower and equipment.

It is strange that Hitler, who had overcome the Maginot spirit by realizing that a successful defense depends not so much on fortifications, but more on mobile forces making proper use of the defenses, now reverted to the French misconception. He not only declared cities in Russia to be "local strongpoints," but also announced the whole army group in Kurland as a "Fortified Area" and therefore failed to extricate it in good time. The same also occurred to Field Marshal Walter Model's army group in the Ruhr basin. In order to maintain and relieve Budapest, another of his famous "fortresses," he squandered his last operational reserves, which were badly needed in the West as well as in the East. The drama of Stalingrad was now repeated all over Europe.

Since the Blitzkrieg was checked in Russia and in North Africa, and above all, since Hitler had intervened more and more in the conduct of war, scarcely any new strategic ideas were cultivated. Hitler, despite his enthusiasm for technical matters, remained obsessed by his own experience of the First World War. From a purely strategic viewpoint, since 1941 things had just muddled on.

However, the over-orthodox application of Ludendorff's "total war" conception, as absorbed by Nazism, during this war reached an intensity of atrocities unsurpassed by Genghis Khan's march of conquest and the Thirty Years' War, which prevented, *a priori*, any attempt at finding a political solution to the war.

NOTES

1. MGFA—IIIW 59/3—OKW/WFSt/L IV: Chefsachen: "Barbarossa," p. 176. F.H.Qu., den 21/12/41. Fernschreiben an OKH (Op.Abt.). Cf. also Franz Halder, *Kriegstagebuch*, Stuttgart, 1962, vol. 3, p. 360.

2. MGFA—IIIW 59/3, *op. cit.*, p. 179. OKW/WFSt/Op(H). F.H.Qu., den 28/12/41.

3. B. H. Liddell Hart, *The Other Side of the Hill*, London, 1956, p. 210.

4. Führerbefehl vom 8. September 1942 über grundsätzliche Aufgaben der Verteidigung (OKH/Gen.St.d.H/Op.Abt[I], Nr. 11153/42g. Kdos.), printed in *KTB des OKW*, Frankfurt/Main, 1963, vol. 2, pp. 1292–1297.

5. Felix Steiner, *Die Armee der Geächteten*, Göttingen, 1963, p. 153.

6. Frido von Senger und Etterlin, *Krieg in Europa*, Köln, 1960, pp. 295–296.

7. B. H. Liddell Hart, *op. cit.*, p. 299.

8. *KTB des OKW*, *op. cit.*, vol. 6, p. 524.

9. Colmar von der Goltz, *The Nation in Arms*, London, 1906, pp. 107–108.

10. Halder, *op. cit.*, vol. 3, p. 121.

11. *KTB des OKW*, *op. cit.*, vol. 2, p. 1297.

12. *Vide* chapter 19.

13. B. H. Liddell Hart, *op. cit.*, p. 237.

14. In Directive No. 68.

15. B. H. Liddell Hart, *op. cit.*, p. 212. For the "Demyansk Cauldron," cf. Edgar Röhricht, *Probleme der Kesselschlacht*, Karlsruhe, 1958, pp. 131 ff.

16. A. Bullock, *Hitler. A Study in Tyranny*, Harmondsworth, Middlesex, 1962, pp. 685–686.

17. Percy Ernst Schramm, "Das Ende des Krieges," in *Die deutsche militärische Führung in der Kriegswende*, Arbeitsgemeinschaft für Forschung des Landes Nordrhein-Westfalen, Heft 118, Köln, 1964, p. 38.

18. BA/MA—HO8–46/111:3.

19. Quoted in K. Zeitzler, "Stalingrad," in S. Westphal, ed., *The Fatal Decisions*, London, 1956, p. 123.

20. *Ibid.*, p. 126.

21. *Vide* chapter 15, under "The Revival of Schlieffen's Fear of Gaps."

22. Cf. Peter de Mendelssohn, *The Nuremberg Documents*, London, 1946, p. 77.

23. *On War*, V, 16, p. 347.

24. S. Westphal, ed., *op. cit.*, p. 138.

25. He who wants to read more about Stalingrad is referred to Field Marshal Paulus' own account (ed. W. Görlitz), *Ich stehe hier auf Befehl!*, Frankfurt/Main, 1960, Zeitzler's account in S. Westphal, ed., and von Manstein's memoirs.

19

Case 9: The Ardennes Counteroffensive: The Last Attempt

One can hardly establish any influence of military theory in connection with the Ardennes offensive, in the winter of 1944–1945. Nevertheless, this operation provides a striking example of lack of principles and theory in the conduct of war. The investigation of the German spring offensives in 1918[1] has already revealed the results that are to be expected from warfare conducted by opportunistic gambling, and not based on sound political and military judgment. Since it is obvious that in 1944 the Germans had 1918 in mind, the repetition of the basic failures is indeed surprising, the more so, since Clausewitz had so clearly established the relationship between the offensive and the defensive.

THE REASONS FOR THE GERMAN COUNTEROFFENSIVE

In the last quarter of 1944 it was obvious to any objective observer that Hitler's "Fortress Europe" was crumbling. Gradually, the size of that "fortress" became identical with the territory of Germany proper. Moreover, Germany's military strength was dwindling even more rapidly than the decline of its territorial possessions. Hitler, who, like Schlieffen, was obsessed by a *fureur de nombre*, ignored the depleted state of his formations and, instead of replenishing the existing decimated divisions, incessantly formed new ones, giving them bombastic names in lieu of proper equipment. Closing his eyes to the superiority of his adversaries and, above all, to their superiority in the air, he made himself believe that his opponents would also reach the end of their tether. Hitler doubted whether his enemies in the West could sufficiently cover their front, which stretched over 800 kilometers. He therefore held the opinion that by selecting a spell of bad weather, which would prevent the utilization of airpower, Germany, even at that late time, could concentrate adequate forces in order to inflict on the Western powers a decisive defeat.

Hitler maintained that if the German offensive thrust was aimed at Antwerp, this would deprive the Anglo-American armies of the necessary port facilities, split up the British forces from the American, and might result in a second British

Dunkirk. Also, as in 1940, he decided on the Ardennes as the break-through sector. In fact, the Ardennes were only weakly held by American troops because Eisenhower had not intended to launch any operation there. Surprise was considered to be essential for the success of the offensive. However, in case of success at least twenty-five to thirty hostile divisions would be annihilated, together with the destruction of a vast amount of vital war material, stockpiled in the area for the further assault on Germany, for which there could be no replacement.

General Blumentritt summarized five reasons for Hitler's decision:

1. He hoped to take the Allies by surprise . . .
2. To raise the spirit of the German people . . .
3. To gain time for the creation of new war material and weapons.
4. He wanted to make the approach to the Ruhr district more difficult for the enemy.
   . . .
5. He saw that in the east and the west collapse was threatening. . . . German forces on the eastern front were no longer capable of stopping the Russian attack. On the other hand . . . he hoped . . . to throw the Allies into confusion by an offensive which was to come as a complete surprise.[2]

On 11/12 December 1944, at a conference with the commanders who were to take part in the offensive, Hitler stressed the point that further defensive conduct of the war could only delay the final decision, but never change the situation absolutely. In order to achieve this, only one chance remained, namely, to stake everything on one card—the offensive. For that purpose the prospects in the West were more favorable than in the East. The distances to be covered were shorter and would require less fuel; the theater of operations was smaller and limited by the coast. Above all, the English and the American leaders— military and political—were less obstinate than the Russians and would give in. The Western powers might become convinced that the claim for "unconditional surrender" was no longer feasible and would therefore accept a compromise peace. This would split the hostile coalition. He, Hitler, was in the meantime prepared to risk even a temporary enemy break-in near Metz until the effect of his own offensive could make itself felt.[3]

THE CONTROVERSY OVER HITLER'S PLAN

Field Marshal von Rundstedt, at that time again Supreme Commander West (OB West), was opposed to any German offensive in the West at that juncture. He was in favor of adopting a German defensive attitude, ceding the offensive step to the Allies, and at the same time assembling strong Panzer reserves for a concentric counterstroke after the enemy had deployed its forces. This was, in essence, a Clausewitzian idea.

However, Hitler refuted this suggestion, which he regarded as a useless waste of effort. He stuck to his concept of the "great solution," namely, the offensive aimed at Antwerp. He did not heed the fact that his plan bore no relation to the actual proportion of his forces to the enemy's. In fact, "the forces used in the Ardennes offensive were the last penny in the pauper's purse."[4] It was the commitment of the very last German reserves that could be assembled for any action in any direction.

No wonder that the German military experts in the West (not in OKW) shrank at the "great solution" and wanted it replaced by a less ambitious and more realistic one—the "small solution." They suggested directing the first phase of the operation against Liège. Should that step meet with success, then, circumstances permitting, by wheeling to the right, the British could be forced to withdraw their front.

COMPARISON WITH THE "SPRING OFFENSIVES" OF 1918

Although in Hitler's planning and conduct of the Ardennes offensive there exist many similarities to Ludendorff's conduct of the offensives in the spring of 1918, General Blumentritt drew attention to some basic differences. "In 1918 Germany was able to concentrate nearly all her forces in the west, for Russia had concluded peace," wrote Blumentritt. More divisions, artillery, and material were available at that time. The political attitude toward Germany in 1918 was not so destructive as in 1944. The great potential strength of America was only beginning to make itself felt. The German western front in 1918 was short and the troops stood in adequate strength. In 1918 there was no devastating air force. From the starting point of the offensive, near St.-Quentin, to Amiens was only fifty miles as the crow flies. In 1944 it was ninety-five miles to Antwerp. In 1918 the offensive began in the middle of March and on easier terrain. In 1944, on the contrary, the offensive was to pass over the rough, mountainous country of the Eifel and the Ardennes in December, along ice-bound and snow-covered roads. In 1918 the troops were still unbeaten and had suffered few reverses. When, therefore, 1918 and 1944 are compared, it is clear that conditions in the First World War were much more favorable for the Germans than in 1944.[5]

Indeed, all these differences had been correctly observed. Nevertheless, it is obvious that Hitler was thinking in terms of the offensives of 1918. First of all, Hitler, like Ludendorff, nourished illusions that, by attacking on the seam of the Allied armies, he could split the hostile coalition and drive the British into the sea, which would result in the readiness of the enemy to conclude a peace of compromise. On considering the political differences, mentioned by Blumentritt, this *idée fixe* of Hitler's was all the more astonishing.

A second similarity was in the neglect of diversionary attacks at unassaulted sectors in order to tie down enemy forces that could otherwise rush to the support of the attacked front, which in fact happened in 1918 as well as 1944.

In 1918 the assault forces and their command were not shaped by military requirements, but by domestic political considerations.[6] This was the case in 1944 also. Two Panzer armies were to lead the attack—the Fifth Panzer Army, commanded by General Hasso von Manteuffel and the Sixth SS-Panzer Army under SS-Oberstgruppenführer Josef (Sepp) Dietrich. The latter had, in the past, been commander of the "Leibstandarte SS Adolf Hitler," and his army was to consist of SS-Panzer divisions, whereas the Fifth Army would be formed by non-SS armored divisions.[7] Hitler had assigned to the SS Army what he expected to be the decisive role in the offensive; and even after the Sixth Army came to an early standstill, whereas the Fifth met with success, Hitler not only did not switch forces from the former to the latter, but also pushed further reinforcements into Dietrich's sector, without having any more success there. Hitler simply wanted "his Waffen-SS" to deliver the decisive blow.

Hitler, like Ludendorff, could not decide to withdraw his forces in good time, after the breakdown of the offensive, and like Ludendorff, he paid for an indecisive short gain in time with heavy losses and the destruction of valuable forces (this time armored formations!), which he would need so badly in the future. It was the same "no withdrawal" all over again, and this time on absolutely valueless ground.

Finally, having lost the momentum of his offensive at Bastogne, he resorted to Ludendorff's remedy of achieving partial successes by hitting successively at different places in order to eventually shake the hostile front and bring it to collapse. Accordingly, Hitler now ordered a second offensive from Zweibrücken–Bitsch in the direction of Zabern, with the ultimate goal of pushing down the Rhine valley and there destroying as many American divisions as possible. This attack would be followed by a third in Upper Alsace, with the same aim of destroying further American divisions. In order to have sufficient reserves at hand for the execution of these operations, he began rushing German troops from Finland. He hoped, as Ludendorff had done, that the destruction of so many American divisions would turn the scales in Germany's favor, and that the offensive in the direction of Antwerp would eventually be resumed.[8] Needless to say, these were all pipe dreams of the "greatest strategist of all times."

It is of interest that many of Hitler's orders in connection with the Ardennes offensive were lifted directly from Ludendorff's pamphlet, "The Offensive in Position Warfare" (Angriff aus dem Stellungskrieg).[9] Moreover, on 18 November 1944 OKW advised Supreme Command West to take precautions against secret preparations becoming known to the enemy through deserters and prisoners of war, as had happened in 1918. OB West and all his front line units were ordered strictly to report immediately any suspicion that the enemy might have recognized the offensive preparations. Attention was drawn to the fact that in July 1918 the German front line troops were aware of enemy counterpreparations, while the High Command remained in the dark and had therefore ordered the execution of the assault.[10]

That Hitler really had a repetition of the 1940 break-through in the Ardennes in mind is obvious from an order to the Army Archives in early October 1944 to transfer to OKW the documents relating to the operations of the Sixth and Fourth Armies in May 1940, especially an appreciation of the ground for the advance in Luxembourg and southern Belgium, prepared in January 1940.[11] Had he really not grasped the fact that the circumstances had changed drastically, even with regard to the ground? Then, with the intention of launching the offensive in the spring or early summer, and backed by a considerable Luftwaffe, the narrow and steep mountain roads were considered practicable. Now, in midwinter, and under bad weather conditions, deliberately chosen on account of lack of air power, the icy roads became a nightmare for the tracked units as well as for the wheeled, and helped the anti-tank defenses of the enemy. In no circumstances whatsoever, in that season of the year, would the ground aid an operation based on surprise and speed. Moreover, these road conditions imposed a heavier toll on petrol consumption than had been planned. One should also bear in mind that the fuel requirements were, in any case, inadequately covered from the beginning.

In 1918 Ludendorff could, with a certain amount of justification, allow himself to gamble because Germany was freed from the menace of the Russian front. Hitler's gambling in 1944 was completely unjustified in face of the pending Russian winter offensive. By delivering in the West a "pin-prick"—as Halder called it[12]—he had squandered his last mobile reserves.

NOTES

1. *Vide* chapter 10.

2. Günther Blumentritt, *Von Rundstedt. The Soldier and the Man*, London, 1952, p. 266.

3. Reported by General Hasso v. Manteuffel, C-in-C Fifth Panzer Army, a key figure in the offensive, in "Die Schlacht in den Ardennen 1944–1945," in H. A. Jacobsen and J. Rohwer, *Entscheidungsschlachten des zweiten Weltkrieges*, Frankfurt/Main, 1960, p. 539.

4. Franz Halder, *Hitler as War Lord*, London, 1950, p. 66.

5. G. Blumentritt, *op. cit.*, pp. 269–270.

6. *Vide* chapter 10, under "Command Arrangements for the Offensive."

7. Both armies also had infantry divisions at their disposal.

8. Cf. W. Warlimont, *Im Hauptquartier der Wehrmacht, 1939–1945*, Frankfurt/Main, 1962, pp. 521–522.

9. *Ibid.*, p. 516.

10. *KTB des OKW*, Frankfurt/Main, 1961, vol. 4, p. 440.

11. *Ibid.*, p. 431.

12. F. Halder, *op. cit.*, p. 66.

20

The Relationship Between Policy and War in Nazi Germany

Throughout this study much importance has been attached to Clausewitz' postulate of the primacy of policy over war. It therefore seems appropriate to begin this last chapter with an investigation of Hitler's attitude to Clausewitz.

HITLER AND CLAUSEWITZ

Hitler, who was an autodidact in every field, had acquired a remarkable military knowledge through reading books on military matters. People who knew him during the early twenties revealed that he had read Clausewitz' *On War* at that time and could quote from it at length. In fact, even in *Mein Kampf* he had once referred to Clausewitz,[1] but not in connection with any important problem of warfare. As early as 9 November 1934, in a speech at Munich, he snapped arrogantly at his generals: "None of you have read Clausewitz, or, if you have, you have not understood how to apply him to reality."[2] This was a clear attempt to stress his superior knowledge in the sphere of strategy, as compared with the soldiers' purely professional outlook.

During the war, however, he referred to Clausewitz very seldom. In Hitler's famous "Table Talks," as far as they are recorded, the great philosopher of war was never mentioned.[3] Only in Hitler's political testament, drawn up on 19 April 1945, the day before the dictator committed suicide, he urged his followers to continue the struggle against the enemies of the Fatherland, "faithful to the creed of the great Clausewitz."[4] As on all previous occasions, no specific reference to, or quotation of, any particular part of Clausewitz' teaching was made. Even from this short survey it is obvious that Hitler, in fact, had never penetrated the depths of Clausewitz' philosophy.

However, some people believed, at certain times, that Hitler had fully understood *On War* and conducted his campaigns in accordance with Clausewitz' thoughts. In 1940, after the collapse of France, Karl Linnebach, the famous editor and interpreter of Clausewitz in the inter-war period, maintained:

We can, as Clausewitz has pointed out, choose different roads on war. We can, for instance, direct our intentions to the aim of doing as much harm as possible to our enemy in the economic field. But that is not the direct road. . . . This is exactly what happened to our enemies. The Führer has forged the sharp sword of the German army and welded the whole German nation together, into one great arm, in which—to use one of Clausewitz' metaphors—the army forms the edge, the people the steel blade. Our enemies, on the other hand, thought that, behind their protective wall of concrete and wire entanglements, an elegant rapier would suffice as a weapon. They believed that they could win the war . . . without a bloodshed.

Linnebach not only held that Hitler had understood Clausewitz and that the Allies had had to pay for not listening to the latter, but he also insisted that the Germans "had drawn the right conclusions from the First World War."[5] It seems now, in retrospect, that both assumptions had been stated prematurely.

Hitler had not only overlooked the importance attached by Clausewitz to the defensive in general and to flexible defense in particular, and disregarded the latter's warning against a war in Russia, but as well as this he had not heeded a conclusion reached by Clausewitz as early as 1807, at a time when the latter was still a prisoner of war in France; that "great, vast extending conquests are extremely difficult to defend in our times, therefore the most clever people believe that they should not be undertaken at all."[6] The young subaltern Clausewitz had already fixed his mind on attaining the possible, whereas Hitler always indulged in striving after the impossible.

However, Hitler departed from the general usage of the post-Napoleonic era, in which, according to Schlieffen, a triumvirate—consisting of Monarch, Statesman, and General—was to conduct war. By holding the offices of Head of State, Chancellor, and Supreme Commander of the Armed Forces in his own hand, Hitler had returned to the times of Friedrich the Great and Napoleon without paying attention to the changed circumstances in the sphere of politics as well as in the sphere of warfare. In 1936 a syndicate of General Staff officers at the Wehrmachtakademie was asked to suggest an organization for supreme leadership in Germany in case of war. They maintained that for the conduct of total war, the authoritarian state, free from parliamentarism, was the ideal solution. Nevertheless, the burden of modern war was considered to be so tremendous that the head of such a totalitarian state must be assisted by additional "leaders" in particular branches. It was suggested that three positions be established under the over-all domination of the Head of State:

1. The General, to whom the primacy among the three should be given and who should also be nominated as Deputy Head of State.
2. The leader of the Economy, who should, by his measures, render the achievement of victory possible (although the armament industry would remain under the General's direction).
3. The Leader of the People.[7]

No wonder that Hitler had not adopted such a system, which sought too vital a part for the soldiers.

However, as a matter of fact, Hitler had restored the unity of policy and war after a long period of discord between the two in German history. But it was not exactly this kind of unity that Clausewitz had in mind. For Hitler was greatly influenced by Ludendorff's dictum of policy subordinated to the conduct of total war,[8] and although embodying both functions in his own person, he believed, as did his predecessors, that politics had to keep quiet until victory was reached.

If one looks back on Germany's history, one will discover that during the Wars of Liberation, the statesmen—Stein and Hardenberg—worked in harmony with the soldiers—Scharnhorst and Gneisenau. During the Wars of Unification there was concord between Bismarck and Roon, the Minister of War. Moltke, the Chief of the General Staff, despite certain controversies, cooperated fully. In Wilhelm II's era a vast and fateful gulf opened between the statesmen and the soldiers. The relationship between the Chancellors—Bethmann-Hollweg, Michaelis, and Count Hertling—on the one hand and Falkenhayn and Ludendorff on the other became one of overt hostility,[9] until finally the soldiers gained the upper hand. In the short-lived Weimar Republic the reciprocal attitude was one of suspicion on behalf of the politicians toward the generals and one of reserved loyalty in the opposite direction. A new stage in the relationship was reached by the total dictatorship of Hitler.

HITLER AND THE GENERALS

After the interrogation of German generals, Liddell Hart reached the conclusion that "the German General Staff had little influence with Hitler compared with what it had exercised in the Kaiser's time, and that it tended to be more of a brake upon his aggressive plans than an impetus to them."[10]

Hitler had gradually reduced the influence of the General Staff, not only because he knew that most generals were not converted to National Socialism, but also because he felt that the army sought to maintain its special position in the State, which, of course, could not be tolerated by him. Moreover, he was afraid that the generals, trained by the General Staff in sober and logical thinking, would oppose his adventurous expansionist plans. After the termination of the Polish campaign in 1939, Colonel General Keitel explained to Colonel W. Warlimont the strange phenomenon of why Hitler had not consulted OKH, as he should have done, prior to his decision to attack France later in the same year. It had been known to Hitler for a long time, Keitel said, that OKH was opposed to any war with France. Hitler knew that the former Chief of the General Staff, General Beck, had, during the Czechoslovakian crisis of 1938, warned against any conflict with France because Germany would for many years remain inferior to France. That was also the reason why Beck, who did not believe in the possibility of war with France, had planned to spread the erection of the German western defenses—the Westwall—over a period of ten years. Such slow progress was completely contrary to Hitler's own political plans. When, in the autumn of 1938, he discovered the army's intention he sacked the Inspector of Pioneers and Fortresses, General Förster, and assigned the task of erecting the Westwall to his own Inspector General of Building Concerns, Dr. Fritz Todt.[11] That was the beginning of the famous "Organisation Todt."

It was also the first of many future steps in by-passing the army and curtailing its functions. This was done by the creation of the "OKW theaters of war," which were conducted directly by Hitler, as Supreme Commander of the Armed Forces, without any say in them by OKH. Other devices in this process were the creation of Waffen-SS divisions, independent of OKH in many respects. The Waffen-SS units were eventually organized in army corps and even armies and thus became an army inside the army. Besides the SS, Göring was allowed to create his own Luftwaffe-Feld-Divisionen (Air Force Field Divisions), which, despite being used as normal land forces, remained indirectly under the control of the Luftwaffe, at the expense of OKH (in the case of the German airborne divisions this control was complete). On the other hand, in the first years of Hitler's Germany, OKH tried to preserve the detached position of the army within the State. The leading generals held the Schlieffenian opinion that defense policy (Wehrpolitik) was the exclusive domain of the armed forces, rather than the task of the leading statesman. General Beck, during his term of office as Chief of the General Staff of the Army, tried to withhold from OKW, i.e., from Hitler's staff as Supreme Commander, any information about the army's planning for future war. Relations between the two institutions—OKH and OKW—were strained to such a degree that General Beck prevented his officers from communicating officially with OKW.[12]

However, parallel to the absorption of the German governmental functions by the Nazi party, Hitler managed to push the military out of the political sphere and succeeded in confining them more and more to purely military-technical matters. The various stages of this process are well known: the Blomberg affair of February 1938, which gave Hitler the opportunity of himself assuming the office of Supreme Commander and eliminating the position of Minister of War; the removal of General von Fritsch, C-in-C Army, which, while passing unopposed by the generals, convinced Hitler that no further organized opposition of the army was to be expected; finally, the dismissal of Field Marshal von Brauchitsch, C-in-C Army, in December 1941, enabled Hitler to assume also direct command over the army. However, on the other hand Hitler could not decide on establishing an effective Supreme Command with full executive powers. Therefore, OKW became some kind of private military office for Hitler, rather than an effective instrument of execution. Field Marshal Keitel, Chief of the OKW, was merely the head, or perhaps even the secretary, of Hitler's private cabinet. If some critics had called Schlieffen's relationship with the Kaiser "Byzantinism," then Keitel's relationship to Hitler was one of absolute servitude. Hitler had overcome the ancient antagonism between soldiers and politicians by maintaining both spheres in his own hands. Yet he had degraded the military from responsible partners in decision making to mere receivers of orders and their blind execution. Bernhard von Lossberg, in charge of army affairs on Operations Staff OKW, revealed that Hitler had ordered strict separation of military and political matters, even in the highest staff—OKW—which should have been concerned with the reciprocal aspects of political and military issues. The use of the term "military-political situation" was forbidden by Hitler because under his regime there were no "military politics." Either a specific matter was a military one, the dictator maintained, and therefore the concern of soldiers only, or it was purely political and was then the other way round.[13] In fact, the professional perfectionism of the German officers had already reached such a degree that most of them consented to this separation of spheres.

It was the tragedy of the German generals that Hitler's opponents always played into his hands, and that he therefore so often proved to be right in his adventurous gambling, contrary to the proper judgment of his professional advisors. Therefore, the latter's arguments lost more and more of their impact on Hitler. "A combination of Hitler's often brilliant intuition, with orthodox and methodical planning of the General Staff could have been highly effective," wrote Alan Bullock, and added: "But this was ruled out by Hitler's distrust of the generals."[14] Indeed, it was one of the ironies of history that Hitler's mistrust of the generals was a direct continuation of the same attitude of the politicians of the Weimar Republic. Only the motivations were different: The pacifist Republicans regarded the generals as potential warmongers; Hitler was afraid lest they might hamper his aggressive aspirations.

POLICY AND WAR UP TO THE RUSSIAN CAMPAIGN

It is obvious that Hitler's policy up to 1941 succeeded in paving the way for military actions. The Anschluss of Austria, in 1938, resulted in the territorial encirclement of Czechoslovakia from the north, west, and south. That rendered any Czechoslovakian resistance a hopeless attempt from the beginning. The final occupation of Czechoslovakia in 1939 closed the ring around Poland, leaving the latter only an outlet to Russia. However, Hitler was aware that Poland's rulers would not come to terms with Russia. Moreover, the Ribbentrop–Molotov Pact secured the victory of German arms over Poland even before a shot was fired. At the same time, Hitler succeeded in holding back the Western Allies from invading Germany by a simple bluff: distributing exaggerated information about the strength of the Westwall, which was in fact in an unsatisfactory state of preparedness. When he finally turned to the west and attacked France, his back was secured by the agreement with Russia. There is no reason to believe that the Russian attitude to Germany would have changed, had Hitler embarked on the conquest of England. This would merely have been consistent with the political and military course so far adopted.

One cannot deny that until the end of the campaign in France, Hitler had acted completely in accordance with Clausewitz' principles (although with regard to long-term international politics, the wisdom of the partition of Poland and the violation of Danish, Norwegian, Belgian, and Dutch neutrality may be doubted!). From his own revision of the draft for "Operation Green" (war against Czechoslovakia), it is obvious that he had steered that political course on purpose. He wrote then: "It is my unalterable decision to smash Czechoslovakia by military action in the near future. It is the business of the political leadership to await or to bring about the suitable moment from a political and military point of view."[15]

It is also of interest that prior to the surprising Blitzkrieg successes in Poland, Norway, France, and the Balkans, Hitler had not shared Schlieffen's illusion of a short war. At a commanders' conference on 23 May 1939 he raised the question: "Short or prolonged War?" and replied:

Armed forces as well as political leadership have always striven for a short war. However, against that, the political leadership has to dispose for a war of ten to fifteen years' duration. In 1914 the opinion was held that a prolonged war could not be financed. Nowadays the same ideas again turn the heads of many people. On the contrary, every State can take it as long as it is necessary, if it does not suffer an immediate considerable weakening (as for instance by loss of the Ruhr district).[16]

On the other hand it has already been learned that, betrayed by his fantastic successes hitherto, Hitler turned to attack Russia in the belief that he could finish the job in four to five months.[17] This time, as in 1914, no dispositions for a prolonged war had been made. It appears that while Hitler had so far succeeded in the war by applying Schlieffen's encirclement methods, he also came to accept the latter's belief in a short war.

A by-product of Hitler's own conduct of the war, not only on the political level, but also on the military, was the fact that, repeatedly, the soldiers, even those of his own staff, were left in the dark about political developments. From Warlimont's, Lossberg's, and Greiner's accounts from OKW, as well as from Guderian's reports from the battlefield, it is apparent that the soldiers were not informed about the secret military clauses of the Molotov–Ribbentropp Pact. The disclosure of these arrangements at the moment the Russian troops were already advancing, created delicate situations. This was also the case with regard to the Hitler–Molotov conference of November 1940. The Defense Department, the most important department in OKW, already occupied with the preparations for the Russian campaign, had not the slightest information about what was going to be discussed with the Russian Commissar for Foreign Affairs.

A basic feature of Hitler's rule since the early days of his party leadership until his death was the policy of *divide et impera*. The same principle was applied to his direction of the war. Being himself the Supreme Commander of the Armed Forces he had delegated little authority to the Chief of the Supreme Command, Field Marshal Keitel, and to the Chief of Operations Staff, General Jodl. They were therefore not entitled to settle disputes between the services. It was always necessary to ask Hitler's decision. This procedure was, in many a case, too protracted, in addition to sometimes compelling Hitler to deal with minor problems not worth the attention of a Head of State. One should add to the confused situation Göring's special position as Commander-in-Chief of the Luftwaffe; the Luftwaffe had, owing to Göring's special relationship with Hitler, many advantages over the other services, and many a decision was reached outside the normal military hierarchy. For this state of affairs one should attribute the fact that the commanders-in-chief of the two other services could hardly ever achieve a balanced view of the general situation, which was, after all, essential for reaching proper conclusions. Thus the formation of policy remained firmly in Hitler's hands.

This also explains the astonishing fact that in the Second World War, similar to the First, Germany had no comprehensive plan for war. Hitler himself had not laid down such a plan, and therefore nobody was allowed to shape one, nor dared press Hitler to do so.

However, since Hitler's judgment had hitherto always proved right, despite the divergent views of the military experts, he tended more and more to throw military advice to the winds, and he became arbitrary in his decisions on an ever-increasing scale. When he reached the fateful decision to attack Russia, prior to the elimination of England, the generals resigned themselves to this step, and only Grand Admiral Raeder, who had a more global outlook than his colleagues of the army, tried to change Hitler's mind.

POLICY AND WAR SINCE THE RUSSIAN CAMPAIGN

With the decision to attack the Soviet Union while leaving an undefeated Great Britain behind his back, Hitler had left the firm ground of Clausewitzian principles. Policy no longer provided for the victory of arms. Moreover, Hitler had deviated from his own declared principle of waging war on only one front at a time. Germany's economic and manpower potential was as unfit for an armed contest on several fronts as it was in the First World War. Hitler, however, tried to convince himself, and his subordinates, that his opponents were exaggerating their war production, and that in fact Germany was superior to them in this field too.[18]

There is no doubt that, at the time, there was neither a political nor a military necessity to attack Russia. Moreover, Russia had faithfully made valuable economic contributions to Germany. Russia would probably not have intervened in Germany's war against England.

One result of the invasion of Russia was the fact that Hitler became so absorbed in the conduct of the war on the eastern front that he paid little attention to his other theaters of war. Only the defeat in North Africa and the Allied invasion of Sicily and Italy forced him abruptly to remember that he was involved in a world war. His underestimation of sea power, traditional to German military thinking,[19] was equally matched by his underestimation of American power.

Hitler, like Ludendorff and Hindenburg twenty-four years earlier, did not reckon with a major American intervention on the European continent. Neither had he supposed that America would speed up its mobilization and war production in so short a time. In 1917 Ludendorff saw no other alternative against the stranglehold of the British Navy than the launching of the unrestricted submarine warfare, even if it should bring the United States into the war against Germany. Even if one disagreed with Ludendorff over the soundness of such a decision, one cannot deny that there was a reason behind it. However, one looks in vain for the political or military wisdom of Hitler's declaration of war on the United States on 11 December 1941. It was characteristic of Hitler's relations with his generals that the latter learned about Hitler's declaration of war on the United States from the news, broadcast over the radio.

The scope of the General Staff's actions was further curtailed by the fact that from the Russia campaign onward, OKH had to confine itself to the conduct of the war on the eastern front. All the other theaters of war, even Finland, which was closely linked with the war in Russia, became OKW theaters of war. In fact, the General Staff was relegated to the status of the Supreme Command of a particular theater of war and lost its universal outlook and direction of affairs. Hitler had succeeded, where Allied pressure after Versailles had utterly failed, in destroying the German General Staff. On the other hand OKW had no say on the eastern front and never became a real substitute for the battered General Staff of the Army. "The responsibility for the conduct of operations was thus divided," said Alan Bullock, "and the strategic picture of the war as a whole remained the concern of Hitler alone."[20] No wonder that as early as 4 August 1941 the Chief of the General Staff of the Army complained that he lacked the necessary basis for his planning, namely, the clear knowledge of the political goals and intentions.[21]

Hitler, occupying himself more and more with the conduct of operations, convinced of his own military genius, gradually renounced any political actions and staked everything on martial achievements. This was reflected in Goebbels' diary in the summer of 1943: "We are doing too much on the military and too little on the political side of the war. At this moment, when our military successes are none too great, it would be a good thing if we knew how to make better use of the political instrument. We were so great and resourceful in that way at the time of our struggle for power; why shouldn't we achieve mastery of this art now?"[22]

There were, and still are, opinions that Hitler might also have succeeded in Russia had he not adhered to inhuman methods in his warfare and, above all, in the administration of the occupied territories. Nothing would be gained for the purpose of this study by pursuing this hypothetical assumption. However, one thing is crystal clear, as von Manstein put it, namely, that the strategist Hitler, striving for the quick termination of the war in Russia, was frustrated by the Eastern policy of the politician Hitler.[23]

WAS IT POSSIBLE TO NEGOTIATE A PEACE SETTLEMENT?

The Allies' demand for Germany's unconditional surrender, which prevented Hitler from giving in and made him carry on with the war until Germany's final destruction, also prevented the repetition of a "stab-in-the-back" legend

Despite this "unconditional surrender" war aim of Germany's opponents, Hitler played with the idea of achieving a "draw" in that bloody war. He had inherited from Schlieffen a great admiration for Friedrich the Great. Hitler considered his and Germany's situation as analogous to Prussia's situation during the Seven Years' War (1756–1763). Although badly shaken and fighting against superior foes, the Prussian king managed to stand his ground until changed political circumstances created a basis for the Treaty of Hubertusburg (15 February 1763). The political event that had turned the tide in Friedrich's favor was the death of Elizabeth III of Russia, whose successor, Peter III, was an admirer of the Prussian king and therefore deserted the anti-Prussian coalition. Hitler already living in a world of imagination and hallucinations, believed so much in the analogy with Friedrich the Great that he considered President F. D. Roosevelt's death on 12 April 1945 as the equivalent of the Russian Csarina's death and as foreboding the longed-for Treaty of Hubertusburg.

Even so clever a general as von Manstein had picked up Ludendorff's ideas of 1918 that the delivery of massive partial blows, resulting in the enemy's heavy losses and his yielding of huge numbers of prisoners, would make the enemy prepared to compromise.[24] Only by taking into consideration purely military factors could German soldiers—von Manstein was not alone in his belief—dream of achieving a "draw." They had overlooked Clausewitz' postulate of the unity of policy and conduct of war, and the primacy of policy in the framework of that unity.

NOTES

1. Cf. Adolf Hitler, *Mein Kampf*, London, 1939, p. 544.

2. Quoted in Prof. W. Hahlweg's introduction to the 16th ed. of *Vom Kriege*, Bonn, 1952, entitled "Das Clausewitzbild einst und jetzt," p. 42, and also in G. Beyerhaus, "Der ursprüngliche Clausewitz," *Wehrwissenschaftliche Rundschau*, Jg. 3, H.3 (March 1953), p. 110.

3. Cf. Dr. Henry Picker, *Hitlers Tischgespräche im Führerhauptquartier, 1941–1942*, Stuttgart, 1963 (new rev. ed. by P. E. Schramm), or another version *Hitler's Secret Conversations*, New York, 1961 (Signet Book, paperback).

4. *KTB des OKW*, Frankfurt/Main, 1961, vol. 4, p. 1668.

5. Karl Linnebach, "Vom Geheimnis des kriegerischen Erfolges," *Wissen und Wehr*, 1940, vol. 3, pp. 442–445. Linnebach was the editor of the two inter-war editions of *Vom Kriege*—the 14th ed. in 1933 and the 15th ed. in 1937, to which he also wrote an introduction and comments.

6. From an article, "Skizze zu einem Operationsplan für Österreich," written by Clausewitz as a prisoner of war in France in spring 1807. Quoted in Karl Schwartz, *Leben des Generals Carl von Clausewitz und der Frau Marie von Clausewitz*, Berlin, 1878, p. 71.

7. BA/MA—W10-1/14. "Wie hat sich das Fehlen eines gemeinsamen Oberbefehls über die verschiedenen Wehrmachtsteile bei den Mittelmächten und bei der Entente ausgewirkt? Einfluss auf den Gang der Ereignisse. Von dieser historischen und kritischen Betrachtung ausgehend sind allgemeine Grundsätze für die Spitzengliederung einer Grossmacht in der Lage Deutschlands aufzustellen." Vortrag gehalten am 24. April 1936 an der Wehrmachtakademie von der Arbeitsgemeinschaft I: Oberst d. Generalstabs v. Uthmann, Oberstleutnant d. Generalstabs Kessler, Oberstleutnant Matzky, p. 89.

8. *Vide* chapter 14.

9. Schlieffen and the younger Moltke merely ignored the political agencies.

10. Liddell Hart, *The Other Side of the Hill*, London, 1956, from the preface to the 1956 ed.

11. Cf. H. Greiner, *Die Oberste Wehrmachtführung 1939–1943*, Wiesbaden, 1951, p. 97.

12. Cf. P. Bor, *Gespräche mit Halder*, Wiesbaden, 1950, p. 77.

13. B. v. Lossberg, *Im Wehrmachtführungsstab*, Hamburg, 1949, p 33.

14. A. Bullock, *Hitler. A Study in Tyranny*, Harmondsworth, Middlesex, 1962, p. 666.

15. *Ibid.*, p. 447.

16. Quoted in H. A. Jacobsen, *1939–1945. Der zweite Weltkrieg in Chronik und Dokumenten*, Darmstadt, 1961, pp. 111–112.

17. *Vide* chapter 16.

18. Cf. Hitler's explanation in the conference of 9 Jan. 1941, as quoted by H. Greiner, *op. cit.*, pp. 340–345, from the war diary of Defense Department OKW.

19. *Vide* chapter 6.

20. A. Bullock, *op. cit.*, p. 665.

21. Franz Halder, *Kriegstagebuch*, Stuttgart, 1962, vol. 3, p. 153.

22. Quoted in A. Bullock, *op. cit.*, p. 692.

23. Cf. Erich von Manstein, *Verlorene Siege*, Bonn, 1955, p. 173.

24. *Ibid.*, p. 476.

Epilogue

Germany lost two world wars despite the fact that in both instances Germany entered the war with a highly trained and well-equipped army at its disposal.

The reasons for the defeat seem to be similar in both cases. During the First World War, from the outbreak, or rather from the planning phase, up to the very end the war was handled as a purely military matter. The pre-prepared plan and the technical requirements for setting it in motion were so rigid that when the probability for its execution emerged on the international horizon, no space for political maneuver was left. The politicians surrendered unconditionally to the military. Captivated by the stupid belief that politics have no say in the conduct of war, the statesmen waited for their time to come, after the termination of hostilities, instead of striving incessantly for the creation of a favorable political atmosphere for a settlement. In such circumstances the bankruptcy of warfare became automatically the bankruptcy of politics also, as Clausewitz had predicted. Schlieffen's military-technical approach triumphed over Clausewitz' sounder view that policy and warfare are closely interwoven spheres and that policy is the dominating factor. Even a superficial survey of the political scene of 1914 will reveal that Germany had already lost the war before the first shot was fired. Because the war was lost on account of international political relations, German military achievements were all the more remarkable. However, the latter could not turn the tide. They could only prolong the war.

It was an outstanding feature of Hitler's conduct of the opening phase of the Second World War that clever politics paved the way for military success. However, when the dictator became intoxicated by his unexpected and unprecedented military achievements, he neglected the political field and embarked on purely military adventures. The attempt was again made to solve the bloody dispute between nations and ways of life on the martial level alone. It is not, therefore, hindsight to say that even before its actual outbreak, Germany had also lost the Second World War. It was simply predicted by Clausewitz' theory of the relationship of policy and warfare.

If the direct question is put whether there was any influence of the theories of Clausewitz and Schlieffen on the German conduct of the two world wars, the answer is in the affirmative. There is no doubt that Schlieffen's attitude of conducting war as a purely military affair provided a decisive contribution to failure. Closely linked with this blunder was Schlieffen's obsession with the enemy's annihilation by means of encirclement as the only possible strategic solution. On the other hand the fact that the Germans had not understood Clausewitz' philosophy, and therefore had never heeded his theory or the practical implications to be derived from it, was without doubt a vital factor in Germany's defeat. One is continually struck by how valid and unsurpassed Clausewitz' theory still is, although almost 150 years have elapsed since its formulation. No new doctrines have so far been formulated. In fact, what other postulate could have replaced Clausewitz' maxims about the relationship between policy and war?

There are dangers for one who tries to establish historical analogies. No historical situation is similar in all its details to another. The mosaic of historical events is generally so complicated that the smallest detail, if wrongly interpreted, is likely to distort the whole picture. Nevertheless, it appears that history has the mission to teach. For this purpose it is necessary to draw conclusions.

From the German example, investigated by this study, the conclusions to be drawn for the situation of the State of Israel are simple and obvious, almost commonplace. It would be a folly to believe that Israel's problems can be solved on the battlefield alone. The problem is, above all, a political one, as are all relations between nations, people, and ideologies. War is but one means in the wide range of political interaction. However, in order to make war an effective factor at the statesman's disposal, should he be compelled to resort to it, efficient, highly trained, and well-equipped armed forces are essential. Their very existence is a political factor of the first order. Military strength is likely to convince the adversary that a bloody contest may not pay off. It is certainly hard for soldiers to realize that despite their professional expertness, they are dominated by "silly civilians." Likewise, politicians tend to shrink from exercising their legitimate say in military matters. But proper cooperation of soldiers and statesmen, and the unconditional recognition of the armed forces as an instrument of statecraft are vital. The German example—as manifested in two world wars—is too appalling to ignore. Therefore, Israel's statesmen and soldiers must have the wisdom to apply the necessary relationship of policy and warfare to any future armed clash that might be forced on it. Prudent statecraft that knows how to use the military instrument, which on its part must be efficient, is likely to secure success.

A final word to the soldiers: Nothing is more destructive in the field of military art than the establishment of dogma. Germany has paid a terrific price for Schlieffen's Cannae obsession. An open and versatile mind as well as the ability to judge any situation on its own merit is a necessary requirement of generalship and for the conduct of troops at every level of command. There are no "patent solutions" or Schlieffenian "gospels of victory" in so bloody a business as war.

Bibliographical Essay

GENERAL REMARKS ON SOURCES

In preparing this book material from the following German archives was used:

* Bundesarchiv/Militärarchiv, formerly Koblenz, now in Freiburg im Breisgau;
* Berliner Hauptarchiv, formerly Preussisches Geheimes Staatsarchiv, Berlin-Dahlem;
* Dokumentenzentrale des Militärgeschichtlichen Forschungsamtes, Freiburg im Breisgau. Most of the documents that were previously stored here are now kept in the Militärarchiv.

Unfortunately for the purpose of present-day research, von Clausewitz' papers, which were in the custody of the Army Archives at Potsdam until the end of the Second World War, have since disappeared. It is not known whether they were destroyed by the air-raids on Potsdam on 14 April 1945 or whether they disappeared in another way. However, early secondary sources, especially Karl Schwartz, *Leben des Generals Carl von Clause-witz und der Frau Marie von Clausewitz*, Berlin, 1878, 2 vols., give a clear picture of these private papers and a certain number of quotations from them. On the other hand, von Clausewitz' manuscript of *Strategy*, which was edited and published by E. Kessel in Hamburg in 1937 under the title *Strategie aus dem Jahr 1804 mit Zusätzen von 1808 und 1809*, is filed in BHA under Rep. 92 Nachlass Gneisenau M52, and the manuscript of von Clausewitz' lectures about the "Small War" is in the possession of the Münster (Westf.) University Library and was edited and published in 1966 by Professor Werner Hahlweg in *Schriften—Aufsätze—Studien—Briefe, Dokumente aus dem Clausewitz-, Scharnhorst- und Gneisenau-Nachlass, sowie aus öffentlichen und privaten Sammlungen*, vol. 1, Göttingen, 1966. Additional Clausewitz papers were edited and published by W. Hahlweg under the title *Verstreute kleine Schriften*, Osnabrück, 1979. In fact the complete edition of von Clausewitz' work, in ten volumes, appears to be sufficient for a compre-hensive evaluation of von Clausewitz' theory.

With regard to von Schlieffen, in addition to his printed works, his papers can be found at least in all three above-mentioned archives under the topic of Schlieffen, as well as in other collections, for instance, among the papers of General Wilhelm von Hahnke, von Schlieffen's aide-de-camp and son-in-law, and General Wilhelm Groener. The orig-inal manuscript of the various versions of the Schlieffen Plan is kept in Freiburg, and from a study of these, it appears that Gerhard Ritter was in error at some points in his published version of the plan.

The First World War, as far as the subject of this book is concerned, is well documented by private papers kept in all three archives mentioned (for instance, the papers of W. Groener, M. Bauer, M. Hoffmann, and others), which to a certain extent compensate for the destruction of the official files in Potsdam.

There is, however, one very important exception: the Younger Moltke. None of the German archives holds any original Moltke papers. Moltke's memoirs and papers (Helmuth von Moltke, *Erinnerungen, Briefe, Dokumente, 1877–1916*, Stuttgart, 1922), published by his wife, present a very unsatisfactory selection. From information provided to me by the Moltke family, it appears that the papers of the Younger Moltke had been destroyed by his eldest son at the time the latter fled from Berlin in 1945. However, the archives in Koblenz contain an open letter of Moltke's son, Adam von Moltke, to Walter Görlitz, written in order to refute the latter's presentation of Colonel General H. von Moltke and his term of duty as Chief of the German General Staff in his book Walter Görlitz, *Der deutsche Generalstab*, Frankfurt am Main, 1950 (the relevant chapter reads ''The War without a General''). Furthermore, I was kindly given access by Mrs. Eva Schotte-von Moltke, the late Adam von Moltke's daughter, to an unfinished and unpublished manuscript of her father, in which the latter attempted to rehabilitate his father, the Younger Moltke, and which sheds some light upon Moltke's relationship with Schlieffen. However, the principal explanation of Moltke's conduct of the initial phase of the First World War is, in fact, to be found in Schlieffen's writing.

The inter-war publications of the Schlieffen school (cf. Appendix B to Chapter 12), as well as the private papers of the central figures of this school, shed light upon the actions of this group and illuminated various aspects of the First World War. In the same way, they foreshadowed future events. This was also the case with the documents of the *Wehrmacht Academy*, kept in the Militärarchiv.

For the purpose of this book there was no lack of documentation with regard to the Second World War. Of particular interest is the draft of a still unpublished article, prepared in June 1940 by General Friedrich von Rabenau, at the time Chief of the Army Archives, analyzing the Blitzkrieg campaigns of 1939–1940.

For the German documents, which the Allies captured in 1945, and which were temporarily held in the United States, but were returned to the Federal Republic of Germany, the following publications rendered valuable information:

1. Weinberg, G. L. (ed.). *Guide to Captured German Documents*. Alabama, 1952.
2. Weinberg, G. L. (ed.). *Supplement to the Guide to Captured German Documents*. Washington, D.C., 1959.
3. American Historical Association, Committee for the Study of War Documents. *Guides to German Records Microfilmed at Alexandria, Va*. Washington, D.C., 1959.

A full bibliography of the subject of this book would need too much space. Therefore, the following books and articles are only a selection of publications, that were mainly used in this study. It has sometimes proved difficult to decide in which category to include a particular book or article.

Carl von Clausewitz

Carl von Clausewitz' own writings

Carl von Clausewitz' main work was published in ten volumes after his death under
the title *Hinterlassene Werke des General Carl von Clausewitz über Krieg und Kriegführung*. The first edition of these collected works was published in Berlin in the years
between 1832 and 1837 and a second edition appeared in Berlin between 1853 and 1863.
Volumes One to Three comprise the famous treatise *Vom Kriege* from which, in addition
to many popular and abridged editions, until now 19 "recognized" editions have been
published. The four post-World-War-II editions (sixteenth to nineteenth) were edited and
provided with a historical-critical introduction and an epilogue by Professor Werner
Hahlweg. The only reliable English translation so far is the Princeton edition Carl von
Clausewitz, *On War* (edited and translated by Michael Howard and Peter Paret), Princeton,
N.J., 1976. This edition comprises "Introductory Essays" by Peter Paret, Michael Howard, and Bernard Brodie, and a "Commentary" by Bernard Brodie.

The other volumes of von Clausewitz' works are:

Volume 4:	*Der Feldzug von 1796 in Italien*;
Volumes 5 and 6:	*Die Feldzüge von 1799 in Italien und der Schweiz*;
Volume 7:	*Der Feldzug von 1812 in Russland, der Feldzug von 1813 bis zum Waffenstillstand und der Feldzug von 1814 in Frankreich*;
Volume 8:	*Der Feldzug von 1815 in Frankreich*;
Volume 9 and 10:	*Strategische Beleuchtung mehrerer Feldzüge von Gustav Adolph, Turenne, Luxemburg und andere historische Materialien zur Strategie.*

In 1922 Hans Rothfels edited a selection of Clausewitz' political essays and letters
under the title *Politische Schriften und Briefe*, München, 1922.

Eberhard Kessel published in 1937 von Clausewitz' essay "On Strategy" in *Strategie
aus dem Jahr 1804 mit Zusätzen von 1808 und 1809*, Hamburg, 1937.

The well-known Clausewitz expert Werner Hahlweg, as already mentioned, edited
what in fact amounts to two additional volumes of von Clausewitz' writings: *Schriften—
Aufsätze—Studien—Briefe. Dokumente aus dem Clausewitz-, Scharnhorst- und Gneisenau-Nachlass sowie aus öffentlichen und privaten Sammlungen*, vol. 1, Göttingen,
1966; and *Verstreute kleine Schriften*, Osnabrück, 1979.

The prestigious German military periodical *Militärwissenschaftliche Rundschau* published in March 1937 a special issue of the full text of two letters of von Clausewitz to
a certain Major Roeder: "Zwei Briefe des Generals von Clausewitz. Gedanken zur
Abwehr." In 1977 Joachim Niemeyer, an assistant of Professor Werner Hahlweg, edited
a collection of von Clausewitz' letters in connection with the occurrences in October
1806 and added comments: Carl von Clausewitz, *Historische Briefe über die grossen
Kriegsereignisse im Oktober, 1806*, Bonn, 1977.

Clausewitz Biographies

Karl Schwartz, *Leben des Generals Carl von Clausewitz und der Frau Marie von
Clausewitz*, Berlin, 1878, 2 vols., although of low scholarly value, is still the most

comprehensive biography of von Clausewitz and contains much valuable documentation. Karl Linnebach, who became editor of the inter-war editions of *Vom Kriege* and had access to the Clausewitz family archive, edited during World War I a biography: *Karl und Marie von Clausewitz*, Berlin, 1916. After the First World War he published a biographical essay: "Clausewitz' Persönlichkeit," *Wissen und Wehr*, Jg. 11(1930), H. 5.

Interpreters of von Clausewitz

These are legion. Suffice to mention here the most important ones:

Aron, Raymond. *Penser la guerre. Clausewitz.* Paris, 1976.

Beck, Ludwig. *Studien.* Stuttgart, 1955.

Blaschke, R. *Carl von Clausewitz. Ein Leben im Kampf.* Berlin, 1934.

Caemmerer, R. v. *Clausewitz.* Berlin, 1905.

Collins, E. M. "Clausewitz and Democracy's Modern Wars." *Military Affairs* 19, no. 1 (1955): 15–20.

Elze, Walter. *Clausewitz.* Berlin, 1934.

Espesito, V. J. "War as a Continuation of Politics." *Military Review* 34, no. 11 (Febr. 1955): 54–62.

Fabian, Franz. *Clausewitz. Leben und Werk.* Berlin (East), 1957.

Freytag-Loringhoven, Frhr. v. *Die Macht der Persönlichkeit im Kriege Studien nach Clausewitz.* Berlin, 1905.

———. *Kriegslehren nach Clausewitz aus den Feldzügen 1813 und 1814.* Berlin, 1908.

Gembruch, W. "Zu Clausewitz' Gedanken über das Verhältnis von Krieg und Politik." *Wehrwissenschaftliche Rundschau.* Jg. 9, H. 11(1959), pp. 619ff.

Greene, J. I. *The Living Thoughts of Clausewitz.* London, 1945.

Hahlweg, Werner. "Lenin und Clausewitz." *Archiv für Kulturgeschichte.* Bd. 36 (1954), H. 1, pp. 30–59; H. 3, pp. 357–387.

———. *Carl von Clausewitz. Soldat—Politiker—Denker.* Göttingen, 1969.

Hartl, Maria. *Carl von Clausewitz, Persönlichkeit und Stil.* Emden, 1956.

Hennicke, Otto. *Clausewitz.* Berlin (East), 1957.

Kessel, Eberhard. "Zur Entstehungsgeschichte von Clausewitz' Werk 'Vom Kriege'." *Historische Zeitschrift* 52(1935), pp. 97ff.

———. "Carl von Clausewitz." *Wissen und Wehr.* Jg. 18 (1937), H. 11, pp. 700–706; H. 12, pp. 763–773.

———. "Zur Genesis der modernen Kriegslehre." *Wehrwissenschaftliche Rundschau.* Jg. 3, H. 9 (1953), pp. 405–423.

———. "Die doppelte Art des Krieges." *Wehrwissenschaftliche Rundschau.* Jg. 4, H. 7 (1954), pp. 298ff.

Leeb, Wilhelm v. *Die Abwehr.* Berlin, 1938.

Leinveber, A. *Mit Clausewitz durch die Rätsel und Fragen, Irrungen und Wirrungen des Weltkrieges.* Berlin, 1926.

Lenin, W. I. *Clausewitz' Werk "Vom Kriege."* Berlin (East), 1957.

Liddell Hart, B. H. *The Ghost of Napoleon.* London, 1933.

Linnebach, Karl. "Vom Geheimnis des kriegerischen Erfolgs." *Wissen und Wehr* 21 (1940), pp. 442–445.

Metzsch, H. v. *Clausewitz Katechismus.* Berlin, 1941.

Nohn, E. A. "Clausewitz contra Bülow." *Wehrwissenschaftliche Rundschau*. Jg. 5, H. 7 (1955), pp. 323–330.

———. "Der unzeitgemässige Clausewitz." *Wehrwissenschaftliche Rundschau*. Beiheft 5 (Nov. 1956).

Paret, Peter. *Clausewitz and the State*. Oxford, 1976.

Pilcher, T. D. *War According to Clausewitz*. London, 1918.

Reinhardt, W. *Wehrkraft und Wehrwille*. Berlin, 1932.

Rosinski, H. "Die Entwicklung von Clausewitz' Werk 'Vom Kriege' im Lichte seiner 'Vorreden' and 'Nachrichten'." *Historische Zeitschrift* 51 (1935), pp. 278–293.

Rothfels, Hans. *Carl von Clausewitz. Politik und Krieg*. Berlin, 1920; reprint: Bonn, 1980.

———. "Clausewitz" in E. M. Earle (ed.), *Makers of Modern Strategy. Military Thought from Machiavelli to Hitler*. Princeton, N.J., 1943.

Schering, W. M. *Die Kriegsphilosophie von Clausewitz*. Hamburg, 1935.

Stamp, Gerd (ed.). *Clausewitz im Atomzeitalter*. Wiesbaden, 1962.

Vad, Erich. *Carl von Clausewitz. Seine Bedeutung heute*. Herford, 1984.

Alfred von Schlieffen

Alfred Count von Schlieffen's Own Writings

Alfred von Schlieffen's essays of military thought were published in the following compilation: Feldmarschall Graf Alfred von Schlieffen, *Cannae*, Berlin, 1936 (3d ed.). His service papers were published in two volumes on the eve of the Second Worl War: A. v. Schlieffen, *Dienstschriften*, Berlin, 1937/1938, 2 vols. Eberhard Kessel edited and published after the Second World War a collection of his letters: Generalfeldmarschall Graf Schlieffen (ed. E. Kessel), *Briefe*, Göttingen, 1958. The German historian Gerhard Ritter published in 1956 for the first time the full text—various drafts and versions—of the so-called Schlieffen Plan. An English translation with an important foreword by B. H. Liddell Hart was published two years later: Gerhard Ritter, *The Schlieffen Plan. Critique of a Myth*, London, 1958.

Schlieffen Biographies

The documentary evidence shows that Hugo Rochs' biography of Schlieffen was on behalf of the Schlieffen family (Rochs was at one time a Regimental Surgeon under Schlieffen's command): Rochs, Hugo, *Schlieffen*, Berlin, 1926.

Interpreters of von Schlieffen

The publications of the inter-war Schlieffen school are given in Appendix B to chapter 12 of this book and will not be reported here. Additional relevant publications are:

Bernhardi, Friedrich von. *On War of To-Day*. London, 1912, 2 vols.

———. *Deutschland und der nächste Krieg*. Stuttgart, 1913.

Bircher, Eugen, and Bode, A. W. *Schlieffen: Mann und Idee*. Zürich, 1937.

Boetticher, Friedrich von. *Schlieffen*. Göttingen, 1957.

Bredt, Joh. Victor. *Die belgische Neutralität und der Schlieffensche Feldzugsplan*. Berlin, 1929.

Delbrück, Hans. *Geschichte der Kriegskunst im Rahmen der politischen Geschichte*. vol. 1: *Das Altertum*. Berlin, 1900 (In this volume A. v. Schlieffen discovered the battle of Cannae!).

Elze, Walter. *Schlieffen*. Breslau, 1928.

Falkenhausen, Frhr. von. *Ausbildung für den Krieg*. Berlin, 1902–1904, 2 vols.

———. *Der grosse Krieg in der Jetztzeit*. Berlin, 1909.

———. *Flankenbewegung und Massenheere*. Berlin, 1911.

Foerster, Wolfgang. "Hat es eine Schlieffenplan-Legende gegeben?" *Wehrwissenschaftliche Rundschau*. Jg. 2, H. 12 (Dec. 1952), pp. 601–605.

Freytag-Loringhoven, Frhr. von. *Krieg und Politik in der Neuzeit*. Berlin, 1911.

———. *Politik und Kriegführung*. Berlin, 1918.

Grosser Generalstab. Kriegsgeschichtliche Abteilung I. *Der Schlachterfolg, mit welchen Mitteln wurde er erstrebt*. Berlin, 1903 (This is a study instigated by von Schlieffen and typical for the era of his term of duty as Chief of the General Staff of the Army).

Hahnke, Wilhelm von. "Zum Schlieffen-Plan und Moltke-Aufmarsch." *Militär-Wochenblatt*. Jg. 110 (1925), no. 2.

Kiliani, E. v. "Die Operationslehre des Grafen Schlieffen und ihre deutschen Gegner." *Wehrkunde*. H. 2, 1961, pp. 71–76; H. 3, pp. 133–138.

Mantey, Friedrich von. "Umfassung, Umgehung und Durchbruch. Eine Schlieffenstudie." *Wissen und Wehr*. Jg. 12 (1931), H. 10, pp. 569–590.

Müller-Brandenburg, H. *Von Schlieffen bis Ludendorff*. Leipzig, 1925.

Senger und Etterlin, F. M. v. "Cannae, Schlieffen und die Abwehr." *Wehrwissenschaftliche Rundschau*. Jg. 13, H. 1/2 (1963), pp. 26–43.

Stahl, Friedrich-Christian. "Der Grosse Generalstab, seine Beziehungen zum Admiralstab und seine Gedanken zu den Operationsplänen der Marine. Aus Anlass des 50. Todestages des Generalfeldmarschalls Graf von Schlieffen am 4. Januar 1963." *Wehrkunde*. Jg. 12, H. 1 (1963), pp. 6–12.

Wetzell, Georg. "Schlieffen—Moltke (der Jüngere)—Bülow." *Militär-Wochenblatt*. Jg. 109 (1925), no. 44.

Printed Primary Sources

Heiber, Helmuth (ed.). *Hitlers Lagebesprechungen*. Stuttgart, 1962.

Jacobsen, Hans-Adolf (ed.). *Dokumente zur Vorgeschichte des Westfeldzuges 1939–1940*. Göttingen, 1956.

———. *Dokumente zum Westfeldzug 1940*. Göttingen, 1960.

Kriegstagebuch (KTB) des Oberkommandos der Wehrmacht (OKW), 1940–1945. Frankfurt a. Main, 1961–1965, 4 vols. (7 tomes).

Ludendorff, Erich. *Urkunden der Obersten Heeresleitung über ihre Tätigkeit 1916–1918*. Berlin, 1922.

Das Werk des Untersuchungsausschusses der Deutschen Verfassungsgebenden Nationalversammlung und des deutschen Reichstages 1919–1926. Berlin.

Books on Military Theory and Military History

The number of publications of this category is tremendous. Here are listed only those that were used in this study:

Blumentritt, Günther. *Strategie und Taktik*. Konstanz, 1960.

Caemmerer, R. v. *The Development of Strategical Science during the 19th Century*. London, 1905 (The original German edition was published in Berlin, 1904).

Craig, Gordon A. *The Politics of the Prussian Army, 1640–1945*. Oxford, 1955.

Earle, Edward Mead (ed.). *Makers of Modern Strategy*. Princeton, N.J., 1952.

Erfurth, Waldemar. *Die Geschichte des deutschen Generalstabes von 1918 bis 1945*. Göttingen, 1957.

Görlitz, Walter. *Der deutsche Generalstab*. Frankfurt a. Main, 1950.

Goltz, Colmar von der. *The Nation in Arms*. London, 1906 (1st German ed.: 1883).

―――. *The Conduct of War*, London, 1899.

―――. *Jena to Eylau*, London, 1913.

Hagemann, Ernst. *Studien zur Entwicklungsgeschichte der deutschen Kriegstheorie*. Berlin, 1940.

Hahlweg, Werner (ed.). *Klassiker der Kriegskunst*. Darmstadt, 1960.

Hubatsch, Walther. *Schicksalswege deutscher Vergangenheit*. Düsseldorf, 1950.

Justrow, Karl. *Feldherr und Kriegstechnik*. Oldenburg, 1933.

Krauss, Alfred. *Theorie und Praxis in der Kriegskunst*. München, 1936.

Meier-Welcker, Hans. *Deutsches Heerwesen im Wandel der Zeiten*. Arolsen, 1954.

Mette, Siegfried. *Vom Geist deutscher Feldherrn. Genie und Technik 1800–1918*. Zürich, 1938.

Nickerson, Hoffman. *The Armed Horde*. New York, 1940.

Ritter, Gerhard. *Staatskunst und Kriegshandwerk*. München, 1956–1964, 3 vols.

Rosinski, Hans. *The German Army*. Washington, D.C., 1944.

Spaulding, O. L.; Nickerson, H.; Wright, J. W. *Warfare*. Washington, D.C., 1937.

Steiner, Felix. *Von Clausewitz bis Bulganin*. Bielefeld. 1956.

Vagts, A. *A History of Militarism*. London, 1959 (rev. ed.).

Memoirs and Diaries

Almost all the acting German personalities of the period dealt with in this study have published their memoirs sooner or later. Although they are subjective and biased, they provide an important component for a better understanding of the problems under investigation. Since these memoirs cannot be listed here, the reader is therefore referred to the notes of the relevant chapters.

Secondary Sources

Since these are legion, it would exceed the scope of this work to list them all. Again, the interested reader may locate them in the notes of the various chapters.

German Military Pamphlets

This is a very important category that enables one to trace the impact of theory upon the actual conduct of war as intended by the General Staff. The pamphlets used in this study were:

Instruktionen für die höheren Truppenführer, 1885.

Exerzier-Reglement für die Infantrie (Ex.R.f.d.J.) from 29 May 1906–D.V.E. Nr. 53.

Vorschriften für den Stellungskrieg für alle Waffen: Teil 8: *Grundsätze für die Führung der Abwehrschlacht im Stellungskriege* from 1 Sept. 1917. Teil 14: *Der Angriff im Stellungskrieg* from 1 Jan. 1918.

Führung und Gefecht der verbundenen Waffen (F.u.G.) 1921-D.V.Pl. Nr.487.

Truppenführung (T.F.), 1933–1934–H.Dv.300/1.

Kriegführung (K.F.), draft manuscript of 3.1.1938.

Index

About the Author

JEHUDA WALLACH, a Colonel (Res.) in the Israeli Defense Forces, is Professor of Military History at the Aranne School of History, Tel-Aviv University. He has published widely in German, English, and Hebrew and is the author of *Israeli Military History: A Guide to the Sources* and the editor of *We Were Like Dreamers: Essays on the Israeli War of Independence*. He has written over seventy articles on military history and military matters.